When considered as a social phenomenon, literacy is remarkably difficult to define, because its functions, meanings, and methods of learning vary from one cultural group to the next. The vast majority of literacy research has been based on middle-class European or American children. In this volume the author has chosen to focus on Moroccan children whose parents are unschooled, whose language is often different from that used in the classroom, and whose first instruction often involves rote religious instruction. These children – and their Third World counterparts around the globe – represent the majority of the world's children, and yet international education policy is hampered by a lack of understanding of literacy among such youth. By exploring the ways that literacy is conceptualized and measured using both qualitative and quantitative methodologies, the author is able to offer new interpretations of literacy development and socioeconomic development that have broad ramifications for the future.

Literacy, Culture, and Development

Literacy, Culture, and Development

Becoming Literate in Morocco

DANIEL A. WAGNER
University of Pennsylvania

CAMBRIDGE
UNIVERSITY PRESS

Published by the Press Syndicate of the University of Cambridge
The Pitt Building, Trumpington Street, Cambridge CB2 1RP
40 West 20th Street, New York, NY 10011-4211, USA
10 Stamford Road, Oakleigh, Melbourne 3166, Australia

First published 1993

Printed in the United States of America

Library of Congress Cataloging-in-Publication Data
Wagner, Daniel A., 1946–
Literacy, culture, and development : becoming literate in Morocco / Daniel A. Wagner.
p.   cm.
Includes bibliographical references (p.   ) and index.
ISBN 0-521-39132-6 (U.S.). – ISBN 0-521-39813-4 (U.S. : pbk.)
1. Literacy – Morocco. 2. Literacy – Social aspects – Morocco.
I. Title.
LC158.M8W34   1993
302.2′244 – dc20   92-46214

A catalog record for this book is available from the British Library.

ISBN 0-521-39132-6 hardback
ISBN 0-521-39813-4 paperback

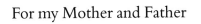

For my Mother and Father

Contents

Preface

In 1968–70, ten years before the Morocco Literacy Project (MLP) began, I served as a Peace Corps volunteer in Beni-Mellal, at the foot of the Middle Atlas Mountains in Morocco. My primary mission was to assist in the surveying and building of small irrigation canals, work that required travel into rural mountainous areas. It was exciting at times, and exasperating at others, for work was often held up by bureaucratic entanglements far beyond the reach and even comprehension of the naïve outsider that I was. But the experience was an important one. Because of it, I decided to reorient my upcoming graduate studies from experimental toward cultural issues in psychology. Shortly after beginning graduate school in the U.S., I was fortunate to discover the field of cross-cultural research in psychology and education. A few course credits later, a *Let's Learn Spanish* paperback in my coat pocket, and ridiculous heavy boots on my feet in a land where sandals were de rigueur, I set off to join a team of researchers from Rockefeller University to conduct some preliminary work of my own, which included a study of schooling and memory development in a Mayan community in the Yucatan Peninsula of Mexico.

About a year later, with the help of a dissertation fellowship from the Social Science Research Council, I was off to Morocco for a 2-year stint of fieldwork on the effects of schooling on the development of memory and perception. Unlike my work in Mexico, where I was a true outsider, the Moroccan work benefited tremendously from the network of personal relationships that I had established during my earlier years in that country.

In particular, because I was interested in assessing the cognitive skills of children and adults who had never attended school, the mountainous areas where I had worked previously seemed ideal as a base of operations. One of my good friends worked in al-Ksour, which I decided to make a central location of my work, a decision that influenced the efforts of the MLP much later on. Also, because I was interested in memory development, a Moroccan friend suggested that the "best memory experts" were those individuals who attended Quranic schools. Following through on this suggestion not only enhanced my dissertation focus on individual differences in memory but also led to a series of studies on Islamic schooling extending well beyond the boundaries of the Middle Atlas and Morocco itself.

Five years later, after another summer of work as a Fulbright-Hays visiting lecturer in Morocco, I began a long-term collaboration with Abdelhamid Lotfi, then a doctoral student at the University of Pennsylvania. With funding from the Ford Foundation and the International Development Research Centre (Canada), we traveled to Indonesia, North Yemen, Egypt, Senegal, and Morocco, conducting a comparative study of Islamic schooling and its effects on children's learning. During our peregrinations, we began to understand why memory skill was so greatly valued in these schools, as primarily a route toward certain kinds of sacred knowledge and Arabic literacy skills. We also realized that our research only skimmed the surface of these several contrasting societies, and that what was needed was a more in-depth approach to learning in a single society.

Given our backgrounds, Morocco seemed the ideal place. We applied to the U.S. National Institute of Education (now the Office of Educational Research and Improvement) and the National Institutes of Health for a multiyear study of schooling, cognitive development and literacy acquisition, eventually called simply the Morocco Literacy Project. However, my friend Lotfi was soon tapped to be the youngest-ever university dean in Morocco and could not contribute much of his time to the MLP. Fortunately, some of the faculty members at the newly revamped Faculty of Educational Sciences (FSE) at the University Mohamed V (UMV) in Rabat were interested in becoming a part of the project. Although the faculty members were optimistic and energetic, the bureaucratic nightmares of the old Peace Corps days began to reappear. Eventually, an agreement of cooperation was signed by Penn and UMV, and a subagreement was worked out between FSE and Penn's Graduate School of Education. In a hierarchically and centrally organized society like Morocco, it is crucial to have all official approvals in order. Indeed, our Moroccan colleagues commented that, ironically, the bilateral university agreement gave our project more latitude in working in various rural regions and in schools at different levels than they themselves normally had. In order to enhance this bilateral effort, we were able to organize, with funding from the United States Information Agency, an exchange program that brought about a dozen Moroccan professors for short visits to Penn, and a half-dozen Penn professors taught and did research in Morocco. This rather substantial amount of bilateral university activity – probably the most extensive in the history of U.S.–Moroccan university relations up to that time – helped to create a remarkably good climate of cooperation between the two institutions.

Getting the work to happen

While deciding on a general research topic and securing the requisite grants and permits needed to do a study are necessary conditions, these tasks clearly do not suffice for carrying out a project. Shortly after the grant awards were made, a graduate student in education, Jennifer Spratt, with a background in the social sciences and 2 years of Peace Corps service in Morocco, joined the team. Soon after, Brinkley Messick, who had just completed his doctorate in anthropology and also had Morocco Peace Corps experience was engaged to direct field research for the start-up of the project. Both Spratt and Messick were fluent in Moroccan Arabic and French, and their broad training was ideally suited for the complexity of the tasks we sought to undertake in the field. As principal adviser to the team, Abdelkader Ezzaki, currently a professor of education in Morocco, was then completing his doctoral studies in educational psychology at Temple University, a sister institution to Penn in the Philadelphia area. With this core team, and additional faculty consultants from both universities, research assistants, and a cadre of field researchers, we were set to begin the work of the project in late 1981, which included almost 6 years in the field and three years of data analysis.

Overall, this description of the historical trajectory of the MLP might look like an orderly progression, where rational decisions were made and consequences clearly foreseen. Although there is truth in such a description as we tried to rationally guide the efforts of the project, luck or what Moroccans term *baraka* (divine grace) often played a key role at decisive junctures.

Acknowledgments

In writing this book, which is the product of work undertaken by literally dozens of individuals over almost 10 years, I cannot overstate my appreciation for all who helped to make it possible. This was a project that often called on team members to go beyond the call of duty and to invest of the heart. It was a project that was not without its frustrations, scientific, bureaucratic, and personal.

My greatest professional debt in the research work is to Jennifer E. Spratt, who was assistant director of the project, and who stuck with it through thick and thin, investing summers, weekends, and more into making this the best work it could be. At the same time, her good humor and good sense made it a pleasure for all of us to persevere when the going got tough. Jennie, whose passion was anthropology, and who ended up a skilled statistical methodologist, is the kind of person who makes things happen through sheer will.

There were many others, of course, who made this work possible. Our professional consultants included Boubker Ben Omar, Scott G. Paris, Abdelkader Ezzaki, Mohamed Mellouk, Susan S. Davis, Jeanne Chall, and Harold W. Stevenson. Our research staff at the University of Pennsylvania included Veysal Batmaz, Layla Bianchi, Mark Decker, Diane Eyer, Gary E. Klein, Marilyn Liljestrand, Janet Marcus, Brinkley Messick, Amy Shargel, Bonnie Stewart, Iddo Gal, Beverly Seckinger, and Fabienne Tanon. Field research assistants were (Moroccans) Rachida Abdou, Abderrahim Benallal, Bouchra Benghazala, Zhor Harfi, Hafida Khamar, Naima Lachgar, Mustafa Majdi, Mouh Ou Ben Ali, and Fatima Tamezoujt; (Americans) Jeannine Anderson, Heather Graham, Christine Hauser, Deborah Kapchan, Elizabeth Letts, Elizabeth Moore, and Cynthia Visness. Our thanks also to a number of Moroccan friends of the project, including Umm Aicha, Fatima Badry, Hussein Aggour, Mohammed Nejmi, Ali Oudadess, Hadda Ou Moussa, and Yahya Tamezoujt, to name just a few. Jennie Spratt and Beverly Seckinger also provided some of the vignettes (ethnographic examples) utilized throughout the book. David Hogan provided helpful suggestions on the title of the book.

As noted, the Morocco Literacy Project was undertaken under the auspices of a bilateral accord between the University of Pennsylvania and the University Mohamed V. I would like to express my appreciation to the officials of each university for their kind support over the years of the project. In particular, I thank Abdellatif Benabdeljlil, Abdelkader Lahjomri, and M'hamid Zayimi, and former dean of Penn's Graduate School of Education Dell Hymes for their personal interest in supporting the MLP. The U.S. Peace Corps in Morocco also provided exceptional assistance by "seconding" several volunteers to work on the MLP during the period from 1983 to 1985.

Naturally, none of these acknowledgments would have been possible were it not for the funding of the Ford Foundation and the International Development Research Centre (Canada) for early support of the work of Abdelhamid Lotfi and myself in a comparative study of Islamic education from which the MLP issued. The project itself was principally funded by major grants from the (former) National Institute of Education (Grant #NIE-0128) and the National Institute of Child Health and Human Development (Grant #HD-14898); support for the final writing was provided, in part, from the U.S. Department of Education (Grant #R117Q00003). Many thanks again to Jennie Spratt, who drafted some of the original project papers and read and commented on the manuscript, making many valuable suggestions. Editorial assistance was provided by Christie Lerch. Julia Hough at Cambridge University Press helped to guide this project to its present conclusion. Naturally, all responsibility for any remaining errors is mine alone.

Finally, and above all, I must thank my wife and children for their patience and support over the decade of work that eventually led to the publication of this book.

A note on Arabic transliterations

For various historical reasons, the Arabic-language transliterations used in this volume do not conform to the existing standards set by Middle East specialists. Morocco has a history of research by Francophone scholars who have transliterated Arabic in North Africa with certain characteristics that do not conform to the practices of "pure" Arabists. For example, the use of the apostrophe to stand for the long vowel in certain Arabic letters is now standard practice in some professional journals, but it is not widely used in the research literature on Moroccan society. Furthermore, even though there may be a preferred English spelling of certain names, such as Marrakesh, the present volume primarily retains the Francophone spelling, Marrakech, so as to conform to prior traditions.

Previous publication of some of this research

Parts of this book have appeared in a number of chapters and articles over the years during and subsequent to completion of the Morocco Literacy Project. I am grateful to the publishers for allowing me to use some of these materials in the present volume. These publications include the following: Wagner, D. A. (1990). Literacy assessment in the Third World: An overview and proposed schema for survey use. *Comparative Education Review, 33,* 1, 112–138. Wagner, D. A., Messick, B. M., & Spratt, J. E. (1986). Studying literacy in Morocco. In B. B. Schieffelin & P. Gilmore (Eds.), *The acquisition of literacy: Ethnographic perspectives.* Norwood, NJ: Ablex. Wagner, D. A., & Spratt, J. E. (1987). Cognitive consequences of contrasting pedagogies: The effects of Quranic preschooling in Morocco. *Child Development, 58* (5): 1207–1219. Wagner, D. A., & Spratt, J. E. (1988). Intergenerational literacy: Effects of parental literacy and attitudes on children's reading achievement in Morocco. *Human Development, 31,* 359–369. Wagner, D. A., & Spratt, J. E. (1993). Arabic orthography and reading acquisition. In J. Attariba (Ed.), *Culture and cognition.* Hillsdale, NJ: Erlbaum. Wagner, D. A., Spratt, J. E., Gal, I., & Ezzaki, A. (1989). Reading and believing: Beliefs, attributions, and reading achievement among Moroccan school children. *Journal of Educational Psychology, 81,* 283–293. Wagner, D. A., Spratt, J. E., & Ezzaki, A. (1989). Does learning to read in a second language put the child at a disadvantage? Some counter-evidence from Morocco. *Applied Psycholinguistics, 10,* 31–48. Wagner, D. A., Spratt, J. E., Klein, G. D., Ezzaki, A. The myth of literacy relapse: Literacy retention among Moroccan primary school leavers. *International Journal of Educational Development, 9,* 307–315. Spratt, J. E., Seckinger, B., & Wagner, D. A. (1991). Functional literacy in Moroccan school children. *Reading Research Quarterly, 26,* 2, 178–195. Spratt, J. E., & Wagner, D. A. (1986). The making of a *fqih:* The transformation of traditional Islamic teachers in modern times. In M. White & S. Pollack (Eds.), *The cultural transition: Human experience and social transformation in the Third World and Japan* (pp. 89–112). New York: Routledge & Kegan Paul. Wagner, D. A. (1990). *Literacy and research: Past, present and future.* Special issue of *Literacy Lessons* for the 1990 International Literacy Year. Geneva: IBE/UNESCO. Wagner, D. A. (1991). Literacy as culture: Emic and etic perspectives. In E. M. Jennings & A. C. Purves (Eds.), *Literate systems and individual lives: Perspectives on literacy and schooling.* Albany: SUNY Press.

1. Domains, questions, and directions

Oum Fatima and print

Oum Fatima has labored virtually every day of her 55 years. With four children and a chronically ill husband unable to help financially, she could only hope to bring in money by doing housecleaning in the wealthier homes of the labyrinthine *medina* (or old city) of Marrakech.

Beyond regular washerwoman duties, it was normal for Oum Fatima to handle a gamut of contacts between the "outside world" and the home and children for whom she worked so hard. Such activities varied enormously. On some days the mailman would arrive with letters; Oum Fatima would deliver each to the addressee, knowing simply by the type of handwriting or script used – Arabic or French – who should receive which letter. Once a month the "electric man" would arrive to collect money for the month's charges; Oum Fatima handled this affair with just a question or two, drawing money from an earthenware jar in which she stashed odd coins and bills in anticipation of his visits. At the *souk* (market), Oum Fatima's skill in mental arithmetic and bargaining was legendary. Not only could she switch effortlessly between the several parallel currency units in use – dirhams, francs, and riyals (a base-five system) – but her ability to negotiate the lowest possible price made her a well-known figure in the *derb* (quarter). To those of her social class, as well as to those "higher up," Oum Fatima was a woman worthy of great respect.

Never having gone to school, Oum Fatima could neither read nor write in any language, nor could she do simple arithmetic on paper.

Although both local educators and international policymakers would call Oum Fatima illiterate, most people in her *derb* consider her a shrewd bargainer, astute with money, and among the most competent individuals they know. To the specialists and policymakers, Oum Fatima would be "happier," "better off economically," and "a better mother" if only she could read and write. And, more broadly, Morocco would be a "better country" if all of the Oum Fatimas were literate. To her neighbors she is an intelligent, hardworking woman who has coped remarkably well under adverse social and economic circumstances and has done an extraordinary job in raising her children. How do we interpret Oum Fatima's ability and behavior in this single, limited snapshot of her life? Such contrasting perspectives on and dimensions of literacy – whether cultural, social, individual, economic, or linguistic – represent a recurrent and central theme in this book.

Literacy is a remarkable term. While it seems to refer simply to individual possession of the complementary mental technologies of reading and writing, literacy is difficult to define in individuals and to delimit within societies, and the term itself is charged with emotional and political meaning. Not long ago, newspapers and scholars referred to whole societies as "illiterate and uncivilized," in effect equating these words; and the term *illiterate* still carries a negative connotation, sometimes reinforced by agencies determined, in their own words, to "stamp out" or "eradicate" illiteracy.

Defining literacy as an individual phenomenon was once thought to be easy; one simply tested for reading and writing skills. Such "simplicity" soon became controversial, as specialists began to argue over which tests were most appropriate, most valid, most psychometrically sound, and so forth. Major debates continue to revolve around such issues as what specific abilities or knowledge reflect literacy ability and what levels can and should be defined for measurement. In an effort to deal with this confusion, UNESCO coined the term *functionally literate* as a person who "has acquired the knowledge and skills in reading and writing which enable him to engage effectively in all those activities in which literacy is normally assumed in his culture or group" (Gray, 1956: 19).

But, though functional literacy has a great deal of appeal because of its implied adaptability to a given cultural context, the term can be very awkward for research purposes. For example, it is unclear in an industrialized nation like Great Britain what level of literacy should be required of all citizens: Does a coal miner have different needs than a barrister? Fundamental to all of these tests, however, is the idea that literacy is composed of a set of human skills, each of which could be measured, studied, and taught.

At a broader level, the United Nations and other agencies interested in social change sought to infer literacy skills from school attendance records: People who have attended a certain number of years of formal public schooling are assumed to be literate. We now know that such assumptions are misleading. As we shall see, the number of years of schooling tells us rather little about what an individual actually learns during that time period and even less about how much of that learning is retained after leaving school. For example, should we assume an equivalent degree of literacy among individuals who have (a) just completed fifth grade of primary school, (b) just completed 5 years of primary school but reached only third grade due to 2 repeated school years, and (c) completed fifth grade 10 years ago?

When considered as a social phenomenon, literacy is even less well defined, because its functions, meanings, and methods of transmission vary from one cultural group to the next. Whether Oum Fatima is illiterate or literate or somewhere in between depends on one's frame of reference. More than a decade ago, Scribner and Cole (1981) suggested that a comprehensive definition of literacy extend beyond the skills approach to include as well the knowledge necessary to apply literacy skills "for specific purposes in specific contexts of use" (p. 236). Thus, they sought to understand literacy practices that involve both social knowledge and cognitive skills.

As social scientists have sought to examine cultural differences in behavior, an important conceptual distinction emerged – that between the emic and the etic concepts. First discussed by Pike (1966) and then elaborated by Berry and Dasen (1974), this distinction is crucial. *Emic* concepts are those that can be understood only within a single cultural system or society, and can be measured only according to criteria relevant to that single system. *Etic* concepts are those that are deduced or derived from a position outside of any particular system, and have as a primary goal the analysis of more than a single society. An etic perspective on literacy assumes that such skills as decoding, picture matching, and reading instructions on a medicine bottle have substantially the same meaning and cultural functions for all individuals and cultural groups. An emic perspective on literacy assumes that different types of meanings, social functions, and skills are associated with literacy in different societies. An emic definition of literacy in Morocco, for example, would incorporate Oum

Fatima's script-recognition skills, as well as her skills at complex calculations across local currencies. That these literacy practices are thought of – by actors and local observers alike – as constituting literate behavior supports taking an emic definition of literacy into account.

The etic and the emic are frames of reference that may be quite helpful in understanding diverse perspectives on literacy, but they are also contrasts that are ultimately artificial. All literacy practice incorporates both emic and etic elements. One could, for example, create a script-recognition test and apply it widely around the world, thereby producing an etic test from a locally derived emic reality. It is not our goal to split such fine epistemological hairs. Yet both the individual and social approaches to literacy, and its definitions, rely heavily on one frame of reference or another.

Before considering our own approach to the study of literacy, it is useful to provide an overview of the multiple ways in which literacy has been conceptualized. Each general perspective – the historical, the economic, and the educational – has been the subject of numerous studies. How these broad arguments have been posed by researchers over the years is an essential first step in understanding why literacy has become an increasingly critical issue around the world.

Literacy in history

Turning points in the production of literate materials – from the Dead Sea Scrolls to the Gutenberg Bible to the word processor – have served as markers of social change. In addition, historical changes in society have greatly influenced people's use of literate materials. One example was the use of legal documents by thirteenth-century British landlords to control the intergenerational transfer of property (cf. Clanchy, 1979). Another was the critical role that the French Revolution played in promoting liberty of the press, which in turn played a role in unseating the king (Darnton, 1990). Such historical accounts of literacy argue that reading and writing, often as separate activities, are implicated in crucial social and cultural changes. That clergymen of many of the world's great religions were also the possessors of one or both of these skills also signifies not only the "restricted" (Goody & Watt, 1968) nature of literacy but its social and moral power as well.

On the one hand, history makes us aware that in Europe and elsewhere literacy has been implicated in sweeping changes in religious, educational, and political culture and institutions. On the other hand, this emphasis on literacy as a factor in important world events can blind us to the fact that, in contemporary societies of both the developing and industrialized worlds, literacy may also serve to maintain traditional elements of culture. Morocco, as we shall see, provides an interesting case in point: It contains dimensions of literacy that reflect its stance part way between each of these worlds.

Literacy and economic development

Literacy advocates often take it for granted that the rise of a literate populace was a major historical factor in the economic development of industrialized Europe. Though this commonly held belief has now come under strong criticism by some historians (e.g., Graff, 1987), many international agencies still assume that universal literacy will bring a parallel economic well-being to the contemporary Third World (e.g., the United Nations' World Declaration on Education for All, 1990). This assertion derives from two quite different presuppositions. The first applies the historical view of literacy to economics, asserting that literacy is an active, important component in the process of social development and causally linked to economic growth. Because literacy changes attitudes and brings new information to people previously deprived of sources of information beyond their village limits, the theory goes, they develop new cognitive abilities and modern attitudes that enable them to adopt the social behaviors needed in a modern industrialized society (Inkeles & Smith, 1974).

The second assumption is that literacy and formal schooling are equivalent. Citizens of Third World countries will need, it is claimed, 4 to 6 years of primary schooling if their countries are to attain sustained economic growth. A threshold number of years of education is required for more or less permanent literacy to be acquired by the individual (cf. Fagerlind & Saha, 1983). Little empirical research has been done to support such claims of literacy retention, a topic we explore later in this book. Overall, cross-national comparisons using national census data to show that (presumed) literacy rates (based mainly on statistics on school attendance) predict economic growth (expressed by the gross national product, or GNP) reveal that, with few exceptions, countries with high economic growth rates are those with a highly educated and literate population. The flaw in such arguments is that we cannot be sure of the direction of the relationship between literacy and economic growth. Is literacy a cause or a consequence of economic growth, or is it simply unrelated? And what is the quality of the literacy data used in such analyses? There are a number of comprehensive reviews of this question (e.g., Anzalone, 1981; International Development Research Centre, 1979; Wagner, 1990), and almost every one points to the absence of in-depth empirical studies of literacy in the Third World.

In short, the foremost problem regarding the consequences of a given literacy rate in Third World countries seems to be in knowing how to measure this rate in the first place. The surprising, if not alarming, fact is that we have very little reliable information on national literacy rates for most Third World societies. Needless to say, without such knowledge any comparison of rates and their consequences becomes meaningless.

Literacy and cognition

Ever since European explorers made it their *mission civilisatrice* to bring imperial culture and education to the peoples whom they saw as poor, uncivilized, ignorant, and illiterate savages, the definition and introduction of literacy have had broadly political, cultural, moral, and instructional dimensions. Of course, what constituted savagery depended greatly on the perspective of the colonists who did the categorizing (and who, we might note, also did the writing about the categorizing). A century or two later, when public education began in Europe, the same discourse appeared in the *patries meres* themselves. How were the ruling classes to provide for the poor, uneducated, and illiterate masses at home?

Inherent in the use of the term *illiterate* in such descriptions of the poor, destitute "others" to differentiate them from "us," the literate people, was a veiled claim to moral and cultural superiority, which did not reflect sustained interest in the betterment of the peoples they ruled. Nonetheless, the term *illiteracy* was certainly a good deal more accurate two or more centuries ago, when the "civilized world" appeared to comprise so few societies, than it is in the 1990s, when our awareness of cultural diversity is so much greater and our skepticism about claims to cultural superiority so much more conscious. Today we know that the various communities of the contemporary world are so varied that simple dichotomies, such as literate versus illiterate, fail to capture the realities of the cultural practices that individuals engage in, whether schooled or unschooled. This argument, which has been made forcefully in recent years by Heath (1983), Scribner (1987), and Street (1984), among others, needs to be balanced as well by an understanding of the various forms in which literacy ability can appear and by an awareness that it can be measured in various ways.

As anthropologists and psychologists began to study the effects of modernization on traditional peoples, they also began to search for the causes of the differences in human thought, perception, and logic that were reported by intrepid explorers. Among the first to investigate systematically the cognitive consequences of literacy was Alexander Luria, a Soviet psychologist who studied the impact of literacy campaigns on the thinking of peasants during the Russian Revolution (Luria, 1976). His work, and that of other psychologists and anthropologists over the next several decades (e.g., Goody & Watt, 1968), lent support to the notion of a "great divide" between the cognitive worlds of those who are literate and those who are not.

More recent work, particularly that of Scribner and Cole (1981), suggests that any cognitive consequences of literacy are likely to be quite specific to the types of literacy acquired and much more narrowly defined than the major contrast suggested by a "great divide." Their work in Liberia found that what constitutes knowledge and thinking skills is culture specific and situation specific, with illiterate and literate Liberians showing substantially similar cognitive abilities. Although the issue of literacy's cognitive consequences was not a major focus of our research, some of our results bear on related areas (as described in chapter 6 and appendix 1).

Another major domain of interest in literacy and cognition concerns the impact of children's cognitive skills on learning to read. Ever since the development of intelligence tests in the middle of the nineteenth century, specialists have sought to understand the degree to which school-based learning, and reading acquisition in particular, are dependent on children's intellectual development. This focus on the cognitive prerequisites for literacy development has become an important area of educational research in most Western countries, as is evident from a perusal of Pearson's (1984) *Handbook of Reading Research*. Over recent decades, some researchers have sought to tie reading difficulties to particular cognitive "deficits" in visual perception, memory ability, and problem-solving skills, and others have suggested that overall intelligence or IQ may be at the root of reading "failure." I use quotation marks around the words

deficits and failure because there is great disagreement as to the appropri-
ateness of such terms, which carry some of the same negative connotations
ascribed to illiteracy.

Regardless of one's academic specialty, there is little question that test
scores of reading achievement among children are highly related to test
scores of cognitive skills. This finding is yet another source of disagreement among researchers who would prefer to see differences among
groups as "explainable" either by individual cognitive factors or by sociocultural factors. As it happens, we know remarkably little about the combined impact of such variables in Western societies and far less in the
developing world.

Literacy and schooling

Until fairly recently, most specialists thought of literacy as predominantly a
consequence of formal schooling. After all, a major pedagogical goal of
school curricula the world over is the teaching of reading and writing. It
comes as no surprise, then, that most research on reading and writing
focuses on the questions of how the individual learner acquires these skills
and of what pedagogies to use for teaching them. Where resources are
available, mainly in Western Europe and North America, considerable
effort has been devoted toward trying to improve the ways in which
reading and writing are taught, how these skills can be systematically (and
psychometrically) measured, and how to intervene clinically with children who do not adequately keep up with the norms for learning such
skills in school.

Historians and anthropologists now have shown us that literacy is often
transmitted outside the normal channels of schooling. For example, as
early as the sixteenth century, reading was said to be widespread in areas of
Sweden without schools – a consequence of family efforts to read the
Bible at home (Graff, 1987). In contemporary Liberia, the Vai people still
teach each other the indigenous Vai script, completely outside of any
schooling experience (Scribner & Cole, 1981), and the Native American
Cree of northern Canada maintain the use of their syllabic script as a
source of cultural identity (Bennett & Berry, 1987). Furthermore, before
the rise of mass public education in the nineteenth and twentieth centuries, literacy was provided by other social institutions, most notably
religious schools: Jewish, Christian, Islamic, and Buddhist schools are
among the best-known examples. These schools shared a number of

characteristics, including the presence of a master and his apprentices, often with children, adolescents, and adults clustered together in the same class. Teachers were almost always male, and they had considerable power over their charges, as well as in the community at large. Of these, only the Islamic Quranic schools, such as those described in this book, are still widespread today.

Much out-of-school literacy learning takes place at home. If parents or older siblings are literate, younger children can learn a great deal about the functions and uses of writing, and even how to employ them, before setting foot in school. In the United States, there has been a dramatic increase in research on the nature and influence of home learning of reading and writing skills. It has been found that families in which parents read storybooks to their children (Teale & Sulzby, 1987) and provide helpful learning environments (Snow, Barnes, Chandler, Goodman, & Hemphill, 1991; Heath, 1983) tend to produce children who learn to read well in school. In Morocco, as we shall see, the influence of parental or family literacy is complicated by the fact that few older family members are literate; how a child learns to read and write at home or school in such circumstances is another focus of our interest.

Defining literacy

In view of the multitude of experts and published books on the topic, one would suppose that there would be a fair amount of agreement on how to define literacy, but such is not the case. Most specialists agree that the term connotes aspects of reading and writing, but major debates continue to rage about what specific abilities or knowledge count as literacy and what levels to employ for measurement (cf. Venezky, Wagner, & Ciliberti, 1989). As noted earlier, the term *functional literacy* has the advantage of being applicable to any cultural context; but defining literacy as functional does not tell us how to set the goal of a national literacy program, nor does it specify what kind, or level, of functioning is appropriate for all citizens in a given society.

Another reasonable approach – viewing literacy as an ability possessed in some degree by all citizens – was suggested in another UNESCO report (1957: 18): "(L)iteracy is a characteristic acquired by individuals in varying degrees from just above none to an indeterminate upper level. Some individuals are more literate or less literate than others, but it is really not possible to speak of literate and illiterate persons as two distinct categories." Yet this definition remains too broad to help us in measuring literacy. Innumerable specialized literacy skills – from "reading" a stop sign to interpreting Shakespeare – are in use in the world every day, for dozens of orthographies, and in hundreds of languages.

Our definition of literacy must include some idea of how such literacy skills can be measured. UNESCO, which provides worldwide statistical comparisons of literacy, relies for its literacy measurements almost entirely on data provided by its member countries; these, in turn, are based on national census information, which typically relies on measures of literacy ability by self-assessment questionnaires or years of primary schooling, neither of which reliably measure literacy (UNESCO, 1992). Newspaper-reading skills have been used as a baseline in some countries, but these tests also suffer from a lack of reliability. If the test emphasizes comprehension, it may grossly underestimate literacy, especially if the text is in an official language not well understood by the person being tested. On the other hand, if a person is simply asked to read a passage aloud, with little or no attempt to measure comprehension, the test may overestimate literacy.

A better solution would be to design a battery of tests for a given society to evaluate literacy skills, from low to high levels – tests that would be applicable across the complete range of possible languages and literacies in the society, so that a continuum of measurement possibilities can be achieved.[1] Whatever the definition of literacy, it is our view that the terms *illiteracy* and *illiterate* carry so many negative connotations that they ought to be avoided. In this book, when we want to refer to someone who has limited literacy skills, we will generally employ the term *nonliterate,* though even this term can be employed only on the rare occasions where individual competencies and knowledge do not exist at all.[2] As may be seen in the vignette of Oum Fatima, her skill in recognizing the differences between the Arabic and French scripts and her use of others' literacy skills constitute literate *behavior,* much as an American college student makes use of "literacy specialists" to improve a job résumé. In this book, Oum Fatima would be at the low end of low-literate but would not be nonliterate.

As may be clear from this discussion, an underlying problem in defining literacy concerns basic research methodology. Part of the uncertainty over the definition of literacy has resulted from the different scholarly approaches used to study the subject. The methodologies chosen by each researcher naturally reflect his or her disciplinary training. Both qualitative and quantitative approaches (as described in chapter 4) – for example, psychological experimentation and anthropological observation – have value in helping us to understand literacy, but disciplinary boundaries make it difficult for agreement to be achieved in the single domain of literacy. There is no easy resolution to this problem, but it is clear that both a broad-based and flexible conceptualization and definition of literacy and a cross-disciplinary research design are required.

Because literacy is a cultural phenomenon, adequately defined and understood only within each culture, it is not surprising that definitions of literacy may never be permanently fixed. Whether literacy is thought of as including computer skills, mental arithmetic, or civic responsibility, for example, will vary across countries, depending on how leaders of each society define this most basic of basic skills. Researchers can help in this effort by trying to be clear about which definition(s) they choose to employ in their work. As noted, our work considers literacy to be both a social and an individual phenomenon: *social* in that social practices are shared among members of a given culture, and *individual* in terms of the specific set of attitudes and learned behaviors and skills involved in encoding, decoding, and comprehending written language.

Literacy research and policy

Beyond the difficulties inherent in the debates on definitions, however, there are several areas in which scholarly interests intersect with the world of policy. The year 1990 – the year in which most of the writing of this book was completed – was declared by the United Nations to be International Literacy Year (ILY). The major event of the ILY was a world conference entitled Education For All held in Jomtien, Thailand, which focused attention on literacy research and literacy policy for the next millennium. We will return to such policy matters later in this book, but it is important, at the outset, to understand how our research work intersects with certain basic policy questions.

Within the Morocco Literacy Project, we had three main research-policy interests. First, we wanted to explore different ways of conceptualizing and measuring literacy in cultural context. Rather than simply translate methodologies used previously, we sought to rethink the categories of literacy and illiteracy, as well as the various ways in which assessment could be undertaken. Second, we wanted to understand better the nature of literacy acquisition in children living in a developing country. Because the vast majority of previous research (and subsequent theories) on reading acquisition is based on middle-class European or American children, it seemed essential to gather concrete information on Moroccan children, taking advantage of the natural fact that most parents were unschooled, that the home language might be different from that used in the classroom, and that initial instruction might involve rote religious teachings. These Moroccan children – and their Third World contemporaries around the globe – make up the majority of the world's children, and yet international education policy is hampered by a lack of understanding of literacy among such youth.

Finally, we sought to understand what children retain from literacy instruction after they leave school. Whereas this question has been largely ignored in the United States because most children remain in school through high school (though this statistic appears to be rapidly changing in urban America), children in many Third World countries typically average less than 5 years of primary schooling, with only a minority of children going on to secondary school. We wanted to learn more about what knowledge and literacy skills children retain after dropping out of school. If governments wish to impart what they term "permanent" literacy skills among their citizenry, how much instruction is required for such skills to be maintained?

These and related questions were important motivators for our work. But we had no illusions that we would solve such problems in a general way, as we worked in a small corner of a society that itself represents a small and (ultimately) unique corner of the world. Yet, at the same time, we felt that this work – though scholarly in its origins – could generate new thinking about literacy policy in cultural context and could be a theoretical, methodological and empirical beginning of more such applied efforts in other parts of the world.

Literacy in cultural context

Most studies of literacy focus on the context of schooling, as though this were the only social factor that influences literacy. Though schooling is the easiest element to study (as it provides a ready-made sample and is, after all, the locus of most formal training in literacy), formal schooling is only one factor that imparts literacy in society. Our perspective suggests a much broader approach to the cultural context in which literacy is socialized, including such factors as age, gender, environment, and language background. Each of these factors became an important focus of our efforts, and each helped to determine the sample of children we sought to study in Morocco.

In order to gain a comprehensive understanding of emic, or culture-specific, dimensions of literacy in Morocco, we needed to employ ethnographic methods of observation and interview to understand better urban and rural environments, parental attitudes, and the role of Islamic education. Because Moroccan society offers considerable contrast with typical Western societies, it seemed an ideal context within which to consider this problem. Yet we must also reiterate the ordinary dimension of the contexts that were studied. These were typical schoolchildren, from average homes in communities where parents "get by" economically and partake of local cultural events and rituals, and where the government "does its best" to provide a decent education within limited means. Although some aspects of Moroccan cultural life may seem exotic to the Westerner, there is little, of course, in the Moroccan experience that seems unusual to the Moroccans themselves.

Telling the tale

There are different ways of telling such a tale. Chronology of events, longitudinal change in the children's samples, and method-results-conclusions – each has its advantages. In telling this tale we have chosen to use a bit of each of these "ways in" to the study of literacy in Morocco. As happens with large-scale studies like this one, there are literally mountains of data points, and it is easy to discourage not only the generalist but also the reader who wishes to know something of how it really is, to get a flavor for the place.

We begin, therefore, with two ethnographically based chapters that provide a sense of the contexts of what is termed the Moroccan culture of literacy. Wherever possible, detailed examples, vignettes, are provided to give a sense of the Moroccan reality. Chapter 4 encompasses the methodologies used, the samples selected, and the experimental designs employed in the project. Chapters 5–7 make up the first major set of studies on literacy acquisition in Moroccan schoolchildren, from preschool through the end of primary school. Chapters 8–10 consider various dimensions of literacy acquisition, including such fundamental questions as first and second literacy acquisition, functional approaches to literacy, and the critical issue of literacy retention.

In Chapter 11 the relationship between literacy and poverty in Morocco is discussed, based primarily on data from national surveys and international agencies. Chapter 12 considers the linkages between research and policy and suggests some directions for policy and planning for literacy and education in Morocco and other developing countries. Chapter 13 summarizes the key findings of the book and suggests further avenues for exploration.

Notes

1 See also Wagner (1990) for a proposed schema for the development of literacy assessment at the household level in developing countries.
2 Chapter 11 uses the term *illiteracy,* because Moroccan and international economic policymakers employ this term in discussions about national statistics.

2. Language and literacy in Morocco

At the gas station

It is a bright sunny April day as Si Mohamed, a government agent of *Eaux et Forets* (water and forests department), drives his office car into the brand new Afriquia gas station in Berrechid. When Allal, the gas station attendant, has filled the gas tank, Si Mohamed asks for a *facture* (receipt) to submit for reimbursement. Allal rummages briefly through his leather money bag and carefully extracts a pad of blank *factures* and a blackened rubber stamp with the station's name and address. With a deep breath he exhales on the rubber stamp, moistening it slightly, and then presses it with deliberation into the *facture* paper. This small rubber stamp, like tens of thousands all over Morocco, serves as the guarantor of official literacy in Morocco. Allal, who cannot read or write, then hands the stamped paper to Si Mohamed, who fills in the date, the amount of gas, and the price.

Mohamed and Allal have just engaged in a joint literacy act, one that is representative of literacy in Morocco and in many other parts of the world that stand, like Morocco, midway between what is labeled traditional and modern. Today, literacy is possessed, understood, and used by many more than a small elite, even in countries where the majority can neither read nor write.

Two millennia of languages and literacies in contact

To discuss the history of language and literacy use in Morocco is to trace the history of the northwest corner of the continent of Africa (see Figure 2.1).

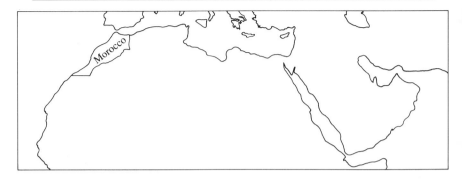

Figure 2.1. Regional map of northwestern Africa.

Strategically located at the southern gate of the Strait of Gibraltar, Morocco has been a crossroads where great civilizations of the ancient world met and commingled. Greeks, Phoenicians, Romans – all made their way to Morocco as they moved westward across the Mediterranean Sea, eventually working their way down the northern coast of Africa from Egypt to Libya to the Maghreb (literally, "the West" in Arabic). The process of conquest and counterconquest in Morocco began as early as 1000 B.C. and, if we include the protectorate (colonial) period, did not end until the mid-twentieth century (Laraoui, 1977).

Berber and other languages of pre-Islamic Morocco

The earliest known inhabitants in what is now Morocco were the Berbers, who until relatively recently were a nomadic people who also engaged in organized agriculture. The Berber people were in fact spread across the entire southern coast of the Mediterranean, extended well into what is present-day Libya. The Berber language is a member of the Hamitic family of languages (which includes Ethiopian), whereas Arabic is a Semitic language. Thus, in spite of almost a thousand years of contact between the two languages, Berber bears virtually no semantic or syntactic similarity to Arabic, with the minor exception of some vocabulary borrowing (Boukous, 1977; Galand, 1979). Berber is spoken in three dialectal forms – *Tamazight, Tashelhit,* and *Rifi* – usually associated with particular geographic regions of Morocco, though recent internal migrations have led to much greater Berber dialect contact than in previous centuries. Although official statistics on the number of native Berber speakers in

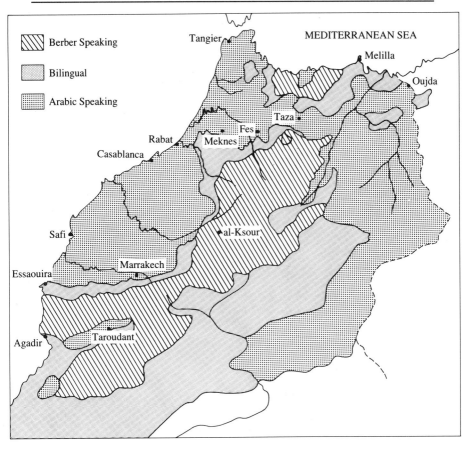

Figure 2.2. Linguistic map of Morocco. Adapted from Montagne (1931/1973).

Morocco have never been gathered, estimates range from about 30% to more than 60% of the population (Moatassime, 1974; see the linguistic map of Morocco in Figure 2.2.)

The politics of Berber language use in Morocco is particularly sensitive, as in much of North Africa. Until the end of the French protectorate in 1956, colonial authorities attempted to divide and conquer Morocco by emphasizing cultural and linguistic differences between Berbers and Arabs. A College Berbere was established in Azrou, in central Morocco, that offered a bilingual program of French and Berber language subjects, to the exclusion of Arabic. With Independence, nationalist feeling came down strongly against what it saw as a divisive colonial language policy;

from that time until the present, Berber has not been authorized at any level in the Moroccan educational system. Various authors have argued that there is a policy of cultural discrimination against the Berber-speaking populations, and riots have occurred in neighboring Algeria, where similar linguistic policies obtain (Moatassime, 1974; Montagne, 1931/1973).

From what is known of the linguistic ecology of Morocco, it appears that the major concentration of Berber monolinguals, predominantly women and young children, is located mostly in the mountain and desert regions. Nowadays, most Berber-speaking men become bilingual in Moroccan Arabic due to schooling, contact with the media, and increased migration to urban areas. This bilingualism in men has led many to predict (and decry) the eventual demise of Berber language and culture in Morocco. Berber is usually considered to be an unwritten language, and the available contemporary publications on Berber language are usually transliterated into Arabic or French (Roman) scripts. Yet, an ancient alphabet (*Tifinagh*) does exist for the Berber language, but it was mainly used for inscriptions; it is virtually unknown in contemporary North Africa.[1]

When the Romans arrived in Morocco about 500 B.C., they established colonies for the export of grain back to Italy, and they called Morocco the imperial "breadbasket." Besides the construction of aqueducts and thermal bases, the Romans also brought the Latin language and script to Morocco, and Roman inscriptions can still be seen in various ruins of north-central Morocco. However, unlike the conquerors to follow, the Romans were generally uninterested in linguistic dominance, and no effort was made to provide education or literacy to the Berber-speaking populace. Thus, with the eventual departure of the Romans, some time in the early part of the next millennium, little beyond architecture remained of their presence.

At about the time of the Roman departure, Jewish groups apparently moved into southern Morocco, settling mainly in the Anti-Atlas foothills and the Middle Atlas range. Their geographic origin remains unknown, but they may have traversed the Sahara laterally to the south of Morocco with salt caravans that traveled from the Red Sea to Timbuktu and Mauritania. Some historians suggest that they came from Yemen, in southern Arabia, where an important Jewish community existed, or from elsewhere in the Byzantine Empire (Laraoui, 1977: 75). The Jews brought the Hebrew script, but there is little evidence that the script was widely used in ancient times. Apparently, these Jews became assimilated into the Berber population and spoke Berber, retaining Hebrew only for religious purposes.[2] These Berber and Jewish communities remained intact in their isolated rural mountains for centuries following the Arab conquest. Thus, even up to the time of our research in the 1980's, Berber has remained the lingua franca in numerous regions of Morocco. Today, though, it is coming under increasing pressure from the Arabic language used exclusively by the modern education system.

Islam and the Arabic language in Morocco

The great Islamic conquest of northern Africa reached Morocco in the eighth century, before gaining strength to move on to invade, with the help of Moroccan reinforcements, the Spanish peninsula in the ninth and tenth centuries. To speak of a "conquest" suggests a much more complete hegemony than was ever the case in Morocco. Although all subsequent national leaders proclaimed adherence to Islam, there always remained significant resistance to the Arabic language and cultural values that the Islamic invaders attempted to impose on the Berber populations of Morocco. The settlement of the Arabic-speaking populations in the coastal towns and connecting river valleys helped to maintain contact with the rest of the Islamic dominions, and at the same time reinforced the maintenance of Berber traditions in rural and mountainous areas.

Unlike their Roman predecessors, however, the Islamo-Arabic invaders sought cultural domination along with political hegemony. The strong linkages between the Arabic language and Islam (as evidenced by the Quran itself) made such a domination inevitable as long as Islamic leaders ruled the country. To enhance the spread of the religion, as in all conquered lands, Islamic schools were created to train future leaders and to increase Islamic learning in the general populace. A more complete discussion of such schools is provided in chapter 3, but it is important to realize here that all these schools utilized the Arabic language, as this was the written language of the Quran. To understand the Quran – to be a good Muslim – was to be literate in Arabic. This simple fact has been decisive in the gradual domination of Arabic over Berber, which has taken centuries to achieve.

The Arabic-speaking invaders spoke what is now termed literary or Standard Arabic (termed *fus-ha*), which was quite similar to that of the written Quran. Over the many centuries of separation between the conquered territories (such as Morocco) and the Arabian Peninsula, various dialects developed. Moroccan Arabic may be regarded as part of a continuum of varieties spoken throughout the Arab world in which the degree of resemblance and mutual intelligibility among varieties decreases with geographic distance. Certain phonemes in Moroccan Arabic have no counterpart in Standard Arabic, and other phonemes, distinct in Standard Arabic, may be collapsed into one in Moroccan Arabic (e.g., *t/th; d/dh)*. On the syntactic level, Moroccan Arabic is more liberal with inflections and word order and allows more economy with function words than does Standard Arabic. In its vocabulary, Moroccan Arabic makes freer use of loanwords from foreign languages, especially French and Spanish. These dialectal differences result in some common practical difficulties in the Arabic-speaking world – for example, Moroccans speaking in dialect would find it difficult to understand Jordanians speaking in their dialect, and vice versa.

The difficulty in communication across the Arabic-speaking countries, when added to the tremendous cultural value placed on knowledge and recitation of the Quran, led to a long effort to utilize Standard Arabic as the official language of the country and the language of the mass media and school instruction, an effort that continues up to the present. Because of its association with Islam and the written Quran, spoken Standard Arabic enjoys considerable prestige among both Moroccan Arabic speakers and Berber speakers, even though only a minority can speak it fluently (Grandguillaume, 1983). With the exception of monolingual Berber speakers, Moroccan Arabic remains the predominant spoken language used for informal and everyday communication; still, it remains largely unwritten and is restricted to the oral medium (Salmi, 1987).[3]

In addition to variation in spoken Arabic, its written form may also be considered as having two varieties, classical and Standard. The classical variety is that of the ancient, religious, or formal texts, with the Quran as the ultimate example. Usually Standard Arabic is the modern written form taught in schools in Morocco and other Arabic-speaking countries. The differences between the classical and Standard written Arabic are modest relative to the rather large differences between the spoken dialects and spoken Standard Arabic (Ferguson, 1959).

European invasions of Morocco

The French, already a colonizer in Algeria since the middle of the nineteenth century, began a military intervention that led to the establishment of a French Protectorate in Morocco from 1912 until 1956; the protectorate allowed for a certain amount of autonomy, as Morocco, unlike neighboring Algeria, was never considered to be an integral part of France. On the other hand, France definitely took seriously its *mission civilisatrice,* a key component of which was the spread and dominance of the French language. As part of this policy, the French began to establish public schooling with the French language as the only vehicle of instruction. Although both Arabic and Berber eventually became part of the school curriculum (for reasons that were more political than educational), the French language became ever more important in government bureaucracy, the modernizing economy, and for school advancement. The French permitted certain traditional aspects of society, such as Islamic religion, law, and the Quranic schools to continue functioning during colonial rule.

As early as 1860, the Spanish also invaded Morocco, occupying Tetouan, but limited their intervention to the northern tier of the country. In the 1930s, following a major insurrection, the Spanish ceded political control to the French, who ruled Morocco until independence and the restoration of the monarchy.

The contemporary language situation in Morocco

Present-day Morocco is a multilingual society in which three language systems coexist: Arabic, Berber, and French. The degree of multilingualism exhibited by a Moroccan is affected by such factors as degree of urbanization, geographic and ethnic origin, and level of education. In the large urban centers, Arabic and French are widely used side by side, and code switching – the use of two languages interchangeably – is often engaged in by educated Moroccans. In contrast, French is rarely heard in rural areas, where Arabic and Berber predominate. As noted earlier, there is considerable bilingualism in the Berber-speaking areas of Morocco, with Berber men most likely to be able to speak both Arabic and Berber with fluency.

Jamal's return

Eight-year-old Jamal has just returned to his hometown, al-Ksour, from France, where his Berber family lived while Jamal's father worked at an automobile factory. Jamal speaks French and Berber fluently, but almost no Arabic. Now he attends a primary school in al-Ksour, and when he tries to read and write in Arabic, he often makes mistakes. When another student corrects him too harshly, the teacher admonishes all of the boys never to say "You're wrong" or "This is wrong": "We come to school to learn, and no one knows everything." The boys nod in agreement, but several of them cannot resist making fun of Jamal's poor Arabic.

There used to be many students like Jamal in the schools of al-Ksour. According to the head of his school, when he first started working there in the mid-1960s, teachers often had to explain the lessons in Berber for students from outlying rural areas. Now, however, almost all of the children come to school with some knowledge of Moroccan Arabic. One reason why Jamal's parents returned to Morocco was that they wanted him to learn Arabic and be educated in his own country's schools. But it is difficult for Jamal at first. Today, Jamal asks his friend, Hafid, if he wants to watch the soccer match with him and his brothers at a neighbor's house, where they can all speak Berber. Hafid remembers how anxious and confused he felt during his first year at Quranic school, before he could understand much Arabic. Now Hafid is one of the best students in his class.

Although the French governed Morocco for less than 50 years, they left a lasting impact on many aspects of society, including language and literacy. Because virtually all publications, from newspapers to textbooks to government forms, were in the French language, it became extremely difficult, even several decades after independence, to create a literate infrastructure in the Arabic language. Now, as noted, Standard Arabic is the official language of government, schooling, and literacy, even though French remains a secondary official language and may still be seen on many government forms.[4] Thus, although some Moroccan children in elite preschools and private primary schools may receive much of their instruction in French, and their parents may speak French at home, they are the exceptions to a legacy that is now under pressure from a national educational policy termed Arabization (cf. Grandguillaume, 1983). This policy, which involves the gradual, systematic replacement of instruction in French by instruction in Arabic, is well underway in Morocco and is complemented by a simultaneous policy of Moroccanization of the teacher corps (Hammoud, 1982).[5]

Today, therefore, the principal language of literacy for most Moroccans is Standard Arabic. This is the case whether a student comes from a Moroccan Arabic-speaking or Berber-speaking milieu. French is learned as a second or third language and a second literacy when children enter third grade of primary school; and instruction in French consists of at most 8 hours per week of reading and writing instruction through the fifth grade. For the rural population, access to spoken or written French is gained almost entirely in school, except for television and radio. Very few parents of the children in our study could speak, read, or write French. French language and literacy proficiency becomes more important in high school and university, where certain scientific subjects are still taught in that language. In urban areas, such as Casablanca, Rabat, and Marrakech, French remains omnipresent as a second language and second literacy. Billboards, newspapers, and storefronts are covered with print in French. But, due to the influx of poor and nonschooled families into these urban areas, it is not unusual to find a rather marked bifurcation along social class lines in French language use. Furthermore, in the late 1980s, with increased schooling in Arabic and the continuing departure of Europeans, the use of the French language and linguistic competence in French seem to be on the wane.

In sum, the government has chosen a policy of promoting the ascendancy of the Arabic language, while at the same time trying to maintain French as the language for the modern economy, or what is sometimes called the "window on the world," a way of connecting with European life, culture, and economic development. Our discussions with local schoolteachers, government officials, intellectuals, and individual students suggest a common sense of anxiety over this policy, which seems to have reduced the quantity and quality of French in the country but has not replaced French materials and abilities with equivalent Standard Arabic materials and abilities.

Arabic literacy in traditional Morocco

In traditional areas of Morocco (past and present), a man may be considered literate if he has memorized and can recite the Quran and perhaps write down Quranic verses, even though he may not actually comprehend the sense of what he has read and written. The term in Moroccan Arabic often used to describe one who is literate is *qari,* meaning "one who reads," but also "one who has studied" or "one who has gone to school." The same broadness of meaning occurs with the verb root of this word, *qara'a* (to read), which is also used to mean "to study" and "to go to school." For Arabic, the semantic domains of literacy – reading, study, and formal schooling – are thus bound together. Another common verb, "to read" – particularly at the beginning stages – is *hafadh* , meaning more exactly "to memorize"; this semantic linkage seems to provide an emic rationale to many children, parents, and teachers who believe memorization is a basic part of education. To Americans, literacy without reading or reading as memorization is difficult to comprehend. In practice, however, we found that parents often invoked such terminology, believing, for example, that a child who does well in rote memorization of the Quran will be a good reader.

In traditional Morocco, as in perhaps most societies, literacy is much more than simply being able to decode or encode a string of speech. Important parts of Moroccan culture are literally built on the concept of literacy. Social standing, and what has been called "cultural capital" (Bourdieu, 1977), or the kind of knowledge possessed by an individual, is intimately linked to literacy in Morocco. Of course, as formal education and Arabic literacy skills reach more and more of the population, there will be an observable decrease in the exceptional respect given to those considered literate. It is, in cultural terms, what has been called the law of diminishing returns. Yet there remain many parts of Morocco – and statistics suggest that this is still the large majority of the population – where the traditional value of literacy remains high, where the *qari* are still a revered class of people.

Taking the bus

The impressive, newly built Marrakech bus station has more than 31 ticket counters for different bus lines and destinations. Numbered signs in Arabic and French quickly indicate, to the literate, where to buy the desired ticket. Exit gates and individual bus quays are also systematically numbered, and one can easily find a bus to Casablanca, following the clearly marked signs: "ligne Casablanca" ticket counter, exit gate no. 2, bus quay no. 10.

When Hammou stepped timidly into the bustling station, with the intention of buying a ticket to Skhour des Rehamna to visit relatives, he went to the first window he saw and asked if the bus were going there. The Beni-Mellal ticket seller – used to such requests – patiently instructed him where to go, pointing in the general direction of a row of counters to the left. Hammou wandered unsurely in the direction indicated, asking other travelers waiting in lines the same question until he was rescued by a man whose prime function at the station appeared to be guide and information giver, who shepherded him to the right counter. There, too, another man of unclear occupation, lounging by the counter, asked Hammou where he planned to go, as he did the other clients in the line.

Ticket in hand, Hammou asked again for directions to the waiting bus, and was offered such information, even when he didn't ask: from the ticket seller, from the doorman (who guarded the exit to the quays against those without valid tickets), and from porters. Having found his bus, and finally settled into his seat, Hammou surveyed his surroundings.

The inside front of the bus was adorned with signs indicating the bus driver's tastes and concerns. A gaudy cardboard hand of Fatima (*khamsa*) and a tiny sequined slipper hung from the rearview mirror; and a phrase from the Quran was painted with a flourish in red above the windshield for *baraka,* or blessing. A smaller sign, painted less elegantly, admonished the passengers against smoking or spitting. A few faded postcards taped to the dashboard and a decal of a bathing beauty completed the decor.

Next to him, Hammou found a Western-dressed, bespectacled young woman immersed in a book – no doubt a Marrakech University student preparing for exams during a weekend visit home. A handful of other people were reading: three or four well-dressed businessmen with Arabic and French newspapers; a teenage girl looking over a popular *cine-roman* magazine (containing series of photographs from a film or television program, with comic-book captions providing the dialogue); a young man studying his notebook and a sheaf of stencils. But, for the most part, the bus was filled with people chatting amiably with their neighbors and sharing food, farmers discussing the weather and the year's crop yield, women with nursing or sleeping babies, and others gazing pensively out the window.

When Hammou noticed me (JS, an American researcher) reading beside him, he asked if I were a university student. I nodded. "God help you," he said in Arabic, thinking I was Moroccan. "You [the students] hold the progress of our country in your hands." I had to smile in embarrassment as I held the illustrated cover of an Ian Fleming paperback out of his view.

This sketch of Hammou's bus ride provides several key observations concerning the culture of literacy in Morocco. First and foremost, we see how nonliterate Hammou maintains considerable respect for and appreciation of the powers of literacy. Second, the bus's decor presents two very distinct uses of writing: The Quranic inscription was an aesthetic and comforting security measure, conferring *baraka* on the bus, while the notice of activity restrictions had a practical, though less spiritual, purpose. Passengers reading on the bus were few, but some of the variety of reading materials available to them is represented: newspapers for information, notebooks and stencils for schoolwork, heavily illustrated magazines and comics for entertainment. Finally, in many public situations, though reading skills might be advantageous for efficient action, the need for them is commonly circumvented by planned-for and equally acceptable substitutes. This ability to get by without literacy skills (often through tactics that may be quite sophisticated) has been noted in other societies, and tends to be especially prevalent where mediators of literacy are at work.[6]

Literacy mediators

The variety of situations in which literacy comes into play in both traditional and contemporary Morocco is mediated by literate individuals and particular social institutions. We observed literacy mediators in many households in al-Ksour, ranging from that of a divorced Berber woman (often joined by her daughter and a friend with a grandson) to a family of eleven; primary breadwinners included a migrant factory worker in France, a taxi driver, a woodcutter, a small merchant, and a bathhouse owner. We found that the literacy uses and needs of individuals and families in Morocco appear to vary more in frequency or degree of need than in the domain or type of literacy engaged. For example, most Moroccans are obliged to deal with the Moroccan government (i.e., literate) bureaucracy, but a civil servant has literacy needs virtually daily, whereas a farmer's wife may require literacy only for registering her newborn son. In the same vein, a Quranic school teacher uses what we term "religious literacy" skills (such as knowledge of the uses of Quranic text) continually, but most Moroccans, as Muslims, make only occasional use of such skills, in prayer and during events such as yearly Islamic festivals. This claim is not meant to imply that each individual accomplishes (or negotiates) his or her literacy needs in the same way. For example, the Quranic school teacher may know several different styles (*tajwid*) of reciting the Quran, as well as various commentaries or interpretations of the Quran itself. On the other hand, although many Moroccan men and women have memorized parts of the written Quran (considered a form of literacy practice) for the purpose of recitation or prayer, they may not actually be able to read the Quran with comprehension. Clearly, there are tremendous qualitative differences between these Quranic school teachers and the "average" Moroccan with some training in religious literacy.

Public writers

Available statistics on adult literacy in Morocco based on UNESCO and national government figures for public education, state that more than

60% of the adult Moroccan population (over 15 years of age) cannot read or write with fluency in any language.[7] Traditional mediators of literacy, which originated in earlier centuries when only a handful of specialists fulfilled the literacy needs for almost everyone else, are likely to maintain a strong presence in contemporary Morocco. Among the important literacy mediators are the several distinct professions of public writers – literate individuals who provide a "literacy service" in exchange for money or other social goods. Many Moroccans still rely on such writers, in addition to the more informal appeals to neighbors, friends, and others. Three types of public writers are still common in Morocco: notaries, "modern" public writers, and Quranic specialists (or *fqihs*).

Moroccan society has an elaborate legal culture based on written law, including both the Islamic Shari'a, or sacred law, and modern legislative law. Formal written documents are required for a wide range of legal undertakings, such as property transactions, marriage, inheritance, and other business dealings. To prepare such documents, one must go to the notary (*adil*).

Notaries have a long history in the Middle East, where they have served not only as the writers of legal documents but also as court witnesses (Tyan, 1959; Wakin, 1972). Notaries are trained in Islamic law, and there are several published manuals that guide them in the correct formulation of the various document types; however, they are required to pass a government test. In Marrakech, notaries used to work out of shops in the marketplace, near streets where private houses doubled as judges' courts, but now the notaries of Marrakech have been gathered together in buildings of the Ministry of Justice adjoining the courts. Notaries still write contracts and other documents in longhand, use many of the old formulations, and sign in their distinctive, stylized manner. Whereas a document written by a modern public writer requires registration in a municipal office to be considered binding and have any evidential value, a notarial document has the force of six witnesses. Those notaries who charge high fees tend to fill the documentary needs of bourgeois merchants and upper classes, who have property and estates to distribute and manage; the lower classes will utilize an expensive notary only in cases of substantial importance, such as in a major land or marriage dispute.

Notaries have long been part of urban life in the Middle East and North Africa (see Messick, 1993), but public writers of a second, general variety did not emerge as a distinct profession in Marrakech until late in the period of colonial rule. These so-called modern public writers, who operate out of marketplace stalls and are not regulated by the government, provide services mainly for the lower classes. Their appearance on the scene was an indicator of expanding literacy needs, especially in less bourgeois segments of the population. As literacy needs increased, the nonliterate and low-literate population needed ready access to specialists who could not only write from dictation but also provide the proper form required by various documents. In sharp contrast to notaries, who are highly educated in traditional law, modern public writers often have very little formal education and only self-taught legal expertise. They are further distinguished by the "modern" character of their work: They frequently use typewriters (Arabic and French) to fill out the ever-expanding variety of bureaucratic forms, write personal letters, and prepare the most elementary of legal agreements. Compared with high-status notaries, public writers rank low in social esteem, another sign of their link to the newly literate lower stratum of Moroccan society.

The third type of public writer is the *fqih* healer, who writes amulets and does astrological and numerological calculations for curing (as distinguished from the Quranic school teacher described in chapter 3). Like the notary, the professional *fqih* has a lengthy heritage in the Islamic world and can consult reference manuals for guidance in providing services. But, unlike the notaries, whose place in Moroccan legal life seems secure even amid contemporary societal change, the *fqih* healer is losing ground to the modern medical profession. Nevertheless, such *fqih*s are of interest for several reasons. First, their profession requires a complex understanding of the Arabic alphabet and its relation to numbers. Second, as curers, these men tend to retain their popularity most with the lower classes, our sample population. Third, curing and writing amulets were traditional part-time activities of Quranic school teachers, some of whom are also curer *fqih*s. Finally, *fqih*s who primarily specialized in curing also provided general writing and reading services for people in their local neighborhoods, and the principal textual material for amulets and other written cures was the Quran itself.

Medical matters

Aisha, suffering from chronic arthritis, finally decided to take her problem to the *fqih*. Her sister agreed to accompany her to Si Hariri's house one morning. Si Hariri is well known in al-Ksour as a Quranic school teacher and also enjoys a reputation for his effective traditional remedies for common persistent ailments and domestic problems. He has gained his knowledge of herbal recipes and amulet writing from his own Quranic master, having requested such lessons in order that he might supplement the meager income he anticipated in his career as a Quranic school teacher. Si Hariri's small library of the Quran, Hadith, Shari'a, and Sheikh Kishk's theme-based collections of Quranic and Hadith quotations also includes two little yellow paperbacks, *Al-Kutub as-Safra,* the indispensable reference books of the traditional healer.

He is well aware of the skepticism and disdain for his craft among modern doctors, the Westernized younger generation, and many of his scholarly colleagues who disagree that such activity is within the bounds of legitimate Islamic practice. He counters such disapproval with the proof that many have come to him after trying unsuccessfully the medicine of modern doctors, and have found relief in his combination of herbal teas and applications to fight the physical symptoms and "writing" to exorcise the spirits (*ar-riah*) that are causing the problem.

After listening patiently to Aisha's description of her symptoms, punctuated by her sister's vivid testimony, Si Hariri concluded that she was undoubtedly under the influence of spirits. He solemnly told her that he would have to prepare certain materials for this problem, and that she was to come back the next day. Upon her return, the *fqih* presented Aisha with three small packets wrapped in newspaper. The first two packets contained various herbs to be applied to the swollen joints and drunk in the form of herbal teas. The third packet held six pieces of notebook paper, one of them folded carefully into an inch-square "book" (*kitab*), as Si Hariri referred to it. It was an amulet, with a special inscription inside it, and was to be worn close to the patient's body, on a necklace or inside the belt, or under her pillow at night for 10 days. Each of the other five papers was marked with letterlike but illegible scrawls in a watery, brownish ink, a thinned version of the wool-based *smakh* used with the traditional *luha* or writing board typically used by children in Quranic schools. The patient was instructed to dunk one of the papers in slightly salted water and rub it until the ink had been washed off. The water mixture must then be drunk, and some of it sprinkled on the affected areas and forehead. She was to repeat the process with the remaining papers each day, for a total of five days.

Across town, Zineba, too, was suffering from another flare-up of rheumatism in her wrists and ankles. She called her 16-year-old son Said to the drawer where important papers were kept, and requested that he find, read, and translate for her the medical prescriptions collected during visits to several doctors. When he reached the prescription written by a certain doctor from a neighboring town, she laid it aside, recalling that this remedy had once been particularly efficacious.

Paper in hand, Said set off for the pharmacy, with his mother's instructions to buy the particular brands of painkillers and deep-heating rub specified in the prescription. When he returned home with the medicine, Zineba requested that Said read and translate the accompanying literature to her so that she could follow the dosage and application instructions carefully. For Zineba, the idea of entrusting her medical matters to anyone but a modern medical doctor was unthinkable.

In these two scenes of women seeking health care, two very distinct uses of the written materials may be observed. In the first, the writing – the amulet, the soaking papers – is itself the medicine; in the second, the prescription is saved as a record and is a means for procuring medicine, and the instructions provide information. The difference between an amulet and a prescription also serves to represent the extremes of literacy use in traditional and modern thought. The amulet, produced by a *fqih* educated in astrology, numerology, and the traditional medical sciences, offers cure or protection via the power inherent in numbers and related letters, via the blessing of Quranic text, and by calling on the action of spirits. The modern prescription, produced by a medical doctor trained in a European medical school, is anchored in a different tradition of medical thought. Here, traditional medicine and modern science use the power of the written word for similar purposes that are achieved through radically different functions of print.

The literate bureaucracy

As is the case in virtually all countries, the national government plays the primary role in increasing citizens' literacy needs in Morocco. Bureaucracy is an obvious element, as the government seeks to establish greater control over taxation, internal and external movements, and legal issues. In addition, the government dispenses social services, such as water and electricity, as well as postal and health services. The proliferation of government forms for all types of controls and services is one of the more shocking aspects of contemporary life to the older generation of Moroccans.

Candidates for every manner and kind of job must now present dossiers containing a range of public documentation, from birth certificates to a police form, as well as diplomas and transcripts. Older people, especially in the lower social strata, have no record of birth, but for the younger generation such documentation is mandatory. In addition, Morocco has instituted a national identity card and marriage and birth documentation (*hala madaniya*) for heads of families, which is designed to help the government keep track of each member of the society. As for public services, not only do piped-in water and electricity networks now reach into many rural areas, but the bill collection system is computerized, as it is for taxes on such personal items as television sets. The post office, following the French tradition, is a center not only for mail but also for telecommunications and the sending of postal money orders.

This wide spectrum of modern government activity, all requiring some degree of literacy, was introduced in the colonial period, and now reaches Moroccans in every social class. Similarly, the economy makes increasing literacy demands on job seekers. Some occupations that demand high levels of literacy have expanded rapidly in recent years – for example, nursing, pharmacy, office work, teaching, and banking. But beyond these obviously "literate" types of employment, many other jobs also require some forms of literacy. In urban shops, for example, most clerks need to be able to decode price and other product information on packaging, and merchants have to keep records of sales volume and inventories, and of credit given to favored clients. Another example of how such literacy needs are met was observed at the taxi station at al-Ksour.

A taxi driver

Aziz, a taxi driver whose route is between al-Ksour and a neighboring town, awaited his *nuba* (turn taking) as orchestrated by Moha, the station master. In a small spiral notebook, Moha would register the arrival and departure and origin and destination of every taxi that rolled into his station. Depending on the day of the week, specific rules designed to give local and out-of-town drivers a fair share of the market dictate which taxis may collect passengers in al-Ksour and which may only discharge them. Referring to his notebook, Moha would usher the groups of waiting passengers to the taxis whose turn it was.

Aziz looked forward to the days when the occasional Western traveler would share the ride, for then he could display and exercise his knowledge of spoken French. He had learned the language informally while working with the French in the early 1950s, in a small commercial venture, after some exposure during his few years of primary school attendance. One was impressed by this simple country man's proficiency in the spoken language and even more so when he carefully read aloud the written French instructions for installation and use of a newly purchased fire extinguisher for the car.

Following Aziz into his home, one finds that his literacy skills do not always meet the task at hand. During a heated argument with his son over a notice written in Arabic and sent home from school, Aziz squinted hard over the note as though from poor eyesight. He then demanded that another son read it aloud to him, for he himself was literate in French but not in Arabic.

Aziz the taxi driver will find himself in an increasingly awkward position in the face of the government's present policy of making Arabic the sole language of literacy in the public sector. In homes, different literacy tasks require varying levels of skill, for which particular family members are recruited. Uneducated parents often depend on their literate children to read for them. In one family, for example, a teenage high school student was called on to read an address, written in an unfamiliar hand, on a letter incorrectly delivered to the house. His elderly uncle, only partially literate, had examined it for a while but was unable to determine the mistake. This same man, however, could decode numbers well enough to attend to his electric bills himself. Later, a female cousin visiting the family recruited the same high school student to write out an address for a letter to a friend.   In the "medical matters" vignette related earlier in this chapter, it is useful to note the role of mediators in the two events. At the traditional healer, the client was accompanied by a family member, both for moral support and the dictates of propriety. Her own manipulation of the medicines, written and otherwise, did not require literacy skills; all she needed was a good memory for oral instructions. In the second case, the son's mediation or participation in the event, through his interpretation of written materials, was crucial for the procurement and correct use of the medicines. Alone, Zineba would never have located the required prescription or known how to use the drugs. Fortunately for Zineba, her schooled son conveniently filled the gap between her own skills and the requirements of the situation.   The impact of this new intergenerational pattern of family literacy, with the child as literacy mediator for the parent, is a topic central to literacy and education in many Third World countries.[8]

Material culture of literacy

The *material culture* of literacy refers to the technology and products of literacy in a given society, that is, the instruments and physical means connected with literate activities (see also Heath, 1980; Szwed, 1981). For example, a literacy instrument that is at once the symbol of the Quranic school and its principal physical medium is the individual writing board, the *luha*. In the traditional Quranic school each pupil had his personal *luha*, identified by the loop of colored string used to hang it on the wall in the schoolroom. *Luha*s were handmade by a small group of town craftsmen in several standard sizes, from very small, intended for alphabet learners, to large, for advanced students in memorizing and studying texts beyond the Quran itself (Wagner & Lotfi, 1980). On a large *luha*, for example, the lines of a grammar treatise are written widely spaced – this is the part to be memorized – and in between, at an angle, the teacher writes his commentary, which is not meant to be memorized.

*Luha*s are still sold in the Marrakech marketplace, but the buyers now come primarily from rural areas. In town, the wooden *luha* is almost completely replaced by individual modern slates, used with chalk, or by a large blackboard (*sebora*) for the classroom, or both. Even the individual slate, although still referred to as *luha,* is differently conceived: It is for practice and is brought home with notebooks and readers. The blackboard at the front of the classroom is a material embodiment of a conceptual change in the organization of the Quranic school; the emphasis is now on the group and lesson uniformity, rather than, as with the traditional *luha,* a somewhat more private, individualized endeavor.

Several centuries ago, during the height of the Ibn-Yusuf college (*madrasa*), numerous booksellers had their stores near this venerable scholarly center in Marrakech. However, as in many other parts of the Arab world, a secular tradition of literacy eventually developed and learned to coexist with the religious literate tradition. In addition, the distribution and genre of such literate materials also changed over time. Until as recently as 30 years ago, books available in booksellers' shops in Marrakech were confined to Islamic subjects, such as works on religion, Islamic law, Arabic grammar and letters, and Arab-Islamic history. Now the trade in books, in both volume and genre, indicates greatly increased popular participation in reading.

Some traditional bookstores are still to be found in the poorer quarters of the old city (*medina*) of Marrakech. In other bookstores, however, located primarily in the new city, older Arabic genres are joined on the shelves by contemporary Arabic works, published either in the Levant or North Africa, and by books in French and, to a lesser extent, in English and Spanish. These contemporary publications represent the introduction of a wide range of new subject matter, both scholarly and popular. The expanded horizon of literate materials available ranges from novels (Western and Middle Eastern, in French and Arabic) to the sociology of Marx. In comparison with the traditional genres, these newly accessible titles represent a distinct development of secular reading interest. Although books are quite expensive at bookstores in the Gueliz (the modern part of the city), there is a flourishing street-vendor market in used books located in Jama'a al-Fna, the great central square of the old city. In addition to the regular vendors' stalls, at the beginning of the school year there is a lively trade in schoolbooks among student buyers and sellers.

As with the secular book trade, the history of newspaper and magazine publication in Morocco is confined to the present century, with the development of newspapers being closely tied to the country's modern political history. One interesting aspect is the role of newspapers as tools for communication – of nationalist views in the colonial period and now of government information – to the general population. Newspapers, it is said, are influential only where there is a public that either reads or receives ideas through other literate individuals. A comparison of early nationalist papers to present-day ones reveals a rise of popular interests that extend beyond purely political matters. Just as the book trade developed in a secular direction from a traditional specialization in Islamic subjects, so the newspapers have now gone beyond politics, their initial raison d'être, to include sports, cultural affairs, and world news. A parallel diversification is found in magazines, some of which are photo-story publications that require little or no literate skills for appreciation.

Campaign publicity is a third example of printed matter for literate and nonliterate consumption.

Electioneering

Overnight, the city of Marrakech had been swathed in multicolored sheets of paper – slapped in rows on walls, hanging from wires strung over passageways and avenues, festooning storefronts, in one case cleverly arranged to spell out the slogan "God, the State, and the King." On closer inspection, each sheet is seen to be printed with the photograph, name, and party platform details of a candidate for public office. The colorful scene announces not a carnival or holiday but the campaign for coming local elections of city and regional representatives and other officeholders.

The variety of colors, apart from attracting attention, serves a very practical purpose for the largely nonliterate constituency. On election day itself, as explained by a knowledgeable though nonliterate mother of eight, voters are given a booklet of color-coded tickets, one for each candidate.

Those who cannot read the name of their preferred candidate have only to match the color of the ticket with that of the candidate's posters, fliers, and election information booth, tear the ticket out, and place it in the voting box. As the multitude of candidates exceeds the number of available solid pastel colors for preparing stencils and posters, many candidates even have a two-color code scheme: lavender with a yellow vertical stripe, sky blue with a green bar, gold with a brown one. Even in rural areas, visual and oral politicking goes on during the preelection period. Similar to but more pervasive than the elephant and donkey visual symbols for the American voters, the color code system described here is a necessity, and an official recognition of the diversity in literacy levels of the Moroccan voting public.

The material quality of printed matter has also gone through a long evolution. Books are familiar objects, the physical embodiments of a lengthy literate tradition – at least in the experience of the lettered traditional elite. For the lower social stratum, the literate tradition was confined to the Quran, and this was an object not necessarily to be read but to be retained in the household for the *baraka* it holds as the word of Allah. In many traditional families, the Quran is still found hanging on the wall in a decorated bag.

Although we do not know how common such practices were in the precolonial period, advertisements, posters, notices, banners announcing or celebrating a public event, graffiti, street signs and writing on storefronts are now in Marrakech and, to a lesser extent, in al-Ksour as well. These public writings are in Arabic or French or both, and run the spectrum of usage from the most secular movie posters to official government announcements and nonofficial ones such as those witnessed during the election campaigns, to religious phrases from the Quran and other sources on banners in front of mosques, especially during Ramadan, the month of fasting. To what extent individuals make use of such literacy available in the environment is still an open question. In the United States, where there is written material attuned to children's interests on each box of cereal and virtually covering the urban landscape, a number of studies are beginning to demonstrate the importance of such literate "ecologies" (Ferreiro & Teberosky, 1982; Mason & Allen, 1986). In Morocco and other Third World countries, differences between rural and urban ambient literacy provide fertile ground for studying the effects of literacy outside the classroom, as we shall see in subsequent chapters.

Before completing this brief sketch of the material culture of literacy in Morocco, we would be remiss if we failed to note a dimension of literacy that has appeared via the latest and most pervasive new element of mass media – television. Thought sometimes in the West to be the embodiment of a nonliterate tradition, television in Morocco has managed, much like that of secular trade books, to link itself to the prestige of religious literacy. The extremes of traditional and modern material forms of literacy may be seen in the presentation of the Quranic text on television during Ramadan. This modern communication medium, generally thought of as placing few literacy requirements on the viewer, now reaches the homes of Moroccans of all socioeconomic levels. Moroccan television is structured in its use of classical Arabic and French in newscasts and other programming, so that literate individuals generally have had more direct access. But the appearance of Quranic passages on the screen accompanied by an audio portion of chanted recitation brings together the oldest and newest media while at the same time placing new demands – in terms of both written Arabic and oral Standard Arabic – on the home viewer. It may well be the case that the contemporary increase in Standard Arabic syntax and the utilization of Standard Arabic vocabulary (in lieu of Moroccan dialect) may be due more to television watching and listening (including Egyptian soap operas) than to the use of Standard Arabic in the classroom.

"Restricted literacy": Past and present

The pattern of traditional literacy we describe in Morocco could be characterized as "restricted" (Goody, 1968), as only a small, elite segment of the society was literate and actively engaged in reading and writing. In the present century, however, the social distribution and culture of literacy have been transformed, accelerated by the colonial French and by the establishment of a national school system.

It is worthwhile to consider for a moment this term *restricted literacy*. Sometimes used in a judgmental sense in terms of the haves and the have-nots, this characterization obscures the fact that many people who are said to be illiterate *do* use literacy, even if indirectly, as we saw in the vignette of Oum Fatima in chapter 1. People clearly vary in terms of personal literacy skills, but those who are completely nonliterate often have access to literate persons for their required needs; and, as will be seen in our research, nonliterate mothers have many well-honed beliefs about literacy and education.

Historically, to be nonliterate was not perceived with a negative stigma, although it can be in contemporary Morocco. In traditional Morocco, the demands literacy placed on individuals were fewer and more limited, and there were individuals, institutions, and social mechanisms for satisfying those needs. As we have seen, both transmission and reception of literate media passed through a range of formal and informal mediators – from public writers and Quranic scholars to literate neighbors and relatives. In large rural families in traditional Morocco, it was not uncommon to select one son to pursue the life of a *fqih,* while his brothers concerned themselves with cultivation or pastoralism and his sisters worked in the house or tent. An important difference between then and now is one of attitude: Today literacy is often perceived as an individual's personal need and right, whereas it once was something a person as a member of a group or neighborhood might accomplish indirectly through mediators. Historical and ethnographic data lead to the conclusion that in traditional times (up until perhaps the mid-twentieth century), Moroccans did not conceive of literacy as something that ought to pertain to every individual. Now, however, the ideology of personal literacy has made a remarkably strong mark on public consciousness at all levels of Moroccan society. As one primary school teacher told us: "A person without literacy is like a soldier without bullets."

Stability and change

In sum, what we see in Morocco is a kaleidoscope of rapid change, but within a context of rich cultural values that change slowly over time. Many features of traditional literacy remain, even as attitudes and behavior concerning literacy and education are undergoing dramatic evolution. Is this a uniquely Moroccan situation, or is this a phenomenon that has much in common with other parts of the world? There is, of course, no more of an answer to this question than to the parallel question of whether Moroccan culture has much in common with other cultures. Naturally, there is much in common, and much that is different. However, it is our thesis that we cannot, and should not, leap to the general without understanding some of the specifics of literacy in cultural context. Morocco may have more in common with Algeria than with the United States, but the Moroccan experience is unique in its sociohistorical development, in what "counts" in the society, in its educational infrastructure, and so much else. Western or other assumptions about literacy must give way to everyday understandings of literacy, for ordinary people in ordinary situations.

In our approach to studying literacy in Morocco, we have tried to consider the phenomenon of literacy from both individual and social-cultural perspectives. A spectrum of literacy uses and mediators, we have seen, exists, and these have changed over time, especially in the direction of secular and popular content and access. The concrete technology of literacy – its material culture – is also changing, shifting toward the modern, while never entirely abandoning the traditional. In addition to the increased use of the Arabic language, Moroccan society, once characterized by a pattern of restricted social distribution of both the skills and use of literacy, is moving steadily in the direction of generalized and popularized literacy. To understand the nature of literacy in Morocco is to travel a long way toward understanding the complex and variegated culture of Moroccan society. The central factor in these changes in language and literacy use is the dramatic expansion of government schools. In chapter 3 we trace the rise of modern education from its historical roots in traditional Islamic schooling.

Notes

1   Various Berber groups have attempted to revive the use of Berber script as part of an effort to support a renaissance of Berber language and culture in Morocco. These efforts have been only partly successful, given government resistance to any change from Arabic linguistic dominance in all facets of Moroccan cultural life.

2   A second, much more widely known Jewish migration occurred in the fifteenth century, during the Spanish Inquisition, when thousands of Jews, who had flourished under the relatively benign regimes of the Andalusian Muslims, were forced to flee from southern Spain to Morocco. This second group of Jews tended to be urbanized, highly educated, and relatively well-to-do people. They settled in the great cities of Tangiers, Meknes, Rabat-Sale, and Marrakech, unlike their coreligionists, who still dwelled mainly in uneducated poverty in the rural countryside. This second wave of Jewish immigration established a significant urban literate community that co-existed well into the twentieth century alongside the Islamic religious community. For further discussion on the history of Jewish life in Morocco, see Zafrani (1969), Ayache (1980), and Shokeid (1982).

3   Some attempts have been made in recent years to publish newspapers and magazines in the Moroccan dialect. Though completely feasible from a linguistic perspective, there is great resistance among the national leadership to move away from the long-term effort toward Standard Arabic in both spoken and written forms.

4 Indeed, since the advent of computerized electric and tax bills and the like, French has been in the ascendancy due to the ease with which its script can be utilized by such information technology. Considerable efforts are now being made to adapt the Arabic script to new technologies.

5 Since 1956, when Morocco was declared a "sovereign Muslim state, whose official language is Arabic," policymakers have sought to Arabize a number of domains that formerly functioned primarily in French. A series of policies, devised by successive officials in the Ministry of Education, has resulted in the gradual Arabization of the public schools. As of the 1984–1985 academic year, the schools had been Arabized through the second year of first-cycle secondary school – that is, all subjects were taught in Arabic, except for French itself, which was taught as a second language. Although French is no longer used in the primary schools as the language of instruction for math and science, the fifth-grade day, for example, is divided such that one instructor teaches both French and math and another teaches a variety of Arabic language subjects (e.g., grammar, recitation, composition, and the like), as well as other school subjects that are studied in Arabic. See a further description of classroom language use in chapter 3; see also Seckinger (1988) for a discussion of some of the problems encountered in the process of Arabization.

6 Anzalone and McLaughlin (1983) found a similar phenomenon among low-literate adults in the Gambia.

7 Statistics on adult literacy are provided by UNESCO, and are usually based either on school attendance figures or on responses to national census questions, such as "Can you read and write?" Neither source is very reliable as an indicator of literacy levels in a society (Wagner, 1990), but such statistics are usually the only data available for national and cross-national comparisons. Estimates of the official adult literacy rate in Morocco are provided in chapter 11.

8 Patterns of intergenerational literacy have rarely been reported, but see Wagner and Spratt (1989) for a description of data for Morocco. This issue is also addressed in chapters 6 and 11 of this volume.

3. The cultural context of schooling

[Quranic schooling] was held in mosques, or in rooms about the town be-
longing to them, . . . in which all sit on the ground, the teacher facing his
pupils, whose bare pates are all within reach of the switch in his hand. Instead of books or slates, each one is provided with a thin board, narrowed to
the lower end. . . . One of the bigger boys being set to teach them to write
the alphabet which they have already been taught by ear, the letters are
written out on the board for them to copy. The lessons are then read aloud
by all together, rocking to and fro to keep time, some delighting in a high
key, others jogging in lower tones. (Meakin, 1902: 304)

Most educational systems in the Third World have been heavily influenced by centuries of colonial rule, and Morocco is no exception. Though
the Spanish influence in northern Morocco has diminished substantially
since independence, the French educational system has provided the base
on which much of Moroccan public education has been built. And yet, the
present educational system was preceded also by almost a thousand years of
Islamic education that provided a network of educational institutions that
in some ways still exceeds the reach of modern public schooling. Both the
modern and traditional systems of schooling have evolved over decades of
contact between teachers, students, and pedagogies within Moroccan
society. Competition and even rivalry are still apparent in the kinds of
remarks made about these institutions, and no comprehensive picture of
education or literacy in Morocco can be drawn without some understanding of each of them.

To describe schooling in any country often seems to involve reciting the
kinds of statistics provided by ministries of education: numbers of students, teachers, classrooms, by grade, and so forth. It is of interest to note,
for example, that in 1988, 72% of all 7 and 8 year olds had spent at least
some time in primary school, whereas this figure was only 46% in 1970.
Similarly, for at least 1 year of secondary schooling, the figures are 31% and
11%, respectively. Thus, there has been a dramatic increase in school
enrollment over the last two decades. Nonetheless, the statistics also show

that female enrollment lagged about 50% behind that of males, and that only about one in three students who enter primary school actually reach secondary school (sixth grade). Dropouts before the end of primary school vastly exceed those who finish. Statistics, then, tell us a story of the success in increasing initial enrollments as well as the tragedy of the many, many students whose initial hopes were dashed.

But there is another way to tell this story. To describe the cultural context of schooling, we need to enter into the lives of the children and families who interact with these sometimes strange but powerful institutions. The most effective and realistic way to portray the nature of schooling is to understand it through the actors who take part in the process. We provide, therefore, a series of vignettes based on the lives of two families whom we shall visit throughout the chapter.

Two families

The Hamrani family is typical of many Marrakech residents. The Hamranis moved to this city of a half-million residents 14 years ago from an outlying village, because changing patterns of land use, periodic droughts, and a growing population had made subsistence farming less and less viable. Although many such newly urbanized families are of Berber or mixed Arab–Berber linguistic and cultural heritage, the Hamranis are Arabic speakers, like the majority of families in Marrakech. Their standard of living, as gauged by the possession of a refrigerator and television and by utilities such as electricity and running water, is higher than that of typical rural families.

The Tamandat family lives on the outskirts of rural al-Ksour in the foothills of the Middle Atlas Mountains, up a winding unpaved road packed down by years of travel by horses, donkeys, goats, and people and laced with ruts carved by fast-flowing rainwater. It takes the Tamandat children longer than many of their in-town classmates to walk to school. They have no running water, electricity, or television, nor much access to newspapers, magazines, or other reading materials. Both parents are primarily Berber speakers themselves, and the Tamandat children spoke little if any Arabic before going to school. Because Ahmed Tamandat, the father, sells his wheat at the *souk,* he has learned to speak fluent Moroccan Arabic, a fact of which he is proud. On the other hand, he cannot read or write Arabic.

As in many parts of the Muslim world, Islamic schooling in Morocco predates modern formal schooling by almost a millennium, beginning shortly after the great Islamic invasion. It has played a crucial historical role in the training of the nation's youth and continues to reach about half the number of the young children who go on to the modern school system. Although such traditional Quranic schooling may have touched the lives of most Moroccans, its impact – relative to the modern school – remains little understood either within or outside the country. Any discussion of the social and cognitive consequences of such traditional schooling necessarily depends on an adequate understanding of its varied roles in the lives of children and families.

Historically, Quranic schools had no form of government regulation. They were essentially the private enterprise of individual *fqihs*, instructors who contracted for payment directly with students' parents or a village community and who taught in a time-honored method handed down through the generations. *Fqihs* typically carried a single important credential: They themselves had memorized the Quran.

To a considerable extent, the Islamic educational system in Morocco can be said to be embodied in its teachers. The Quran is believed to be the actual word of God and is meant to be recited aloud (Quasem, 1982). Learning to recite can only be accomplished with the help of a master skilled in phrasing and pronunciation conventions. Although much independent study of the text may also take place, it cannot replace the training and oral modeling provided by the *fqih*. Students in search of the higher levels of Islamic education, such as exegesis, grammar, and law, traditionally traveled great distances to study with a scholar reputed to be particularly learned in one of these disciplines. A student's program of study at this level consisted not of attendance at one particular institution but a series of apprenticeships with individual scholars who might be scattered across the country. Similarly, there was no single "diploma" describing and capping one's course of study. Instead, a documentation of the scholars with whom one had worked (*ijaza*), sometimes including their recommendation and notice of satisfactory mastery of material, was the standard proof of education; and it carried weight depending on the reputations of the scholars worked with. In many cases an individual's reputation, along with a known history of study with renowned scholars, was more important in attracting students to establish one's own school than any document that one might possess (Eickelman, 1978). To this day the Quranic school is often any available space – a garage, a rented room – in which a master and his students can convene. The importance of the teacher is such that the school itself is often referred to simply by the name of the *fqih* who teaches there.

The centrality of the role of the teacher in traditional Morocco is a theme present at all levels of Islamic learning. In the words of one informant – himself a tailor and former Quranic school teacher – and known as a *fqih* in his community:

> I think that in everything, you need a teacher. It is possible to study by yourself, but it would be much easier with a *fqih*. For example, if you are traveling on a road you don't know, if you go by yourself without asking you might know some of it. But if you ask someone, "the teacher of the road," he will show you the easiest way to go.

The range of meanings ascribed to the term *fqih* is particularly important and requires some clarification at this point. How may we differentiate among the Quranic school teacher, the traditional healer (described in chapter 2), and the proverbial "wise man," – all popularly known in Morocco as *fqih*? In its literal sense, the term designates a scholar of Islamic jurisprudence. But in common Moroccan usage, it signifies more generally an individual with a certain level and type of religious knowledge, usually attained through formal religious schooling. Just what knowledge is required, however, depends on both the scholarly level and the social conditions of the community in which he operates. For example, in a rural or low-income urban area with a low adult literacy rate or little religious scholarship, an individual may be recognized as a *fqih* on the basis of his own "more than average," but still very limited, religious and literacy training. This same level of training, however, would not be sufficient to earn him the same title in a more literate or scholarly circle.

In our interviews, the qualifications for becoming a *fqih* were frequently defined in broad, imprecise terms, open to considerable interpretation:

> The *fqih* . . . knew religion in general. . . . His head was like a sea, he could talk about every field. That is why he was a *fqih*. . . . The Quran states that if someone is good with Allah, Allah makes him a *fqih* of religion, a *fqih* of both religion and life. A *fqih* is someone who is very knowledgeable about both religion and life. He knows what to do in life and after death.

According to another informant, "the *fqih* is someone who instructs people in their religion and guides them in their religion." Thus, whereas a *fqih* may be found in many areas of employment – prayer leaders at the mosque, charm writers, merchants, tailors, bathhouse owners, even soldiers – the title of *fqih* still retains the sense of "teacher" (cf. Spratt & Wagner, 1986).

During the years of French colonial rule (1912–1956), the vast system of Quranic schools (known variously in Morocco as *kuttab*s, *madrasa*s, *jami*s, or *msid*s) was caught up in a succession of reforms. Quranic schooling then went into decline, first with the rise of the colonial and nationalist schools and then with the tremendous expansion of the national public school system. Quranic schools, with a few rural exceptions, now function as preschools, because children, who may attend for as long as 3 years, are legally required to transfer to public primary schools at 7 years of age. In a royal decree of 1968, King Hassan II launched a campaign called Operation Quranic School. Emphasizing the importance of Quranic schools in introducing the country's youth to the Quran and to Islamic beliefs, the king urged the Ministry of Education to upgrade and standardize Quranic instruction and required all children to attend a Quranic preschool for at least 2 years. Although these standards were not universally applied, after 1968 it became more common to find blackboards, class lists, and elementary arithmetic added to Quranic instruction. The 2-year preschool attendance requirement also led to a great increase in the number of children in the *kuttab*s, which now accept girls on an equal basis with boys, who used to be the only clientele of these traditional schools.

Quranic pedagogy

Amina goes to the kuttab

Up the road from the weekly *souk* (market) in rural al-Ksour is the *masjid* (mosque) Sidi Ahmed ben Youssef. A small concrete room above the mosque serves as a *kuttab*, its walls unpainted and unadorned. Two windows on one side of the room admit a bright but indirect light, and a handful of plants in old powdered milk cans line one windowsill. A blackboard hangs from another wall, facing three worn straw mats and two rows of low wooden stools behind them.

Classes are taught by Si Khalidi,[1] a *fqih* in his mid-40s, who usually dresses in a brown flannel *djellaba* (Moroccan outer robe) with the hood up. Si Khalidi lives with his wife and children in a house adjoining the *kuttab*. He is known to the community as both a *fqih* and a tailor of *djellaba*s, who sets up his sewing machine at the *souk* every Sunday. Like most other *fqih*s, Si Khalidi finds the nominal monthly fees paid him by the parents of his charges insufficient to support his family, and tailoring provides an important supplementary income.

Today is a Thursday in fall, early in the school year, and Si Khalidi is teaching in the *kuttab*. It is nearly two o'clock in the afternoon, and when he comes down the steps from his house to unlock the school door for the afternoon session, there is already a small crowd of children waiting outside. Among them is Amina Tamandat. Amina and her friends line up outside the door, two by two, and enter noisily, taking seats on the mats and benches and rummaging through their bags for slates and chalk. They range in age from 4 to 7 years.

This afternoon's session begins with the recitation of a previously memorized *sura* (chapter of the Quran). Si Khalidi begins, punctuating the rhythm of his words with periodic taps of his stick on the blackboard in the front of the simple room. After a few syllables, the children join in, chanting loudly in near unison and repeating the same three-note pattern for each *aya* (verse). Next, children are called on to recite individually. The youngest ones stammer over the unfamiliar words, and the older students continue more smoothly, but all of them speak loudly, some even shouting, in a style and tone of voice distinct from that of conversation. The best students are motioned to the front of the room to recite for the rest. Amina is not among them today, though she is often one of the first to memorize a new *sura*.

It is now time for letter-writing practice. Today the Arabic letter *ghain* is presented. It is written on the blackboard under the heading "letters" (*huruf*) in several combinations, with each of the short and long vowels, and then in three common words. Pointing to each example with his stick, Si Khalidi models the corresponding sound, and the class repeats in unison. Long-vowel syllables are enunciated in two tones, emphasizing the length of the vowels. This time Amina is chosen. She strikes the board with the stick and pronounces each syllable and word in the same declamatory recitation voice.

Before dismissing the class, Si Khalidi offers a few reminders about morals, manners, and politeness. Children must respect their parents, he says, advising them to kiss their parents on the hand when they arrive home and to behave themselves. Amina and other Berber-speaking children are still having a hard time understanding all of this, because the *fqih,* who comes from the Arabic-speaking plains, knows only a few words of Berber.

Most parents say that Si Khalidi is a "good" *fqih*. He is a devout Muslim, prays five times daily at the *masjid,* and is also familiar with "modern school pedagogy." His interest in keeping up with the times is reflected in his efforts to teach the alphabet, encourage comprehension, and include elementary arithmetic in his teaching – elements of contemporary Quranic schooling that did not exist only one or two decades ago. How did this change come to pass for Si Khalidi, a middle-aged man whose schooling was exclusively in Islamic institutions? As he indicated, modern public schooling is becoming more central in the lives of the family than the 1 or 2 years of *kuttab* experience is, and parents have let him know that they think that, in addition to the critical task of teaching Islam, elementary academic skills are also useful. So, for many *fqihs,* children, and parents, the *kuttab* has now become more like its contemporary cousin, the secular preschool. And yet, the Quranic pedagogical techniques of rote recitation and in-unison chanting, as well as strict obedience, have been maintained, coming into the present from a long and distinguished past.

As almost lyrically described in the quotation from Meakin at the beginning of this chapter, writing on the wooden *luha* – predecessor of the small chalkboard slates used in Si Khalidi's *kuttab* – was a central feature of traditional Quranic schooling. The traditional *luha* was washed with a dissolved clay solution (*selsal*) that provides an off-white writing surface when it dries. The teacher would write the material to be memorized on the student's board in a black ink made of burnt wool (*smakh*). Occasionally, he might correct the student's writing effort by adding marginal notes on the *luha*. If, later in the day, the student was able to recite the text without looking at his *luha,* he would be permitted to wash the writing off and apply a new white coat, which will be ready for a new text the next day. Working from his own *luha,* each student would proceed at an individualized pace. In the old days, when a youth successfully memorized a significant portion of the Quran, a special ceremony marked this achievement. The *luha* was elaborately decorated for this occasion, often with floriated calligraphy or square Kufic script, to symbolize an important intellectual event in the boy's life. Thus decorated, the *luha* came home from the school and was retired from use. For the most part, the days of the wooden *luha* are now gone from the *kuttab,* as are the reed pen and burnt-wool ink. Such materials are now used only in the more remote mountain areas of the country and in the few higher-level Quranic schools still in operation (Eickelman, 1985; Wagner & Lotfi, 1980).

Aside from the practical difficulties inherent in the instruction of so sacred a text to restless young children who cannot be fully conscious of its religious value, there is another problem in reading the Quran. The language of the text is considered to be the finest example of pure classical Arabic, but as such it is remote from the children's practical linguistic world of spoken or written Arabic. In addition, the Quran is highly abstract and metaphorical and thus conceptually inaccessible as well. It is not surprising, therefore, that little effort is made, even today, to ensure children's comprehension; the "impossibility" of initial comprehension continues as an important rationale for the initial rote acquisition and recitation of the text. Because of Islamic tradition, there are no visual aids in Quranic text. Also, as a sacred text, the Quran is immutable; there is, for example, no pedagogical tactic of presenting vocabulary in other or simpler contexts to facilitate comprehension, though the shorter *suras* are presented first, because they are thought to be easier for children to memorize.

Even in Quranic preschools today, beginning sessions of Quranic memorization are rarely accompanied by study of the written representation of the verses being learned or practiced. The decoding and writing lessons on the classroom's blackboard are usually limited, as described in Si Khalidi's *kuttab,* to individual letters. Typically, this written material is studied first by repeating it orally, followed by the class's chanting in unison and then individually. Finally, writing exercises on children's individual slates may entail copying a letter (or letters) from the blackboard. Thus, we see here an instance of "bottom-up," letter-to-blend-to-word instructional techniques, similar to those in modern Western classrooms, being used extensively in a setting where rote memorization techniques were once the primary method.

Quranic schooling and thinking

[Islamic education] . . . trains the memory and the power of reasoning – always in formal methods – and then give to neither any adequate material on which to work. The memory is burdened with verbatim knowledge of the Quran . . . and the reason is exhausted in elaborate argumentations therefrom deduced. (MacDonald, 1911: 288–9.)

Memorization of the Quran harkens back to the time when the Prophet Mohamed, who was illiterate, was said to have received the Book orally from the Archangel Gabriel and recited it to his early companions, who then committed it to memory. It was not until some years after the Prophet's death that the Book was set down in writing (as-Said, 1975). Recitation of Quranic text came to be an integral part of Muslim prayer, and it is important as well on many other ritual occasions. One who has memorized the Quran in its entirety is still highly respected and is considered to possess a blessing or *baraka* as a "carrier" of the Quran (Eickelman, 1978; Wagner, 1985). The act of memorization is, for many believers, the cornerstone of the faith; the decline in memorization in contemporary times is considered by some Muslim scholars to be indicative of an erosion of belief.

Many observers, both Western and Muslim, of Quranic schooling are not nearly as sanguine about the merits of rote memory and recitation. Hardy and Brunot (1925), who worked in the French colonial education administration in Morocco, claimed that the Moroccan child with Quranic schooling is so "exuberant with his memory that his imagination is smothered" (p. 8). They go on to say that memory is the only "mental faculty" that is well developed, and "the Moroccan child is capable of retaining without excessive effort, sentences and even entire chapters [of the Quran], without understanding" (p. 8). In more recent times, Zerdoumi has suggested that "Quranic school imposes on [the child] a purely mechanical, monotonous form of study in which nothing is likely to arouse his interest. The school thus tends to curb his intellectual and moral activity at the precise moment when it should be developing rapidly" (1970: 196). We will return to this issue in chapter 6.

Contemporary change in Quranic schools

Besides the national government's campaign to standardize Quranic pre-school education, a second reason for this shift in Quranic pedagogy is the increasing concern to prepare children for primary school entrance by acquainting them with the types of activities and situations they will encounter there. Periodic training programs for some Quranic school teachers, organized in the 1980s by UNICEF and held in local primary schools, used to provide access to new teaching techniques in reading, writing, and arithmetic. It should be noted that this intervention did not include significant financial support, a situation that created considerable resentment among some Quranic teachers. The *fqih*'s salary, the school's materials, and sparse classroom accommodations are supported almost entirely by contributions from the neighborhood, by the nominal, customary fees from parents of attending children, and in some cases by a percentage of the collected revenue of the religious community, the *habous*.

The Quranic school classroom is still an austere place, with children required to sit still for sessions of 2½ to 3 hours. But the legendary pitiless ogre, claimed by many adults to have traumatized them severely in their own childhood, was seldom encountered among the teachers we met

Girl in a Quranic school in al-Ksour.

As in the Moroccan home, children always remove their shoes and sandals before entering the traditional preschool.

Children in the traditional preschool use slates to show the teacher their classwork.

Classroom arrangement in a Quranic school in al-Ksour, with boys on one side of the room and girls on the other.

Children in a public school in Marrakech.

The classroom of a traditional Quranic school in al-Ksour.

Traditional Quranic schools in Morocco now have many of the accoutrements of contemporary schools, such as classroom blackboards and modern posters. Children still sit on the floor, however, on reed mats.

Traditional public notary (*adil*) in Marrakech.

Traditional Islamic teachers (*fqihs*) are the mainstay of the system of religious preschools in Morocco. A *fqih* in al-Ksour.

Quranic scholar and chanter of religious songs in al–Ksour.

A traditional preschool teacher and his family in al-Ksour.

The primary route to becoming a *fqih* over the centuries was to spend long years memorizing and studying the Quran.

Quranic scholar studying with *luha*.

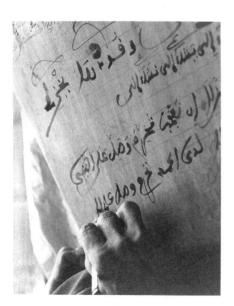

Close-up view of *luha* for Quranic study.

A *luha* used for advanced Quranic study in Morocco.

during our research. In most cases present-day Quranic school teachers were themselves educated in the traditional way – with the wooden *luha,* hours of study from before dawn to sunset, the master's ever-vigilant and far-reaching rod, and even permanent scars from a teacher's penchant for neck pinching as a disciplinary measure. Despite their own experience in school, about half of the teachers we observed appear to have embraced at least some of the modern methods and content as more practical for the children and tend to use praise and nonthreatening correction methods to direct behavior rather than the scare tactics of old.[2]

Even with these changes, there remain marked differences between the Quranic preschools and the modern preschools (*rawd al-atfal*) found in larger towns and cities and administered privately or by government ministries. The modern preschools have also increased in number as a function of the royal decree of 1968. Further, their teachers are predominantly women, whereas only a small number of women have joined the formerly all-male ranks of Quranic school teachers.

Modern secular preschooling

Hicham goes to kindergarten

Last year, at age 5, Hicham Hamrani attended a Quranic school not far from his home in the Marrakech *medina* (the *casbah,* or old fortified part of the city). Now he goes to the nearby *rawd al-atfal* (literally, garden of children), where his sister Atiqa had gone before she entered primary school. This preschool is located in a traditional style *medina* house, with two floors, and built around a central courtyard in which a lemon tree grows. Unlike in Quranic schools, where children from 3 or 4 to 7 years of age are grouped together for instruction, this preschool features age-graded classes where teachers tailor their activities closely to the levels of their students. Hicham's classroom is a long, narrow room on the second floor, with a blackboard at one end and a door and window on the right side leading to a balcony overlooking the courtyard. The white walls are decorated with student artwork, some visual-aid charts of letters and arithmetic symbols, and a bulletin board showing the week's activities and notices to the teachers. Pencils, pens, chalk, crayons, glue, games, and the children's individual French and Arabic notebooks are arranged on a shelf at the front of the room, and the other three walls are lined with child-sized chairs.

It is nearly 8 A.M., and Lalla Fatiha is shepherding the 6 year olds upstairs to class. She is a 15-year veteran of preschool teaching, with a junior high school education herself. Despite her lack of formal preparatory training, Lalla Fatiha is considered by parents to be a dedicated teacher, at once efficient and affectionate with the children.

The children are instructed to get out their slate boards – identical to those used in Si Khalidi's *kuttab* – for Arabic writing practice. Starting with individual letters, Lalla Fatiha tells them to write *sa* on their slates, a letter they have already studied. After a moment, she raps the blackboard with her knuckles, whereupon the children immediately stop writing and raise their slates to their forehead for her inspection, again as in the *kuttab*. She names the children who have made mistakes, then asks leading questions to prompt the students to correct their own and others' errors (e.g., "How many "teeth" are there in the Arabic letter *sin*?"). She also praises good work, especially in cases where students had been previously mistaken but have now corrected their errors. For each letter practiced, Lalla Fatiha calls on three students who have written the letter correctly to come up to the blackboard and write the letter for the class to see. Hicham has made no mistakes today, and when Lalla Fatiha chooses him to write the last letter studied on the board, he guides the chalk intently, if rather shakily, and returns, beaming, to his seat.

Moving to arithmetic, Lalla Fatiha writes three addition problems on the board, then reads them aloud, pointing carefully to each symbol as she reads it. The students repeat aloud in unison, then copy each equation onto their slates. Lalla Fatiha shows them how to figure out the problems by drawing and then counting, little hashmarks on their slates – for example, / / / / / / + / / / / / = ? (6 + 5 = ?). Today she spends several minutes explaining and re-explaining the procedure to a new girl who is just learning the number symbols and is confused by the concept of addition. Hicham is sitting next to the girl and shows her his own slate, pointing out the hashmarks and counting with her. Several students are then chosen to read the equations in Standard Arabic, because the number names in Moroccan Arabic employed in the local *kuttab* are not accepted in Lalla Fatiha's *rawd al-atfal*.

The morning session closes with the recitation of three short Quranic *suras*. These are said in unison by Lalla Fatiha and the students, in the same three-tone chant as that used in the *kuttab*. The class recites in unison a state-mandated National Awareness text in Standard Arabic honoring the king, the flag, and the Islamic Kingdom of Morocco. When the recitation is over, Lalla Fatiha dismisses the class, sending them down the stairs to line up at the door, where some will be met by a parent or older sibling and others will walk home on their own. Hicham lives only a few minutes' walk away, and goes home with a neighbor.

Compared to the single, unadorned *kuttab* classroom where up to 75 students of different ages are led by a single male Quranic school teacher, even the most modest *rawd al-atfal* appears to be a much more stimulating place. With the children grouped according to age in separate classrooms and with separate teachers, the modern preschool teacher can concentrate on types and levels of activities deemed appropriate for the age group she is responsible for. The Quranic school teacher, on the other hand, delivers his daily fare of Quranic recitation, decoding, writing, and math instruction to a group of children ranging widely in age, receptiveness, and length of attention span. As we have seen, the modern preschool teacher also offers a greater variety of activities to her limited age-range class: oral expression and reading and writing practice in Arabic and sometimes French; arithmetic, memorization and reciting of secular songs, and perhaps an hour a week of Quranic material; but also handicrafts, drawing, painting, role playing, and perceptual drills in the form of games such as card matching and puzzles. Clearly important is the preschool's emphasis on spoken Standard Arabic, which will be needed in primary school; many of the *fqihs*, though fluent in the similar classical Arabic of the Quran, are more at ease in Moroccan dialect than in conversational Standard Arabic.

Despite its material and pedagogical distance from the *kuttab*, the *rawd al-atfal* has retained the methods traditionally used in Quranic schools to teach the decoding and writing of Arabic letters, letter combinations, and words. It has also retained the methods used for memorizing the Quran and secular texts – rote repetition and recitation. A major difference, however, lies in the variety of activities that fill the school day. In the modern preschool, no more than half an hour per morning or afternoon is devoted to Quranic recitation; the rest of the session is used for crafts, oral expression, instructional games, or math instruction. In the Quranic school, the largest portion of the school day is spent on decoding and writing activities and on Quranic practice, and few or no other activities are included.

Modern public schooling

As noted in chapter 2, the French protectorate established a system of modern public education patterned entirely on that of metropolitan France, with the French language as the medium of instruction. Although various reforms have been carried out since independence (especially in terms of Arabization), much of the French educational legacy is still viable in the public schools. Primary schooling in Morocco is composed of the first five grade levels of Moroccan public education.[3] The nationally pre-scribed curriculum includes Arabic reading and writing, math, science, religion, and civics/history at all five grade levels and French language and literacy instruction during the last three grades of primary school. At the end of every year, pupils undergo an evaluation to determine promotion to the next grade level; at the end of grade 5, a nationwide major examina-tion (the feared *shahada*) is held, determining promotion to secondary schooling. As in many other Third World countries, grade repetition in Morocco is quite common, ranging from 15% to 25% in grades 1 to 4, with up to 50% at grade 5, as a consequence of the *shahada* (SEP, 1988; Spratt, 1988). One result of this restrictive system of promotion is that a majority of students fall below expected grade level after a few years of schooling.[4] A schematic overview of the schooling system is shown in Table 3.1.

Atiqa and Hafid at the primary school

Right after lunch, without taking tea with the rest of her family, 11-year-old Atiqa Hamrani hurries back to Madrasat Omar Khayyam for the af-ternoon session. There are so many students at her school that the classes are divided into two shifts, which operate at different times of the day. In Marrakech, this school once served as a bleach factory, then as a *funduq* (hotel for traveling merchants), before finally opening its doors as a gov-ernment primary school in the fall of 1960. Like most of the schools in our study, it has no library, but each class has a cooperative trading/lending arrangement through which students bring in books and maga-zines from home and exchange them with their classmates.

Atiqa's fourth-grade classroom is upstairs, with windows looking out over the leafy courtyard. The walls are decorated with commercially made visual aids, bilingual in French and Arabic, depicting "the butcher," "the airplane," "the port," "the postman," and "the horse." A picture of King Hassan II, young and serious in the early 1960s, looks down from above the blackboard, and a crinkled plastic Moroccan flag is tacked up beside him. The teacher's desk, in the front of the room, is covered with a flowered oilcloth, and the year's program of lessons, meticulously penned into ruled squares in both Arabic and French, is neatly taped to the front, facing the class.

There are 28 boys and girls in Atiqa's class, about average for fourth

Table 3.1. Grade levels and exam schedules in Moroccan schools

Preschool
    Quranic (*msid, kuttab*)
    Modern (*rawd al atfal, jardin d'enfants*)
Primary school (*madrasa, école primaire*)
    Cours preparatoire (CP)
    Cours elementaire (first year; CE1)
    Cours elementaire (second year; CE2)
    Cours moyen (first year; CM1)
    Cours moyen (second year; CM2)
Shahada[a] leading to CEP (*certificat d'etudes primaires*)
Junior high school (*adadiyya,* collège)
    First-year secondary (1AS)
    Second-year secondary (2AS)
    Third-year secondary (3AS)
    Fourth-year secondary (4AS)
Brevet[a] leading to CES (*certificat d'etudes secondaires*)
Senior high school (*tanawiyya, lycée*)
    Fifth-year secondary (5AS)
    Sixth-year secondary (6AS)
    Seventh-year secondary (7AS)
Baccalaureat[a] leading to diploma signifying completion of secondary school

Note: See note 3, this chapter, for subsequent changes in school structure.
[a]Selection examination.
Source: After Dichter (1976).

grade classes in Marrakech. Most of the girls have on pink or white school smocks over their regular clothing, but a few are wearing *djellabas.* As they take their seats, Lalla Saadia, Atiqa's teacher, instructs them to get out their slates and store their book bags under their desks. Lalla Saadia teaches math and French.

This afternoon's math lesson begins with a review of the distance and quantity terms in French (*metre, kilometre, decilitre*). Lalla Saadia poses questions, writing equations on the board for the students to copy onto their slates and solve. After a moment, she raps her knuckles on her desk and they lift their slates for her inspection. As the students work on their slates, Lalla Saadia encourages, corrects, and explains in Moroccan Arabic, but equations are read off the board and solved aloud in Standard Arabic. After this review, she sends Atiqa and another girl to fill buckets with water from the spigot across the courtyard, for a demonstration on liquid volumes and capacities.

When the girls return, Lalla Saadia asks them to pour the water, from a cup to a 2-liter plastic water bottle, from the bottle back into the cup, from one bottle to another, and so forth, as she makes up problems and asks questions: "How many cups of water are there in one bottle?" How many deciliters are there in two liters?" The students pay close attention and nearly leap out of their seats to shout the formulaic answers in Standard Arabic. When several problems have been demonstrated, and a fair amount of water sloshed onto the floor, Lalla Saadia picks two more students to empty the buckets into the planters in the courtyard, and sets the rest of the class to solving problems from the blackboard on their slates. Fifteen minutes later, it is time for a break, and the students file down to the playground for 10 minutes before returning to the classroom for the rest of the afternoon session.

The last subject of the day is French language. The class turns to a text in their reader about a 1970 World Cup soccer match between Morocco and Mexico, and Lalla Saadia reads it aloud. When she asks questions, the students raise their hands and stand to respond as usual, but this time vie for her attention in French (addressing her as "*Madame, Madame*" rather than "*ustada, ustada*" [teacher] in Arabic). Then the class practices the text by repeating it, one sentence at a time, one student after another. After each sentence has been repeated several times, Lalla Saadia writes the new vocabulary words on the blackboard, along with synonyms that the class has already studied (e.g., *le score* = *le resultat*) or brief definitions, and the students copy these into their notebooks. She also asks questions about vocabulary ("What is the opposite of *vieux* [old]?") and grammar ("What are the endings of the third group of verbs in the imperfect tense?"), expecting the students to know not only the grammatical rules but also the French terms for discussing them.

. . .

Meanwhile, that same morning in al-Ksour, Hafid Tamandat was also on his way to primary school. The school was founded in 1957, and its most impressive feature is a large, shady central playground. By the time Hafid arrives, dozens of boys are milling around outside the school's gate, some buying penny candy or sunflower seeds from the vendor who is always stationed outside.

There are 33 boys in Hafid's class, one of the larger fifth-grade classes in the school. Some of the first-grade classes have as many as 48 students, but almost two in five of the children will drop out or be dismissed from school by fifth grade.

Hafid sits in the front row, next to his friend Youssef. The wooden desks, each with two seats, are ranged in four columns, facing the black-board. The teacher's desk is in the right front corner, near the window. Sunlight brightens the classroom on the side where the windows are, and four light bulbs hang bare from the ceiling. The walls are decorated with a disparate assortment of pictures culled from magazines – a soccer team, several individual players, a smiling blond girl sitting on a pile of hay and petting a white horse, two men doing karate, a lakeside landscape with sailboats and white houses in the distance, hunters on a hillside and skaters on a frozen pond below, a nun looking piously down at her clasped hands. A few commercial visual aids like the ones in Atiqa's Marrakech classroom (these are of doctors and nurses during surgery) and postcards from Morocco and abroad are displayed. The year's program of lessons is posted on a bulletin board at the front of the room.

Si Mustafa, Hafid's teacher, instructs history, geography, and civics, as well as Arabic language arts. He is proud of his own fluency in Standard Arabic, and tries to instill a similar love and respect for the language in his students. It is a clear spring morning, and Si Mustafa greets his class as the boys jostle to their seats. He chooses three students to write their brief compositions on the blackboard, and others to read them aloud for correction. When an error is found, the rest of the students jab their hands into the air, pleading loudly for the teacher to call on them, until he designates one to answer.

When the lights sputter out for 2 or 3 minutes, no one seems to notice; undependable electricity is a fact of life in al-Ksour. Si Mustafa instructs the class to get out pen and paper and write a short composition about the causes and consequences of urban migration, advising them to write quickly but not to stray from the subject. Si Mustafa gives a short lecture on organization: "For our subject, there are causes and effects. It's like going to the doctor with a stomachache. He would ask, 'What did you eat?' – that's the cause – and then move on to the symptoms, the effects." Afterwards, he begins a discussion on the relative merits of city versus country life. Hafid says that he would rather live in a city, with cafés and cinemas and wide, paved streets, but other students counter that cities are expensive, too big, and confusing. Hafid is not convinced, and says he wants to live in Casablanca.

It is time for more language study. Si Mustafa tells the class that, for the upcoming *shahada,* the Arabic portion will last 2½ hours, including the reading of short texts and answering questions on them. Si Hammou writes a paragraph on the board entitled "The Sun," leaving it un-voweled,[5] then calls on students to go to the board and write in the vowels, one sentence at a time. The vowels are written in pink chalk to distinguish them from the white letters of the text. Si Mustafa explains the trickier vowelings and drills common spelling errors. He warns the class that lots of their al-Ksour classmates will not make it to secondary school unless they memorize their lessons.

Families and schooling

The Moroccan household is becoming the locus for new education and literacy activities. Although schooling is not the only cause of the changes occurring within Moroccan family structure, nevertheless it seems intimately related to such changes. Schooling is one factor – along with the demographic explosion, rapid urbanization, and fundamental economic change – that is changing Moroccan family life.

Within the Moroccan family, the arrival of a younger generation of literate and schooled men and women has led to a generation gap between children and their parents. In our sample of families, a first generation of literates must now relate to their parents, who grew up in a world of restricted traditional literacy. In modern Morocco, where literacy counts in dealing with the structures of power in the wider society, children have partially reversed the old pattern of parent-child authority in the family. It is the younger literate or biliterate (Arabic and French) generation that now provides access to new sources of information, through literacy skills that interpret and mediate the outside society for their low-literate, non-literate, or monoliterate (Arabic, Quranic Arabic, or French) parents. In this sense, one of the most significant discontinuities between home and school is expressed within the family itself: between literate and nonliterate generations.

Even though they themselves were raised in a generation and a social class that did not have high literacy expectations, many parents tend to have adjusted their nonliterate and unschooled worldviews to the new dictates of a more literate contemporary Morocco. Whether in an encouraging or threatening manner, most Moroccan parents place great value on school achievement. Although they may not be able to help their children actively with schoolwork, many parents have rapidly internalized the modernist ideology of education and literacy because it has built so well upon traditional educational values. Surprisingly, it is the generation of children now in school who are experiencing the frustration of Morocco's pyramidal educational system, maintained by a high proportion of examination failure and matched by a corresponding lack of job opportunities in the marketplace. It is ironic that in the parallel rise of literacy-related expectations, and frustrations, it is generally illiterate parents who hold firmly to expectations while their literate children must live the frustrations. The parents' generation seems at once more locked in tradition and more confident in the ideology of change.

Literacy and schools have also affected gender roles. In earlier times in Morocco, a conception of gender differences in behavior and qualities of mind tended to support traditional child-rearing practices and also had direct implications in the sphere of literacy. The traditional worldview, which rigidly distinguished the male/public and female/private/domestic domains, meant that boys went to Quranic school and girls learned domestic skills. Although the percentage of girls attending school in Morocco is still lower than that of boys (in relation to total numbers of school-age children), especially in rural areas, the concept of an exclusively male right to education has now been superseded by a policy of universal access. To the extent that literacy is a tool of power in the public realm, and to the extent that it "opens doors," it may be a vehicle for restructuring the gender-based division of labor (women in the house, tending to children; men outside, working for wages) both in the general society and within the family (see Lerner, 1963, for an early discussion of this question).

Connected to the changing identity of women in Moroccan society and culture is the gradual move toward nuclear rather than extended family living and toward a higher divorce rate. Literacy, once the privilege or expectation of elite males, is now much more accessible to the men and women of Morocco's lower strata. For example, in pursuit of formal education and employment, a small but growing number of young, un-married women are leaving their parental homes to live in school dor-mitories and rented rooms. Such an event, virtually unheard of a generation ago, and still without widespread sanction, directly challenges the traditional dictate that a girl must remain in the house of her parents until marriage.

As of 1988, about 12% of all adolescent females had some secondary schooling, providing them with some literacy skills not only in Arabic but also in French. Furthermore, our ethnographic interviews suggest that the younger generation of Moroccan women have a special motivation to learning French, as it is one of the few ways they can gain some personal independence at home and in their future married life. This is true both psychologically and economically. Psychologically, access to French pro-vides an opportunity to read literature, go to films, and talk to foreigners in the French language, which is also seen as Western-oriented and more egalitarian toward women. Economically, many jobs are open only to Moroccans who are bilingual and biliterate, and such secretarial positions, a small but rapidly growing sector of the job market, are particularly attractive to such women. As a consequence, these young and often un-married women find themselves in a situation without rules or precedent to follow, as they are still the first generation. The effects of such novelty and liberty on the social structure of Morocco are still to be determined but are already thought to be profound.[6]

Homework constitutes another important intrusion of the formerly public world of schooling and literacy into the once-bounded and private world of the family, dating from the institution of the public school system. In his examination of the ibn-Yusuf *madrasa* of Marrakech in the 1930s, Eickelman (1978) showed the importance of informal peer group learning in the form of study sessions among Quranic school students outside the confines of the formal lesson. Just as there are observable analogues in the area of rote memorization between the pedagogies of the traditional Is-lamic *madrasa* and the contemporary secular public schools, we find a similar continuity in peer learning, displaced, however, from the tradition-al Quranic school dormitory to the individual family dwelling. In both the Hamrani and Tamandat families, siblings commonly helped one another in school homework.

Moroccan public school students study constantly, utilizing in their home efforts many of the strategies observed in the schools. As mentioned earlier, memorization is the principal tactic for learning lessons, and oral recitation is the method by which the student checks his or her knowl-edge. In fact, although many contemporary Muslim educators trained in Western pedagogical methods consider rote memorization to be a debilitating remnant of an archaic system of instruction, we observed rote memorization as a prime learning strategy well into the university. To acquire a text – here secular classroom notes, not the sacred Quran – students repeat it outloud over and over or, less frequently, read and reread it silently. Rote memorization of public school materials also occurs out-side the house during the annual examination season in the late spring. Students can be seen in serious concentration as they promenade singly in public gardens or stroll near streetlamps in the evenings, eyes riveted to their open notebooks, lips mouthing the text. As it is in the West, school homework is becoming a central event in Moroccan family life.

The cost of schooling also affects families, particularly as poor families become part of a consumer economy. Although public schooling is ostensibly free in Morocco, students must provide all of their own materials, including textbooks, a considerable expense for low- to middle-income families. Each succeeding year is more expensive than the last, the higher grade levels requiring longer, and therefore more expensive, books, and more of them, because of the greater number and variety of subjects studied. Whenever possible, families preserve and pass on books from older siblings to younger, and classmates sometimes pool their resources and buy books together. Thus, even as the possible financial rewards of schooling become better known among the poor, the difficulties of getting past the examination hurdles must be weighed against the real costs to families of limited means.

The Tamandats look to the future

Nineteen-year-old Abdulhamid Tamandat sometimes helps with literacy tasks in his family. Last night his mother, Fatima, had a stomachache, and she asked Abdulhamid to examine the label on the medicine she had taken last time and see if it was still a "good" prescription. She often wishes now that she had gone to school herself, but when she was a child, during the preindependence era, her own parents' views on schooling were no different from those of most of al-Ksour's families. The only schools in town were those run by the French, and Fatima's parents had no interest in sending any of their children, girls or boys, to a place that might prepare them to serve the French, draft them into the French army, or, as legend would have it, even convert them to Christianity. She remembers stories of neighbors who went to great lengths to keep their children out of the French schools. One girl was sent away to the mountains to herd sheep, and another, disguising herself as an old woman, had her chin tattooed and dressed up in a *haik* and big slippers stuffed with paper. Though Fatima's own parents never resorted to such measures, their sentiments were the same: School would corrupt their children, and they did not want to send them there.[7]

Later, as they saw the sorts of opportunities available to those with school diplomas, the Tamandats came to regard education as the key to a better future for their children and increasingly invested their hopes and resources in their children's schooling. Though her older daughters never went to school at all, Hafid's mother is determined that some of her children will stay in school long enough to earn diplomas and find jobs in the

modern sector, preferably civil service jobs, with such social benefits as
health insurance.

Abdulhamid already feels the weight of family responsibility on his
shoulders, and is very conscientious about his studies. As the general level
of education rises, and the already bleak employment market swells with
growing numbers of qualified job seekers, Abdulhamid is developing the
double-edged attitude common to contemporary Moroccan adolescents:
An education won't necessarily ensure him a secure future, but lack of an
education will almost certainly mean a more precarious one. If he successfully passes his *baccalaureat* exam this year, Abdulhamid will be the first
Tamandat to attend university. The odds, however, are not very good.[8]

If the lives of the Tamandat children from al-Ksour and the Hamrani
children of Marrakech were projected into the present (it is almost a
decade since they were first interviewed) we would likely find that the
trend toward a more literate Morocco has continued. The younger children no doubt have received more schooling than their older brothers and
sisters, and dramatically more than their parents. What this increase in skill
and knowledge means, in the context of continuing life in a rural village or
teeming *medina,* where the average is now almost a fifth-grade education
(rather than a second or third grade), remains obscure for the observer as
well as for the children themselves. The issue of the level of schooling and
literacy that should/ought/needs to be acquired is one that may or may
not have direct consequences for these families "on the ground." What
will this generation's new skills get them in the economic marketplace?
What will it get them in terms of citizens' participation in the national and
international scheme of things? These are questions to which we shall
return again. Nonetheless, from this description of the cultural context of
schooling, we learn something of what goes on in the daily lives of most
Moroccan children. What we do not know from such qualitative analyses
is how variations in background will allow some children to achieve in
school and others to fail; or whether differences in the home, in parents'
education, in language background or gender, or in their own schooling
experience (such as attendance in Quranic preschools) will preclude or
secure certain opportunities in school and beyond.

To address these more specific and more empirical sets of questions, we
developed a research strategy that involved comparisons of contrasting
samples of children and families, and methods for evaluating what was
being learned and when. Chapter 4 describes how we went about this task.

Notes

1 The honorifics *Si* (a variant of *Sidi, my lord*) and *Lalla* (often referring to a woman who has gone on the pilgrimage to Mecca) may be used alone or to preface given names, and connote respect.

2 See Spratt and Wagner (1986) for a discussion of the changing roles of *fqihs* in contemporary Morocco.

3 As of 1990, the government extended primary schooling to six grades. The national exam, *shahada,* was eliminated after our research was completed.

4 The high dropout rate is a major issue in Moroccan education and one that directly affected our sample of primary school children, as described in chapter 4; dropouts present a problem to any longitudinal study of schooling in the Third World.

5 Depending on the nature of the text, Standard Arabic may or may not be voweled; proper understanding of the vowel system is an important part of learning to read in Arabic. Further discussion of this issue is provided in chapter 5.

6 For more information on the changing roles of Moroccan women, see Davis (1984), Dwyer (1978), Mernissi (1975), and Spratt (1988).

7 See Dichter (1976) and Spratt and Wagner (1986), for similar stories of resistance to attending the French schools.

8 In a speech delivered on June 18, 1987, King Hassan II announced that the *baccalaureat* exam would be abolished the following academic year, to be replaced by three end-of-trimester exams administered for each subject studied. If a student's overall average on these exams over the 3 years of senior high school were sufficiently high that student would receive a high school diploma. These measures were intended to curb the high rates of repetition and attrition and thereby alleviate the cost of "wasteful" additional years of schooling. The decision was made following the most dismal *baccalaureat* results in history: Of the students who sat for the first session of the exam for the 1986–1987 academic year, only 11.45% passed.

4. Doing fieldwork in Morocco

As graduate students we are told that "anthropology equals experience";
you are not an anthropologist until you have the experience of doing it.
But when one returns from the field, the opposite immediately applies: anthropology is not the experiences which made you an initiate, but only the
objective data you have brought back. (Rabinow, 1977: 4)

Choosing the problems

Not unlike the anthropology student Rabinow so aptly describes, our
research team sought not only the experience of doing the work and an
appropriate methodology of inquiry but also the objective data that could
answer the "important questions" about literacy in Morocco. We felt that
there were four major questions to address: What are the functions of
literacy in a society like Morocco? How do Moroccan children and adolescents acquire and retain literacy, taking into account the many within-
country factors such as family background, native language, gender, and
preschooling? What international policy issues could be addressed from
such a project on literacy in a developing country? What kinds of
methods – old and new – could be developed or adapted for use in a study
of literacy in Morocco? Let us consider briefly what was involved in each
of these questions.

The first question followed on interest in understanding the cultural
nature of literacy learning. More than a century of work exists on the
cognitive and pedagogical aspects of successful and not so successful reading acquisition in Western countries and in Western (Indo-European)
languages. Thousands of studies have considered the impact of neurologi-
cal, perceptual, intellectual, curricular, and other factors involved in promoting or hindering the acquisition of reading and writing in the
individual child. However, until recently, we knew rather little about the
cultural functions of literacy in society. How do individuals (parents,
teachers, children, office workers) view their own literacy capacities and

those of others? Studies began to show that social variables such as cultural attitudes and values concerning literacy, "mismatches" between home and school environments, and language preference had an important impact on whether children in school or adults in basic education programs, would learn the curriculum being taught (e.g., Reder & Green, 1983; Heath, 1980). Others showed that literacy was so prevalent in the home that many children had substantial contact with literacy long before they began formal instruction and that there were major sociocultural differences in such contact (e.g., Heath, 1982; Wagner, 1983c). Given our intention to work in Morocco, we found it of particular interest that so little research had been done on the cultural functions of literacy in developing countries. Further, as discussed in the previous two chapters, there is a great deal about literacy in Morocco and elsewhere that is emic and tied local cultural knowledge.

The second question focused more directly on the learning processes involved in the acquisition and retention of literacy: What are the cognitive and social prerequisites for learning to read in Arabic? By cognitive factors, we were interested in basic intellectual skills, such as perception, logic, early decoding abilities, language fluency in Arabic and/or Berber, and so on. With regard to social factors, we wanted to go beyond concern with broad cultural factors and their general impact on literacy in societal context. We sought to understand and empirically measure the importance of parental education, years of Quranic schooling, literacy ecology (e.g., number of books in the home), and the like on specific reading abilities. Furthermore, we thought that it would be crucial to follow a sample of children over the entire primary school period and beyond in order to have a more comprehensive picture of the developmental processes at work. Finally, there had been frequent claims about how children with only a few years of formal schooling may lose what modest literacy skills they had acquired; given the high dropout rates in Moroccan schools, we thought that literacy retention would be a key issue to study. We could find no longitudinal acquisition and retention research of this kind in a Third World setting.

As a third problem area, we had a tremendous opportunity to provide some direction to policymakers concerned with educational planning in Third World countries. Prior experience suggested that policymakers often bemoan the fact that they themselves have little time or resources to answer certain questions crucial for effective educational policies. For example, one key UN program officer in Morocco wanted to know the impact of Quranic preschooling on subsequent school learning, because he had to make a decision on whether to continue a training program for *fqihs* that had been put into place. Yet he had only anecdotal information to guide his decision making. Others complained that projects such as ours – with funding principally from scientific agencies – tended to ignore practical and policy dimensions for national development, because funding for such studies was intended for "basic research." Although this was certainly the case for the Morocco Literacy Project (MLP), we had decided from the project's inception to link research with policy questions wherever possible. This interest eventually encompassed the policy issues concerning the impact of Quranic preschooling, the importance of teaching in a first or second language, the value of additional years of schooling for the retention of literacy skills, and how literacy and poverty can be understood in the Moroccan context.

These three general questions absorbed considerable initial thinking, but it soon became clear that research questions could not be divorced from the methods to be developed and employed. Some specific issues seemed intractable. For example, how could we find out the impact of literacy on individual income unless we conducted a 15-year longitudinal study – and especially if people would not tell us how much they earned? By contrast, other questions seemed much easier to address, even though they had never been studied previously. To understand the impact of Quranic preschooling on beginning reading ability, for example, seemed to call for the relatively simple research strategy of comparing children who did and did not attend such preschools. In reality, this problem was not trivial, for it required access to Quranic schools, new methods for evaluating children's reading skills using Quranic texts, bi- and trilingual researchers, and so forth. It soon became clear that creating appropriate methods was going to be a major part of project work.

Searching for methods

Our general approach was to employ and combine the disciplinary methodologies of anthropology and psychology; that is, we used both ethnographic and quantitative methods. In traditional social science accounts of literacy, anthropologists typically collect in-depth ethnographic accounts of single communities while trying to understand how literacy is woven into the fabric of community cultural life. Little or no attempt is made to quantify levels of particular literacy abilities. In contrast, cognitive and educational psychologists typically choose to study measurable literacy skills, using tests and questionnaires. Thus, whereas anthropologists primarily use *qualitative* descriptions to construct a persuasive argument, psychologists tend to use *quantitative* measures and inferential statistics to substantiate claims beyond a given level of uncertainty. Precedent for a dual or combined approach, which is still relatively rare in the social science literature, is probably best exemplified by the work of Michael Cole and his associates (Cole, Gay, Glick, & Sharp, 1971; Cole & Means, 1981; Scribner & Cole, 1981).

In traditional research on culture and psychology, the interpretation of group differences in behavior and beliefs has long been a problem. For example, how should we interpret Rivers's (1905) finding that unschooled persons growing up in South Indian islands are less susceptible to visual illusions than are British university graduates? How do we interpret the finding that on certain logical syllogisms, unschooled Africans use a concrete form of reasoning rather than the abstract form preferred by American college sophomores? These "differences" – assuming that they have been reliably measured – may be interpreted in a number of ways. First, one might claim that because the South Indians show less susceptibility to illusion, they are less developed cognitively and thus more "primitive" than educated Britons. On the other hand, the apparent fact that South Indians resist erroneous perceptual inferences may lead to the conclusion that they see more truly and therefore have superior visual systems. In the second case, there is little question that Western society tends to prefer abstract thinking over context-specific thinking, and numerous researchers have concluded that American college sophomores are "better" thinkers than unschooled Africans. But how certain can we be of the superiority of abstract solutions, when life decisions are far from abstract? As has been pointed out elsewhere (Cole & Means, 1981; Wagner, 1982a), there are no easy solutions for determining the relative importance and validity of differences between any two groups of individuals.

There are at least two important ways to reduce what Campbell and Stanley (1963) term the "threats to validity" of comparative differences. One is to reduce the number of perceptible differences between the comparison groups, thereby approaching the ideal experimental model derived from the physical sciences, which suggests the manipulation of a single variable while holding all others constant. Although it is difficult if not impossible to exclude variability in social life, one can reduce variability by avoiding large multivectored cross-cultural differences, and favoring the study of within-culture contrasts. One example would be to study differences between schooled and nonschooled individuals who reside in the same country, thereby reducing the number of potential confounding variables.

One may also reduce the threat of alternative explanations of differences if the pattern of differences is not monolithic. That is, if American college sophomores performed "better" than Africans on all cognitive tests, we ought to be skeptical about the American students' "superiority." On the other hand, if the findings showed theoretically predicted differences in perceptual development but not in memory, we might be more likely to reject the hypothesis that there were biases in the tests or in the methods of testing. In the MLP, the fact that no single group or set of groups was consistently superior or inferior on the entire range of tasks was fortuitous in this regard, helping to refute the contention that some groups might have been aided or hindered systematically by the testing context, language of testing, or the tester's own behavior.

Our general strategy was to try to obtain qualitative and quantitative information that would mutually address the main questions of the project. We adhered to the traditions of anthropology when engaging in participant observation in homes and clinical interviews and viewing culture through the local perspectives of individuals in their daily lives. Similarly, when we addressed such questions as the impact of Quranic schooling on subsequent literacy achievement, we adopted and adapted experimental psychological methods that called for the random selection of children who had or had not attended such schools, and tested for empirically reliable consequences with objective testing methods. But beyond these two traditions, we attempted what has variously been called "ethnographic psychology" (Cole, 1975) or "cultural psychology" (Stigler, Shweder & Herdt, 1990). This often involved the local adaptation of experimental tasks and procedures that blended experimental and ethnographic approaches. For example, given our interest in how children learned to read in Arabic, we employed principles derived from research on European languages to develop innovative measures that were based on unique characteristics of the Arabic script. Finally, we used standard sociological methods to create structured questionnaires in multiple languages so that we could interview parents and children about relevant "facts" in their lives (number of children, years of education, attitudes concerning language and education, and the like). A detailed summary of our test construction methodology is contained in appendix 2.

Brief summary of empirical studies

Before we describe the research field sites and sample populations used in the project, it is important to provide the theoretical rationale for their selection in the empirical studies of the MLP. This can be achieved most clearly by providing here a summary list of the central questions we chose to explore; other background information and details on each of the research designs are given in subsequent chapters.

Chapter 5. What is the nature of Arabic reading acquisition? Are there particular characteristics of the language and its script that make Arabic easy or difficult to learn? Is there a pattern of skill development in Arabic reading acquisition? Are early measures of individual reading skills predictive of subsequent literacy development?

Chapter 6. What background factors affect literacy development in Moroccan children? Are there effects of preschooling experience, gender, or urban-rural environments? What are the effects of "home factors," such as family socioeconomic status and parental education? Are children's other skills, such as math, affected similarly or differently from reading skills?

Chapter 7. What is the nature of children's (and parents') knowledge and beliefs about literacy? Do such beliefs affect reading acquisition? Are beliefs about literacy specific to certain sectors of Moroccan society, or can such beliefs be seen in a much broader context?

Chapter 8. Do children with different first languages (Berber or Moroccan Arabic) develop Arabic literacy skills at the same or different rates? How does schooling (including preschooling) intersect with rates of development? What are the possible effects on second literacy (French language) acquisition? Is the prior acquisition of Arabic literacy (in Arabic script) related to subsequent acquisition of French literacy (in Roman script)?

Chapter 9. How is school-learned literacy related to functional literacy needed for everyday life? Are children and adolescents able to use school-based skills effectively to deal with household literacy needs? What pedagogical lessons can be drawn from a functional perspective on literacy development?

Chapter 10. Who drops out of school, and for what reasons? What is the marginal academic value of staying in school? What is the impact of dropping out on the retention of literacy skills learned in school? Is there short-term or long-term loss in literacy skills, and does such loss vary by gender and environmental experiences?

Chapter 11. Based on national demographic statistics, how literate are adults in contemporary Morocco? How do these data compare with those

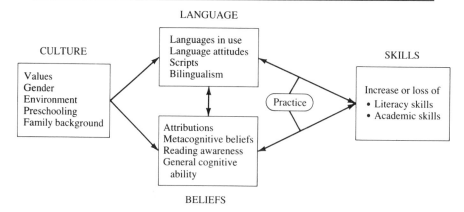

Figure 4.1. Schematic overview of the project.

for other countries in the region and the Third World? How does literacy vary on a regional basis, and what are the economic and poverty indices related to literacy? Will demographic trends in schooling lead to a fully literate Moroccan population over the next few decades?

These concerns may be, and have in the past, been considered to be discrete questions in search of answers in one society or another. In the MLP, we investigated them in the light of a comprehensive study with overlapping methodologies and population samples. To understand better how the various pieces fit together, see the schematic overview of the project shown in Figure 4.1. It is important to emphasize that our research strategy was to try to answer as many key questions, especially those with policy ramifications, as possible within the samples, methods, and human resources that we would muster. We were ambitious, knowing that this type of large-scale longitudinal effort was unusual in the developing world and had never before been attempted in Morocco. As happens in such cases, our data collection sometimes outstripped the human resources available to digest it completely.[1] Even so, it took almost 3 years after data collection stopped for all of the data relevant to the central thesis of this volume to be analyzed.

The research field sites

In choosing field sites for the project, we needed to balance a number of competing concerns. Because the project was formally linked with the University Mohamed V, in the coastal capital of Rabat, it would have been convenient to locate our work in that growing city of more than a half-million inhabitants. But there were drawbacks as well. The majority of the city's population had immigrated to Rabat over the past several decades, making the population too heterogeneous for the kinds of contrasts we sought to make. As noted earlier, we were looking for a more traditional Moroccan way of life and for a population sample that was "typical" and "stable" in the sense of income, attitudes, language use, and educational aspirations. Naturally, such an ideal type was unlikely to be found, for most parts of Morocco had undergone major social changes over recent years. Nonetheless, we knew and were often told *"plus ca change, plus ca reste le meme"* (the more things change, the more they stay the same). So, though traditional Moroccan values and life-styles could be found, Rabat was not likely to provide us with such a sample population.

On the other hand, some of our questions required samples that could be found almost anywhere in Morocco. For example, it was easy to find children learning to read in Standard Arabic, because all Moroccan children are required to do so. Similarly, it was not difficult to find a sample of children for whom the rate of school dropout was elevated, as this, too, was common in much of Morocco. Yet other criteria were not so easily met. For example, we wanted to find contrasting urban and rural field sites that were different on dimensions that we thought might matter in a study of literacy, such as the availability of books, newspapers, and general print media in the children's home environment. We also needed to find children in the same town who spoke either Berber or Moroccan Arabic as a native language, but not both.[2] We also sought contexts that provided preschooling (Quranic and modern) for some, but not all, children, as we wanted to contrast those who had and had not gone to such preschools. Finally, and importantly, we needed field sites where we were likely to be well received. The following is a brief description of the two field sites we selected.

Marrakech

Marrakech is one of the great and famed cities of the world, as well as a former capital of Morocco. With settlements dating to prehistoric times, the city gained prominence in the twelfth century under the Almohad dynasty, at which time great earthen and stone walls were constructed around the central part of the *medina* (city; in this case, the old city). The prestige of Marrakech was enhanced by the construction of the great Koutoubia Mosque, completed in Andalusian style in the fifteenth century and still dominating the city today.

Located near the foothills of the High Atlas Mountains, from where it receives unusually ample supplies of water, Marrakech is also at the edge of the Sahara, which formally begins on the other side of the 14,000-foot-high mountain range. The city was a hub at one end of a major caravan route that traversed the Sahara on its way to West Africa. These commercial and travel linkages also help to explain the presence of a significant amount of sub-Saharan African influence in the physiognomic characteristics of some Marrakech families, a probable consequence of a substantial slave trade over the centuries.

In recent decades, and particularly since the creation by the French of the "new city" beyond the old *medina* in the 1930s, Marrakech has grown rapidly, with a population in excess of a half-million people. Its poorest inhabitants are immigrants from nearby villages, people who sought work in the many small trades that have expanded with the tourist trade in Marrakech. The city is considered by locals and tourists alike to be one of the most beautiful places in Morocco. The old *medina* still maintains the allure of the traditional *casbah,* with winding and narrow alleyways of teeming crowds at dawn and dusk, and where no cars may pass. There is the great square, Jama'a al-Fna (literally, place of the dead), where criminals were executed in ancient times and where now acrobats, fruit sellers, local folk, and foreigners gather in the early evening. There are the palm-lined streets and fancy villas in the new city and the immense palaces of the royal family.

From the perspective of our research, Marrakech offered an excellent urban field site. There were lots of schools, and lots of children. Both Quranic and modern preschools were in abundance. And, in spite of the influx of people from nearby villages, Marrakech retained much of its traditional past as an Arab city. As part of the study, we were able to locate a half-dozen elementary schools and the same number of preschools in which to carry out our initial work. Because of its large and relatively accessible population of children, and the mobility of its families (leading to sample attrition), we generally included more children in the urban Marrakech samples than in the rural samples.

Al-Ksour

Al-Ksour is a small rural town of about 5,000 inhabitants nestled in the foothills of the Middle Atlas Mountains, about 150 miles north of Mar-

Many schools rely on individual slates on which children write their lessons. A slate is similar in use to the *luha,* common in traditional Islamic schools.

The testing of fifth graders in Marrakech classrooms utilized test booklets prepared by the project team.

Boy answering questions about newspaper article in everyday literacy test.

Children taking tests in school courtyard in al-Ksour.

Schoolmaster in a Marrakech modern preschool (left) with one of the project staff.

The old bazaar (*souk*) of the urban *casbah* of Marrakech.

Village mosque in rural Morocco.

A late afternoon conversation in al-Ksour (with the author).

rakech near the road to the ancient city of Fes. Until a new road was built, just before our work began, al-Ksour had been relatively isolated from commercial and administrative activities in the region and from the provincial capital of Beni-Mellal. Yet its strategic location, at the threshold of Berber-speaking territory in the mountains, led the French army to make it a garrison town for the control of the Berber mountain tribes during colonial times.

Although most houses have electricity, almost half are without running water, and it is not unusual to see women, young and old, carrying buckets and earthen jars to and from the common water fountains in the various neighborhoods. Al-Ksour has a weekly *souk,* where villagers do their major shopping and mountain people come to sell their handmade wares or agricultural products.

Al-Ksour is traditionally a Berber town, with most of its original inhabitants coming from families with roots in the Tamazight tribes of the Middle Atlas Mountains. However, its increased contact with Beni-Mellal and the Arabic-speaking plains below has meant that numerous non-Berber families have settled in the town over the past couple of decades. There has been no linguistic census (local or national), so we can only estimate that somewhat more than half the population speaks Berber in the home; and some of these families are bilingual (with one parent a native Berber speaker and the other an Arabic speaker). It remained, in the 1980s, a town that was excellent for the linguistic comparisons we wished to carry out.

Al-Ksour is also a town with a strong Muslim tradition. There are numerous *kuttab*s, and only a single modern preschool catering primarily to the children of the few "bourgeois" Arabic-speaking families. With the coolness of the mountains next to the warmth of the plains, it is also a pleasant town in which to reside, a fact not lost on the French colonials who stayed in the area for almost four decades.[3] According to local historians, but never to our knowledge put into print, the Berber-speaking populations in the mountains above al-Ksour were among the greatest fighters against the colonial French army, resisting complete conquest until well into the 1930s.

As noted in the preface, al-Ksour was where I had worked on my dissertation research and before that as a Peace Corps volunteer. It was, therefore, a town in which we had many contacts and likely access to research assistants, as well as to Quranic and public schools.

Sample populations used in the study

Three cohorts of children were used in the project: a group of children who had just finished preschool and were about to enter primary school (Table 4.1); a group of primary school children (Cohort 1), selected in first grade and followed over 5 years (Table 4.2); and a group of fifth graders (Cohort 2) followed over 3 years, some of whom went on to secondary school and some of whom dropped out (Table 4.3). Each of these samples is described here, with further details provided in the relevant chapters that follow.

Preschool sample. The preschool sample was utilized for the study of children's emergent Arabic literacy skills prior to formal training in primary school, as well as for an early comparison of the reading skills of children attending different types of preschool. The sample included 146 children all of whom were just completing their second year of traditional Quranic preschool or modern preschool. These same preschools were the ones that normally served the children who eventually attended the primary schools used for the selection of Cohort 1. Boys and girls, in roughly equal numbers, averaged approximately 6 years of age, which was old relative to American preschool children but typical in Morocco, where many children do not begin primary school until about age 7.

Cohort 1 sample. The children in Cohort 1 were selected for the 5-year longitudinal study, which contrasted subsamples by gender, prior preschool experience, and language background (in al-Ksour). The children, 350 boys and girls, were in grade 1 of primary school in either Marrakech or al-Ksour. Because obtaining accurate data on each child's preschool attendance was crucial for the research comparisons, we first collected this information from the children themselves, then checked it against school records (if available), with individual Quranic preschool teachers, and finally with the children's parents. Because formal records were not always kept at the preschool level, the convergence of these four sources of information was used to determine a child's placement in the appropriate preschool category.

Assigning children accurately to Moroccan Arabic and Berber monolingual subsamples was also a nontrivial matter. Because in al-Ksour many children were bilingual or partially bilingual, even though we chose only monolingual children to avoid the complexities of bilingualism, the determination of language competence among 7 year olds was not an easy

Table 4.1. Preschool sample

Environment	Rural	Urban	
Preschool	Quranic (PRQ)[c]	Quranic (PUQ)	Modern (PUM)
Subsample size:[a]	44	48	54
Gender			
Boys	28	24	24
Girls	16	24	30
Age at time of assessment[b]	6.0	6.0	6.0

[a]Total N = 146.

[b]Age of preschoolers, based on preschool teachers' estimates, is approximate, as preschools did not normally keep formal records on students.

[c]PRQ = preschool age, rural, Quranic; PUQ = preschool age, urban, Quranic; PUM = preschool age, urban, modern preschooled.

Table 4.2. Primary school sample (Cohort 1)

Environment	Rural				Urban		
Preschool	None		Quranic		None	Quranic	Modern
Language	Berber (RNB)[a]	Arabic (RNA)	Berber (RQB)	Arabic (RQA)	Arabic (UNA)	Arabic (UQA)	Arabic (UMA)
Subsample size[b]	27	23	56	60	29	66	89
Gender							
Boys	13	11	30	29	12	33	44
Girls	14	12	26	31	17	33	45
Mean age at time of assessment	7.4	7.4	7.4	7.4	7.3	7.2	7.1
Mean years of preschooling	0.1	0.1	1.1	1.6	0.1	1.7	1.9

[a]Acronyms of the seven comparison groups: RNB = rural, non-preschooled, Berber-speaking; RNA = rural, non-preschooled, Arabic-speaking; RQB = rural, Quranic, Berber-speaking; RQA = rural, Quranic, Arabic-speaking; UNA = urban, non-preschooled, Arabic-speaking; UQA = urban, Quranic, Arabic-speaking; UMA = urban, modern preschooled, Arabic-speaking.

[b]Total N = 350.

Table 4.3. Primary/secondary school sample (Cohort 2)[a]

Environment	Rural	Urban
Sample size	178	286
Gender		
Boys	92	150
Girls	86	136
Mean years of age	12.9	12.7
Age range	11–15[b]	11–15
Total N = 464		

[a]This sample was drawn from 464 fifth graders, most of whom went on to secondary school. Those who dropped out (N = 72) became the school dropout sample, described in chapter 10.

[b]The age range in the fifth-grade sample is quite wide, due to a high rate of grade repetition. Such a range is typical in the Moroccan educational system, indicating that the average child had repeated 1 year of primary school and some children had repeated 2 or more years.

matter. Here, too, we used converging evidence from various sources to determine language background: the child's own report of his or her parents' native tongue and family language use; a short conversational language test in spoken Moroccan Arabic and Berber; and the results on the Moroccan Picture Vocabulary test of Moroccan Arabic language ability. Fortunately, there were highly significant correlations among all of these language assessment procedures in the establishment of reliable language categories.

Cohort 2 sample. Cohort 2 was selected from fifth-grade classrooms in the same schools from which Cohort 1 was originally drawn, in order to ensure general comparability. We utilized the sample of older children who remained in school to extend the age range of our inquiry into belief systems, functional literacy, and so forth. In addition, we utilized Cohort 2 to study children who dropped out of school at the end of the school year to track their literacy skills downstream in the retention study.

Due to their broad range of grade repetition histories prior to inclusion in the study, children in Cohort 2 were necessarily more heterogeneous than those in Cohort 1, in terms of age range and total number of years spent in school. As a consequence, it was necessary to create more levels of test difficulty, so as to avoid both floor and ceiling effects. This was made more complicated by the fact that the dropout sample would receive no further formal schooling, whereas the in-school children would continue to be taught reading, writing, and other relevant subjects, which had direct effects on the skills we wanted to measure. Details of how we handled this problem are described in chapter 10.

A rather different sort of problem occurred when the Moroccan government made an unexpected change in grade repetition policy in the very year (1985) in which we sought to study school dropouts. During the entire decade prior to our study, approximately 30% to 40% of all fifth graders generally failed the *shahada* (primary school exit exam), and thus were kept back from secondary school; many of these students (as well as others) dropped out of school at that time. In 1985, we chose a sample of 464 fifth graders and gave each a complete assessment with tests and interviews. However, at the end of that year, only 72 of the original 464 had actually dropped out, or only 15% of the sample. Thus the result of the government's unanticipated change of policy was to reduce the expected dropout sample by half; furthermore, there was little we could do about it, for we had chosen the baseline sample of children almost 6 months earlier. This policy change may have been wise from an educational perspective (see Spratt, 1988, for an alternative view), but its consequence for our study was that the dropout sample ended up smaller than we had hoped for broad policy generalizations, even though many results turned out to be statistically reliable.

Parent interviews. We had originally sought to interview a sample of households of the children in Cohort 1, having been told that parents from the poorer social classes in Morocco would be uninterested or averse to being part of a research study. Furthermore, we knew that a 2-hour home interview would take at least a half-day, or more if return visits were required. With the expected delays, cups of steaming hot mint tea, and neighbors and relatives coming and going in the household, our expectations for such interviews were modest – we hoped to collect as many as 30 or 40 home interviews. As it happened, the mint tea did flow freely, and friends had a tendency to visit when we dropped by – in al-Ksour we were the most exciting local event of the week. Yet we soon discovered that word of mouth (what Moroccans wryly term the "Arab telephone") had spread throughout both of our field site communities, and contrary to our expectations, we were asked by more and more families to drop by *their* homes.

Thus, though we only completed about 50 home interviews in the first 6 months of work, more than 250 further interviews were completed over the next 6 to 12 months. Overall, we interviewed more than 90% of Cohort 1 families, though we were able to use only 289 for statistical analyses, owing to missing data or inappropriate classifications.

All parent interviews were conducted in the household of the child, often with the child present. In most cases we were able to interview the mother of the child, who was expected to provide the most informed answers about family members; as it happened, fathers were seldom at home during the usual daytime interviews. Because of strong cultural taboos against male outsiders entering the household, we generally chose female field assistants who would be able to elicit the best information in a family setting. We also discovered that teams of one Moroccan and one American woman were optimal for this kind of work. The prestige of the foreigner helped to open doors and provide a "naïve" perspective that put most mothers at ease, and a local Moroccan woman, often known or known of in the community, added an element of cultural security and language competence. Together, these teams were remarkably effective in gathering what we found to be interesting and highly reliable data on the Moroccan family.

The interviews themselves consisted of a comprehensive series of questions concerning educational attainment in the family (grandparents, parents, and children), language background and preferences, occupation and socioeconomic status data, and a broad inquiry concerning parents' attitudes about education, literacy, pedagogy, religion, and the future. The parent interview questions are provided in appendix 3.

Sample attrition and school year/grade terminology. As noted, grade repetition in Morocco is quite common and leads to considerable variation in children's grade level attainment over time. In Cohort 1, for example, out of 350 children in grade 1 during the first year of the study, it was found 5 years later that 109 had dropped out of the sample due to failure or sample attrition; of the remaining in-school sample, 50 (22%) were in grade 3, 98 (43%) were in grade 4, and only 80 (35%) were in grade 5. In Cohort 2, out of 464 children first tested when all were in grade 5, it was found 2 years later that 146 (31%) had dropped out of the sample (mainly due to the *shahada* examination); of the children remaining in school, 129 (28%) were in grade 6 and only 189 (41%) were in grade 7.

Because sample children in each cohort were tracked over years of the project, it is easier and more accurate to refer to "years" of schooling rather than "grade level attained." It may be noted, for example, that Cohort 1 and Cohort 2 year 5 samples differed substantially: Cohort 1 children were actually spread over grades 3, 4, and 5, because of repetition during the 5 years of the study; by contrast, Cohort 2 year 5 children were all actually in grade 5 (the first year of Cohort 2 testing) and were, on average, 1½ years older than the children of Cohort 1 (due to repetitions in earlier grades). No comparisons were intended (or made) between the two cohorts of year 5, so that this instructional difference had no bearing on project conclusions.[4]

Culture, testing, and going forward

Over the years, much has been said about the difficulty of testing across cultures, making testing "fair," and the promotion of culture-free tests. It was the sense of our research team that there exists no fool-proof way to resolve such issues. We adopted a strategy for conducting fieldwork and testing that was not only reasonable (so we thought) but also expedient (in terms of helping us get the job done). Our approach was to limit the danger of misleading comparisons by reducing such contrasts to within Morocco rather than across nations (with the minor exception of cross-national trends, discussed in chapter 11). We further sought to preserve the anthropologist's attitude of skepticism toward the tests we would create and employ. Would children or adults really understand what we were trying to get at? If so – or if not – how would we even know? What kinds of safeguards could we build into the testing to inform us about the problems inherent in our measures?

Our efforts to resolve these kinds of questions involved several elements: first, not be in a hurry; second, pilot-test all instruments; and finally, talk with children, parents, and teachers about what we were doing and solicit their help. We cannot claim, of course, that we successfully resolved all threats to the validity of our data or our methods of analysis. After almost a decade of fieldwork and data analysis, we felt that both the qualitative and quantitative data of the project were at the top end of reliability and validity for this type of study.

As we began the project, our preoccupations with finding field sites, meeting with colleagues at the Moroccan university, and creating tri-lingual testing and interview materials soon gave way to the press of selecting the schools and the children. It is to this effort that we now turn.

Notes

1 As mentioned later in the text, we collected large amounts of data on individual differences in reading and cognitive skills, interview data from the children, the parents, and their schoolteachers, and a compendium of ethnographic field notes. We attempted to use as much of these data as possible, but found, in the end, that there still remained data "leftovers."

2 Although the study of early bilingualism (Berber and Moroccan Arabic) and literacy acquisition would have been fascinating, our resources did not permit such an investigation. As discussed in chapter 8, our interest in studying the impact of the Berber language on Arabic literacy development led us to eliminate from the study those children who were found to be fluent bilinguals in both Berber and Arabic before going to school.

3 Over the past half-century, French and Arab "settlers" in al-Ksour were interested in other aspects of cultural life in their market town. Among these was the strong tradition of "free women," or prostitutes, mostly of Berber origin, who provided entertainment, especially to out-of-town visitors. As did several other towns in the Middle Atlas foothills, al-Ksour attracted many men on market day in search of distraction. Although to our knowledge there is little written about this activity, which is considered contrary to Islam, few would question the commercial importance of prostitution to the town. Furthermore, because divorced or "fallen" women (usually having borne children out of wedlock) have little other means to survive, such commerce provided a living for women who would otherwise have found employment virtually impossible. By the early 1990s, it appeared that such prostitution in al-Ksour had declined under government and police pressure.

4 Such sampling variations affected the proportion of children with different curricular experiences in each year of the study and therefore precluded an extensive (8-year) longitudinal examination of the results, as did the use of grade-appropriate tests designed to match particular grade levels of the samples of children. Consequently, an assessment of change using identical tests (see, e.g., Rogosa, Brandt, & Zimowski, 1985) was not feasible. To enable comparisons between measured reading skills across different years, we constructed standardized reading achievement scores in each grade. Further information on test construction is provided in chapter 5.

5. Learning to read in Arabic

Amina goes to school

Amina Tamandat just today has begun first grade in al-Ksour, and has brought home her paperback textbook, *Qiraati* (My reading), which the school provides for each student. As she enters her house, she calls to her older brother, Abdulhamid, to come and look at her first very own book. There are lots of letters printed in black and highlighted in places with pastel colors of red, green, and blue. A few letters are printed almost an inch tall, and they are the ones used in the examples for practice. Because she has gone to the local Quranic preschool, she knows all the letters on the page and begins to pronounce all the simple words that use the key letters. She is proud that she can say most of them, and she repeats them over and over, to the considerable pleasure of her brother.

Understanding literacy acquisition in Morocco necessarily requires in-depth knowledge about the nature of the Arabic script and how children come to learn to decode, encode, and comprehend Arabic as a written language. From our ethnographic work, we had a relatively good idea of the circumstances in which children and adults come into contact with written materials, from advertising to textbooks. What was less obvious was whether learning to read in Arabic involved the same cognitive skills as, say, learning to read in English or French or Chinese.

Library research and communication with Arab educators had led us to conclude that there was a surprising dearth of research on Arabic reading acquisition. This was surprising, for at least two reasons. First, along with English, French, and Chinese, Arabic is one of only a handful of recognized international languages. A national language in more than two dozen countries and a religious or second language in many others, Arabic is spoken by an estimated 250 million persons. Second, according to UN estimates, the Arabic-speaking world has one of the highest rates of illiteracy, averaging, in 1990, about half of all adults. Nonetheless, we could find little scientific study of Arabic reading acquisition in children or adults published in an education journal, even in the Arab world.[1]

Thus, as we planned our work, we sought to establish some benchmarks for testing Arabic literacy achievement and for understanding how children acquire prereading and more advanced reading skills in that language. To accomplish this goal, we first had to understand similarities and differences between the Arabic language and the Indo-European languages on which are based most of the Western scientific understanding of reading acquisition.

Arabic orthography and reading

Scientific interest in the relationship between orthographic systems and the acquisition of reading may be traced to the hypothesis that certain writing systems offer easier access to literacy than others. Comparative work on this topic has concentrated on distinctions across broad linguistic features, such as whether a particular writing system employs an ideographic, syllabic, or alphabetic orthography or script (Downing, 1973; Henderson, 1984; Kavanaugh & Venezky, 1980). Ideographic scripts, used by the Maya and Egyptians in their ancient hieroglyphics, employ pictorial symbols to stand for particular words or ideas. Chinese is one of the few ideographic scripts still current today, though the Chinese government is making a major effort to employ alphabetic versions of Chinese as well. Syllabic scripts, such as cuneiform, use symbols to represent syllables or sound clusters. These were the precursors of the modern alphabetic writing systems and included such languages as Assyrian and Phoenician (Micholowski, 1993).

Alphabetic systems (including all Indo-European languages), which utilize letters to represent specific sounds and that when combined into meaningful sound clusters become "words," are considered by many specialists to be the ideal system in which to write. Some scholars, such as Havelock (1976) have even suggested that the origins of intellectual thought and democracy may be traced to the adoption of an alphabetic system of writing by the Greeks. A more recent version of this argument suggests that it was not simply the alphabet that led to the Greek intellectual revolution, inasmuch as other alphabets such as Hebrew and Arabic existed at the same time as Greek or even preceded it. Rather, according to Skoyles (1988), the fact that Greek was the first alphabet to use a complete vowel system in its alphabet facilitated the pronunciation of previously unknown words. By contrast, both Hebrew and Arabic, while utilizing only few vowel letters as well as voweling or vocalization marks in religious texts, usually did not provide voweling pronunciation guides to the reader, thereby rendering more difficult pronunciation, interpretation, and fluent reading of unfamiliar materials.

Nonetheless, there is growing evidence that literacy, even in languages and orthographies as distinct as English and Chinese, is acquired by schoolchildren in roughly the same amount of time and with similar overall difficulty (Stevenson, Stigler, Lucker, & Lee, 1982), a conclusion based on the general pattern of school-related achievement and the extent of reading disabilities in the school-age population. However, the degree to which the processes of reading acquisition may differ across diverse languages and writing systems, as well as across the life span, remains a question in need of further research (Wagner, 1993). As further suggested by Skoyles (1988), differences in particular orthographies, such as Arabic, may affect the ease or difficulty of reading acquisition.

The Arabic script is composed of a 28 letter alphabet, and it differs in certain important ways from the Roman alphabet. The letters of the Arabic alphabet represent only the consonants and long vowels of spoken Arabic; the short vowels are represented only by additional diacritical marks – and sometimes not at all (see Figure 5.1a). These short vowel markings can be read in various ways, depending on a word's meaning, tense, voice, function in the sentence, and other features, which often must be guessed from the context. In theory, there is strict sound–symbol correspondence between the letters on a page and their spoken equivalent in Arabic, considerably greater than that found in English with its many irregularities.[2] Because short vowel sounds are normally provided only in the Quran and in children's reading materials, the average reader of books and newspapers must bring to the text a considerable additional knowledge of vocabulary, syntax, and, in many cases, contextual interpretation in order to obtain correct vocalization and comprehension. Advanced students practice on unvoweled texts as preparation for "adult reading."

Quranic text with diacritics   Newspaper text without diacritics

Figure 5.1a. Vowels of the Arabic alphabet. The letters in the words in the left panel include diacritical vocalization marks. The letters in the right panel, typical of newspaper and textbook writing, do not include such marks.

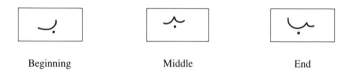

Beginning   Middle   End

Figure 5.1b. Letter forms of the Arabic alphabet. Letters in the Arabic alphabet have different forms, depending on their position – at the beginning, middle, or end of a word.

However, for children just learning to read, incorrect vocalization is expected to lead to serious problems in comprehending texts that lack diacritics.

In addition, certain letters are similar in shape and are distinguished only by a single stroke or dot, representing sounds that may be phonologically indistinct in Moroccan Arabic; thus, certain letter pairs present special confusion for the beginning reader (e.g., *sin/shin; sin/sad; dad/dha; jim/za*). Furthermore, the form of a particular letter can differ, depending on its position (beginning, middle, end) in a word (see Figure 5.1b). Because spacing between words is optional, such orthographic features as the use of letters in their terminal form (i.e., at the end of a word) tend to signal "word boundaries." We hypothesized that the ability to recognize these specific features of letter forms would be critical to decoding and comprehending text.[3]

Thus, as part of our effort to understand the early stages of reading acquisition, we needed to develop reading tests that would reflect the particular features of Arabic orthography. Searching for previously developed Arabic reading tests, we found only simple adaptations of standard American-style reading tests, such as word decoding and paragraph comprehension. Though such tests could be adapted to the Moroccan setting, we also sought to create innovative measures that would take into account the particular properties of the Arabic language and script.

Assessing prereading skills

Given the importance of understanding children's beginning or prereading skills, we spent considerable time and effort trying to develop tests that would shed light on the emic or internal characteristics of the Arabic script but that would give results comparable to those from early reading measures used for other scripts (the etic perspective). Guided by the work of researchers working with other orthographies (e.g., Aaron & Joshi, 1989; Clay, 1979; Feitelson, 1966, 1967, 1980), we first sought to determine the prereading skills that children acquire in learning to decode the Arabic script.

The Early Reading test

The Early Reading test is a composite of subtests that could provide a quantifiable measure of the beginning of Arabic literacy. These reading tasks[4] were created to measure the child's knowledge of the orthographic concepts of "letter" and "word" and of Arabic letter and word boundaries. The tasks did not require complete knowledge of the Arabic alphabet, nor did the child need to know how to read real words. As such, these tasks are for children at the prereading stage, where they come to recognize that some forms of pictorial (orthographic and nonorthographic) displays begin to have a special relationship to literacy in Arabic. It should be reiterated here that the typical floor or lowest performance level of learning among our sample population of Moroccan children might be expected to be below that found in same-age American children (because of differences in home literacy experiences), and therefore we constructed tasks to capture the very beginnings of literacy knowledge.[5] A description of the test items measuring concept and boundary knowledge in Arabic orthography follows (see Figure 5.2).

The *Letter Concept (LC) task* asked the child to find the letter from among a series of three items, each of which included a letter and two other items (number, picture, or other symbol; see Figure 5.2a). This task is intended to show whether the child has a concept of the term letter, and

a. Letter Concept (LC): "Where is the letter? Please point to it."

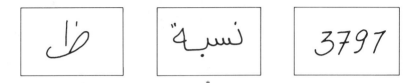

b. Word Concept (WC): "Where is the word? Please point to it."

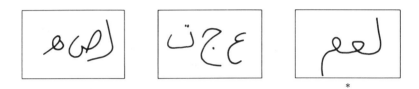

c. Letter Boundary (LB): "Which box has a correctly written word in it?"
(Nonsense strings of letters are employed of which only one choice has
letters correctly connected to form a word.)

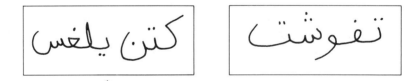

d. Word Boundary (WB): "Which box has two words in it?"
(Again, nonsense items were used; individual items employed spacing or
final-letter forms to indicate that the letter string was necessarily two words.)

Figure 5.2. Concept and boundary tasks in Arabic orthography. (a) Letter Concept; (b) Word Concept; (c) Letter Boundary; (d) Word Boundary. (Asterisk indicates correct answer.)

whether he or she knows how to distinguish letters from numbers or other symbols or representative drawings. To a child with even a modest familiarity with Arabic script, this task ought to be (and was) easy. But in rural al-Ksour and among preschoolers, we suspected that some children might not have this basic knowledge of the Arabic alphabet.

The *Word Concept (WC) task* imposed the additional requirement that the child be able to distinguish single words from nonwords (multidigit numbers, other symbols, or designs; see Figure 5.2b). Again, we expected relatively high performance on this task.

The *Letter Boundary (LB) task* required the child to choose which of three words was written correctly with regard to proper letter form and connecting strokes between letters. By taking advantage of the specialized rules governing the way that Arabic letters are connected in cursive script,[6] we were able to create artificial wordlike clusters that employed correct boundaries between letters and others that employed incorrect boundaries. Some artificial words were correctly connected and written according to the orthographic connection rules, whereas the non-word-like clusters violated one or more of the rules. It was decided that such artificial or nonsense (the term typically used by experimental psychologists) words would be useful in preventing confusion over whether a child's correct choice was based on the recognition of a previously known specific word or due to an understanding of Arabic writing conventions. To the best of our knowledge, this was the first use of cursive letter connection rules in Arabic literacy assessment. In Figure 5.2c, the example shown employs three Arabic letters, but only the item at the right employs correct connectors between letters.

The *Word Boundary (WB) task* examined the child's ability to discern features of writing that signal the end of one word and the beginning of another. Again, using artificial words (so that the correct word is not simply the only real Arabic word), we created sets of grouped letters, some of which *must* be two words because of an orthographic boundary, and others that, with no required boundary, might be a single word (Figure 5.2d). In each case, both artificial words used a normal between-letter space convention to separate the two groups of letters so that the space (alone) was not a sufficient indication (as it would be in English) that two separate words were required.

Both boundary tasks are good examples of emic literacy measures, because they could only have had utility in the study of Arabic orthography. Neither of the tasks had ever been used for assessing early Arabic

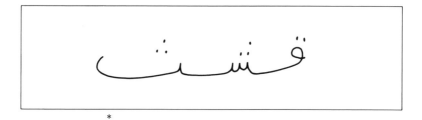

a. Letter recognition: "Where is the 'Tha'? Please point to it."

b. Letter form: "Which two letters have the same sound?"

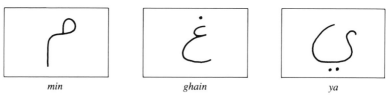

min   *ghain*   *ya*

c. Letter identification: "Which is this letter?"
   (Both correct sound and correct name were counted as correct responses.)

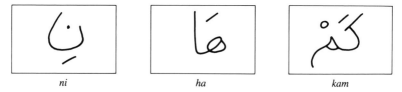

ni   *ha*   *kam*

d. Letter-vowel pronunciation: "Read this."

Figure 5.3. Letter Knowledge tasks. (a) letter recognition; (b) letter form; (c) letter identification; (d) letter-vowel pronunciation. (Where appropriate, asterisk indicates correct answer.)

literacy skills. Though such measures hold considerable promise, they have yet to be utilized elsewhere for Arabic reading assessment.

The *Letter Knowledge (LK) task* was designed to evaluate young children's knowledge of Arabic orthography at the level of a single letter. In this set of measures, children were asked to demonstrate knowledge about particular letters. All items (a–d) were combined into a single Letter Knowledge score. A discussion of the items follows (see Figure 5.3.).

Letter recognition. In the Arab world there has been a greater historical dependence on the cursive (and handwritten) script than in the West. One consequence of this long calligraphic tradition in Islam is the remarkably stylized and variable written forms in Arabic. This observation led us to ask whether this variability could create problems in letter recognition among Moroccan children. In this subtask (shown in Figure 5.3a), we chose letter combinations that followed orthographic rules but were, again, artificial words, so that children with whole-word recognition abilities would not have an advantage in letter naming over other children. Eight Arabic letters in various positional configurations were utilized in the task. Because a letter of the Arabic alphabet may appear in up to four different forms, depending on the letter and its position (initial, medial, final, or independent), this task measured a young reader's ability to recognize a letter regardless of its configuration, and is, necessarily, a key component of Arabic decoding ability.

Letter form. Because Arabic letters can take different shapes depending on whether the letter occurs at the beginning, middle or end of a word, we also assessed the child's ability to recognize a given letter when presented in different configurations. Across the six items, target and foil (incorrect) letters (connected in wordlike clusters) were chosen for increasing similarity of form, such that the last few items presented letters that were more easily confused by less skilled readers. An example is provided in Figure 5.3b.

Letter identification. Naming of letters is a common early reading skill in English. Most American children are capable of a nearly perfect performance by 4 to 5 years of age. As in the United States, in Morocco a good deal of letter learning – learning the formal names and not just their sounds – takes place in formal classroom situations. However, observations led us to suspect that American children get much more of this type of practice at home than our sample of Moroccan children did. The naming of individual letters has been found to correlate highly with later reading achievement in English (Chall, 1983). To test this finding in Morocco, we asked children to identify individual letters presented in written form by giving the letter name or its sound (see Figure 5.3c).

Letter-vowel pronunciation. This subtask (shown in Figure 5.3d), analogous to the simple sounding out of letters in English, is complicated in Arabic by the diacritical marks, which can radically change the pronunciation of any consonant. For example, changing the diacritical bar under the letter *n* to a bar over the letter would change a *ni* to *na*. Moroccan children receive extensive practice on such vocalizations once they enter preschool and primary school, but the amount of practice received at home seemed to vary considerably in the homes we studied, and was quite limited in homes with nonliterate parents.

Vocabulary knowledge

The *Moroccan Picture Vocabulary (MPV) test* is similar in format to the well-known Peabody Picture Vocabulary test, although shorter (25 items; see Figure 5.4). Its purpose was to assess young children's knowledge of common words in Moroccan Arabic. Because no reading or writing was required, the MPV served as a measure of oral Moroccan Arabic vocabulary skills. The MPV seemed important because substantial research with other written languages had shown a strong relationship between spoken vocabulary and reading performance (Downing, 1973). Furthermore, the MPV also provided an important empirical baseline measure for children whose first language was Berber; thus, the MPV was also used to validate self-assessed and parent-assessed oral Arabic language skills of the children in our sample. Finally, as noted in chapter 2, some specialists had claimed that Moroccan Arabic is so different from Standard Arabic that it would be of limited help in learning to read. A strong correlation with subsequent reading performance would help to dispel this claim.

Assessing reading skills in school-going children

The line drawn between prereading and subsequent reading skills in school-going children is an arbitrary one. Reading researchers typically have created such a boundary by the employment of certain tests that measure the literacy skills of what is termed the mature or skilled reader. Our tests of subsequent or standard reading skills, used in various forms for assessment in each cohort in the study, were based on Arabic words and syntactic structures derived from first- through fifth-grade Moroccan pri-

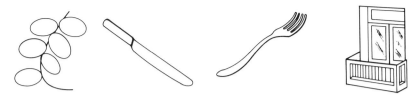

Figure 5.4. Moroccan Picture Vocabulary test. Question: "I'm going to show you some pictures on each page of this book. Then I want you to point out where the picture that I'll ask you about is. Where is the knife?"

mary school reading primers. All measures were pretested (changed and refined) with small groups of Moroccan children from the same schools as our sample children but who were not included in the formal study.

The first battery of tests, drawing on first- and second-grade curricula, was administered to the children in the spring of their first year in primary school. A more difficult battery of tests, drawing on material from third- to fifth-grade primers, was developed and employed in years 3 and 5 of the longitudinal study of Cohort 1.[7] Following is a description of these tests, with corresponding examples shown in Figure 5.5.

The *Word Decoding (WD) test* was utilized as a measure of decoding skill at the single word level. It required the child to read outloud a series of real Arabic words. Each word was presented to the child individually, on a white card; the child's response to each item was scored as incorrect, partly correct, or correct. Of the 16 items on the test, the first 6 provided complete vocalization diacritics while the remaining 10 items did not. These latter items therefore required the child to rely more heavily on whole-word recognition and prior experience, as would be the case in newspapers or other adult materials.[8]

The *Word-Picture Matching (WPM) test,* modeled on the Gates-MacGinitie test (1965), was designed to measure the child's ability to recognize and comprehend text at the single word level. The WPM required the child to choose the written word, among three choices (years 1 and 2) or four choices (years 3 and 5), that "named the picture" (Figure 5.5b). The WPM contained 12 items in years 1 and 2 and 25 items in years 3 and 5. Like the WD task, the WPM was administered to the preschool sample only once and to the longitudinal sample in alternate forms across years 1 and 2 and years 3 and 5 of the study. In addition, response foils for the task were selected to provide either orthographic

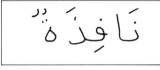

naa fidatun (window) jarii dah (newspaper)

a. Word Decoding (WD): "Read this word."

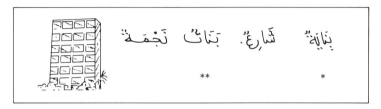

** *

b. Word-Picture Matching (WPM): "Which word names the picture? Point to it please."

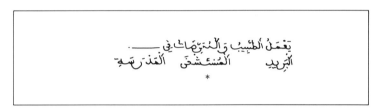

c. Sentence Maze (SM): "Which of these words best completes the sentence?"

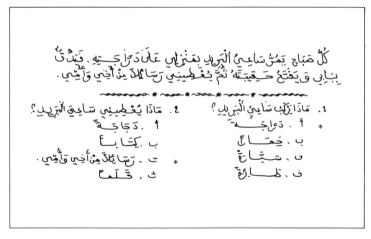

d. Paragraph Comprehension (PC): "Read this story. Then read each question and choose the best answer according to the story."

Figure 5.5. Arabic standard reading tests. (a) Word Decoding; (b) Word-Picture Matching; (c) Sentence Maze; (d) Paragraph Comprehension. (Asterisk indicates correct answer; double asterisk indicates orthographic error as described in text.)

similarity or no obvious similarity to the correct response, so that the relative frequency of orthographic and nonspecific errors could be calculated and analyzed for each student.[9] In the example, the orthographic error is indicated with a double asterisk.

The *Sentence Maze (SM) test,* a common measure of reading comprehension at the sentence level, consisted of a series of sentences, each one with a single word missing. The child was asked to select from an adjacent list of three words (or four words, in years 3 and 5) the one word that best completed each sentence (Figure 5.5c). The 30-item test was constructed so that the correct choice required a knowledge of four specific types of skills: (1) knowledge of appropriate voweling or case ending; (2) ability to distinguish between words with the same (triliteral) root but not the same meaning; (3) knowledge of feminine/masculine and singular/plural grammatical transformations; and (4) knowledge of appropriate verb tenses. As with Word-Picture Matching, the SM test was presented in a paper-and-pencil, multiple-choice format for older children (in years 3 and 5 of the study).

The *Paragraph Comprehension (PC) test* comprised six short paragraphs about familiar topics, with each paragraph followed by three to five multiple-choice questions (Figure 5.5d). Across two alternate forms test paragraphs included topics drawn from school primers such as the zoo, the postman, the train, the lunar calendar, fruits and their benefits, and visiting the Valley of the Kings at Luxor. The length of passages ranged between 25 and 65 words, with comprehension questions increasing in difficulty with each grade level, from relatively literal questions (where information to answer the questions could be obtained directly in the text) at the third-grade level to more inferential questions (where information had to be obtained by inference from the idea units in the text) for the fifth-grade level passages.

An *Arabic reading (AR) achievement score* was calculated from a composite of each of these tests administered in a given year. Given our longitudinal approach, subsequent testing necessitated more difficult questions. Thus, to create a reliable overall reading achievement score, we found it useful to standardize the scores of each test in a given testing year through the use of z-scores, which then produced a child's score as a standard unit of variance from the mean of the sample. An important advantage of this technique is that it is possible to combine tests of different lengths and difficulties, as all tests may be expressed in the same standardized units. We used this method to create AR achievement scores for each year of the study; these were particularly useful in regression analyses, as they represented the most reliable estimates of reading ability.

Overall, these tests of reading in Arabic spanned a broad range of skill, from a beginning knowledge of what is writing to a sophisticated understanding of implicit meanings in written text. Although some of our tests were adapted from similar tests used in European languages, others made quite specific use of the unique features of the Arabic language. In this way we sought to bridge emic and etic perspectives in literacy assessment and to provide a profile of the variability that exists in Arabic literacy acquisition in Morocco.

Results for the preschool and first-grade sample

To understand beginning reading and the transition to primary school, we compared Arabic test scores of the preschool sample with the first graders of Cohort 1. The latter group of children were, on the average, about 1 year older and had completed a little more than half of their first year of primary school.[10]

A preliminary goal was to determine if our various tests were statistically related to one another, for this would be an indication that the skills we intended to measure were in fact providing reliable measures of different facets of reading acquisition.[11] For the preschool sample, we found strong correlations among the Morocco Picture Vocabulary, Letter Concept, Word Concept, Letter Knowledge, and Word Decoding tasks (see Table 5.1). For the primary school sample, we found high correlations among individual early reading subtests, particularly the Letter Knowledge, Word Decoding, and Word-Picture Matching scores. On the whole, these correlations support the construct validity of the tests, as well as their utility in differentiating levels of subsequent reading ability.[12]

As expected, major differences were found between the scores of preschool and first-grade children on all reading tasks (see Figure 5.6).[13] The pattern of better performance among first graders held across tasks and suggests the dramatic effectiveness of 1 year of primary schooling in promoting the development of reading skills, although the older age of the first graders makes it difficult to separate out maturational effects. Most striking is children's performance on the critical Word Decoding test, where preschoolers failed almost completely and first graders made substantial gains.

Table 5.1. Correlations among Arabic reading test scores

Preschool sample[a]

	1	2	3	4	5	6	7
1. LC[b]							
2. WC	.32						
3. LK	.29	.29					
4. LB	.01	.19	−.05				
5. WB	.12	.22	.03	.08			
6. WD	.22	.22	.68	−.02	.04		
7. WPM	.11	.00	.18	.05	.07	.23	
8. MPV	.18	.30	.29	.07	.01	.20	.08

Longitudinal primary school sample[c]

	1	2	3	4	5	6	7	8	9
1. LC/1									
2. WC/1	.09								
3. LK/1	.13	.34							
4. LB/1	.05	.22	.29						
5. WB/1	.01	.30	.26	.16					
6. WD/1	.05	.25	.83	.23	.17				
7. WPM/1	.11	.29	.60	.30	.25	.54			
8. MPV/1	.13	.32	.41	.24	.21	.34	.31		
9. AR/3	.20	.24	.67	.28	.16	.62	.45	.38	
10. AR/5	.23	.16	.57	.22	.09	.49	.32	.39	.82

Note: $r > .20$; $p < .05$; $r > .25$, $p < .01$ when $N > 100$.
[a]N (listwise) = 144. Two children were not included owing to missing data.
[b]See text discussion for meaning of abbreviations. Numerical suffixes: 1 = year 1; 3 = year 3; 5 = year 5.
[c]Total N = 350. Exceptions owing to pairwise analysis: AR/3 with earlier scores, N = 262; AR/5 with earlier scores, N = 228 (N = 218 with AR/3).

Because both samples had subsamples that differed in terms of urban and rural environments and in terms of preschool experience (modern, Quranic, or none), it was possible to compare test performance across these groups as well, independent of age differences. Several of these tasks are shown in Figure 5.7. For the preschoolers, there were few differences in test performance by region, type of preschooling, or gender.[14] However, in the primary school sample, a recurrent pattern was evident for Letter Knowledge, Letter Boundary, Word Decoding, and Word-Picture Matching measures: Urban children generally outperformed rural chil-

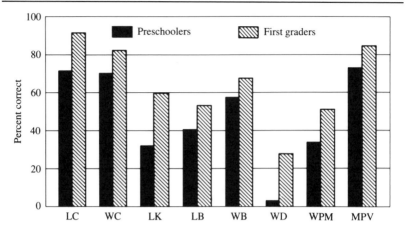

Figure 5.6. Year 1 Arabic reading test score means for preschoolers and first graders.

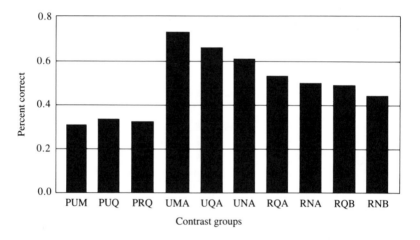

Figure 5.7a. Letter Knowledge test by preschool and first-grade subgroups. (Subgroups are described in the text in chapter 4.)

dren, Arabic speakers outperformed Berber speakers, and preschooled children outperformed nonpreschooled children.[15] Of particular interest again was the Word Decoding test (Figure 5.7c), which showed quite large differences between the urban and rural subsamples and between Arabic- and Berber-speaking groups.[16] Because the decoding of written language

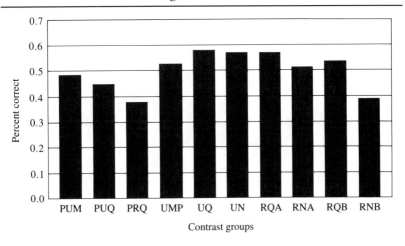

Figure 5.7b. Letter Boundary test by preschool and first-grade subgroups

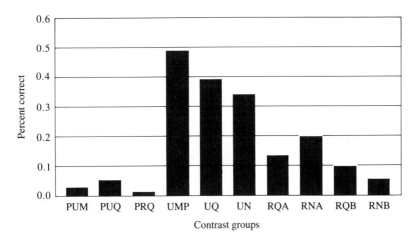

Figure 5.7c. Word Decoding test by preschool and first-grade subgroups

into speech is central to reading an alphabetic script like Arabic, these findings were an early clue to the kinds of problems that some Moroccan children encounter in literacy acquisition. However, these first comparisons of preschool and primary school children were limited by the cross-sectional nature of the analysis; the 5-year longitudinal study de-

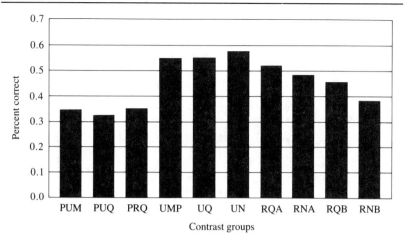

Figure 5.7d. Word-Picture Matching preschool and first-grade subgroups

scribed in the next section more powerfully tracks literacy development as it takes place over time.[17]

Results of the longitudinal study

Early reading skills and subsequent reading achievement

Within the primary school sample (Cohort 1), there were strong correlational relationships between first-year reading scores (particularly Letter Knowledge, Word Decoding, Word-Picture Matching, and Morocco Picture Vocabulary) and subsequent reading achievement in years 3 and 5. When we performed a hierarchical regression analysis to assess the independent contributions of particular first-year skills on reading achievement in years 3 and 5 (Table 5.2), we found that Letter Knowledge and Word Decoding made the most significant contributions to later performance. Results of the regression analysis were equivalent regardless of the order of entry of test scores (first or last among same-year tasks). Letter Boundary, Word Boundary, and Word-Picture Matching test scores explained more modest amounts of variance, even when entered first in the regression model. Overall, the reading tests used in first grade predicted more than 60% of the variance in Arabic reading in year 3 (AR/3) and more than 45% of the variance in year 5 (AR/5).

Our findings in Morocco are consistent with the results of studies in

Table 5.2. Hierarchical regression analysis: prereading scores on Arabic
reading achievement in years 3 and 5

Arabic reading in year 3 (AR/3)	Adj. R^2	R^2 chg.	F
1a. LK 1[a]	.425	.425	193.90
2a. LK 1 + LB 1 + WB 1	.427	.002	1.50
1b. LB 1 + WB 1[b]	.076	.076	11.76
2b. LB 1 + WB 1 + LK 1	.427	.351	159.46
3a. LK 1 + LB 1 + WB 1 + WD 1/2	.622	.195	134.44
4a. LK 1 + LB 1 + WB 1 + WD 1/2 + WPM 1/2	.648	.026	19.53
3b. LK 1 + LB 1 + WB 1 + WPM 1/2	.522	.095	52.64
4b. LK 1 + LB 1 + WB 1 + WPM 1/2 + WD 1/2	.648	.126	92.53
N = 262			

Arabic reading in year 5 (AR/5)	Adj. R^2	R^2 chg.	F
1a. LK 1	.309	.309	102.66
2a. LK 1 + LB 1 + WB 1	.311	.002	1.22
1b. LB 1 + WB 1	.032	.032	4.75
2b. LB 1 + WB 1 + LK 1	.311	.279	91.95
3a. LK 1 + LB 1 + WB 1 + WD 1/2	.450	.139	58.01
4a. LK 1 + LB 1 + WB 1 + WD 1/2 + WPM 1/2	.464	.014	6.80
3b. LK 1 + LB 1 + WB 1 + WPM 1/2	.366	.055	20.73
4b. LK 1 + LB 1 + WB 1 + WPM 1/2 + WD 1/2	.464	.098	18.53
5. LK 1 + LB 1 + WB 1 + WD 1/2 + WPM 1/2 + AR/3	.662	.198	149.74
N = 228[c]			

[a] Numerical suffixes: 1 = year 1; 1/2 = average of years 1 and 2 (see note 7); 3 = year 3; 5 = year 5. Underlining indicates the task(s) producing the change in R^2 for that step.
[b] Version "b" of the hierarchical regressions provides an alternative entering of the variables in question when two or more tests are presented in a single year.
[c] N drops to 218 for step with AR/3.

North America and Europe showing that children's early reading skills are critical for subsequent success in literacy development. Children who have such skills as early as first grade, or even in preschool, consistently showed superior abilities 5 years later. We also found that certain skills, such as knowledge of the alphabet and word decoding, seemed to be more important than other early reading skills in predicting subsequent reading ability.

Error analysis and decoding in Arabic

From results showing the importance of word decoding skill, we suspected that beginning readers in Morocco might need to rely heavily on phonetic sounding out of Arabic text. When combined with the observation that many children showed an imperfect mastery of the alphabet (based on the results of the Letter Knowledge task), we were led to hypothesize that children who made mistakes in letter recognition might be particularly susceptible to certain kinds of problems in the decoding of Arabic and that certain children might be prone to phonetic decoding mistakes. To test this hypothesis, we reanalyzed data from the Word-Picture Matching test, which was designed to assess the degree to which particular types of errors were made because of orthographic similarity to the correct matched word (i.e., mistakes in letter recognition) or other types of errors.

Thus, we performed an error analysis of Word-Picture Matching test responses to examine the relative importance of orthographic errors in children's responses. The relative frequency of orthographic errors was 13.6% higher than would be expected by chance, thereby supporting the hypothesis that orthographic features of Arabic script may be common stumbling blocks for word comprehension among many young readers of Arabic.[18] Further, to assess the long-term importance of orthographic errors in Arabic reading achievement, we identified four distinct groups of students, differentiated by whether they made many or few errors and by the type of error they made. In this post hoc analysis, children with many *orthographic* errors demonstrated some knowledge, albeit imperfect, of the Arabic orthographic system (making errors equivalent in English to choosing "can" instead of "cat" when shown a picture of a cat); those with many *nonspecific* errors could not demonstrate even this level of decoding knowledge, and tended to make non-specific errors based on pure guessing or on semantic confusions (such as choosing "dog"); the other two contrast groups of children were identified as simply *high* or *low* in terms of errors made of any type.[19]

When these four categories of students were compared on Arabic reading achievement, the pattern of results remained remarkably stable over the 5 years of the study (see Figure 5.8). Although children in the low error group were, as expected, superior in performance to all other groups in all years, the mean score of the orthographic error group improved over time and was significantly better (by year 5) than that of the nonspecific error group and the high error group.[20] Those children who were particu-

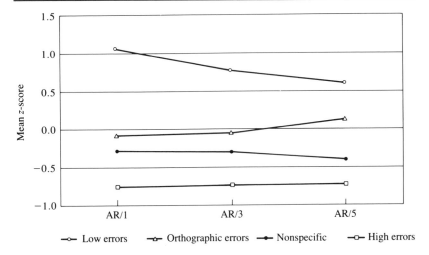

Figure 5.8. Arabic reading achievement scores by Word-Picture Matching error groups in years 1, 3, and 5.

larly sensitive to orthographic similarities – and, thus, were especially susceptible to errors provoked by foils which were spelled similarly to the correct matched word – eventually became superior to the other groups of children who read least well among the sample.

Preliminary conclusions

Our test results led to four broad conclusions. First, during the pre-school to primary school period, across a wide variety of tasks, a consistent developmental progression was found in Arabic reading ability. On the whole, first graders were superior to preschoolers, and especially so on the Letter Knowledge and Word Decoding tasks. We also found some preliminary indication (discussed further in chapter 6) that factors such as urban and rural residence, preschool experience, and maternal language influence reading performance in the first grade of primary school. Each of these variables appeared to affect the process by which children gain access to print, both in an individual psychological sense (e.g., by shaping motivation or by influencing the child's familiarity with the language of literacy) and in a sociocultural sense (e.g., by providing or limiting access to written materials, literate parents, and other literacy mediators).

Second, certain early reading skills were especially predictive of later reading performance in primary school. In particular, as in English, letter knowledge and decoding skills were among the best early indicators of subsequent reading achievement in Arabic. In particular, we found that knowledge of Arabic letters, their transformations, and their pronunciation in year 1 predicted more than 30% of the variance on reading achievement 5 years later. Furthermore, early word decoding skills at the single word level explained an additional 14% of the variance of year 5 reading achievement. This predictive power is considerably greater than that found in reading studies in European languages in the United States or Europe (e.g., Bradley & Bryant, 1983), which claim that about 10% to 12% of subsequent reading is due to such decoding skills. Our measures of Letter and Word Boundary skills also predicted subsequent reading ability, though the restricted range of the tasks (only four items in each) limited the predictive power of these measures.[21]

Third, the error analysis of scores for the Word-Picture Matching test provided additional support for the hypothesis that decoding skills are critical for subsequent reading acquisition. Children who tended to make many orthographic errors demonstrated partial competence in decoding skill (even if they came up with the wrong answer) and later showed better reading skills than children whose errors appeared more random. The use of error analysis – linked to the specific characteristics of Arabic orthography – was particularly valuable here, as reliance on correct answers only would not have provided an indication of processes by which a child arrived at his or her choice. A child's errors can clarify the kinds of strategies brought to bear on the problem of word decoding on comprehension. In this case, decoding skills were found to be an essential part of the reading process; lack of such skills prevented children from connecting the printed word to their knowledge of spoken Arabic.

Finally, as with all correlational data, we cannot be certain that decoding skills per se are those that are most crucial to teach to beginning readers of Arabic. In the United States, for example, there is continuing debate as to the merits of the phonics or decoding approach to reading (Adams, 1990; Chall, 1983). This debate, it should be noted, revolves primarily about the relative importance of decoding skill; very few specialists claim that decoding skill is of little importance in reading alphabetic scripts. There is substantial reason to believe that beginning to read in Arabic may necessitate an even greater reliance on decoding skills than beginning to read in English. As noted earlier, this might be expected from the closer link between spelling and sound correspondences in Arabic than in English, the difficulty of decoding when vocalization diacritics are absent, and the emphasis on oral reading performance both in the preschool and primary school settings. Overall, we found ample evidence to suggest that early letter recognition and decoding skills are critical in Arabic literacy acquisition in Moroccan schoolchildren.

Understanding reading acquisition in Arabic

Despite the high rates of reported illiteracy in the Arabic-speaking world, there is an astonishing lack of research on Arabic reading acquisition. The relationship between the Arabic language and Islam as a religion has received considerable attention, as have the traditional religious pedagogies for teaching Arabic in Quranic schools, but relatively little work has been done to understand the relationship between literacy, Arabic orthography, and the distinct varieties of Arabic spoken in the contemporary Middle East and North Africa. The present research suggests some directions for future investigations in this domain.

Our findings indicate that learning to read in the Arabic script has much in common with learning to read in other alphabets. Indeed, the regular letter-sound correspondence in Arabic makes it, in this sense, more similar to Spanish, for example, than to English. We discovered that when Moroccan children have effectively mastered the Arabic alphabet and basic decoding skills, they are well on their way to becoming proficient readers; those who do not achieve such mastery are likely to be at risk for grade failure and school dropout (Spratt, 1988). Error analysis provided a more detailed portrait of the types of reading strategies that beginning Arabic readers employ, indicating that children who could demonstrate knowledge of the relation between symbol and sound were likely to succeed best in higher grades. Finally, the high correlation between spoken Moroccan Arabic (as measured by the MPV) and Standard Arabic reading achievement ($r > .38$; AR/3 and AR/5) suggests that the ability to speak dialectal Arabic is directly related to later Standard Arabic literacy development (see also chapter 8).

In an effort to gain an emic understanding of Arabic literacy acquisition, we endeavored to create assessment instruments that built on its special linguistic and orthographic features. The Letter Boundary task used artificial syllables to test a child's understanding of the possibilities of combining certain letter forms into words; the Word Boundary task used a similar approach to ascertain the child's knowledge of how words are normally distinguished from one another in the highly cursive Arabic script; and the

Word-Picture Matching test made use of orthographically constructed foils that enabled a sensitive Arabic-specific analysis of errors to be undertaken. These tasks may prove particularly useful for the development of future assessment instruments of reading in Arabic.

Before leaving this topic, we should mention other important research questions related to Arabic orthography and reading acquisition that we did not have time to pursue: the question of the degree of utility of diacritical marks for beginning versus proficient readers;[22] the value of simplified orthographies in Arabic;[23] and the role of extensive copying (dictation) in Moroccan writing instruction.[24] In short, much remains to be learned about Arabic orthography and its relation to literacy acquisition, but some significant advances emerged from this present set of findings. We now turn to the important topic of the ways in which social and cultural contexts can influence who becomes a proficient reader and who does not.

Notes

1 Of the few empirical studies of reading acquisition in Arabic, one that has special relevance to early reading in Arabic in Morocco is the work of Badry (1983) on preschool and early primary school children's creative production of novel verbs to express new concepts. Badry's research indicates that preschoolers appeared to have a working knowledge of the transformational rules applied to Arabic word structure, knowledge that the author suggests could be usefully integrated into teaching reading in Arabic. The key issue is children's knowledge of syllabic structure (i.e., what are termed *triliteral* roots) in Arabic. Triliteral roots are present in all regional varieties of Arabic and are important for comprehension of text in literary Arabic; for example, the triliteral root /*ktb*/ forms the basis for the words "book," "school," and "writing" in Arabic, and such knowledge – whether conscious or unconscious – is, according to Badry, an important part of fluent reading.

A recent review of language and literacy in the Maghreb is provided in Ezzaki and Wagner (1992). An empirical study of children's spelling errors in Arabic reading acquisition was undertaken by Azzam (1989).

2 However, rule-governed elisions and differences in regional pronunciation diminish somewhat the strength of the sound-symbol correspondence in Arabic.

3 Modifications in the printed form of Arabic script have been proposed in recent years, both for purposes of improving the efficiency of printing technology in Arabic and with a view to simplifying the reader's task of learning multiple letter forms, diacritics, and key vocalizations. It should be noted,

however, that such changes have not generally been based on empirical research of the reading process, nor are they yet widely used.

4 In the discussion of assessment procedures, we alternately use the terms *tasks* and *tests*. The former generally refers to a limited number of items or questions, usually of an innovative sort (such as the Letter Boundary *task*), thus constituting a procedure that would not stand up to the scrutiny of psychometricians. The term *test* is used mainly to refer to more lengthy assessments, often derived from Western-type measures (such as the Children's Embedded Figures *test*).

5 Like Ferreiro and Teberosky (1982), and following Vygotsky (1978), we could have attempted a detailed description of the scribbling and early writing of children who obtain writing instruments before they begin alphabetic instruction. Our observations suggested, however, that such scribbling was far less common in Morocco, where even school-going children may lack paper and pencils with which to write. If, as these researchers have suggested, such scribbling necessarily precedes literacy acquisition, what are the consequences of not having an opportunity to engage in scribbling? Our research suggests that scribbling is not a necessary prerequisite for literacy, though we have no evidence that it would not lead to some improvement in subsequent literacy learning.

6 See further discussion of cursive writing in the text on letter recognition tasks.

7 The tests were given in April 1983; two alternate and equivalent forms of the tests were used across the 2 testing years to help reduce possible learning effects on specific items.

8 As noted in chapter 4, children in Cohort 1 were assessed in years 1, 3, and 5 of the longitudinal study of primary school achievement. However, we were also able to make an additional assessment of certain reading skills in year 2 of the study. Though most of the data of year 2 are not critical to the overall analysis of Cohort 1 results, certain tasks (notably the WD and WPM tests) were sensitive to the different forms (see note 7) used to control for learning effects across test administrations in years 1 and 2. For some analyses involving Cohort 1, therefore, WD and WPM scores for the 2 years were averaged, producing a "year 1/2" score, in order to minimize differences found empirically in the two forms (as shown in Table 5.2).

9 Nonspecific errors included those that were semantically similar (e.g., house vs. building), as well as various randomly chosen "wrong" words. Orthographic errors, as discussed in the text, are those where foils are spelled similarly, and thus are likely to be due to limited abilities in letter recognition.

10 A description of these samples is provided in chapter 4.

11 Such test intercorrelations are used to establish what psychometricians call *construct validity*. We conducted additional statistical tests to assess the internal consistency of these tests; these split-half reliability levels for the reading tests

were generally acceptable for experimental measures. Alpha coefficients ranged from .565 to .955, with an average of .852.

12 Because the preschool sample was tested only once, scores for these children could not be used to predict reading achievement in primary school.

13 All t tests were significant at the $p < .001$ level.

14 There were several exceptions, however. The preschool group differed by gender on Letter Concept ($t = 2.08$, $p < .05$) and Word-Picture Matching ($t = 2.30$, $p < .05$), with girls outperforming boys on both tasks; and by preschooling within the urban setting on the Morocco Picture Vocabulary test ($t = 2.97$, $p < .01$), with modern preschoolers outperforming Quranic preschoolers.

15 Because of the unbalanced nature of the project design across urban and rural environments (i.e., there were different numbers of subsamples in each community), separate analyses were performed within each community and across urban and rural samples of Quranic and nonpreschooled Arabic-speaking groups.

Independent t tests showed no significant differences by gender across the entire primary school sample for all early reading tasks; thus, cells were collapsed across gender. As for environment and preschooling contrasts among Quranic and nonpreschooled Arabic speakers, main effects for environment only were found, with urban children generally performing better than rural children. Tasks that showed significant differences were Word Boundary ($F = 5.60$, $p < .05$), Letter Knowledge ($F = 9.97$, $p < .01$), Word Decoding ($F = 19.43$, $p < .01$), and the Morocco Picture Vocabulary test ($F = 18.44$, $p < .001$); a trend-level pattern also obtained for Word-Picture Matching ($F = 2.89$, $p < .10$). No significant interactions or main effects by preschooling were found.

For the urban sample, one-way analyses of variance revealed only one significant finding by type of preschool (none, Quranic, or modern), on the Letter Knowledge task ($F = 3.76$, $p < .05$). On this task, modern preschooled children performed best and nonpreschooled children least well; a similar trend-level pattern was evident for the Word Decoding task ($F = 2.36$, $p < .10$).

In the rural sample, contrasts by preschool (Quranic or none) and by home language (Arabic or Berber) were possible. Two-way analyses of variance showed no significant interactions; though the Arabic-speaking group had consistently better performance on all early reading tasks than the Berber-speaking group did, these differences were significant only for the Morocco Picture Vocabulary test ($F = 15.98$, $p < .01$), which confirmed the language group assessments, and for the Word Picture Matching test ($F = 6.52$, p $< .05$); a trend-level pattern on Word Decoding ($F = 2.95$, $p < .10$) was also found. Main effects of preschooling revealed only one significant difference, for

Letter Boundary ($F = 4.09$, $p < .05$), and one trend-level pattern on Word Picture Matching ($F = 3.04$, $p < .10$); on both tasks, Quranic preschooled children performed better than nonpreschooled groups.

16 The WD and WPM tests indicated differences across alternate forms of each test, as one form of each test was "easier" than the other. As mentioned in note 7, we were able to eliminate the effects of the form of the test by averaging.

17 Cross-sectional studies tend to be much easier to accomplish due to the efficiencies associated with completing assessment across multiple cohorts at the same time. Such studies are weak methodologically because they cannot control for the simple fact that each cohort represents a different sample of children. Even if randomly selected, cross-sectional studies may show cross-age and cross-grade differences that reflect sample differences more than differences in development.

18 The expected rate of orthographic errors was calculated as the ratio of the possible orthographic errors to all (orthographic and other) possible errors in the WPM test, multiplied by the actual total errors made by the sample population. The non-orthographic error rate, calculated in an analogous fashion, was found to be 11.6% lower than expected. For a more extensive analysis, see Wagner and Spratt (1993).

19 To differentiate the four contrasting error groups, children's orthographic and nonspecific error scores were divided into rough thirds according to the distribution of scores for each type of error, thereby creating low, middle, and high categories. Using a 2×2 cell design, children whose error scores fell into the low level for both types of errors were classified "low" overall ($N = 72$); children with a high on both types of errors were "high" overall ($N = 42$). Those children whose orthographic error scores were one or two levels higher than their nonspecific error scores were classified "orthographic" ($N = 88$); conversely, those for whom this pattern was reversed were labeled "non-specific" ($N = 96$).

20 Independent t tests indicated that by year 5 the reading performance of children with a high ratio of orthographic errors was significantly higher than those with predominantly nonspecific error rate ($t = 3.11$, $p < .01$); children in the low error group were superior to all other error groups in performance in all years ($t \leq 4.40$, $p \leq .001$).

21 Further development of these tests for beginning readers (children or adults) of Arabic would seem to be warranted. Such low-end or prereading predictors of subsequent reading achievement can provide effective ways to identify beginning readers who have or have not mastered the initial challenge of understanding orthographic rules in Arabic. These measures might also be of value to adult students who are learning Arabic as a foreign language in university settings. This is an area ripe for further investigation.

22 See Navon and Shimron (1984) for a discussion of the importance of diacritical marks and reading acquisition in Hebrew. See also Azzam's study (1989),
undertaken in Abu Dhabi, on primary school reading errors and the role of
diacritics. Finally, the current research of Mohamed Maamouri (private communication) in Tunisia suggests that increased use of vocalization diacritics
may be an important step in reducing Arabic reading problems.

23 Under the auspices of the Arab League, Lakhdar al-Ghazal has created a
simplified script for Arabic that has been utilized for special applications,
particularly with typewriters. Little of this work has been published in scientific journals, though see Ezzaki and Wagner (1992) for a general review. It
appears that some of this work on simplified scripts may be obviated by the
increased use of Arabic language word processors that automatically correct
for beginning, middle, and end forms of Arabic letters.

24 Our measure of the ability to transcribe Arabic (dictation) was not utilized in
the analyses due to unforeseen scoring problems. Thus, this topic remains one
that has received, to our knowledge, virtually no research attention.

6. Social factors in literacy acquisition

In (traditional) religious education, it was said that the students had to memorize the *sura*s, while it was not considered important that they understand them. . . . Here we prepare students to go into modern elementary schools. So we should teach them not only the Quran, but also how to read, write, and count, and also discuss with them the *sura*s in the Quran. Otherwise, if the students memorize only the Quran, they would be blind people. (A *fqih* in al-Ksour)

The acquisition of any human skill, physical or mental, depends on the interplay among a wide variety of factors. Earlier research and our own observations of Moroccan society suggested the possibility that certain social features of children's lives would be related to literacy acquisition in school. Therefore, our research was designed so that these factors might be directly and empirically studied. It was assumed that some of the factors found to affect reading achievement in the West might be related similarly to literacy in Morocco, but we also wanted to study factors specific to Morocco, such as Quranic preschooling. In this chapter, then, we present findings concerning the impact of family socioeconomic status, level of parental education, urban or rural context, gender, and preschooling on 5 years of literacy development in the primary school sample.

Socioeconomic status

Family socioeconomic status, or SES, is often regarded as a powerful factor affecting school achievement. Whether in the United States, Europe, or the Third World, it is taken as common knowledge that children of the middle and upper classes achieve better in school than do classmates who are economically less fortunate. Probably the best known study that makes this point is the *Coleman Report* (Coleman, 1966), which found that such factors as parents' occupation, disposable income, and years of education are more powerful predictors of their children's educational success and subsequent economic opportunity than are factors related to the schools themselves, such as teacher quality or the school district's budget. Coleman's work set a trend that is still much in evidence in Western educational research – namely, that SES, even if defined in widely different ways in disparate studies, is the major predictor of why certain children succeed in school while others do not. Even though Coleman and later researchers (such as Jencks et al., 1972) were not able to disentangle completely the various components of SES, it appears that both occupational status and parental education are the most consistent SES factors predicting of American children's success in primary and secondary school.

In a dissent from the almost universal acceptance of this proposition, Heyneman (1976) published the first of a series of papers suggesting that SES may affect school achievement more in industrialized countries than in the Third World. His in-depth investigation of schooling and achievement in Uganda found evidence that the quality of schools and the availability of textbooks were more important than the education of parents or their income. One possible reason for this difference in results is that there is more variability in SES in the United States than in many developing countries and, conversely, less variability in textbooks. Furthermore, the so-called universal effects of SES must also be examined in light of the usual problem of societal differences and other school quality factors (such as teacher training, facilities and the like) in the meaning of SES. For example, a household annual income of $10,000 in Marrakech or Casablanca may imply a very different kind of SES value than in al-Ksour; in the latter case, the family would be considered relatively wealthy. As a second example, increments of education among the poor may have differing degrees of value than equivalent increments of education among the middle or upper class, as further discussed in chapter 11.

In Morocco, the problem of SES measurement is exacerbated by the rather sharply defined nature of social classes. With a middle and upper class making up only 15% of the population, a lower class (what the French call the *classes populaires*) as much as 75%, and the remainder being the ultrapoor (see chapter 11), life-styles, income, and educational opportunities are radically different between the first 15% and the rest of Moroccans. The middle and upper classes often possess nicely appointed houses or apartments, one or more automobiles, and many of the luxuries of the average American or European family. The popular classes, by contrast, have little disposable income, and their main consumer possessions (as contrasted with land and animals) might include a radio and/or television.

Because we sought to study comparable families from urban and rural communities, we wondered whether urban parents might have a higher SES than rural parents. Differences in geographic and ecological context, we reasoned, might actually be due to SES differences. On the other hand, although we knew that income was higher (on the average) in urban settings, its effects might be counterbalanced by an equivalently higher cost of living. Indeed, parents in rural Morocco often told us that cheap living (*hayat arkhis*) was one of the best reasons for staying in al-Ksour. Another way to limit the confounding effects of SES is to reduce its overall variability (and therefore predictive power) by limiting the sample selection to children from the *classes populaires* in the rural town of al-Ksour and in Marrakech. This is precisely what we chose to do.

To what extent were we able to obtain roughly similar families by SES in al-Ksour and Marrakech? To answer this question, we made use of the parental interview (described in chapter 4 and shown in appendix 3). As may be seen in Table 6.1, the educational levels in both communities appear similar. For example, mothers' education levels were so low that the large majority of mothers in rural and urban families had completed few, if any, years of schooling. There was somewhat more variation in fathers' education within and across communities; whereas the percentage of fathers with Quranic and primary schooling was relatively low, there was, nonetheless, a range of years that might make a difference to the family's children. Similarly, urban families, measured by the father's job classification, also produced some variation. Overall, relatively few SES differences by rural and urban communities were found in our survey research and ethnographic observations.

Thus, by utilizing a strategy of excluding most middle- and upper-class families from the project sample, we were able to reduce but not completely eliminate the potential effects of SES. To measure remaining effects, we drew on our interview data to construct a useful measure of SES. After a number of complex statistical analyses involving factors such as education, home wealth, and so forth, we found that the occupational categorization of the employment of the child's father was both a simple and robust indicator of SES: "high," jobs in government administration or a profession; "middle," jobs in semiskilled or sales positions; and "low," unemployed, farming, or peasant.

Subsequent statistical analyses showed a clear relationship between SES

Table 6.1. Education and occupational characteristics in rural and urban families

	Rural (%)	Urban (%)
What is level of educational attainment of parents?		
a. Mother		
Preschool		
None	86	74
Quranic 1–2 years	11	29
Quranic 3 or more years	1	4
Modern preschool	1	0
Modern public school		
None	87	77
1–3 years primary	4	9
4–5 years primary	5	9
1–3 years secondary	1	3
4–7 years secondary	0	3
1–3 years postsecondary/university	0	0
4 or more years postsecondary	0	0
b. Father		
Traditional Quranic schooling		
None	70	29
1–2 years	10	27
3 or more years	6	14
Modern preschool	1	0
Modern public school		
None	77	57
1–3 years primary	4	5
4–5 years primary	7	13
1–3 years secondary	3	8
4–7 years secondary	5	7
1–3 years postsecondary/university	1	1
4 or more years postsecondary	0	1
Occupation of father		
Unemployed	3	1
Unskilled labor, farming	40	25
Semi- to skilled labor	11	25
Commerce, services	25	27
Administrative	9	6
Traditional/modern professions	5	8
Other		

Note: These data were gathered during home interviews. Mother, aunt, and grandmother accounted for 90%, 3%, and 2% of the respondents to the questions; fathers and other relatives accounted for the remaining 5% of Respondents. Children were in first grade when these data were obtained. This subsample includes 205 families of children in Cohort 1, for whom most of the relevant data were available.

and children's reading achievement that was most apparent among the high and low reading achievers (see Figure 6.1).[1] Among the middle achieving children, there was a fairly even distribution of achievement by SES. Similarly, survey data on household amenities such as access to water and electricity (the best available measures of household income and expenditures) were also predictive of Arabic reading achievement in primary school (Figure 6.2). Again, children who were poor readers in first grade were most likely to have neither running water nor electricity. These effects, too, do not appear to be completely determinant, as many children (25%) with such amenities were in the low-achieving group. Although some indication was found that SES factors play a role in school achievement in Morroco (even when such factors are constrained through sample selection), we can reject the simplistic argument that the "poorest of the poor" will necessarily become the illiterates of the next generation. On the other hand, as detailed in chapter 11, the general educational effects of poverty do tend to repeat themselves across generations.

Parental education

It has long been a truism that literate parents tend to have literate children, but social science research has told us little about how this transfer takes place. Research on the American family suggests, for example, that direct instruction (such as storybook reading) to children may increase both motivation to learn and reading skill (Heath, 1982; Teale & Sulzby, 1987). However, we know much less about the role of direct instruction in other societies and across social classes; and what we do know suggests considerable variation in the consequences of direct parental involvement. For example, among the Kaluli people of Papua, New Guinea, mothers intentionally avoid teaching their children how to read, because it is thought to be "of no purpose" (Schieffelin & Cochran-Smith, 1984). Beyond such anecdotal information, we know remarkably little about parents' instruction of children's reading in other societies. In rural Morocco and in other developing countries, there may be no one at home literate enough to instruct the child; indeed, as noted in chapter 2, primary school children themselves often become the literacy experts for the entire family.

The parent interviews provided a wealth of information on the educational background of the families in the study. Using these data, it was possible to examine the relationship between parents' educational level and children's reading achievement during primary school. In these analyses, children's overall reading scores for the first year of the study were

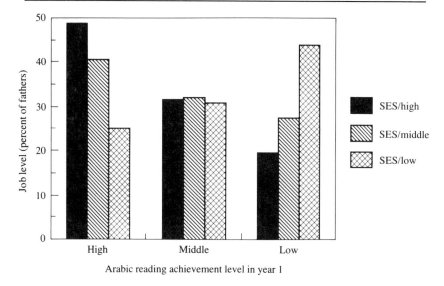

Figure 6.1. Arabic reading achievement in year 1 as a function of SES level.

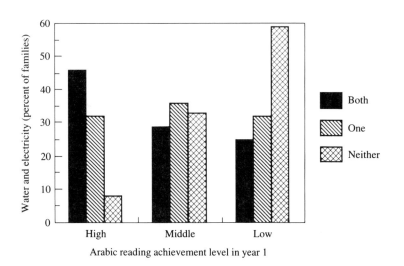

Figure 6.2. Arabic reading achievement in year 1 as a function of household amenities (water and electricity).

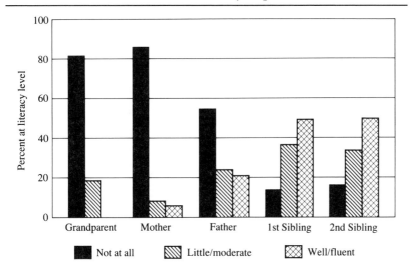

Figure 6.3. Intergenerational changes in self-assessed literacy skill among Cohort 1 children's grandparents, parents, and siblings. ("First sibling" refers to the oldest sibling of the child; "second sibling" refers to the next oldest sibling; N = 295.)

categorized as low, middle, or high (in terms of each third of the distribution of standard scores) and compared across the highest level of education reached by either parent of the child (no schooling, for 49% of the sample; primary schooling only, 33%; 6 years or more, 20%).

By using the interview data about the family members of the sample children in Cohort 1, we found that there had been a dramatic increase in educational attainment levels across generations, reflecting similar national statistical trends as reported by the Moroccan government (Ministry of Education, 1986; see also chapter 11). Only 19% of the Cohort 1 children had one literate grandparent (only 4% had more than one), but 9% of their mothers, 40% of their fathers, and 82% of their oldest siblings had attained at least a moderate level of self-assessed Arabic literacy (corresponding roughly, by our data, to a fourth-grade level in primary school; see Figure 6.3).[2] Furthermore, whereas only 1% of mothers and 12% of fathers had reached the middle of secondary school (ninth grade), 39% of eldest siblings had done so. Intergenerational change in literacy in Morocco reflects the substantial increase in the numbers of children currently attending school, a level more than double that of only one generation ago.

In addition to intergenerational changes, we found that children's reading achievement was strongly related to parental educational level across all

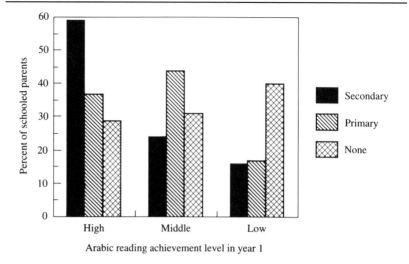

Figure 6.4. Arabic reading achievement in year 1 by parental education level.

5 years of the project (see Figure 6.4).[3] However, even with this clear relationship, we cannot assume that children with unschooled parents are necessarily at risk (in the American sense of the term) of failure and school dropout. Additional analyses revealed that a substantial number of children from families with unschooled, illiterate parents achieved reading scores in the high reading category. In Morocco, probably more often than in contemporary America, it is quite possible to be an excellent achiever with illiterate parents or a poor to midlevel reader from a relatively literate and educated family. Similar cross-generational changes in education and literacy were also common in the United States in the first quarter of the twentieth century where disparities between home and school often existed (Kaestle, 1991). In other words, these findings on intergenerational change probably reflect a transitional period in Moroccan contemporary history, analogous to periods decades ago in Western societies.

Environment, gender, and preschooling

The design of the longitudinal study of Cohort 1 provided an opportunity to compare subsamples that differed markedly by environment, gender, and preschooling experience. Before exploring the results in terms of literacy outcomes, it is useful to review briefly earlier work on these same issues and to consider a few methodological problems that confront such studies.

Rural and urban environments

In the Western research literature, remarkably little attention has been devoted to the rural-urban dimension of educational achievement in general or of literacy in particular. In the United States, most attention has been concentrated on the nature of the urban underclass (Mincy, Sawhill, & Wolf, 1990), largely consisting of Afro-American, Hispanic, or Asian minorities. But beyond this focus on ethnicity in urban America, are there other differences between urban and rural life that might affect educational achievement? Surprisingly, little effort has been made to explore this issue, perhaps due to a judgment that, in industrialized countries with great population mobility and a pervasive communication infrastructure, such differences are likely to be minimal. In the Third World, by contrast, there has long been serious interest in the study of rural environments, from schooling issues to agriculture, as would be expected by the often clear cut differences to be found between rural and urban life in these countries.[4]

Among Moroccans, whether schooled or not, there is a tendency to call someone a *baladi* (literally, from the countryside) who is behind the times or even backward. Rural Moroccans make jokes about their *baladi* ways, though it must be said that they make jokes about their urban compatriots as well! As noted earlier, there are some important differences between urban and rural contexts that go beyond differences in educational level and jokes made by amiable protagonists. Well into the 1980s (when this study was carried out), these differences included the lack of printed media in al-Ksour, as well as no cinema, no magazine store, no newspaper kiosk, and no library. Other differences in print ecology were described in chapter 3 in our vignettes of Moroccan life and society.

Yet there is more to such distinctions in the literacy ecology than the casual observer might see *en passant*. The fact that the numbers of literate individuals and literate materials are so dramatically different between al-Ksour and Marrakech led us to conclude that such ecological differences might be significant predictors of literacy acquisition. Of course, trying to quantify these differences in the literacy ecology is not an easy chore, and we had little prior research upon which to base our efforts. What distinguishes one literacy ecology from the other? As mentioned earlier, there were clear differences between al–Ksour and Marrakech in terms of geography, population size, historical traditions, modes of income generation and the like. There were also differences in parents' education, for public schooling arrived a generation earlier (at least for our sample) in urban Morocco.

To understand better the literacy ecology of our two field sites, we used ethnographic observations in addition to questions in the home interviews. We found, for example, that the amount of print in the ambient environment in Marrakech – such as on cinema posters, advertising publicity, newspaper kiosks, and so forth – is radically different from that in al–Ksour, where the primary source of print is on the labels of certain store-bought goods and in the Quran. Our survey data support this contrast, showing that more than half of the urban sample families had four or more books and magazines in their homes, compared to about a third of the rural families (Table 6.2). As expected, the urban families also had more contact with French written materials than their rural counterparts. Television watching is another important indicator of contact with the literacy ecology, because it provides access not only to spoken Standard Arabic but also to Arabic and French print that appears on the screen (see also chapter 2). Self-assessed estimates of television watching indicated that urban families are almost twice as likely as rural families to watch television on a daily basis. More significantly, more than a third of rural families never watch television, compared to only 13% of urban families, a difference largely due to the lack of TV sets and electricity in rural al–Ksour.

An additional indicator of the literacy ecology may be seen in the types of literacy help – what we termed more generically literacy mediators in chapter 2 – that are available to the families of the sample children in al–Ksour and Marrakech. Although both samples of families tended to seek help most of the time within the household, almost a third of the rural families sought aid outside the family, but only 13% of urban families did so. When literacy mediation was sought inside the household, the mother most often asked a more literate son or daughter for assistance, supporting our conclusions (discussed previously) about intergenerational change. When help was sought outside the family household, as happened more often in rural al–Ksour, most families in each community sought the advice of a literate neighbor or friend. Only a small percentage of the sample families relied on the traditional *fqih* as a mediator – another consequence of the increased level of schooling in much of contemporary Morocco. This observation is in contrast to traditional forms of literacy

Table 6.2.   Literacy ecology in rural and urban families

	Rural (%)	Urban (%)
1. Literacy and media use in the home		
a. Number of types of Arabic written matter in the home (e.g., books and magazines = 2 types)		
1	4[a]	9
2	40	22
3	21	15
4 or more	36	54
b. Number of types of French written matter in the home		
0	33	21
1	37	29
2	17	21
3	7	20
4 or more	5	7
c. Child's use of television		
Never	35	13
1–3 times a week	5	6
Everyday	39	79
d. Mother's use of television		
Never	39	18
1–3 times a week	6	6
Everyday	37	71
2. When necessary, whom do you ask for help in reading and writing?		
a. Choice of inside vs. outside of family		
Inside only	54	65
Outside only	32	13
Both inside and outside	8	13
Never ask/no need	2	6
b. Inside family		
Son/daughter	41	37
Brother/sister	9	7
Spouse	8	15
Never ask/no need	36	27
c. Outside family		
Fqih (traditional Quranic teacher)	6	2
Government worker	0	2
Literate neighbor/friend	36	22
Never ask/no need	50	71

[a]Percentage of responses within rural or urban field site. Some columns add to less than 100% due to missing data or other responses.

mediation described to us by community elders (see chapter 3; see also Wagner, Messick, & Spratt, 1986).

Another potential difference between the rural and urban communities, we surmised, might pertain to the quality of the training of the teachers. We had heard that Moroccan public school teachers in urban communities are more likely to be from urban (and educated) families and tend to be native Arabic speakers as well as conversant in French. On the other hand, we knew that the younger and (presumably) better trained teachers are obliged to work in rural areas before they can eventually transfer to urban schools, which many teachers seek to do for family and professional reasons. The data collected on the sample teachers' study showed that urban teachers were substantially older on average (40 versus 29 years) and more experienced (16 versus 6 years) than their rural colleagues (Table 6.3). However, urban and rural teachers were roughly comparable on educational level attained (4.9 and 5.7 years, respectively) and in the small amount of formal training received (2.7 and 1.4 years).

Other interesting differences were apparent in teachers' attitudes concerning learning and pedagogy. For example, rural teachers were much more likely to say that Berber-speaking children learn differently from Arabic-speaking children, which suggests a greater sensitivity to the context of multilingual al-Ksour. On the other hand, the rural (and younger) teachers claimed to emphasize Standard Arabic when working directly with individual children, whereas urban teachers reverted to dialectal Arabic. The tendency of the young rural teachers to be cognizant of (and obedient to) the government-mandated pedagogy is also evidenced by their much greater insistence on children following the teacher's exact instructions, as opposed to the more flexible learning-by-doing attitude favored by many urban teachers. Finally, it should be noted that urban teachers were more likely to say that boys needed more education than girls. This is counterintuitive when one considers the increased professionalization of women in urban areas, but it may be more reflective of the fact that urban teachers come from an older and probably more socially conservative generation.

Overall, we expected that even if specific environmental effects could not be pinpointed (because so many other factors covary across the two Moroccan contexts), the cluster of factors that distinguish urban Marrakech from rural al-Ksour would likely lead to major differences in literacy development. We were supported in this view by numerous comments made by our urban Moroccan university colleagues, who simply "knew"

Table 6.3. Characteristics of teachers in urban and rural field sites

	Urban	Rural
1. Number of teachers interviewed	23	33
2. Description of teacher's background		
a. Gender		
Male	11	17
Female	12	16
b. Teacher in what type of school		
Quranic preschool	5	5
Modern preschool	3	0
Primary school (first or second grade)	15	28
c. Average age	40	29
d. Percentage of sample married	69	59
e. Maternal language		
Berber	6	8
Moroccan Arabic	17	25
f. Average level of spoken Moroccan Arabic (6-pt. scale)	5.7	5.8
g. Average level of spoken Berber (6-pt. scale)	3.5	3.7
h. Average level of spoken French (6-pt. scale)	3.0	4.2
i. Average level of reading Standard Arabic (6-pt. scale)	5.8	5.7
j. Average level of writing Standard Arabic (6-pt. scale)	5.7	5.6
k. Average level of reading French (6-pt. scale)	3.2	4.6
l. Average level of writing French (6-pt. scale)	3.4	4.3
m. Average years of attendance at Quranic school	4.9	2.8
n. Average grade level of public schooling	4.9	7.9
o. How often do you watch TV each week? (times)	2–3	2–3
p. In what language do you usually watch TV?	Arabic	French
q. Have you traveled abroad?	76	18
r. In travels, to what country did you go (modal response)	France	France
3. Teacher's professional experience		
a. Years of teacher training	2.7	1.4
b. Average number of years as teacher	16	6.3
c. Average years of teacher's public education	4.9	5.7
d. Are you satisfied being a teacher? (% yes)	100	72

Table 6.3. (cont.)

	Urban	Rural
4. Teacher's values concerning learning and pedagogy		
a. Do Berber-speaking children learn differently from Arabic-speaking children? (% yes)	45	73
b. How often do you use Standard Arabic (and not Moroccan Arabic) for individualized instruction? (% time for Standard Arabic)	56	90
c. Do you help your children outside of class? (% yes)	87	78
d. What is best age to teach children to read? (average response in years)	5.5	6.2
e. What is main reason for child to be literate? (modal response)	everyday life	*baraka* (blessing or "cultural capital")
f. In addition to reading by comprehension, how important is memorization? (% responding "memorization")	13	15
g. Which is more important, the child's experience or following the teacher's instructions? (% responding "experience")	2	37
h. To succeed in school, which is more important: native ability or hard work? (% responding "hard work")	19	7
i. Are some children ready to start schooling earlier than others? (% responding "yes")	95	97
j. What makes a good teacher? (modal response)	understanding children	religious dedication
k. Whose responsibility is it to teach a child to read: the teacher or the parents (% responding "teacher")	79	82
l. Who needs more schooling: boys or girls, or do they need the same? (% responding "boys more")	65	15

Note: Levels of language and literacy skill are self-described and part of the interview format.

that life in the countryside was a significant impediment in promoting literacy for rural schoolchildren. What we did not know was the size of the effect, nor whether we could determine particular aspects of the environment that might make a difference.

Gender

In the United States, the study of gender and educational achievement has assumed considerable importance in recent years. One of the best known findings is that boys tend to be superior in math and science, whereas girls excel in reading and writing. These differences, based on both standardized tests and school grades, are statistically reliable, even though the actual differences by gender represent only a few percentage points in the large samples studied (Huston, 1983). In the Third World, gender differences in educational attainment are often seen to be quite large overall: Girls attain lower grade levels, repeat grades more frequently, perform more poorly on standardized tests, and have fewer postschooling job opportunities (Charlton, 1984). The underlying causes of these gender differences, which have been documented in many parts of Asia, Latin America, and Africa, are the subject of considerable debate. Some specialists, like Stromquist (1990), argue that traditional societies are, for the most part, sexist in the way girls and women are treated and that this treatment affects many dimensions of their lives (such as the "overproduction" of children and the inordinate amount of time spent on menial household tasks), that school texts reinforce traditional sex-role stereotypes, and that these factors cumulatively result in continued female subordination and denied access to education in male-dominated traditional societies.

Male and female differences in socialization have also been the focus of a number of Moroccan research studies in recent years (e.g., Davis & Davis, 1989; Mernissi, 1975). Several generalizations follow from this work, and these were confirmed by our own observations of Moroccan school-age girls and various questions posed in the student interview to the sample children in year 5 (when they were about 12 years old). From Table 6.4, it may be seen that the distribution of home environmental factors varies little by gender across the sample (e.g., language use, electricity and running water, distance to school).

However, a closer look at the data suggests certain key differences by gender in the features of literacy behavior in the home. For example, boys reportedly read more frequently in the home than girls do, yet girls were nearly four times more likely to have written a letter than boys (a gender difference that probably could be replicated in the United States as well). In terms of language preference, boys were much more likely than girls to report that they preferred television programs in French, though this finding is confounded with the nature of programming in each language

Table 6.4. Characteristics of boys and girls in Cohort 1

	Boys	Girls
1. Sample size	109	130
2. Description of children's home environment		
a. Language use in home, Berber or Moroccan Arabic (% Berber monolingual)	37	38
b. Is there running water in your house? (% yes)	69	77
c. Is there electricity in your house? (% yes)	69	79
d. Does your family own a car? (% yes)	11	12
e. Does your family own a TV? (% yes)	70	85
f. Does your family own a refrigerator? (% yes)	35	48
g. How long does it take you to get to school? (modal response in minutes)	15–30	15–30
3. Features of literacy in the home (% yes)		
a. Do you spend time reading at home?	82	75
b. How often do you watch TV? (modal response)	everyday	everyday
c. What is the language of your favorite TV program? (% chosen)		
Standard Arabic	37	45
Egyptian Arabic	10	21
French	36	18
d. Does anyone bring a regular newspaper into the home? (% yes)	35	35
e. What kinds of materials do you most like to read at home? (% per item type)		
Nothing	18	25
Newspaper/magazine	21	14
Quran	13	8
Cineroman	0	1
Comics	0	3
Novels/storybooks	46	48
f. Have you ever written a letter? (% yes)	26	82
g. What language did your write in most recently, Arabic or French? (modal response)	Standard Arabic	Standard Arabic
h. How many Arabic language newspapers can you name?		
None	52	59
One or more	30	20
i. How many French language newspapers can you name?		
None	94	98
One or more	2	0

Table 6.4. *(cont.)*

		Boys	Girls
j.	Do you ever read *cineromans?* (% yes) (Note: These are almost always in French)	64	58
k.	What language do you most enjoy reading in?		
	Arabic	50	50
	French	14	12
	Both	36	38
l.	Which language of literacy (Arabic or French) is most important in Morocco? (% French)	31	24
m.	When you help other people to read things, what do you most often help them to read?		
	Nothing	56	62
	Newspaper/magazine	0	0
	Quran	1	5
	Comics/*bandes dessinee*	1	0
	Novels/storybooks	6	8
	Letters	26	18
	Forms and papers	9	4
n.	When you help other people to write things, what do you most often help them to write?		
	Nothing	77	82
	Letters	7	8
	Form-filling	1	2
	Keep diary	4	1
	Math	4	2
4. Attitudes and values			
a.	Do you like school a lot or a little? (% a lot)	90	95
b.	What do you like most about school?		
	Friends	9	5
	Specific subject matter	27	27
	Job prospects	1	1
	General knowledge	25	36
	Your teacher	16	20
c.	What do you dislike most about school?		
	Difficult	2	2
	Teacher too strict	5	6
	Social problems with children	30	23
d.	Who usually gets better grades in school, boys or girls?		
	Girls	6	20
	Boys	12	5
	Same	81	74

Table 6.4. *(cont.)*

	Boys	Girls
e. How far do you hope to go in school?		
Primary certificate	13	14
Middle school certificate	14	17
Secondary (BAC) certificate	33	30
University degree	19	9
f. Why do you think you were promoted in school last year?		
Hard work	94	99
Innate ability	2	1
Easy test	0	0
Good luck	0	0
Good teacher	0	0
God's will	2	0
g. Why do you think you were failed in school last year?		
Did not work hard	58	52
Lack of ability	10	20
Difficult test	10	4
Bad luck	0	0
Bad teacher	4	4
God's will	0	4
h. Do you usually study alone or with friends? (% responding "alone")	72	75

Note: All data taken from the student interviews of Cohort 1. Out of an original sample of 350 children in year 1, 239 student interviews were collected in year 5 of the study. All values are in percentages unless otherwise specified.

medium. For example, French language programs, often dubbed from American Westerns and the like, tend to be more violent than their Arabic language counterparts, and thus more attractive to adolescent boys. Though the sample adolescents reported watching television regularly (at least two to three times a week), more than half of the boys and girls could not accurately name a single Arabic language newspaper, and virtually none could name one in French. This statistic becomes even more striking when compared with the large share of the sample, almost 60% of all boys and girls, who had read *cineromans* (photographic novels) in French.

We also sought to determine the language and literacy preferences of the boys and girls in the sample. One of our hypotheses, based on ethnographic data, concerns the tendency for girls to be more interested in the French language than boys. The data from the student interview, however, showed little of this trend. Indeed, Moroccan youth seem to have a fairly general view that Arabic is the most enjoyable language to read (not surprising, as their skills are far superior in Arabic), but they also feel that Arabic is the most important language to learn. In this latter view, however, boys showed a stronger belief in the importance of the French language for job prospects. It may be, as we shall see in chapter 10, that girls have a more subjective sense of the importance of French and how it affects self-esteem and not simply job opportunities.

Finally, gender differences concerning beliefs about learning and school success are worth noting, and will be explored in greater depth in chapter 7. Here we can observe in Table 6.4 (e.g., item 4g) that though both boys and girls tend to attribute the lack of success to a failure to work hard, girls are about twice as likely as boys to attribute failure to a lack of native ability. The tendency for females to consider themselves perhaps not quite as talented as boys fits with the overall male dominance in Moroccan society. Yet it also contrasts with girls' beliefs that they are more likely to get good grades in school than boys (item 4d). Overall, with respect to attitudes about schooling, one could conclude from our data that there are more similarities than differences among boys and girls. This conclusion is reflected as well in our subsequent analyses of achievement outcomes.

Preschooling

Ever since the growth of the Head Start program in the United States in the 1960s (Zigler & Valentine, 1979), the effects of preschooling on subsequent school achievement have seen a substantial increase in research interest and financial investment. Research on American and European preschool programs has suggested the value of such experience, particularly among disadvantaged groups in society (Woodhead, 1988). In Third World countries, preschools are typically less widespread and empirical research on them far less frequent. Nonetheless, it appears that the effects of preschooling in developing countries are mostly positive (Myers, 1992; Myers & Hertenberg, 1987). However, because such preschooling programs may compete for scarce educational resources in developing countries, research reflects the biases (both positive and negative) that are inherent in the competition for funding.

For this latter reason, and because preschooling (particularly traditional

Quranic preschooling) is so common in Morocco, its study has particular appeal. Our work involved no external intervention however, because all Quranic and modern preschools existed before and after our research was conducted, and we made no effort to intervene in the ongoing nature of the instruction or curriculum. Furthermore, we knew a great deal about the composition of the families that sent their children to preschools, and thus were able to avoid, as described earlier, any obvious confounding of variables such as socioeconomic class with preschooling experience. Our goal in this part of the study was to measure the effects of preschooling (modern, traditional Quranic, or none) on literacy acquisition.

As described in chapter 3, Quranic and modern preschool experience may begin when children are as young as 3 or 4 years of age and continue until they reach age 6, and represents an important introduction to the learning activities, organized curriculum, and strict discipline found in primary school settings. Also, both Quranic and modern preschools provide a first opportunity for intensive exposure to Standard Arabic. For the purposes of the present analysis, there were two major comparisons of interest: First, we sought to understand the long-term impact of Quranic preschooling (by comparing it with no preschooling) on children's literacy and primary school achievement, and second, we wished to compare the potential differences in literacy acquisition between Quranic and modern preschool experience.[5]

An analysis of the effects of environment, gender, and preschooling

In order to address the questions raised in this chapter, children's Arabic reading achievement scores were compared across the varying subsamples of children. In the first major analysis, we observed that the effects of environment appear to be substantial over time (see Figure 6.5). Regardless of age, gender, and preschooling experience, those children attending school in urban areas consistently outperformed their rural counterparts throughout the primary school years, as confirmed by a comprehensive analysis of variance (Table 6.5).

The finding of environmental differences is further confirmed by a comparison of urban and rural subgroups by reading achievement level (see Figure 6.6). Although the largest differences appear in year 1, as expected, the gap remains well into year 5. One interesting aspect of this figure is that the percentage of low (or poor) readers in each region is

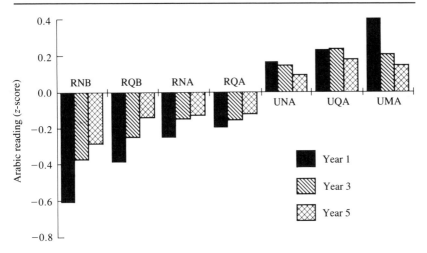

Figure 6.5. Arabic reading achievement scores for seven subgroups of Cohort 1 over years 1, 3, and 5.

roughly the same; such a finding is consistent with cross-national studies and seems to indicate that a combination of psychophysical limitations and common environmental features leads to a substantial number of poor readers in almost every country in the world. One result is the relatively high rate of functional illiteracy in the developing world, even among individuals who have attended primary school.

Of course, low reading achievement in the early years, even in grade 1, has consequences for subsequent reading attainment and for staying in school – as reading in Arabic is the primary measured skill that school authorities use in the selection of students who advance and those who are held back or drop out. Such consequences may be seen in Figure 6.7; first-year Arabic reading scores are quite good predictors of reading level in year 3 and on into year 5, with relatively small numbers of students changing their general level of achievement. Similarly, grade promotion (staying in-grade versus falling behind or dropping out) is directly related to reading achievement in the early grades (see Figure 6.8). In Figure 6.8c, it is clear that children who were high achievers in year 1 are four times more likely to stay in-grade (i.e., fifth grade) by year 5 of the study. Even so, as pointed out in chapter 3, many children – the majority – in our sample fall behind grade level or drop out, as shown on a larger scale in Moroccan national educational statistics.

Table 6.5. Comparisons of reading test scores by sex, region, and preschooling

Test	Sex F	Region F		Preschool (Q vs. NQ) F
Year 1				
LK/1	0.16	20.13[a]	U>R	2.06
WPM/1	0.70	15.94[a]	U>R	0.29
WD/1	0.00	33.49[a]	U>R	0.21
AR/1	0.07	29.83[a]	U>R	0.90
Year 3				
WPM/3	1.23	11.72[a]	U>R	2.99[d]
WD/3	2.46	0.00		1.13
SM/3	0.83	3.70[c]	U>R	0.13
PC/3	0.26	4.36[c]	U>R	0.05
AR/3	1.58	4.85[c]	U>R	1.09
Year 5				
WPM/5	0.44	0.54		0.63
SM/5	0.74	3.91[c]	U>R	0.02
PC/5	2.25	6.26[b]	U>R	0.32
AR/5	1.22	3.63[d]	U>R	0.00

[a]$p < .001.$
[b]$p < .01.$
[c]$p < .05.$
[d]$p < .10.$

Although we undertook complex statistical analyses to compare contrasting groups, it was useful again to compare children categorized into the three categories of reading achievement.[6] As shown in Figure 6.9, both the numbers of children and the shape of the distribution confirm that there were no gender differences over the 5 years of the study in terms of reading achievement. However, there was a modest trend for high-achieving girls to be overrepresented in this group in year 3, but substantially less than boys in year 5. Even though this latter difference was not statistically significant, the general contention that gender discrimination in Morocco increases over the primary school years is supported. Because girls are less likely than boys to go on to secondary school, we have some evidence from these results that substantiate claims that bias toward lower female achievement may begin in the latter part of primary school.

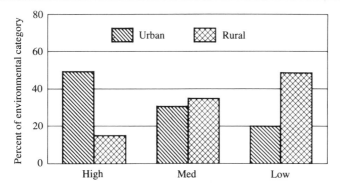

Figure 6.6a. Arabic reading achievement levels in year 1 by environment.

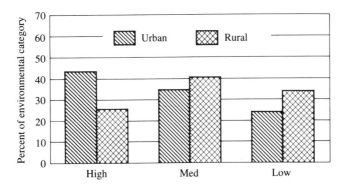

Figure 6.6b. Arabic reading achievement levels in year 3 by environment.

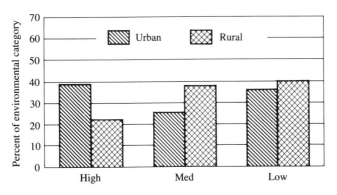

Figure 6.6c. Arabic reading achievement levels in year 5 by environment.

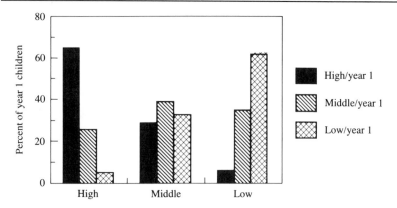

Figure 6.7a. Arabic reading achievement levels in year 3 by year 1 reading level.

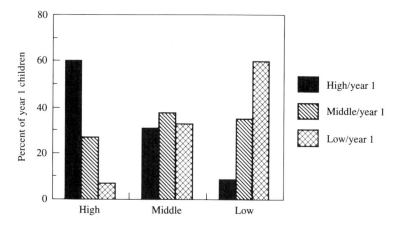

Figure 6.7b. Arabic reading achievement levels in year 5 by year 1 reading level.

Based on the earlier discussion, we might also expect effects of family's socioeconomic background mixed with the three main contrasts of this chapter. In such an analytic context, multiple regression techniques are particularly helpful. However, as with other studies in complex and difficult-to-measure societies (which is most of the world), the actual level of variance predicted in the dependent variables may be quite modest. In this case, gender, region, language, and preschooling predicted (using the measure of R^2) about 16% of Arabic reading achievement in year 1, but this decreased to less than 2% in year 5, with only environment as a significant predictor across all years (see Table 6.6a).[7]

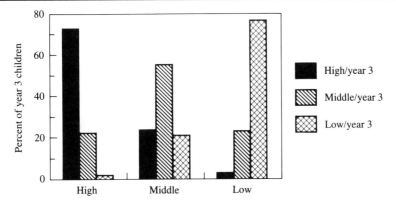

Figure 6.7c. Arabic reading achievement levels in year 5 by year 3 reading level.

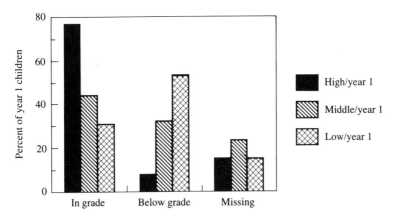

Figure 6.8a. Grade promotion into grade 2 as a function of reading level in year 1. (Note: Missing data represent both school dropouts and children who moved away.)

In a separate regression analysis individual background variables, such as parental education, SES, and literacy materials in the home were used instead of the main categorical variables (Table 6.6b). The results indicate that individual home variables, though they only explain about 7% of the variance after 5 years, have more staying power in predicting future achievement than such usually important factors as gender and environment. Parental education was most important in year 1, while the

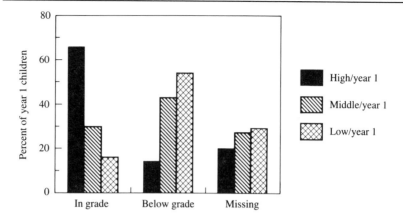

Figure 6.8b. Grade promotion into grade 3 as a function of reading level in year 1. (Note: Missing data represent both school dropouts and children who moved away.)

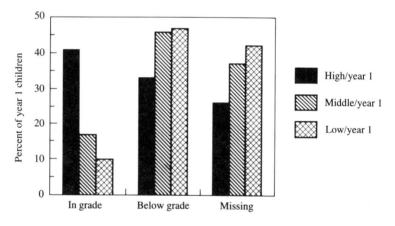

Figure 6.8c. Grade promotion into grade 5 as a function of reading level in year 1. (Note: Missing data represent both school dropouts and children who moved away.)

composite variable for measuring literacy materials in the home (highly correlated with environment and SES factors) tended to predominate in year 5. Finally, when we put both categorical and individual variables into the equation, we found that environment and literacy materials together account for most of the significant statistical effects (Table 6.6c).

As noted in chapter 1, one of our early interests was to investigate the consequences of Quranic preschooling on Moroccan children. The evi-

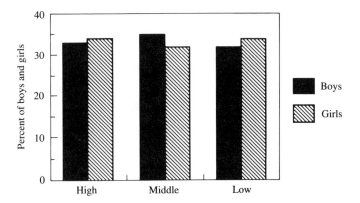

Figure 6.9a. Arabic reading achievement levels in year 1 by gender.

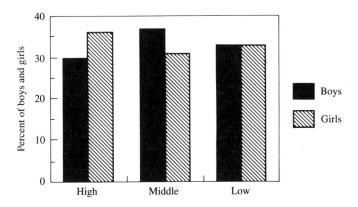

Figure 6.9b. Arabic reading achievement levels in year 3 by gender.

dence from the tests of academic skills showed that, other factors held constant, differences in reading achievement between no preschooling and Quranic and modern preschooling are relatively small, with statistical differences found only among the urban contrasting subsamples (UQA vs. UMA) in year 1.[8] As is discussed in chapter 8, Quranic preschooling is an important mediating factor in bilingual contexts for literacy acquisition.

In addition to academic achievement, the project sought to discover whether there were cognitive consequences to learning in Quranic

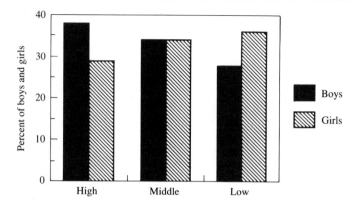

Figure 6.9c. Arabic reading achievement levels in year 5 by gender.

Table 6.6. Regression models predicting reading in Years 1, 3, and 5

(a) Predicting Arabic reading achievement by categorical variables (gender, environment, language, preschooling)

Arabic (AR)	1st year	3rd year	5th year
Predictor			
Constant	0.175	0.125	0.438
Gender	0.013	0.070	−0.119
Environment	−0.499[a]	−0.357[b]	−0.275[c]
Language	0.241[c]	0.137	0.064
Preschool	0.150	0.072	0.058
	Adj. R^2: .158	Adj. R^2: .057	Adj. R^2: .017
	$F(4,345) = 17.37$	$F(4,257) = 4.978$	$F(4,223) = 1.974$

[a] $p < .001$.
[b] $p < .01$.
[c] $p < .05$.

schools, as Scribner and Cole (1981) had found in Liberia. Thus, as part of the general investigation into the effects of preschooling, we developed a subproject on this topic. The results confirmed certain specific effects of Quranic school experience, namely in the area of memory skills; detailed summary of our findings in this area is presented in appendix 1.

Table 6.6. *(cont.)*

(b) Predicting Arabic reading achievement by individual background variables (parental education, SES, literacy materials in the home)

Arabic (AR)	1st year	3rd year	5th year
Predictor			
Constant	−0.429[a]	−0.435	−0.173
Literacy materials	——	——	0.269[a]
Parental education	0.200[b]	0.092	0.052
SES	0.183[b]	0.214[b]	0.061
	Adj. R^2: .070	Adj. R^2: .037	Adj. R^2: .071
	$F(3,290) = 14.24$	$F(3,244) = 9.709$	$F(3,212) = 6.508$

Note: Literary materials in the home is a variable that was assessed only late in year 3, and therefore is regressed on Arabic reading achievement only in year 5.
[a]$p < .001$.
[b]$p < .01$.

(c) Predicting Arabic reading by using both categorical and individual variables

Arabic (AR)	1st year	3rd year	5th year
Predictor			
Constant	−0.043	−0.202	0.217
Gender	−0.017	0.057	−0.112
Environment	−0.480[a]	−0.324[b]	−0.181
Language	0.246[c]	0.150	0.034
Preschool	0.036	0.131	0.008
Literacy materials	——	——	0.249[a]
Parental education	0.086	0.073	0.022
SES	0.168[c]	0.084	0.069
	Adj. R^2: .187	Adj. R^2: .075	Adj. R^2: .067
	$F(6,287) = 13.86$	$F(6,241) = 6.405$	$F(7,208) = 3.651$

[a]$p < .001$.
[b]$p < .01$.
[c]$p < .05$.

Table 6.7. Math performance by rural and urban field sites

Year of Testing	Average Math Score		
	Rural	Urban	Range
Year 1			
Total	7.7	6.7	(0–10)
Year 2			
Total	5.6	5.2	(0–12)
Year 3			
Oral	2.9	2.6	(0–6)
Written	3.8	4.2	(0–12)
Year 5			
Written	6.3	7.2	(0–12)

Note: Urban *N* over years 1, 2, 3, 5 is 171, 143, 130, 115, respectively; rural *N* over years 1, 2, 3, 5 is 162, 142, 130, 128, respectively.

Math achievement

Based on the analysis of reading achievement, one might be tempted to hypothesize that urban teachers, urban schools, and the urban children themselves are somehow superior to their rural counterparts. However, this contention is contradicted by a pattern of results that favored rural children's early performance in mathematics achievement.[9] In math skills, rural groups outperformed the urban groups (see Table 6.7) in the first 2 years of the study, with urban children catching up in year 3 and surpassing only in year 5. A potential explanation for the early rural advantage comes from studies that have found that nonschooled children may be quite skilled in arithmetic as a function of practice in the market and elsewhere (Ginsburg, Posner, & Russell, 1981; Saxe, 1985). In Morocco, it is possible that rural children, especially before schooled math instruction begins in earnest (up to age 8), are given more financial responsibility than urban children, and might go more often to the market for household purchases. It has been reported by Stevenson, Lee, and Stigler (1986) that young Japanese children outperform same-age American children in early math skills, with the favored explanation drawing on parental motivation and school factors (e.g., time on task). In Morocco, this explanation does not seem to apply during the early school years, as reading and math scores are affected in an opposite manner by environment: urban children have high reading and low math, whereas rural children have low reading and high math.

Context and literacy acquisition

What may be concluded from our conjectures about literacy acquisition in countries like Morocco? First, urban environment, independent of SES, had a significant and long-term effect on Moroccan children's learning in school; other factors, such as gender, parental education, and language, tended to dissipate over the years of primary schooling. Second, the positive (though modest) effects of preschooling were roughly equivalent for those for children who had attended modern or traditional Quranic preschools for the same time period. This similarity of effects was likely due to the partial overlap in the nature of curriculum and instruction between these two types of preschooling (as described in chapter 3). Third, we found evidence that individual differences, such as literacy materials in the home, could have important and longlasting effects on reading achievement in school children.

Also impressive were the effects of early reading in primary school on subsequent reading achievement and on staying in school. The data indicate that children who succeeded early in first grade had the best chance of becoming good readers and remaining in-grade. Furthermore, children who are seen as poor readers in the early years seem to become stuck in that category, whether they are from urban or rural environments. This category of low-level readers may have numerous origins, including learning disabilities and the like. In a country like Morocco, where few specialists are available to public school children, the risk of reading and school failure is particularly high.

Nonetheless, as shown in the regression analyses, there is much that we were not able to account for in children's learning of literacy, even though early literacy skills were highly predictive of later literacy skills and of grade promotion. It appears that literacy begets more literacy, but literacy is not simply a matter of the kinds or categories of social and economic background factors so easily invoked in the United States or Europe. What seems more important in the development of literacy is its actual use by children.

But what influences the child's use of literacy? Western research over the last decade indicates that there are important differences in use that stem from beliefs and attitudes about reading and writing. We attempt to explore similar terrain in chapter 7.

Notes

1 The scores utilized for Arabic reading (AR) achievement were described in chapter 5. These groups were created by dividing Cohort 1 into three roughly equal subgroups according to AR performance, as follows: high (N = 117, 87, 77), medium (N = 117, 88, 77), and low (N = 116, 87, 74) for years 1, 3, and 5, respectively. Thus, total sample sizes were 350, 262, and 228 across years, respectively. Thus, in Figure 6.6a, for example, the data indicate that roughly 33% of the total sample of girls was in each of the three subgroups; in Figure 6.9c, by contrast, about 28% of girls were in the high subgroup.

2 Self-assessment refers to the subjective answer given by the respondent in the home (usually the mother) as to the literacy skills of herself and other family members. This measure is clearly less reliable than direct measurement, but testing in the home would have created social dynamics that might have jeopardized other parts of our research, as well as taken too much time away from other issues. It can be noted, however, that the correlation between our self-assessed measures of literacy and years of schooling for family members was uniformly high and statistically significant. In addition, the interviewers on the project staff spent considerable time explaining the need for the respondent to think substantively before attempting an answer. For a further discussion of the pros and cons of literacy self-assessment, see Wagner (1990).

3 Differences across years 1, 3, and 5 were all significant ($\chi^2 \geq 10.19$, $p \leq .05$), with the year 1 effect the strongest ($\chi^2 = 27.62$, $p < .01$).

4 However, see the work of Heath (1983) on literacy use in rural South Carolina. Also, in cross-cultural psychology, there is a research tradition in visual perception that compares individuals' skills who live in so-called "carpentered" (i.e., urban) environments with those who do not. Increased susceptibility to visual illusions has often been found as one consequence of residence in such urban contexts; see Wagner (1982a) for research on environment and perception conducted in Morocco. In the international development literature, one of the major claims in support of primary schooling in developing countries is that rural farmers with even a few years of schooling tend to be more efficient (Jamison & Lau, 1982). This work and other studies supported by the World Bank have had a major impact on national and international policymakers (World Bank, 1988; Berstecher, 1985).

5 This latter comparison could only be made in urban Marrakech (where numerous modern preschools exist among the *classes populaires*).

6 The high-, middle-, and low-achieving groups are described in note 1.

7 The negative value associated with environment simply indicates that urban environment is the direction of the effect.

8 The statistics favoring modern preschooling were significant $p < .05$ only in year 1, for reading achievement AR/1 ($t = 1.32$), as well as for two reading subtests, LK/1 ($t = 2.07$) and WD/1 ($t = 1.67$).

9 In the case of math, the tests over the years of the study typically consisted of two types: notational questions, such as $2 + 3 = ?$, where the child had to supply the correct answer, and story problems, which were read to the child, such as "Jamil had three eggs and gave one to his grandmother. How many eggs did he have left?" These problems varied in difficulty over the years of the study. In the first year, children were also asked two counting problems, in which they had to count outloud the number of stars printed on a page, designed to put children at ease. Mental calculation skill (oral math) was analyzed separately in year 3, but the small number of task items limited useful statistical analyses.

7. Beliefs and literacy

Writing for the record

Nestled in a side street in a certain section of the *medina* in old Marrakech is the *hanout* (small storefront) of an *adl* (public scribe), *Si Abdullah,* who is well known for his skill in handling the "problems of writing" for a wide range of low-literate clientele. A renter asks Si Abdullah for an "official" letter to his landlord, having failed to persuade the landlord to let him stay in his lodging at the usual monthly rate (which has not, thanks to Allah, changed for 15 years). A mother seeks his help to produce a letter assuring a certain school administrator that her son is temporarily out of school "for a good reason."

In each case traditional methods of oral social interaction and persuasion are no longer sufficient to carry the day, or to establish a written record, increasingly important for later follow-up if required. Although both the renter and the mother had attended primary school, they know the importance and power of carefully crafted written documents – the difference between a document prepared by a specialist and one prepared by literacy novices like themselves.

Up to this point we have considered the nature of Arabic literacy in Morocco and the cognitive and social factors that influence its acquisition. Our focus on cognitive skills and social factors is crucial because it provides a way to conceptualize a direct intervention in improving children's learning of literacy skills. Yet it is also becoming increasingly apparent that learning in and out of school is greatly influenced by the beliefs, attitudes, and values that individuals possess. During the last decade or so, primarily in a field called social cognition (Flavell & Ross, 1981), research has shown that what children know and feel about their own abilities and skills may affect whether they succeed or fail in school (Sigel, McGillicuddy-DeLisi, & Goodnow, 1992). This chapter focuses on data we used to understand how the beliefs of Moroccan children and their parents can affect literacy development. To start, we present findings on children's beliefs about literacy and their own cognitive abilities and consequences for school achievement. Then we turn to a study of parental beliefs about literacy and subsequent impact on children's literacy.

Children's metacognitive beliefs and attributions

Around the world, children are exposed to a rich variety of symbols, texts, and instructional procedures, both formally and informally learned. Many children in different cultures, even before schooling, can read and write their own names, identify familiar words, and read connected sentences. Some children may receive a great deal of assistance from parents, whereas others are taught to read by preschool teachers or siblings or friends. Children may also develop notions and expectations about the components of good reading, through exposure to cultural norms and models in the process of socialization. With the exception of the few remaining preliterate societies, and despite the diversity in languages and orthographies, literacy experiences, instructional opportunities, and the age at which skilled literacy is acquired, virtually all children (as well as adults) develop concepts and beliefs about reading and about themselves as "good" or "poor" learners in school. We have noted and described some broad cultural beliefs concerning literacy in different societies (chapters 2 and 3), but empirical links between beliefs and actual learning have rarely been explored in a developing country.

The development of metacognitive beliefs about reading and reading strategies is an important area of research in the West (cf. Baker & Brown, 1984; Jacobs & Paris, 1987). From the research to date, we now know some ways to categorize children's beliefs about literacy: Children learn concepts about print (Clay, 1979; Johns, 1980), structural features of text (Stein & Glenn, 1979), and metacognitive aspects of text-processing strategies (Brown, Armbruster, & Baker, 1984; Paris & Lindauer, 1982). As children learn to read, they notice that some children learn more quickly than others and that reading tasks can be easy or difficult. They begin to acquire concepts about print and the regularity of grapheme-phoneme correspondence. Understanding the parameters and complexity of reading appears to develop at the same time that children receive instruction in reading. Thus, metacognition and reading performance are often correlated (Baker & Brown, 1984).

Still, relatively few studies have been concerned with the young child's emerging beliefs about literacy. We know, for example, that young children often do not understand simple rules for decoding text, such as the directionality of print and the role of punctuation (Clay, 1979). Even 8 year olds may not understand that creating meaning from written symbols is the central purpose of reading and that certain strategies facilitate comprehension (Myers & Paris, 1978). In a review of research on metacognition and reading, Garner (1987) concluded that beginning readers and less competent older readers misconstrue many concepts about print and strategies for constructing meaning. In addition, children's beliefs about reading evolve slowly from their interaction with text and develop considerably between the ages of 6 and 12 years. Furthermore, skilled readers have more accurate concepts and more positive orientations about reading than less skilled readers do (Paris, Lipson, & Wixson, 1983).

Questionnaires have been designed to assess children's metacognitive beliefs and knowledge about reading. For example, Paris and Jacobs (1984) used a structured interview to measure third and fifth graders' understanding about strategies for evaluating, planning, and regulating their own reading. Eight year olds knew significantly less about such reading strategies than 10 year olds did. Furthermore, metacognition was correlated with reading skill; poor readers in each grade had less understanding about the strategies that facilitate comprehension than good readers did. Our work provides parallel findings on the relationship between metacognitive beliefs and knowledge and subsequent reading achievement in Morocco.

Along with metacognitive beliefs, the child's sense of self-competence has been found to develop during the primary school years and, in turn, to influence academic achievement (Harter, 1982). American research has shown that primary school children develop concepts of intelligence as a fixed ability or trait and concepts of themselves as being more or less intelligent than their peers (Dweck & Bempechat, 1983; Nicholls, 1983). Dweck and Bempechat characterized such differences in terms of children who become "mastery oriented" versus "helpless" in academic situations. These concepts about intelligence and self-competence are also related to children's "causal attributions" (i.e., to what they attribute the reasons) for success and failure (Weiner, 1983). During the elementary school years, most Euro-American children appear to shift their causal attributions for school success on tasks like reading from simply "trying hard," or effort, to attributions based on native ability, intelligence, and experience. Thus, an optimistic, effortful 8 year old learning to read may differ in critical ways from a 12 year old who assumes that he or she cannot do math. In this chapter we also examine the relationship between causal attributions and reading achievement among Moroccan children.

Children also develop attitudes about others as learners. Children's socially constructed beliefs or conceptions of a "good" reader may influence beliefs about their own competencies and expectations, because their own performance (and subsequent self-concept) is seen in relation to others' achievements. According to social learning theory, children attend to real and ideal models of behavior in their environment and shape their own behavior in accordance with such models (Bandura, 1977). Thus, a determination of children's perceptions of the characteristics that make up a "good" reader would seem to be an important component of children's beliefs about literacy. In low-literate societies, moreover, where literate adults may be few in the child's immediate environment, a clear sense of such "good-reader" models may be especially important to children's literacy development. Little research links this aspect of social cognition to the domain of reading. Our work is a step in this direction.

In sum, this chapter comprises three interrelated studies of belief systems in children that we thought might influence subsequent reading achievement: metacognitive beliefs, causal attributions, and conceptions of good readers.

Research design

Data from Cohorts 1 and 2 were used in these analyses with the samples shown in Tables 4.2 and 4.3. Sample children responded to measures of metacognitive beliefs about reading, causal attributions, and conceptions of good readers that were developed specifically for the project. Assessments of the cohorts took place near the end of various school years: for Cohort 1 in years 1 and 5; for Cohort 2, in years 5, 6, and 7.[1]

Metacognitive beliefs. Separate age-related measures were developed to assess the metacognitive beliefs of children in first grade (Cohort 1) and in later school years (Cohort 1, year 5; Cohort 2, year 6). The examination of first graders' metacognitive beliefs about reading skills required the development of a simple, easily understood and reliable measure. Three short stories about the "habits of a good reader" were constructed, each of which described pairs of children with contrasting reading habits. The presentation of each story was accompanied by a drawing of the child in the story. Stories were read outloud to the child, who was then required to choose which of the two children in the story would "learn to read better." Children were tested individually; they indicated their responses simply by pointing to the picture of the "better" reader in each story.

In creating the stories, we attempted to contrast features of traditional (Islamic/Moroccan) versus modern (Western or French) perspectives on learning and literacy in the Moroccan school setting. These stories, which formed the Habits of a Good Reader (HGR) scale, contrasted the following types of practices:

> *Individual versus group study.* The collective spirit of traditional Morocco and Islamic education may be said to contrast with the increasing emphasis in modern public schools on competitive individual examinations.

> *Silent versus oral reading.* Traditional Moroccan/Islamic pedagogy has emphasized oral reading practice and recitation skills, whereas modern pedagogy typically supports silent reading practices.

> *Comprehension versus memorization.* Traditional pedagogy has treated text memorization as a goal in itself, whereas modern pedagogy generally stresses comprehension as a more important goal of reading and learning.

The caption for Figure 7.1 illustrates the procedure; a complete listing of questions is provided in Table 7.1 (p. 148), and the results in Figure 7.2. Overall, the HGR assessment was intended to yield a measure of beliefs about modern as contrasted with traditional learning styles.

In order to examine the impact of role models on beginning readers, a measure was developed to assess first graders' conceptions of the typical good reader in Morocco. In contrast to the metacognitive measures of beliefs about hypothetical situations, this scale was designed to investigate stereotypes about learners themselves. Using the same format as the HGR scale, we constructed three stories that formed the Characteristics of a Good Reader (CGR) scale. This scale included the following contrasts,

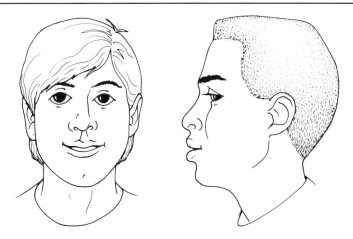

Figure 7.1. Instructions orally given to each child were as follows: "These two boys are both learning to read. This boy [indicate picture of boy at left of card] studies by memorizing his lesson without understanding the words. This other boy [indicate picture of a second boy on the right] tries to understand the meaning of the words but doesn't memorize everything. Which of these boys will learn to read best? Point to his picture." See results in Figure 7.2c.

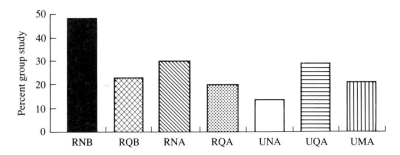

Figure 7.2a. Metacognitive belief questions by subgroup (Cohort 1). Study alone vs. group study

representing well-known emic categories of individuals in Moroccan society:

Arabic speaker versus Berber speaker. Some Moroccan pedagogues claim that native speakers of Berber tend to excel in school due to cultural strengths; others, however, argue that learning in a second language is more difficult.

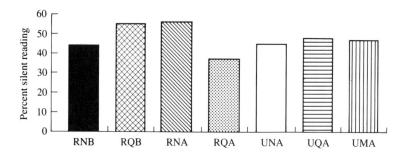

Figure 7.2b. Metacognitive belief questions by subgroup (Cohort 1). Oral vs. silent reading

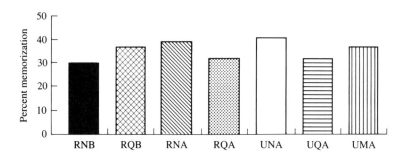

Figure 7.2c. Metacognitive belief questions by subgroup (Cohort 1). Comprehension vs. memorization

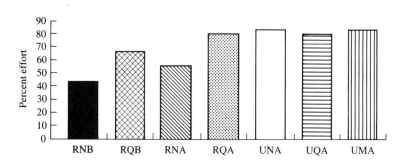

Figure 7.2d. Metacognitive belief questions by subgroup (Cohort 1). Ability vs. effort

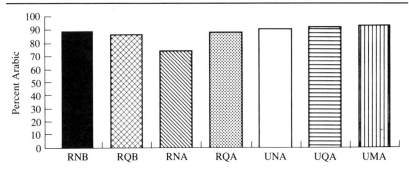

Figure 7.2e. Metacognitive belief questions by subgroup (Cohort 1). Berber vs. Arabic

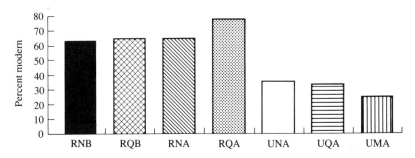

Figure 7.2f. Metacognitive belief questions by subgroup (Cohort 1). Traditional vs. modern

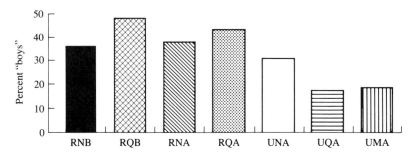

Figure 7.2g. Metacognitive belief questions by subgroup (Cohort 1). Girls vs. boys

Table 7.1. *Metacognitive belief questions for beginning readers*

Habits of a Good Reader (HGR) scale

1. Study alone★ vs. group study:
These boys are classmates. This one always studies by himself at home after school. The other always studies with his friends at home. Which boy will learn to read best?

2. Silent★ vs. oral reading:
These two girls are in the same class. This girl reads silently and tries to understand the meaning of every word. This other girl reads aloud and tries to pronounce each word just like her teacher does. Whose way of reading is best?

3. Memorization vs. Comprehension★:
These two boys are both learning to read. This one studies by memorizing his lesson without understanding the words. The other one tries to understand the meaning of the words but doesn't memorize everything. Who will learn to read best?

Causal Attributions

1. Ability vs. effort★:
These two girls are in the same class. This one is very intelligent. After school she always plays. The other one isn't very intelligent. She works hard at school and studies every evening. Which girl will learn to read best?

Characteristics of a Good Reader (CGR) scale

1. Berber vs. Arabic★:
These other two girls are in the same class. This one always speaks Berber at home. The other one always speaks Moroccan Arabic at home. Both girls work hard in class. Which one will learn to read best?

2. Traditional vs. modern★:
These two boys are both learning to read. One boy goes to the Quranic school. The other boy goes to the modern preschool. Both children work hard in class. Which one will learn to read best?

3. Girls vs. boys★:
These two children are both learning to read. After school the girl helps her mother at home, and the boy helps his uncle in his shop. Which child will learn to read best?

Note: Instructions to the child: "I'm going to show you some pictures of children and tell you something about them. Listen carefully to what each child does, and then tell me which one you think will read best." This scale was utilized only with Cohort 1. Responses with an asterisk★ were assigned a point; see text for further details.

Quranic preschooled versus modern preschooled. Some specialists suggest that the strict pedagogy and discipline of Quranic schooling prepares the child well for primary school learning; others claim that the modern preschool's greater variety of activities enhances the child's general development.

Boys versus girls. Although education in Morocco has been maledominated, girls' participation in schooling has grown rapidly in recent years, as has the perception of improved female performance in school.

Naturally, the intellectual access of first graders to formal debates on these dichotomies is limited; nonetheless, our observations (and subsequent data) indicate that even young children tend to have beliefs on these issues. Preliminary interviews utilizing the CGR scale produced such diverse responses that no predetermined scoring system was developed; rather, an aggregation of items was made during post hoc analyses.

A third measure for the assessment of metacognitive beliefs, adapted to older children, was administered to Cohort 1 in year 5 and to Cohort 2 in year 6. The questions for this measure were derived from the work of Scott Paris and his colleagues (Jacobs & Paris, 1987; Paris & Oka, 1986) and modified for the Moroccan context. A child's score on the 10-item Reading Awareness Index (RAI) indicated the number of times the child chose a response that was expected, based on prior research, to be linked with better reading performance (see Table 7.2, p. 150).

Causal attributions. Children's causal attributions for hypothetical life events were examined along two dimensions: effort versus ability and internal versus external. First graders (Cohort 1) received a single story, in HGR format, which presented a contrast between an intelligent reader who did not study (ability) and a hardworking but less intelligent reader (effort). For this age group, no internal/external attributional assessment was made. The original scale (Harter 1982) was designed to examine the individual's tendency to provide internal versus external rationales for various hypothetical positive and negative life experiences; this scale was modified for our work to incorporate situations pertinent to the Moroccan experience and to include items that contrasted ability and effort attributions within the internal dimension. The 24-item scale, presented orally, was analyzed for two independent scores: Internal/External (IE; 17

Table 7.2. Reading Awareness Index (RAI)

1. Which is harder about reading for you:
   a. sounding out words you haven't seen before, or
   ★b. understanding the grammar of long sentences?

2. If you wanted to improve your reading, would you:
   a. practice reading one book until you memorized it, or
   ★b. read a lot of different books once?

3. What is the best way to read:
   a. skip the parts you don't understand, or
   ★b. never skip anything?

4. What is the best way to remember a long story:
   a. memorize the story word for word, or
   ★b. think about the main things that happened?

5. Which of these is more difficult to understand:
   ★a. the Quran, or
   b. Arabic subject schoolbooks?

6. What do you do first when you come to a word you don't know while reading:
   a. pronounce it aloud and go on to the next word, or
   ★b. go back and reread the same sentence?

7. If you were preparing for a geography test, would you:
   a. memorize the lesson word for word, or
   ★b. try to summarize the lesson in your own words?

8. When you are reading and don't understand a whole sentence, do you:
   ★a. think about what the other sentences in the story are saying, or
   b. ask someone else what it means immediately?

9. If you have to buy a lot of things at the market, is it better to:
   a. repeat the list over and over until you have memorized it, or
   ★b. write it down and take the paper with you to the market?

10. If you are reading a story for homework, do you:
    ★a. read it slowly and try to enjoy it, or
    b. read it as fast as possible and go on to other homework?

Note: Responses with an asterisk were assigned a point. Answering all questions with the asterisked response would give a total score of 10 points; choosing none of them would give a score of zero. The RAI was utilized with both Cohorts 1 and 2.

items) and Effort/Ability (EA; 7 items). For older children (Cohort 1, year 5; Cohort 2, year 6), the Causal Attribution scales (shown in Table 7.3) were adapted from Crandall, Katkovsky, and Crandall's (1965) Intellectual Achievement Responsibility scale.[2]

Table 7.3. Causal Attribution scales

Practice example 1: When a child arrives late at school, is this most often because:
1) s/he doesn't care about arriving on time
2) s/he lives very far away

Practice example 2: If you were playing football, and you fell and cut yourself, would this happen because:
1) you didn't pay attention
2) someone pushed or hit you

A. Internal/External (IE) Scale Questions

(+) 1. If you passed to the next grade, would that be because:
1) you are naturally smart (INT)
2) the teacher liked you (EXT)

(–) 2. When you read a story and forget parts of it, is it usually because:
1) you weren't interested in the story (INT)
2) the story wasn't well-written (EXT)

(+) 3. When you win at a game, does it happen because:
1) you're good at this game (INT)
2) the other player isn't good at the game (EXT)

(+) 4. When you learn something quickly in school it is usually because:
1) the teacher explained it well (EXT)
2) you were paying attention (INT)

(+) 5. If someone tells you that you're bright, is it because:
1) that person likes you (EXT)
2) you can do things well without even trying (INT)

(–) 6. When you cannot work out a math problem, is that because:
1) you were thinking about something else (INT)
2) the problem was especially hard (EXT)

(+) 7. If the teacher tells you your work is fine, is it because:
1) teachers always say such things to encourage students (EXT)
2) you are smart (INT)

(–) 8. When your mother asks you to buy many things at the market, and you forget something, is it because:
1) your mother spoke too quickly (EXT)
2) you have a bad memory (INT)

(–) 9. When you don't do well on a test in school, is it because:
1) the test was especially hard (EXT)
2) you didn't work the day of the exam (INT)

Table 7.3. *(cont.)*

(−) 10. If you didn't pass to the next grade at the end of the school year, would it be because:
1) the teacher was against you (EXT)
2) you didn't try hard (INT)

(−) 11. If someone told you that you were dumb, would that be because:
1) he was quarreling with you (EXT)
2) you were careless and made a mistake (INT)

(+) 12. When someone tells you a joke, and you remember it well, is it usually because:
1) the other fellow knows how to tell jokes (EXT)
2) you tried hard to remember it (INT)

(−) 13. If the teacher told you that you had to try harder, would it be because:
1) the other students get better grades at school than you do (EXT)
2) you hadn't been working hard lately (INT)

(+) 14. If a teacher told you that your work was fine, would it be because:
1) you worked hard on it (INT)
2) teachers often say such things to encourage students (EXT)

(−) 15. When you read a story and don't remember much of it, is it usually because:
1) your memory isn't very strong and you forget easily (INT)
2) the story wasn't well-written (EXT)

(−) 16. When you cannot work out a math problem, is that because:
1) you're just not good at math (INT)
2) the problem was especially hard (EXT)

(+) 17. If you succeeded in life, God willing, would that happen because:
1) you worked very hard to succeed (INT)
2) other people helped you (EXT)

B. Effort/Ability (EA) Scale Questions

(−) 1. When you have trouble understanding something in school, is it usually because:
1) you didn't pay attention (EFF)
2) you are not strong in that subject (ABL)

(+) 2. When you do well on a test at school, which reason is most likely:
1) you always do well on exams (ABL)
2) you prepared well for the test that day (EFF)

(−) 3. If you had a goal to reach in life, but you didn't achieve it, would that be because:
1) you didn't work hard enough (EFF)
2) you weren't smart enough (ABL)

(+) 4. When you read a story and you don't forget it, is it because:
1) you have a good memory for stories (ABL)
2) you liked the story (EFF)

Table 7.3. *(cont.)*

(+) 5. If you had a goal in life and succeeded, would that happen because:
1) you worked very hard to succeed (EFF)
2) you were intelligent enough to succeed (ABL)

(+) 6. When you find the solution to a math problem, is that more likely because:
1) you studied hard before trying the problem (EFF)
2) you are very good at math (ABL)

(−) 7. When you lose a game, does it usually happen because:
1) you don't know how to play (ABL)
2) you didn't try very hard to win (EFF)

Note: Instructions to the child: "I'm going to describe to you some situations that can happen to children your age. I'll also give some possible reasons why each situation might happen, and I want you to tell me which of the reasons I give is MORE likely (or frequent) in your opinion." This scale was utilized with both Cohorts 1 and 2. The symbols (+) and (−) indicate success (+) and failure (−) situations. Abbreviations in the response choices indicate which responses are believed to show effort (EFF), ability (ABL), internal (INT), and external (EXT) attributions.

Results

The beliefs scales used in this study generally did not produce gender or regional differences, and therefore the subcategories of gender and region were collapsed into contrasts that were made by year in school.[3]

Beliefs and reading achievement. The relationship between first graders' beliefs about reading and their subsequent reading achievement (AR/5) was first examined through a series of chi-squares on individual item responses by reading level (representing the low, middle, and high thirds of the distribution of reading scores). By using Arabic reading achievement in years, we were able to get a sense of the long-term consequences of early differences in beliefs (see Table 7.4).

Overall, children in each level of reading performance held "traditional" beliefs on the HGR items, believing especially that competent readers tend to study with others and to memorize (rather than comprehend) text. However, at this age, neither individual nor combined HGR items showed a significant relationship to fifth-grade reading level. This finding is not surprising, as these first graders were, for the most part, very inexperienced readers with little home reading stimulation and few opportunities to learn much about specific reading habits.

Table 7.4. Metacognitive beliefs of first graders and Year 5 Arabic
reading achievement level

Year 5 Arabic reading achievement level[a] (N)[b]	Low (116)	Mid (117)	High (117)	χ^2
(a) Habits of a Good Reader (HGR) scale				
a. HGR1: Best to study alone +[c]	8[d]	9	6	
Best to study with others	25	25	27	1.93
b. HGR2: Best to comprehend +	12	11	11	
Best to memorize	21	22	22	0.28
c. HGR3: Best to read for pronunciation	18	14	15	
Best to read for meaning +	15	19	19	3.78
HGR Total score means (range 0–3)	1.07	1.13	1.10	
(b) Causal Attributions				
Ability	11	9	7	
Effort	22	24	27	5.12
(c) Characteristics of a Good Reader (CGR) scale				
a. CGR1: Arabic speaker +	28	29	32	
Berber speaker	5	4	2	6.27*
b. CGR2: Girl reads better	14	14	9	
Boy reads better +	8	12	17	
No difference	11	7	7	21.44***
c. CGR3: Modern preschooled better +	14	17	20	
Quranic preschooled better	20	17	12	10.66**
CGR Total score means (Range: 0–3):	1.48	1.70	2.07	

Note: *$p < .05$; **$p < .01$; ***$p < .001$
[a]Children's reading achievement scores in year 5 (AR/5) were categorized as low, mid, or high on the basis of their position in the distribution of all subjects' scores; see text.
[b]Due to missing data on specific items, N ranges between 342 and 350 in Cohort 1.
[c] The plus sign indicates which response for each story within the HGR and CGR groups contributed to a child's total HGR or CGR score. An HGR of 3 indicates a "modern" perspective; a CGR of 3 indicates the "ideal" stereotype of a good reader. See text.
[d]Numbers indicate the percent of respondents in each category for each question. The six cell values may not sum exactly to 100 percent due to rounding.

With regard to the single causal attributional story, it was found that most first graders chose effort over ability as more important for achievement (as found among American children of the same age; Dweck & Bempechat, 1983). High-achieving Moroccan children were considerably more likely than low achievers to believe that effort was more important than ability (see Table 7.4b) though this difference did not reach statistical significance.

On the CGR items, better readers were found to hold beliefs that a good reader was likely to be male, modern preschooled, and Arabic-speaking (see Table 7.4c); a composite score combining these responses was also related to first-grade reading level (F [2,347] = 19.40; $p < .01$). Given that children were responding to a set of just three questions, and were only 7 years old at the time of the CGR assessment, this finding is rather remarkable and indicates an emergent belief system as to what type of child is likely to succeed as a young adult in the Moroccan educational system.

As in earlier analyses, we related these outcomes with a variety of background and achievement variables (Table 7.5). In addition, a series of hierarchical regression models provided a more conservative assessment of the contribution of beliefs to reading achievement.[4] The first model, in Table 7.6, included background factors, the CGR scale, and cognitive measures in the prediction of first-grade reading ability for Cohort 1. CGR beliefs were found to predict reading performance, even when entered after parental education, SES, and CGRfit (a variable representing the extent to which the child possessed the actual attributes reflected in the stereotypical good reader). After the inclusion of background and belief variables, cognitive ability still contributed significant additional variance to first-grade reading achievement.[5]

Further analyses showed that metacognitive beliefs and causal attributions were more strongly related to reading achievement among older children than among younger children. The Reading Awareness Index (RAI) showed a substantial correlation with reading achievement for Cohort 2 in years 5 and 7 (Table 7.5). For Cohort 1 (year 5), results of hierarchical regression techniques indicated that the RAI scale played little role in explaining variance in Arabic reading after including background, cognitive, and other belief variables. In Cohort 2 for years 5 and 7, by contrast, RAI beliefs had greater impact (Table 7.7). Parental education and SES had relatively little effect on reading; RAI predicted a small but significant portion of the variance in year 5 and became a stronger predictor in year 7.[6]

Impact of beliefs on achievement: A summary

Our findings showed a significant pattern of relationships between beliefs and reading achievement among Moroccan schoolchildren. The beliefs of

Table 7.5. Correlation matrices of variables

(a) Cohort 1 ($N = 205$)

	1	2	3	4	5	6	7	8	9	10	11	12
1. HGR/1												
2. EA/1	−.22											
3. CGR/1	.03	.27										
4. RAI/5	−.09	−.00	−.07									
5. EA/5	−.02	.03	.05	.01								
6. IE/5	.03	−.01	.07	−.02	.01							
7. AR/1	.06	.09	.32	.02	.04	−.08						
8. AR/5	.11	.06	.16	.07	.07	−.17	.53					
9. Par Ed	.08	.09	.21	.09	−.10	−.02	.17	.14				
10. SES	.00	.12	.10	−.00	.01	−.08	.20	.11	.29			
11. CGRfit	−.08	.28	.26	−.15	−.03	.03	.27	.16	.21	.01		
12. Cog/1	.09	.03	.13	.05	.09	−.10	.28	.35	.08	.12	.06	
13. Cog/5	.10	.02	.16	.02	.08	−.13	.51	.67	.08	.08	.15	.44

(b) Cohort 2 ($N = 300$)

	1	2	3	4	5	6	7	8
1. RAI								
2. IE	.13							
3. EA	.09	.20						
4. AR/5	.15	.12	.14					
5. AR/7	.23	.07	.26	.59				
6. Par Ed	.00	−.02	−.02	.02	−.02			
7. SES	.05	.04	.03	.10	.11	.39		
8. Cog/5	.23	.08	.21	.41	.45	.06	.06	
9. Cog/7	.10	−.01	.06	.28	.23	.02	.04	.33

Note: $r > .19$ significant at $p < .05$; $r > .22$ significant at $p < .01$. For meaning of abbreviations, see text and appendix 2.

first graders about the characteristics of a good reader (the CGR stories) were clearly related to their current and subsequent (year 5) Arabic reading, whereas knowledge of particular reading skills (the HGR scale) was not. In other words, the young child's sense of relatively stable beliefs about the characteristics of successful readers was a more powerful predictor than specific beliefs about learning or reading behaviors. These results are among the handful of studies that link metacognitive beliefs and performance in young beginning readers, and the first we know of in a low-

Table 7.6. Hierarchical regression model to predict reading achievement in grade 1 from background variables and CGR scale

	Adj. R^2	R^2 chg.	F
Par Ed + SES	.07	.07	11.95[a]
Par Ed + SES + CGRfit	.13	.06	19.37[a]
Par Ed + SES + CGRfit + CGR	.17	.04	17.38[a]
Par Ed + SES + CGRfit + CGR + Cog/1	.22	.05	28.26[a]

Note: N = 294, Cohort 1.
[a]p < .001.

Table 7.7. Hierarchical regression models predicting Arabic reading in years 5 and 7

Dependent Variable: Arabic reading (AR/5)	Adj. R^2	R^2 chg.	F
Par Ed + SES	.00	.00	2.84
Par Ed + SES + RAI	.02	.02	6.67[a]
Par Ed + SES + IE	.01	.01	4.03[a]
Par Ed + SES + EA	.02	.02	5.29[a]
Par Ed + SES + RAI + IE + EA	.04	.04	13.04[b]
Par Ed + SES + RAI + IE + EA + Cog/5	.17	.13	63.98[b]
Dependent Variable: Arabic reading (AR/7)			
Par Ed + SES	.01	.01	4.57[a]
Par Ed + SES + RAI	.06	.05	15.76[b]
Par Ed + SES + IE	.01	.00	1.23
Par Ed + SES + EA	.07	.06	20.92[b]
Par Ed + SES + RAI + IE + EA	.11	.10	20.92[b]
Par Ed + SES + RAI + IE + EA + Cog/5	.24	.13	52.78[b]
Par Ed + SES + RAI + IE + EA + Cog/5 + AR/5	.42	.18	92.71[b]

Note: N = 300, Cohort 2.
[a]p < .05.
[b]p < .001

literate developing country. Although much individual variance in CGR beliefs remained unaccounted for, parents, siblings, and the larger society appear to help children learn about the typical characteristics of individuals likely to be literate in Moroccan society. Those who learn the cultural stereotype early on – even if they do not fit the stereotype themselves[7] –

tended to acquire reading more quickly. Here we have an example of what may be termed the socialization of beliefs for literacy in addition to cognitive skill acquisition.

Although knowledge about reading skills (HGR) was unrelated to reading performance in the younger children, metacognitive beliefs about reading skills (RAI) for older children (Cohort 2) was found to be significantly related to reading achievement. Moroccan children who were experienced and successful adolescent readers had acquired some of the same beliefs about the reading process as those found to be effective for successful reading in the United States. Indeed, the relationship between the Reading Awareness Index and reading achievement was stronger in Morocco than in many American studies (Forrest-Pressley & Waller, 1984).[8]

With respect to Moroccan schoolchildren's causal attributions, the data also indicated a pattern similar to that found in American studies. For Cohort 1, the most predictive attribution scale was the IE scale; children who most often chose internal explanations tended to be the more successful readers. In an Islamic country such as Morocco, where the ubiquitous expression *In sha'Allah* (If Allah wills it) has often been interpreted to reflect a fatalistic attitude, this finding takes on particular importance, for those who ascribed failure more often to external factors, beyond their own control, tended not to succeed in school. The EA scale was not as effective in differentiating good readers from poor readers, perhaps because of its restricted range (7 items on the EA versus 17 for the IE scale). Nonetheless, by year 7 (Cohort 2), a strong belief in effort as a reason for success or failure was found to be significantly related to Arabic reading achievement. Finally, unlike some American studies (e.g., Dweck & Bush, 1976), no gender differences were found in causal attributions, nor in the scale's ability to predict reading achievement.[9]

In sum, we can safely say that children's beliefs of various kinds appear to be significantly related to literacy acquisition. Yet we still have little in the way of evidence as to the origins of children's beliefs. We now turn to the most likely source of such beliefs, their parents.

Parents' and children's beliefs about literacy: Are they related?

Western research on parents' attitudes and beliefs about reading and schooling has demonstrated important consequences for children's learning, even if parents do not (or cannot) provide much direct skill instruction (e.g., Goodnow, 1984; Laosa & Sigel, 1982; Miller, 1986; Sigel, 1985). However, most of these studies consider cognitive skills and/or school achievement criteria as outcome variables, rather than literacy. Furthermore, relatively few studies have considered the influence of parental attitudes in cultural contexts outside of America (but see Stevenson & Stigler, 1992, on Japan and China).

During the parental interview, parents were asked 30 questions concerning their attitudes and beliefs about the development and education of their children. These questions were aimed at discovering how parents conceived of the complementary roles of parents, teachers, and schools in the instruction of children. The total set of parental attitudinal questions is listed in Table 7.8; as shown, certain questions were clustered into groups for use as aggregate predictors of children's performance. It should be noted that a subset of these questions paralleled six of the seven metacognitive belief questions asked of the parents' children (Table 7.8a).

Because of the parallel use of questions for 7-year-old children and their parents, the study also provided an opportunity to compare beliefs in both samples. Such a comparison makes particular sense if we assume that children obtain many attitudes and beliefs about learning from their parents. On the other hand, because most of the children in this study were engaged in an endeavor unfamiliar to their low-literate and little-educated parents, their attitudes might be expected to be especially susceptible to experiences encountered outside the family. Compared to American findings, then, one would expect only a modest correlation between Moroccan parents' and children's beliefs about literacy and learning.

Results showed that only one of these questions, involving the choice between the Quranic school and the Western-style preschool, showed a significant positive parent-child correspondence ($\chi^2 = 7.59$, $p < .01$). On this question both the children and their mothers preferred Quranic over modern preschooling. Inasmuch as the type of preschool to which a child was sent is a decision likely to be made, and defended, by the child's parents, this finding is not surprising. The fact that Quranic schooling was preferred overall by more mothers (63%) than first graders (somewhat under 50%) may also reflect a weakening of traditional religious values among the younger generation and a difference in the perceived positive features of the Quranic school for the two groups. The Quranic school's reputation as a place of strict discipline, for example, may well be viewed more favorably by mothers than by first graders.

In a more comprehensive investigation of parents' interview responses,

Table 7.8. Attitudinal questions asked of children's mothers

(a) Metacognitive beliefs about schooling and reading success

    1. Is school success due more to ability or effort?
    2. Who usually does better in school, boys or girls?
    3. What type of preschool do you prefer for your children, Quranic or modern?
    4. Is it better for a child to study alone or with others?
    5. Is it better to study by memorizing a text or by trying to understand it?
    6. Is it better for a child to practice reading aloud or silently?

(b) The importance of reading, schooling, and the role

    7. Why did you send your child to the modern school?
    8. Is it important to learn to read? Why?
    9. What academic level would you like your child to reach?
    10. What is the primary role of the Quranic school teacher?
    11. What is the primary role of the modern school teacher?

(c) Composite attitudinal clusters

A number of conceptually related questions were combined to form attitudinal clusters. Scales were created by adding points for responses that were judged to reflect a given attitudinal direction of each cluster.[a]

Cluster A: Parent vs. teacher involvement in child's education

    12. Is a child's school success due more to the teacher or to the parents?
    13. Is it the duty of the teacher or the parents to teach a child how to read?
    14. Is it the duty of the teacher or the parents to teach a child religion?
    15. Is it the duty of the teacher or the parents to teach a child morals?
    16. Is it the duty of the teacher or the parents to punish the child for wrongdoing?
    17. Is it the duty of the teacher or the parents to teach a child proper public behavior?

Cluster B: Reported involvement in the child's studies

    18. Did your child receive help in reading before s/he entered school?
    19. Do you follow your child's school progress?
    20. Do you do anything special when your child receives a good school report?
    21. Do you do anything special when your child receives a poor school report?
    22. Does anyone help your child with his/her homework?

Cluster C: Progressiveness of "ideal family" views

    23. What is the best age for a boy to marry?
    24. What is the best age for a girl to marry?
    25. What is the best number of children to have?
    26. Should women work inside or outside of the home?

Table 7.8. *(cont.)*

Cluster D: Religious observance in the family
27. Has a member of the family made the pilgrimage to Mecca?
28. How often does the head of the household go to the mosque?
29. How many people pray regularly in the household?
30. Is the Quran ever read in the home?

[a]Scales were derived from points distributed as follows: For questions 12–14, teachers = 0, both = 1, parents = 2; for questions 15–17, teachers = 0, both or parents = 1; for questions 18–22, each yes received 1 point; for questions 23–24, 1 point, respectively, for: age 21 or older, age 18 or older; question 25, 5 or more = 0, fewer than 5 = 1, fewer than 3 = 2; question 26, either = 1, outside = 2; question 27, yes = 1; question 28, sometimes = 1, everyday = 2; question 29, one person = 1, more than one person = 2; question 30, yes = 1.

19 of the questions were combined into 4 distinct conceptual clusters (see Table 7.8c). In a manner similar to the categorization of children's reading scores, a mother's score on each cluster was categorized according to its position in the low, middle, or high third of that score's distribution in the sample. Analyses showed that each of these cluster groups was significantly related to measures of children's Characteristics of a Good Reader beliefs.[10] Furthermore, positive attitudes about parental teaching (cluster A), reported involvement of parents (cluster B), and progressive views of the family (cluster C) were related to Arabic reading achievement in all years ($\chi^2 \geq 7.83$, $p \leq .10$), with especially strong relationships in year 1. Interestingly, the level of reported religious observance in the family (cluster D) showed a curvilinear relationship to children's reading level, with high and low levels of reported religious observance associated with children's reading achievement.[11] Although high religious observance showed the strongest association, suggesting that families with firm religious beliefs encouraged good reading skills, the curvilinear relationship may also reflect a tendency for secular families to have a higher socioeconomic status.[12]

Finally, hierarchical regression analyses were performed to evaluate the independent effects of parental attitudes (the cluster scores) and family background (region, home language, SES, parental education) on children's Arabic reading achievement (see correlation matrix, Table 7.9). When entered first, the attitudinal clusters explained about 10% of the variance in children's year 1 Arabic reading scores, with significant portions predicted by clusters A and C; background variables explained an

Table 7.9. Correlation matrix of background variables and parental attitudes

	1	2	3	4	5	6	7
1. Region/language							
2. Gender	.02						
3. SES	.11	.10					
4. Par Ed	.31	.03	.33				
5. Cluster A	.39	−.01	.19	.27			
6. Cluster B	.30	.03	.18	.19	.17		
7. Cluster C	.42	.08	.01	.16	.23	.26	
8. Cluster D	.00	.18	.13	.11	.09	.05	.02

Notes: $N = 289$, Cohort 1; $r > .19$ significant at $p < .05$; $r > .22$ significant at $p < .01$. Abbreviations: cluster A (parent vs. teacher involvement); cluster B (reported parental involvement in child's studies); cluster C (progressive views); cluster D (religious observance).

additional 9% of the variance. In year 3, about 12% of the variance was explained by the clusters, with each of the four clusters predicting significant portions; the addition of background variables increased the variance explained by only 1%. In year 5, 8% of the variance was explained by the clusters, with clusters B and C predicting significant portions; again, background variables explained virtually no additional variance. Overall, the regression analyses indicated that parental attitudes are useful in explaining part of children's reading achievement, especially for children in primary school.

In sum, though parental beliefs and attitudes about education were found to vary somewhat by educational background, their beliefs predicted not only their own children's metacognitive beliefs but also their children's reading achievement. In particular, it was found that parents with high-achieving children tended to stress parental (as contrasted with teacher's) responsibility in their children's education; hold progressive or modern views toward ideal family structure (such as women's employment, later marriage, and fewer children); report more involvement in their children's school progress; and believe in either traditional religious observance or little religious observance. Whereas the first three tendencies (representing clusters A, C, and B, respectively) may be said to represent aspects of a modernist tendency in Moroccan society and were statistically related to one another, each cluster also predicted independent portions of variance. The findings on cluster D (strength of religious observance) tended to lend support to growing evidence of a split developing in Moroccan society (as in other parts of the Islamic world), between those firmly rooted in Islamic theology and those with a modernist-secularist perspective. Although each of these ideological factions appears to exert a positive influence on the development of their children, those in the middle with regard to religious observance may be the least engaged in promoting their children's education. In other words, parents with strong religious and ethical beliefs clearly care about what their children think and believe, and this can be observed in their children's school performance.[13]

Beliefs and literacy: A reprise

In this chapter we have presented empirical evidence on children's meta-cognitive beliefs and awareness, causal self-attributions, and conceptions of "good" readers, as well as on their parents' beliefs and attitudes. What can we conclude from the examination of the linkages between such varied belief systems and literacy development? Data on the two cohorts, spanning 7 years, yielded a complex pattern of results with important implications. It was found that better readers learn quite early – by first grade – who a good reader is likely to be (male, Arabic-speaking, modern preschooled) in contemporary Moroccan society. At the same time, these children may not know what specific reading habits or behaviors are critical to good reading. However, the most skilled fifth graders were quite aware of what accomplished reading is about, and this knowledge apparently remains important for reading achievement into middle school. Furthermore, data on causal attributions for success and failure provided cross-cultural support for the hypothesis that a strong belief in personal effort can enhance school performance. Over the school years it appears that children's belief systems progress from general notions about who good readers are to encompass beliefs more specifically linked to particular types of skilled cognitive activity.

We also found evidence that parents' beliefs are related to their children's beliefs, but this relationship is not particularly robust. There are, as described in earlier chapters, major intergenerational changes taking place in Moroccan society, changes that create substantial differences in educational attainment and information access between the young and the old. In addition, parental beliefs were directly related to the literacy development of their children in school. For the most part, parents with more "modernist" beliefs seemed to foster more highly literate children. This finding parallels that of the modernization theory approach of Inkeles and Smith (1974), described earlier. Nonetheless, in our work there is a striking difference. Parents interviewed were generally non-literate and families were, for the most part, selected from the lower social stratum of Moroccan society. Relative to prior studies where SES factors clouded (or were confounded with) the research conclusions, it appears that differences in parental beliefs in Morocco cut across environments, and that they are significant determinants of school success even among the poor classes of society. One policy implication is that a change in the beliefs about learning and schooling in the "traditionally-minded" might be an important approach to improving the school learning of their children. We return to this issue in chapter 12.

As we have seen, many factors – cognitive, social, and attitudinal – statistically predict literacy acquisition. It is also clear from the results in this chapter that the typical pedagogical focus on literacy skills training needs to be complemented by attention to metacognitive beliefs and attitudes in children. As we shall see in chapter 8, beliefs are also implicated in the issue of multilingualism and literacy in Morocco.

Notes

1 As discussed in chapter 4, we have chosen to use "year" rather than "grade" as an indicator of the cohort samples over time. Because this chapter utilizes both cohorts, it may be helpful to reiterate, for example, that Cohort 1 in year 5 comprises several grade levels; Cohort 2 in year 7 comprises children mainly in grade 7 but also those who remained in grades 5 and 6 due to repetitions.

2 The individual Arabic reading subtests used in the metacognitive analyses included measures of Letter Knowledge (Cohort 1, year 1), Word Decoding (Cohort 1, year 1; Cohort 2, year 5), Word-Picture Matching (Cohort 1, years 1 and 5; Cohort 2, year 5), Sentence Maze (Cohort 1, year 5; Cohort 2, years 5 and 7), and Paragraph Comprehension (Cohort 1, year 5; Cohort 2, years 5 and 7). Cognitive tests included Concept Identification (Cohort 1, year 1; Cohort 2, year 5), Digit Span Memory (both cohorts, each year), General Information (Cohort 1, year 1; Cohort 2, year 5), Perception (Cohort 1, year 5; Cohort 2, years 5 and 7), and Logic (Cohort 1, year 5; Cohort 2, year 7). An overall cognitive (Cog) score was calculated for each year as the average of z-scores on the cognitive tasks administered in that year.

3 Because no prior assumptions could be made about the degree of consistency across contexts that could be expected in children's beliefs and causal attribu-

tions, the aggregation of specific items into scales was determined by the validity of the individual items. Examination of the percentage of items in each scale in which the "preferred" response (i.e., keyed in the direction of higher reading awareness or internal attribution) was chosen indicated the expected direction in 14 out of 17 IE items in both cohorts; 4 out of 7 (Cohort 1) and 5 out of 7 (Cohort 2) for the EA scale; and 7 out of 10 (Cohort 1) and 9 out of 10 (Cohort 2) in the RAI scale. Overall, children chose the preferred responses with rates of 62%, 57%, and 63% for the three respective scales in Cohort 1 and 62%, 65%, and 70% in Cohort 2. Moreover, the percentage increase across cohorts for the EA and RAI scales (57% to 65%, and 63% to 70%, respectively) indicated a developmental change in the expected direction.

With regard to criterion-related validity, children who selected responses in the keyed direction on an item almost always had a reading achievement score higher than those who selected the other option on the same item, although only a few of those differences were statistically significant. In one extreme example, the preferred reading awareness option on a certain item was endorsed by only 25% of the subjects; nonetheless, this group of children had a mean reading achievement score 0.21 standard deviation higher than that of children who chose the other option.

Further examination of internal consistency revealed that the alpha coefficients for the EA and RAI scales were much lower (Cohort 1: EA = .19, RAI = −.03); Cohort 2: EA = .17, RAI = .15) than the alpha coefficients for the IE scale, which were relatively high (Cohort 1 = .53, Cohort 2 = .62), indicating considerable inconsistency in responses to individual items. This situation, in which both individual and grouped items in a combined scale are good predictors but tend to have low intercorrelations, suggests that the measured beliefs may be situation-specific and may not generalize to other situations. Scores on these scales should be interpreted, therefore, with caution, as they may not reflect a unitary underlying construct; further work should be undertaken to replicate these findings.

4 In projects like this one, in which many variables are related to one another, the order of variable entry in regression analyses becomes a serious question. The relationship between cognitive skills and metacognitive beliefs presents such a problem of order. In these analyses we chose to focus on belief systems not only because they are of central theoretical interest, but also because they offer the potential for intervention. When cognitive variables were entered before belief variables in alternative models, the variance explained by beliefs was often reduced to a negligible amount. One exception was the CGR scale, which remained a significant predictor of first grade reading (3% of the variance) even after cognitive level was entered.

5 Additional analyses showed that the only background variables that influenced CGR beliefs themselves were parental education (4% of the variance explained) and CGRfit (8%). We also explored the possibility that CGR beliefs, and their strength in predicting reading performance, reflected a tendency for better readers to choose CGR responses consistent with their own language background, gender, or preschooling (suggesting an effect of self-confidence). A variable representing the correspondence of the child's CGR beliefs with his or her own characteristics correlated only weakly with reading level in grade 1 ($r = .14$), less so than CGRfit (see Table 7.5a); CGRfit, by contrast, is a four-point scale (including zero) which attributed one point for each of the following characteristics a child possessed: modern preschooling, Arabic home language, and male gender. This finding suggests that belief in one's own attributes was less important in promoting reading performance than recognition of the stereotypical male, Arabic-speaking, modern preschooled model as the "good" reader.

6 The contribution of causal attribution beliefs was also analyzed in these hierarchical regression analyses. For Cohort 1 (year 5), the IE scale explained a modest but significant 3% of the variance in reading ability, whereas attributions to effort (EA scale) explained little variance. For Cohort 2, the effect of the internal attribution scale was smaller than for Cohort 1, whereas the EA scale, after background factors, explained a significant 5% of the variance for reading performance by year 7. Together all beliefs scales predicted a significant 11% of the AR/7 variance (Table 7.7).

In further analyses, each of the RAI, IE, and EA scales was divided into low, middle, and high levels, and ANOVAs were performed to contrast Arabic reading means for each level. Results showed that the RAI scale exhibited a coherent, positive pattern for both cohorts: The higher the child's level on the RAI, the better his or her reading performance. The IE and the EA scales showed similar patterns. Internal responses on the IE scale in Cohort 1, year 5, were significantly related to AR/5, and for Cohort 2, this relationship was also significant with AR/5 but not AR/7. It should be noted that the effort attribution responses on the EA scale were particularly predictive of AR/7 in the urban environment.

7 See note 5.

8 This finding may be a function of wide variations in individual and home literacy found in Moroccan society. Analyses of variance showed that the extreme ends of the RAI scale were particularly effective in identifying good and poor readers, which implies that there is considerable heterogeneity in the reading achievement among students who have a moderate level of reading awareness. For further statistical analyses on this issue, see note 9.

9 For Cohort 1 (year 5), the IE scale explained 3% of the variance in reading ($F = 5.83$, $p < .05$), whereas the EA scale explained little variance. Additional

analyses showed that the RAI, IE, and EA scales were more predictive at the extreme ends of each scale than for the middle majority of subjects. For this reason, each scale was divided into low, middle, and high levels, and ANOVAs were performed to contrast Arabic reading means for each level. When aggregated in this way, the RAI scale exhibited a coherent, positive pattern for both cohorts: The higher the child's level on the RAI, the better his or her reading performance. While not quite significant for Cohort 1, this pattern was significant for Cohort 2 (year 5, $F = 11.60$, $p < .01$; year 7, $F = 7.65$, $p < .01$). Examined in parallel manner, the IE and the EA scales showed similar patterns. Internal responses on the IE scale in Cohort 1, year 5, were significantly related to same-year reading performance ($F = 3.04$, $p < .05$); in Cohort 2, this relationship was also significant ($F = 3.47$, $p < .05$) in year 5, but not for year 7 reading. While effort attribution responses on the EA scale were not significant for Cohort 1, they approached significance for Cohort 2 in year 5 ($F = 2.76$, $p < .10$), and were more predictive of reading achievement 2 years later, in year 7 ($F = 5.82$, $p < .01$). In Cohort 2, significant interactions by environment (year 5, $F = 3.72$, $p < .05$; year 7, $F = 3.16$, $p < .05$) suggested that the scale was more predictive in the urban than in the rural context.

10   In particular, cluster A (the parents' role in a child's education is more important than the teacher's role) was highly associated with children's higher CGR scores ($\chi^2 = 17.37$, $p < .01$); clusters B, C, and D were also related to higher CGR scores ($\chi^2 \geq 9.05$, $p \leq .10$). Out of the five remaining individual attitudinal questions, only question 9 (mother's educational aspirations for her child) was significantly related to the child's CGR beliefs; an aspiration of university education for one's child was positively associated with the child's CGR score ($\chi^2 = 6.56$, $p < .05$).

11   Cluster D: years 1 and 3 were significant at $\chi^2 \geq 10.73$, $p \leq .05$; year 5 was not significant.

12   Parents' metacognitive belief scores (CGR and HGR) were not, however, predictive of children's reading achievement, nor were any of the remaining single attitudinal questions.

13   This notion of strong religious beliefs (in either direction) having an impact on student achievement appears reasonable, but we have not been able to locate other empirical studies that support these findings.

8. Learning to read in a second language and a second literacy

Mouh discovers Arabic

Mouh has come down to al-Ksour from his *douar* (a cluster of houses composing a tiny village) in the High Atlas Mountains to live with his Uncle Khalid in order to attend the town school. At 8 years of age, he is legally a year too old to enter primary school, but his uncle, who works as a guard at the *caïd's* (mayor's) office, knows someone who can adjust Mouh's birth certificate so that enrollment can take place. Mouh's uncle is married to an Arab woman whom he met while stationed as a soldier in the coastal plains near Rabat, the capital. While in the army, Uncle Khalid learned to speak Moroccan Arabic with "Arab soldiers."

In Uncle Khalid's household, Moroccan Arabic is the dominant language. Due to harvesting and household chores in his mountain *douar* home, Mouh has arrived only the week before classes begin in October. He quickly realizes, to his surprise, that all the teachers will speak only in Arabic, using either Moroccan or Standard dialect, neither of which Mouh can speak. Most of his classmates seem to understand what is going on. They can understand the teacher's commands and even know something about the strange-looking writing the teacher is putting on an equally strange black sheet of wood attached to the front wall of the classroom.

Mouh is one of many thousands of monolingual Berber-speaking youngsters who have, before formal schooling, little or no mastery of the Arabic language. Even the old and honored *fqih,* who used to teach the Arabic language in the mosque near the closest market town, died a few years ago; Mouh's *douar,* being very poor, was unable to attract a younger man to replace him. For young Mouh, going to school is going to be a challenge not only in terms of learning the basic school subjects but also in preserving his Berber self-identity.

As discussed in chapter 2, the number of Berber-speaking children attending school taught in Arabic is still quite large in many rural parts of Morroco. Learning and schooling in a second language is exceedingly common in many other regions of the world as well. The remarkable fact is that multilingualism (and even multiliteracy) is the norm rather than the exception in today's world. This is especially so in the Third World, in spite of decades, and even centuries, of effort by colonial and central governments to reinforce and regulate the use of a single (or very few) official language(s).

Within this context of language variation, researchers and policymakers have debated the following question: Does learning to read in the mother tongue, or first (native) language, enhance children's school achievement relative to that of children obliged to learn to read in a second language? About 40 years ago, specialists at a UNESCO conference stated their unequivocal support for the use of mother tongue or vernacular education programs in a classic report:

> *It is axiomatic that the best medium for teaching a child to read is his mother-tongue.* Psychologically, it is the medium of meaningful signs that in his mind works automatically for expression and understanding. Sociologically, it is a means of identification among the members of the community to which he belongs. Educationally, he learns more quickly through it than through an unfamiliar medium. (UNESCO, 1953: 11; emphasis added)

Many specialists consider this issue as basically resolved. There seems little question, on the face of it, that cognitive advantages would result from learning to read in the child's native language. In a native language educational context, children can bring to bear all of their oral language skills (syntactic, semantic, and lexical) to the task of becoming literate. In addition, there are studies that appear to support mother tongue instruction for beginning literacy, such as the work of Modiano (1968) on Mayan-Spanish instruction in Chiapas, Mexico, and that of Skutnabb-Kangas and Toukomaa (1979) in Sweden on Finnish immigrant children. Both of these studies concluded that mother tongue reading instruction facilitated subsequent reading achievement in the second language and in school achievement. However, major reviews of the literature in this area (e.g., Dutcher, 1982; Engle, 1975; Hornberger, 1989; McLaughlin, 1985) present a more complex picture. Dutcher (1982) has pointed out, for example, that the various reasons for explaining success or failure of a given program are highly dependent on the specific nature of the educational/linguistic intervention as well as on the sociocultural context of language use. Such complexities in research on first and second language/literacy learning have recently been described in a study of Turkish schoolchildren learning to read the Dutch language in Holland (Verhoeven, 1990). Though differences in proficiency were found between native and nonnative speakers of Dutch, certain key reading processes were found to operate similarly across both student populations, a topic to which we shall return in the Moroccan case.

Because most contemporary studies of bilingual education have been interventions – in the sense that researchers "create" the learning context by introducing a special native or second language teaching program – it is difficult to separate the effects of the experimenters' involvement with the subjects of their study from the educational and linguistic interventions themselves (the confound known as the Hawthorne effect). In other words, the experimental, and often enthusiastic, nature of the new learning program may be responsible for the heightened achievement of children in such contexts; therefore, the generalizability of the intervention may be severely limited. Furthermore, the dependent variables in such studies often include standardized tests of grade level reading and intellectual development (e.g., Diaz, 1985). Relatively little research has considered the impact of mother tongue language instruction on specific literacy skills, on the relationship between the types of languages and orthographies to be learned, or on the nature of biliteracy development. Thus, in spite of the general tendency of scholars, practitioners, and policymakers to accept the notion that mother tongue instruction is usually best for reading achievement, the research literature provides only limited support for such a general claim.

It is not surprising that mother tongue instruction was and is seen by many as a panacea for minority linguistic groups. Such groups have often been discriminated against politically as well as economically, and are usually at the bottom of the educational achievement ladder in both Western and Third World countries. One of the key issues is disentangling the psycholinguistic question (i.e., the relationship between oral and written first and second language skills) from the social and economic backgrounds of the disadvantaged minority groups. In the Moroccan case, if Berber-speaking children do not achieve as well as Arabic-speaking children, is this for linguistic, psychological, or possibly socioeconomic, educational, or political reasons? Indeed, in an oft-cited study of bilingualism and school achievement in Canada, it was found that high motivation was the key factor in helping children learn from second language instruction (Lambert & Tucker, 1972) . In the Canadian case, French-speaking children in an English-only classroom (in what is termed an "immersion" program) were found to read at least as well in both languages as classmates learning to read in a single language. It was also found that French-speaking children had higher motivation for learning in English than English-speaking children did for learning in French, a distinction that is crucial in such studies.

Yet it was in Africa, not North America, where the 1953 UNESCO document was taken most seriously. With international support, numerous governments developed orthographies for previously unwritten vernacular languages, and these languages were then used in mother tongue first literacy programs for primary school children (e.g., in Nigeria, Mauritania, and Senegal). Although some analysis exists on UNESCO's Experimental World Literacy Program (UNESCO, 1976; Gillette, 1987) and other vernacular literacy programs (Bijeljac-Babic, 1983; Dalby, 1985; Murugaiyan, 1985; Okedara & Okedara, 1992), there is little solid research evidence that children who begin school instruction with such vernacular languages are eventually superior in learning to read and write the target national language (the children's second language), when compared with children who learn to read first in the national language. Unfortunately, the little evidence that exists is clouded by methodological problems in which the motivation, enthusiasm, and bias of those involved in teaching the vernacular might account for most or all of the reported positive effects.

Even if the claim favoring mother tongue literacy were well founded, it is still surprising that almost no research has been directed at the more specific problem to which the key UNESCO document was aimed: How well do children learn to read in a second language (L2) when their own mother tongue (L1) is unwritten? This question is of particular relevance to the numerous Third World countries that have one or more languages in use that are without any "usable" or "efficient" orthographies.[1] Furthermore, studying this question in a naturally occurring (nonintervention) situation in which L1 and L2 literacy learners are attending the same schools and have similar family backgrounds would allow a direct comparison of the two linguistic groups on their reading acquisition. Under such conditions, finding that children learning in L2 lagged behind in literacy and failed to catch up would constitute support for UNESCO's contention that mother tongue literacy is always (and even axiomatically) preferable for beginning school instruction. As the reader might surmise at this point, the Morocco Literacy Project provided an unusually good opportunity to study this question.

We had a second opportunity as well: to study *second literacy acquisition,* which in many societies like Morocco may occur in the child's second or even third spoken language. The relatively few studies conducted on this issue have involved situations in which the first and second orthographies were similar to one another, for example, Spanish and English (Clarke, 1980), or French and English (Cziko, 1978). Surprisingly little research is available on how children who are partially literate in one language/ orthography learn to read in a second language/orthography that is relatively unrelated to the first.[2] Nonetheless, this is precisely the type of multilingual literacy situation that is increasingly common in Third World countries, as well as in ethnic and immigrant communities in the United States and Europe (e.g., Laotian immigrants in Philadelphia or Algerian immigrants in France). Arabic and French literacy acquisition in Morocco also provides a good example.

The central questions raised in this chapter are the following: Does learning to read in one's mother tongue (L1), as contrasted with a second language (L2), enhance reading acquisition? More specific to the present study, do Arabic-speaking children achieve better levels of Arabic literacy skills than Berber-speaking children do during primary school? Do such differences persist in subsequent years of schooling, or do they diminish over time? Does Quranic preschooling facilitate Arabic literacy acquisition differentially for L1 (Moroccan Arabic) and L2 (Berber) learners of Arabic over the years of primary schooling? Finally, to what extent is second literacy (French; Lit2) achievement related to first literacy (Arabic; Lit1) skills? Answers to these questions hold implications not only for Moroccan educational policy but also for other multilingual societies concerned with language and literacy planning.

As discussed in chapter 2, Standard Arabic differs in a number of ways from spoken dialectal Moroccan Arabic. However, in spite of such differences, Moroccan Arabic speakers can be thought of as learning literacy in their mother tongue in the same sense that nonstandard dialectal

English speakers (e.g., African-Americans in the United States; Scottish-English speakers in Great Britain) are learning mother tongue literacy when they learn to read English. Generally speaking, the relationship between any spoken mother tongue and mother tongue literacy may exhibit some differences and have certain consequences (e.g., social acceptance vs. rejection), but the basic phonological, syntactic, and semantic structures are usually highly related. With particular regard to Arabic, Badry (1983) has shown that young Moroccan children can produce novel verb derivations in Moroccan Arabic that parallel rule-governed derivational patterns in Standard Arabic. Similarly, in Tunisia, Maamouri (1983) has pointed to a common lexical core between Standard and Tunisian Arabic varieties, suggesting its systematic exploitation in initial literacy instruction.[3]

At present, Standard Arabic is the official language of schooling and literacy in Moroccan primary and middle schools, with the French language remaining important only for scientific subjects in high school and university instruction. Thus, in contrast to dialectal Arabic-speaking children learning to read in Arabic, Berber-speaking children must learn in a language completely unrelated to their mother tongue. The fundamental similarity between Standard and Moroccan Arabic varieties would be expected, according to much of the research literature, to facilitate Arabic literacy learning among Moroccan Arabic speakers, especially relative to the learning situation of monolingual Berber-speaking children.

Learning French as a Lit2 (and as a second or third language) begins when children enter third grade of primary school, though the principal language literacy in public schooling remains Standard Arabic (see chapter 2). For the rural al-Ksour context discussed in this chapter, access to spoken or written French occurs almost entirely in the school setting, with some additional input from television and radio. As noted, virtually no parents (by self-report) of the rural sample of children could speak, read, or write fluently in French.

Research design

The data analyzed were gathered on the samples of children who lived in al-Ksour, where the Berber and Moroccan Arabic languages are widely spoken and accepted. Children were selected for inclusion in the study only if they were, at the beginning of the study, monolingual speakers of either Arabic or Berber; also, about half of the children in the al-Ksour

Table 8.1. Rural children in the second language/literacy study

	Berber Speakers		Arabic Speakers	
	No preschool	Quranic schooled	No preschool	Quranic schooled
	RNB	RQB	RNA	RQA
Subsample size (Total rural N = 166)[a]	27	56	23	60
Gender	13	30	11	29
Boys				
Girls	14	26	12	31
Mean years of age in year 1	7.4	7.4	7.4	7.4
Mean years of preschooling	0.1	1.1	0.1	1.6

Note: RNB = rural non-preschooled Berber-speaking; RNA = rural non-preschooled Arabic-speaking; RQB = rural Quranic preschooled Berber-speaking; RQA = rural Quranic preschooled Arabic-speaking. All children in this study resided in rural al-Ksour. This is a subsample of Cohort 1, as shown in Table 4.2.
[a]As a longitudinal study, there was attrition in the Cohort 1 sample over the 5-year period of this study. Rural sample size in year 3, N = 130; in year 5, N = 117.

sample differed in Quranic preschooling experience. There were, therefore, four main comparison groups of children in this part of our work: Quranic preschooled Arabic-speaking; Quranic preschooled Berber-speaking; non-preschooled Arabic-speaking; and non-preschooled Berber-speaking (see Table 8.1).[4] For comparison purposes, aspects of French (and other) language backgrounds of the rural and urban samples are shown in Table 8.2.

Arabic and French reading achievement scores were utilized for the longitudinal analyses; cognitive tests included concept identification, memory, general information, and perceptual ability.[5]

Results

Regression analyses showed that virtually no differences in Arabic reading achievement (over years 1–5) were found by SES or parents' educational level, probably due to the relatively limited variability in these factors within the rural environment of al-Ksour. That is, there simply was not much variation in SES among poor rural families, and the great majority

Table 8.2. French (and other) language competencies in rural and urban families

	Rural (%)	Urban (%)
1. Mother's fluency in French		
None	88	87
Very little	2	6
Moderately good	4	5
Fluent	1	0
2. Father's fluency in French		
None	66	57
Very little	9	13
Moderately good	14	24
Fluent	4	1
3. Oldest sibling's fluency in French		
None	25	19
Very little	18	21
Moderately good	24	34
Fluent	5	2
4. Oldest sibling's fluency in another foreign language (mainly English, Spanish, or German)[a]		
None	44	45
Very little	1	3
Moderately good	7	7
Fluent	0	0

Note: Indices are based on self-report responses in the parent interview.
[a]Not all respondents answered this question.

of parents had little or no education. There were also no systematic gender differences. There was, as expected, a significant positive correlation between children's cognitive skills and Arabic reading achievement (see Table 8.3), though no such correlation was found between cognition and French reading level. Finally, as reported in chapter 5, there were no differences by language group in cognitive skills across the years of the study, a finding that allows us to reject the hypothesis that either language sample had superiority in overall intellectual ability.

Effects of mother tongue instruction on reading acquisition

In the first year of the study, Arabic-speaking children outperformed Berber-speaking children in Arabic reading achievement. However,

Table 8.3. Correlation matrix of background and cognitive variables
with Arabic and French reading achievement in rural sample

	1	2	3	4	5	6	7
1. Par Ed							
2. SES	.39						
3. Cog/1	.09	.10					
4. AR/1	.10	.10	.30				
5. AR/3	.11	.06	.39	.55			
6. AR/ 5	.00	.00	.34	.38	.78		
7. FR/3	.18	.02	.09	.28	.55	.31	
8. FR/5	.04	.01	.18	.33	.59	.64	.38

Note: $r > .20$, $p < .05$; $r > .25$, $p < .01$ when $N > 100$. Cohort 1 rural sample sizes for correlations are pairwise, as follows: for Arabic, $N = 112–163$; French, $N = 59–116$.

though the superiority of the Arabic-speaking children was generally maintained in years 3 and 5, the difference between language groups diminished with time and was no longer statistically significant during the later years of primary school (see Figure 8.1).[6] Thus, as hypothesized, there appears to be some advantage to speaking dialectal Arabic as a mother tongue when first beginning to read, but any advantage diminishes substantially over subsequent years of schooling.

Effects of Quranic preschooling

With respect to preschooling experience, the results showed that Quranic preschooled children generally outperformed their non-preschooled counterparts in Arabic reading achievement (see Figure 8.2), even though these group differences were not statistically significant for any year. It was also found that the non-preschooled Berber group (RNB) had the lowest scores over the whole 5-year period, though this gap decreased slightly by the last year of the study.[7] This result supports the claim that Quranic preschooling is particularly helpful to Berber-speaking children, since RQB children performed as well as mother tongue Arabic-speaking children (RQA and RNA) in the study. Furthermore, although Quranic preschooling led to enhanced scores in the early stages of literacy acquisition, the effects were modest and diminished somewhat over time. This finding of the positive effects of preschooling fits with similar findings in developing countries (Myers & Hertenberg, 1987), but also replicates

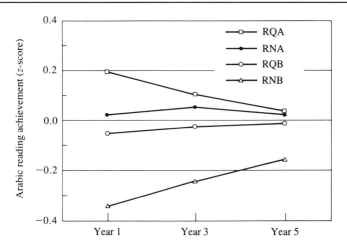

Figure 8.1. Arabic reading achievement (*z*-scores) of rural Arabic-speaking and rural Berber-speaking groups.

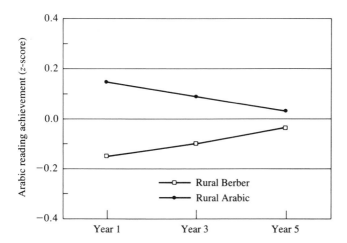

Figure 8.2. Arabic reading achievement (*z*-scores) of rural Arabic-speaking and Berber-speaking groups, by year and preschool. (RNB = rural non-preschooled Berber speaking; RNA = rural non-preschooled Arabic speaking; RQB = rural Quranic preschooled Berber speaking; RQA = rural Quranic preschooled Arabic speaking).

studies showing diminished consequences of preschool experience following entry into primary school (Zigler & Valentine, 1979).

Second literacy acquisition

French instruction in Moroccan public schools does not begin until grade 3 of Moroccan primary school. By year 3 of our study, only 64 children (the 40% of the children who had never failed a grade) were in third grade; these children, certainly among the best students in the rural sample, were tested on French reading that year and again in year 5 of the study. The year 5 assessment also included other children who by that year had reached third or fourth grade (for a total sample of 116). No differences in French reading achievement by Arabic or Berber mother tongue background were found in either assessment year. This result runs counter to the conjecture of some specialists who have claimed that Berber-speaking children would be more motivated and more able to learn French literacy than their Arabic-speaking counterparts.[8] Such a consequence may have been true in the days of the French protectorate when Berbers were particularly encouraged to forgo the study of Arabic altogether and learn only French as a language of literacy.

Preschooling experience, as might be expected, had little effect on learning to read in French, although there was a tendency (marginally significant in year 5 only) for the non-preschooled children to outperform the Quranic preschooled children. This modest effect could be a consequence of the early emphasis on Arabic as a religious language in Quranic schools, which may have a negative effect on motivation for learning French, the former colonial language.[9] We were also interested in the potential transfer of Lit1 skills on the learning of Lit2, and so regression analyses were performed in order to measure the impact of background variables and Arabic reading skill (Lit1) on French reading achievement (Lit2). These analyses indicated that each year of Arabic reading ability contributed a significant additional portion of variance to the French reading score in year 5, supporting the notion of transfer from first to second literacy in an increasing manner over years of schooling (see Table 8.4).

Beyond the general transfer effects of Lit1 on Lit2, we examined measures of specific reading subskills in an attempt to pinpoint further the origin of transfer effects. Regression analyses, which included the various Arabic reading subskills showed that Arabic word decoding skill in year 1

Table 8.4. Regression model for French reading achievement in rural sample

	R^2	R^2 chg.	F
SES + ParEd	.000	.000	0.77
SES + ParEd + Gender	.000	.000	1.42
SES + ParEd + Gender + Lang	.000	.000	0.01
SES + ParEd + Gender + Lang + Presch	.011	.011	3.96[a]
SES + ParEd + Gender + Lang + Presch + Cog/1	.045	.034	4.61[a]
SES + ParEd + Gender + Lang + Presch + Cog/1 + AR/1	.153	.108	13.76[b]
SES + ParEd + Gender + Lang + Presch + Cog/1 + AR/1 + AR/3	.368	.215	34.62[b]
SES + ParEd + Gender + Lang + Presch + Cog/1 + AR/1 + AR/3 + AR/5	.461	.093	17.88[b]

Note: Rural sample (listwise) $N = 107$.
[a]$p < .05$.
[b]$p < .001$.

(WD/1) was by far the best predictor of French reading achievement (FR/3). Because the two scripts, Arabic and French, differ both in form and in reading direction (right to left vs. left to right), this finding appears to support the notion of transfer of alphabetic decoding across highly contrasting orthographies. It should be recalled that Arabic decoding skill was also the best predictor of subsequent overall Arabic reading achievement, as described in chapter 5. In addition, the pedagogical style of learning both Arabic and French is very similar in Moroccan schools, relying on a great deal of rote memorization and oral recitation. Thus, a number of factors may be at work that link Lit1 and Lit2 learning in al-Ksour and that facilitate transfer across skill domains.[10]

Is second language/literacy learning a disadvantage?

Overall, children who are monolingual speakers of Moroccan Arabic and are learning to read Standard Arabic outperformed Berber monolinguals just beginning to acquire Arabic literacy. However, after 5 years of public education carried out entirely in Arabic, both groups of children had acquired roughly the same competence in Arabic literacy. It seems reasonable to conclude that the superiority of the Arabic-speaking children in the early stages of literacy acquisition is due primarily to the substantial similarity and transfer from spoken Moroccan Arabic to written Standard Arabic. This similarity can facilitate the tasks of word decoding and pronunciation, word recognition, and text comprehension for the Arabic-speaking learners. As reviewed earlier, such a mother tongue advantage has been found in a number of other multilingual contexts.

Nonetheless, the Berber-speaking children of the rural sample, monolingual when they entered primary school, made consistent progress toward Arabic-Berber bilingualism during the 5-year course of this study as a function of their increased contact with Arabic-speaking peers in the classroom and in the bilingual town environment. The fact that the gap in Arabic literacy ability closed between the two language groups may be explained at least in part by the Berber speakers' increasing proficiency in Moroccan Arabic, a proficiency that apparently aided their acquisition of Arabic literacy in more or less the same way that it did for monolingual Moroccan Arabic speakers.

The analyses of French (Lit2) acquisition supported the straightforward (yet largely untested) hypothesis that children who perform better in first literacy tend to be better at second literacy acquisition, whether this literacy is in a second language (for Moroccan Arabic speakers) or a third language (for Berber speakers). The finding that Arabic skills explained more than 40% of the total variance in French literacy further suggests that second literacy acquisition is substantially dependent on first literacy acquisition. These findings go well with what Cummins (1979) termed the "interdependence hypothesis": Acquiring a first language/literacy is critical for the acquisition of any subsequent one, because they are based on the same set of underlying linguistic and cognitive skills. Furthermore, the relationship between first (Arabic) and second (French) literacy increased with time, similar to the findings of a longitudinal study of Hispanic bilinguals in the United States (Hakuta & Diaz, 1985). Indeed, the pattern of correlations shown in Table 8.3 indicated that while Lit1 and Lit2 were related from the very beginning of Lit2 acquisition, this relationship actually increased in magnitude as proficiency was gained in each literacy. Finally, we found that cognitive ability was related to Arabic literacy acquisition, but much less so to French literacy, a result that supports the hypothesis that, independent of overall intellectual ability, first literacy learning has a direct impact on second literacy learning.

Languages and literacies working together: A summary

The present findings provide an important counterexample to the generally accepted claim that schoolchildren who must study in a second language are virtually always at a disadvantage – or are, as some say, at risk for failure – in their primary school years. In the present case, Berber monolingual children essentially caught up to their Arabic-speaking peers by the fifth year of primary school.

Why is this so? The Moroccan case differs in several important ways from some previously studied contexts of bilingualism and reading acquisition. First, there is no competing literacy in the Berber language. For rural families and their children, Standard Arabic literacy is the widely recognized key to primary school achievement. Second, social factors such as motivation for learning a second language probably also play a role. As was pointed out, Arabic is the language of Islam, and as such enjoys great acceptance and respect among Muslim Berber speakers. Thus, it is reasonable to suppose that, relative to some other contexts for bilingualism and biliteracy, minimal differences exist between the motivation of the two language groups toward learning to read in Standard Arabic. In the United States, by contrast, a main issue in bilingual education policy is whether Lit1 training should be carried out first in L1 or L2, or in both simultaneously. The kinds of tensions and policy debate characterizing this issue among the American Hispanic community, for example, are virtually absent in the current Moroccan context.[11]

Given the ascendancy of spoken Moroccan Arabic in small-town al-Ksour, Berber-speaking children have a number of significant contexts in which to learn Arabic outside the classroom, thereby reducing their initial linguistic disadvantage vis-à-vis Arabic literacy; these include home television viewing, dealing with the government bureaucracy, and general contact with Arabic-speaking individuals. The situation in which virtually all children are motivated to learn a single national language distinguishes the Moroccan case from that of numerous other multilingual African (and Third World) societies, in which the national, official, or colonial languages may be spoken only in school and official contexts and/or within certain classes of society (e.g., the case of English in Ghana and Nigeria or French in Senegal).[12]

The consequences of the Quranic preschool experience for promoting reading skills were more apparent among the Berber-speaking children of al-Ksour, especially those who did not attend Quranic preschool. These children, who were the lowest in reading ability at the outset of the study, caught up after 5 years of schooling. Our interpretation is that traditional preschooling was particularly beneficial for the RNB group through the provision of additional opportunities to improve oral and written Arabic language skills. That Quranic preschooling had little effect on Arabic-speaking children simply confirms the fact that home-learned (spoken) Arabic skills are more or less sufficient for these children to learn what is required in school, and that additional contact with Arabic in the Quranic school setting had little supplementary effect.

The findings also support the hypothesis that first literacy provides an important underlying structure on which to build second literacy acquisition. This appears to be so even though the two literacies – Arabic and French – are unrelated in terms of orthography, lexicon, and syntax. This particular result seems to suggest that increasing a child's competence in a first literacy – and, in particular, basic decoding skills – may be a good way to promote second literacy acquisition. Because first versus second literacy training is a critical policy issue in many multilingual and multiliterate societies, this outcome may be useful in helping to think about which languages will be most effective to teach.[13]

Many language and education specialists have come to regard mother tongue literacy as the natural "cure" for children from minority language backgrounds who are at risk for school failure. Most of the research on which this assertion is based has come from studies in rather specialized contexts, such as North American bilingual education programs or mother tongue educational intervention programs in a few developing countries. The present findings have considerable potential application, as the majority of complex multilingual societies are located in Africa, Asia, and Latin America, where conditions are often more similar to those found in Morocco than to those of North America. In particular, many Third World countries, especially in Africa, have languages that are either unwritten or that have recently developed orthographies with little available printed materials or literature. In light of the present data, one should not conclude that mother tongue literacy is inappropriate in many linguistic contexts. Rather, the generalization that first language literacy is *axiomatically* best requires serious reconsideration in light of specific contexts of language use and literacy acquisition; in the case of our data in Morocco, this presupposition can be rejected.

Overall, we have found that some of the classic hypotheses concerning language and literacy cannot be applied uniformly to multilingual and multiliterate contexts. In chapter 9, we discover how assumptions concerning school-based and everyday literary skills are in need of reappraisal as well.

Notes

1 Some orthographies may be considered underdeveloped in the sense that very little written or printed literature is available owing to the recency of script creation. In Zimbabwe, for example, both major African languages, Ndebele and Shona, were introduced into the primary school curriculum after independence in the mid-1970s, in a major break with the all-English colonial past. However, a problem still faced by the government is that, even though textbooks were developed using specially developed Roman alphabet scripts for the African languages, few materials outside the school texts are available to read. Thus, both teachers and students still maintain a strong motivation to learn English, given its long literary heritage and postschooling economic opportunities. For a further discussion of the determinants of motivation for learning a colonial versus indigenous literacy, see Lind's (1988) discussion of Mozambique and Wagner's (1987a) description of literacy planning in Zimbabwe.

2 Koda (1987) has conducted some laboratory work in this domain in a study of contrasting samples of college students learning English, Japanese, and Arabic as foreign languages.

3 The issue of dialect and literacy is not, however, without controversy. It has been claimed that some dialects and creoles are "far" enough from the standard form to merit the creation of a separate literacy, possibly with changes in the script itself, and the development of separate versions of school curricula. This has been partially attempted in the United States with Black English, but without success in terms of enhanced student achievement (Labov, 1982). Similarly, it has been suggested that Moroccan children could benefit from instruction in the Moroccan dialect (Salmi, 1987); and, in recent years, at least one newspaper began (intermittently, depending on the political climate) to publish using the Moroccan dialect rather than Standard Arabic. This latter event also sparked rather strong reactions from the government and segments of the public who opposed any attempt to dilute or change the nature of the written language of the Quran as the basis for all Arabic literary forms in Morocco.

4 As discussed in chapter 3, the prevalence of grade repetition in Moroccan schools leads, in a longitudinal study, to considerable variation in grade level over time. Thus, whereas all 166 children in the sample were in grade 1 in 1983, it was found 5 years later that of the remaining in-school sample, 19 (16%) were in third grade, 51 (44%) were in fourth grade, and 47 (40%) were in fifth grade; 49 subjects were lost to sample attrition. Chi-square analyses were performed to determine whether cell ratios differed substantially across grade levels by first language or gender; no significant differences were found. Furthermore, at each assessment, all children had received the same number of *years* of schooling. In addition, the average grade level achieved after 5 years of schooling was the same for both Arabic and Berber language groups (mean grade level = 4.3), and attrition (30%) was also equivalent across groups. Thus, the likelihood that grade level or other changes in the composition of the sample over time might have biased between-group results is quite small.

5 French reading (FR) achievement scores were calculated as the mean of the z-scores of all available reading task scores in a given year. Thus, in year 3, these French tests included LRF, WDF, WPMF, SMF, and PCF; in year 5, the tests included WPMF, SMF, and PCF. (Information on these tests is contained in appendix 2.) Similarly, each child's cognitive score in year 1 (Cog/1) was produced by dividing the sum of z-scores on the individual tests by the number of tests administered (these included CEFT/1, SPD/1, GEN/1, and CID/1).

6 The statistical analyses for data presented in Figure 8.1 were in the form of a 2 × 2 ANOVA. No significant interactions were found over each of the 3 testing

years; the significant main effect for language was found in year 1 only ($F = 6.10, p < .02$).

In order to determine whether longitudinal changes in the sample were responsible for the observed reduction in Arabic reading differences between language groups, the same 2×2 ANOVA model was applied to the year 1 Arabic achievement (AR/1) score for that portion of the sample that remained in the study over the full 5 years ($N = 117$). The general finding was upheld, although weakened, with Arabic speakers exhibiting trend-level superiority in Arabic reading achievement in year 1 ($F = 3.72, p < .10$). Furthermore, an analysis of covariance by language group on AR/1, where cognitive level was controlled, showed that the difference between language groups was still significant for the full year 1 sample ($F = 4.22, p < .05$).

7 Overall ANOVAs by preschooling over each year were not significant ($Fs \leq 1.12, p \geq .29$). The non-preschooled Berber group (RNB), when compared to each of the other groups in year 1, was found to be significantly different from the other groups ($F = 5.19, p < .02$).

8 It has been variously claimed that the phonemic relationship between Berber and European languages such as French and English is closer than that between Berber and Arabic. We know of no research that supports this contention. On the other hand, the status of the Berber-speaking community as an "oppressed minority" (see chapters 2 and 3) might give rise to a hypothesis that Berber speakers would be more motivated to learn French than Arabic as an L2. Although the present results provide no data that address this issue, the status of the Berber language in France and in Algeria might give rise to different results.

9 Claims involving religious motives for learning to read still require further substantiation, even though such a hypothesis is believed by many specialists. In the Islamic case, one need only consider the rise of fundamentalism in Iran, Egypt, and Algeria to see how powerful such religious motives can be in becoming literate.

10 In his study of Turkish- and Dutch-speaking schoolchildren learning to read in Dutch, Verhoeven (1990) found that, in spite of overall achievement differences, both groups of children employed similar cognitive processes in learning to read. In particular, he found that oral proficiency in Dutch was the most important predictor of Dutch (as a second language) reading skill. Although we did not have measures of Moroccan Arabic proficiency after entry into the classroom, our observations tend to confirm the findings of Verhoeven. However, causation is still difficult to determine. For example, in Morocco, oral proficiency (in Moroccan Arabic) among Berber speakers indicates not only a cognitive language ability, but also the degree of cultural assimilation exhibited by the child into the second language culture (i.e., Arab

society), thus implying greater comfort and motivation to learn to read in the second language.

11 For a review of bilingualism, biliteracy, and motivational issues, with a special focus on Hispanic ethnolinguistic groups, see Hornberger (1989).

12 In Morocco, as in other multilingual societies, the use of certain languages in specific contexts is quite common. Termed *diglossia* by Ferguson (1959), the pattern of oral language use is known to vary dramatically by social class, region of the country, and even by gender. In the latter case, for example, our ethnographic observations showed that young Moroccan women with some oral fluency in French tend to use their speaking skills much more frequently than do young men, in al-Ksour as well as in Marrakech and other urban areas. Our interview data further suggest that women who aspire to a more modern self-image and emancipated role in Moroccan society use French as a marker of "liberation." For further discussion on this and related matters, see Spratt (1988).

13 It should be recalled that only basic decoding skills were significantly related to Lit2, not other early reading skills. There is little evidence here that learning other early reading skills would have a salutary effect on later Lit2 achievement, and even less that shows specific forms of transfer across orthographies (e.g., English to Japanese or Chinese). Although some specialists tend to put all first and second language/literacy studies together as if most transfer relationships were equivalent, this generalization is very likely false. More research is required on this important topic.

9. Functional literacy: School learning and everyday skills

Literate prescriptions

The Boularbi family lives in a modest two-room house on the edge of al-Ksour. Mr. Boularbi is almost 60 years old. Since his youth he has worked in the local forestry and charcoal-making business run by his commune. His salary barely keeps food on the table for the family of four, with meat at most once a week. But poverty in al-Ksour does not mean destitution. The Boularbis are proud of what they have accomplished, and that their son has a "real job," working with the local gendarmerie in a neighboring village.

What really concerns the Boularbi family is their health. Mrs. Boularbi has chronic pains in her chest, and Mr. Boularbi was injured in his job 2 years ago, having seriously cut his leg with an ax. Both adults have made numerous visits to the local hospital, but without noticeable relief from the pain. Mr. Boularbi has just come home from the pharmacy with the latest prescription from the nurse. He has been told the number of pills to take in the morning and evening, over a period of weeks.

Even though the prescription is for an over-the-counter drug, it is confusing to Mr. Boularbi. His Arabic reading skills, acquired during Quranic schooling received decades ago, would be of little use in any case, as the complete medical instructions are in French, with only a partial translation into Standard Arabic. The technical terms are, in any event, far beyond the literacy skills of an unschooled woodcutter.

For such medical matters, Mr. Boularbi asks his teenage high school–going son, Mhamid, to decipher the instructions. The young Mhamid makes a serious, potentially injurious error in translation. We wonder what happens when we (the observers) are not around to make the necessary correction.

Literacy skills taught in school may bear only partial resemblance to the kinds of abilities and knowledge utilized in the performance of literacy tasks in everyday life, such as depicted in the vignette about the Boularbis. Whether in America or Morocco, schooling provides only part of the preparation students need to accomplish the literacy tasks of everyday life, as school curricula typically tend to be focused on skill building for subsequent academic learning. Almost since the creation of formal schooling, pedagogues have assumed substantial transfer between school-learned material and real-life activities. In this chapter we explore the interface between school-based and everyday, or "functional," literacy skills.

Definitions of functional literacy, like those of literacy in general, have varied considerably across time and space, attesting to the complexity and context specificity of the term (Levine, 1982). In 1947, to identify "functional illiterates," the U.S. Bureau of the Census analyzed data on years of schooling with self-reported reading and writing ability. With a focus on economic implications, the Teheran Conference of 1965 described functional literacy as being "linked to a vocational training programme and encouraging the rapid growth of the individual's productivity" (quoted in Hamadache & Martin, 1986: 30). This conception formed the basis of the Experimental World Literacy Programme (EWLP), launched in 1967, which was tied to the stated proposition that "reading and writing should lead not only to elementary general knowledge but to training for work, increased productivity, a greater participation in civil life and a better understanding of the surrounding world" (UNESCO, 1976: 10). In practice, however, the EWLP emphasized the connection between literacy and occupational training and paid little attention to these latter, more general goals (see Levine, 1986). At about the same time, Harman argued for "a clearly defined delineation of adult reading requisites and related functional goals," suggesting income tax forms, driving instructions, and job application forms as possible items "which could then become the articulated aim of literacy instruction" and assessment (1970: 237). However, beyond adaptations of children's tests for use with adolescents and adults, little was done until fairly recently in terms of assessing functional literacy.

Almost 20 years later, the National Assessment of Educational Progress (NAEP) conducted a survey that explored literacy skill levels among

American young adults (age 21–25 years). The survey followed a task-based approach, both in its assessment materials and in the recommendations generated by the study's findings (Kirsch & Jungeblut, 1986). Approximately 3,500 young adults were presented with a series of tasks of varying complexity, some of which simulated everyday literacy activities. The simulation tasks were specific to situations that appeared to require literacy skills in the United States, such as reading a menu and filling out a job application. Skills were measured and characterized in terms of three scales – prose literacy, document literacy, and quantitative literacy. The 1986 NAEP report concluded that a strict emphasis on the use of narrative texts in literacy instruction is insufficient preparation for the sorts of complex literacy tasks encountered in contemporary American life, and that out-of-school literacy assessment should go beyond traditional measures of reading comprehension. In spite of this important conceptual distinction, the NAEP study also found that functional literacy (document) ability and school-based (prose) skills were highly correlated ($r =$ .62), indicating an important proportion of shared variance across the two domains of literacy ability.[1]

The nature of functional literacy and its assessment, and the forms of training that might foster its development, are a central issue for literacy planners and educators in the United States and elsewhere. In developing countries, where large portions of the adult population are unschooled and nonliterate, and where the majority of individuals who do go to school receive no more than a fifth-grade education, the functional literacy skills of children attending primary school take on particular importance, providing a major policy rationale for our work in Morocco.

Our research differs from previous studies of functional literacy in a number of ways. Whereas much American research focused on literacy skills for the workplace (Mikulecky, 1982; Sticht, 1975), our study sampled everyday household literacy tasks.[2] Second, whereas other studies focused on adults (the NAEP study, for example, surveyed individuals over 20 years of age), we chose to study the everyday literacy skills of youths 11 to 14 years of age, most of whom were still in school. We targeted this age group because they were often observed in the role of literacy mediators for their household's literacy needs. Third, we sought to understand household literacy among children with varying amounts of schooling and in both urban and rural environments. Although there has been speculation about how the literacy ecology may affect the development of functional literacy skills, few empirical studies have attempted a direct assessment of its impact. Finally, we sought to identify the kinds of household

Table 9.1. Samples for Household Literacy Assessment

(a) Cohort 1 ($N = 218^a$)

| | Urban | | Rural | | |
	Boys	Girls	Boys	Girls	Total
School status at time of HLA[b]					
3rd grade	11	19	10	8	48
4th grade	21	23	23	27	94
5th grade	13	19	23	21	76

(b) Cohort 2 ($N = 453$)[c]

| | Urban | | Rural | | |
	Boys	Girls	Boys	Girls	Total
School status at time of HLA					
5th grade	29	49	40	23	141
6th grade	103	60	36	45	244
Dropout	14	21	16	17	68

[a] N reflects attrition from an initial N of 350.
[b] HLA = Household Literacy Assessment.
[c] N reflects attrition from an initial N of 492.

literacy tasks that pose special difficulties for children of different ages and school experience, as well as the factors in the child's experience that appear to support the development of functional literacy skills.

Research design

Both cohorts of children were involved in the functional literacy assessment (see Table 9.1). All children in the younger cohort had spent 5 years in elementary school at the time of the assessment, but as noted earlier, children had achieved different grade levels (third, fourth, or fifth grade) due to grade repetition. The older cohort differed in terms of number of years spent in school (6 or 7 or more), their grade level achieved by that time (fifth or sixth grade), and whether they were currently attending school. All the school dropouts in this cohort had reached fifth grade prior

a   b

c   d

Figure 9.1. Household Literacy Assessment (HLA) items: (a) letter; (b) newspaper; (c) electricity bill; (d) medicine box.

to leaving school, and had left school about 6 months before they were assessed for this part of our study.[3] In addition to our series of more conventional school reading tests, all children received an assessment of functional literacy skills developed for this purpose as described below.[4]

We designed the Household Literacy Assessment (HLA) instrument from a series of tasks representing the sorts of literacy activities we observed to be commonly practiced in Moroccan households. The HLA measured children's ability to make sense of the written features of four items common in Morocco's literacy ecology: a letter, the front page of a daily newspaper, an electricity bill, and a box of medicine (see Figure 9.1). All materials used were authentic, modified only by the addition of a layer of clear plastic to prevent disintegration from handling.

The HLA was conducted in the fall of the school year, during the administration of the individual student interview. Some students were assessed at school, but the majority were assessed in their homes, where appointments had been scheduled in advance. For a subsample of 205 children in Cohort 2, we also kept a detailed record of the children's

Table 9.2. Household literacy assessment instrument

Item	Questions	
Letter	Q.1	What is this?
	Q.2	Who was this letter sent to?
	Q.3	How much did it cost to send this letter?
Newspaper	Q.4	What is this?
	Q.5	What is the date of this paper?
	Q.6	Read this advertisement. Can you shop at this store at 9 p.m.?
	Q.7	Read this headline. What is it about, in your own words?
	Q.8	Read this short article. What is it about, in your own words?
Electricity bill	Q.9	What is this?
	Q.10	Whose bill is this? In other words, who has to pay?
	Q.11	How much does he have to pay?
Medicine box	Q.12	What is this?
	Q.13	What are some of the ailments that this medicine treats?
	Q.14	How many pills does it say an adult should take per day?

behavior and verbal explanations as they worked through the HLA items. As the HLA was presented, children were asked first to identify each item and then to respond to a number of questions about it (see Table 9.2).

Results

Two analytic approaches were applied to the data. First, error analyses of individual items were made in order to examine variation in specific types of household reading knowledge and skill among children with different school experience backgrounds. The detailed behavioral notes on the subsample of 205 children aided us in the interpretation of the sources of children's errors. Second, linear modeling techniques were employed to determine the contribution of demographic and experience variables to the prediction of household and school literacy. Predictor variables included cognitive level, factual knowledge, gender, age, self-reported literacy activity, urban or rural environment, parental educational level, and SES. The highest grade level attained by individuals in both cohorts and current school status (in-school or dropout; Cohort 2 only) were included as predictors, as we were also interested in estimating the contribution of school experience variables to household and school literacy.[5]

Household Literacy Assessment error analysis

Table 9.3 presents the percentage of correct responses on individual items on the HLA for each cohort by school experience and chi-square statistics indicating contrasts in correct response rates across school experience groups within each cohort. As expected, the percentage of correct responses to the simple identification questions (Q.1, Q.4, Q.9, and Q.12) was quite high for all groups, ranging from 85% to 100% correct. The remaining 10 questions, however, produced considerable differences in performance across the groups. In general, children who had reached the highest grade levels for each cohort were more likely to give correct responses than other children in the cohort – a difference that was statistically significant for seven out of the ten questions for each cohort. This pattern of results supports the widely held assumption that school experience contributes (or transfers) to the acquisition and development of a fairly broad range of household literacy skills. However, such a broad generalization can be misleading, as considerable variability was found within detailed analyses. Specific outcomes for the four basic skill areas tapped by the HLA are discussed in the following section.

Knowledge of spatial print conventions: "What goes where." Many household literacy tasks can be made easier by knowing not only how to decipher print but where to look for it. This knowledge of spatial print conventions, or "conventional knowledge," appeared to be of considerable utility in answering certain questions on the HLA. One such question asked the child to indicate which of the two addresses on an envelope was that of the letter's recipient (Q.2). Following French postal tradition, the letter's destination is written in the center of the envelope, on the same side as the stamp, whereas the sender's address is written across the back flap. Nothing about the addresses would in and of themselves differentiate the sender from the recipient; rather, it is their placement on the envelope that signals this difference. Overall, just under half of the children in Cohort 1 answered this question correctly. In Cohort 2, school dropouts were less

Table 9.3. Percent correct and chi-square results on individual HLA questions by school experience within each cohort

Grade Sample Size	Cohort 1 (N = 218)				Cohort 2 (N = 453)			
	3rd (48)	4th (94)	5th (76)	χ^2	Dropout (68)	5th (141)	6th (244)	χ^2
Letter								
Q.1	97.9	97.9	100.0	——[a]	100.0	100.0	99.6	——
Q.2	56.3	43.6	47.4	2.04	54.4	69.5	65.2	4.60
Q.3	4.2	6.4	10.5	1.97	30.9	33.3	45.5	8.02[b]
Newspaper								
Q.4	85.4	95.7	93.4	——	97.1	95.0	97.1	——
Q.5	27.1	27.7	52.6	13.57[d]	57.4	61.0	73.8	10.25[c]
Q.6	22.9	22.3	32.9	2.76	32.4	37.6	60.9	28.14[d]
Q.7	29.2	44.7	55.3	8.10[b]	51.5	75.2	82.8	28.40[d]
Q.8	29.2	57.5	79.0	30.19[d]	82.4	86.5	91.8	5.76
Electricity bill								
Q.9	89.6	94.7	94.7	——	97.1	97.9	98.4	——
Q.10	0.0	1.1	19.7	26.42[d]	30.9	39.0	67.2	44.22[d]
Q.11	2.1	9.6	17.1	7.21[b]	47.1	46.4	67.1	19.16[d]
Medicine box								
Q.12	85.4	92.6	96.1	——	100.0	97.2	100.0	——
Q.13	0.0	21.3	42.1	29.32[d]	75.0	77.3	84.8	5.18
Q.14	8.3	33.0	46.1	19.26[d]	63.2	54.6	72.5	12.92[c]

[a]Simple identification questions (Q.1, Q.4, Q.9, Q.12) had extremely small cell Ns ($N < 5$) for incorrect responses; chi-square results are therefore inappropriate and are not reported.
[b]$p < .05$.
[c]$p < .01$.
[d]$p < .001$.

likely to respond correctly than children who were still in school, although this difference was not statistically significant. The detailed descriptions from the subset of Cohort 2 showed that more than one third gave the sender's address when asked to state the address of the recipient. Thus, although nearly all children in both cohorts appeared to know that three lines of writing on an envelope were likely to constitute an address (in the context of a questions about a "letter"), many did not appear to know the postal conventions that signaled which one was the recipient's address.

Performance on other HLA items also benefited from knowledge about what goes where. In order to find the newspaper's date (Q.5) or the medicine's prescribed dosage (Q.14), knowing where to look for such information could make a child's search for the correct answer appreciably easier. In the detailed observations of the subset of Cohort 2, we found that 22% could not find the newspaper's date, and 12% could not find the dosage instructions on the medicine box. This inability to locate appropriate information was apparently responsible for numerous incorrect responses (or no response) from many children. In the entire sample, only 36% of Cohort 1 and 67% of Cohort 2 gave the correct newspaper date; 32% of Cohort 1 and 66% of Cohort 2 responded with the correct medicine dosage. On both questions the proportion of children who gave correct responses was significantly greater for children at higher grade levels and for those who were not dropouts.

The electricity bill (Q.9–Q.11) provided a case in which decoding skills and knowledge of print conventions could be useful even without comprehension. When asked to state the name of the person billed (Q.10), computer-printed only in French, a child could obtain a correct answer without understanding French. First, to locate the information, the child could scan the bill in search of the Arabic label *'ism* (name); alternatively, if the child was familiar with the format of such bills, he or she could use knowledge about the conventional position of the billing name and address. If the child could decode the French letters, the name could then be recognized for what it was (a common Arabic name transliterated into the French alphabet) without further knowledge of the French language. However, this question proved to be one of the most difficult for Cohort 1: Only 7% of these children, nearly all of them in grade 5, gave correct responses. In contrast, 53% of the children in Cohort 2, predominantly those in sixth grade, gave the correct answer.

The electricity bill also presented a large array of numbers, detailing such information as volume of electrical power used, unit costs, and amount billed. Although these figures are labeled on the preprinted bill forms in both Arabic and French, the vocabulary items are specialized and typically unfamiliar to young readers. When children were asked to state the payment due (Q.11), many simply looked in the lower right-hand corner of the bill – the conventional position of the billing amount – and asserted that the figure printed there was the amount in question, without appearing to read the label above the numbers in their search for the amount. In total, almost 90% of Cohort 1 and more than 60% of Cohort 2 were unable to find and read this amount correctly. As we shall describe, obtaining the correct answer required knowledge of other print conventions as well.

Knowledge of monetary print conventions. Familiarity with conventions that represent monetary amounts in print can also be important in performing household reading tasks. In Morocco, the numbers printed on stamps, bills, and money represent a system of currency based on the centime (cent) and the dirham (100 centimes = 1 dirham). In oral usage, however, it is common to speak in riyals (from Spanish *real,* coin; 20 riyals = 1 dirham), a traditional unit of currency in use in most areas of Morocco, or in francs (in common usage, 1 franc = 1 centime). Thus, the amount of 10 dirhams may also be referred to as 200 riyals or 1,000 francs. This mixture of numerical systems often requires complicated on-the-spot currency conversions, as we saw in the vignette of Oum Fatima in chapter 1.

In order to read correctly how much it cost to send the letter (Q.3) and the billing amount for electricity (Q.11), a child also had to know the appropriate conventions for representing prices in print. It was possible for children to answer Q.3 correctly if they were familiar with mailing letters and knew that the cost of postage within Morocco was 80 centimes (an item of "common knowledge" at the time the study was done). Thus, when a child answered correctly without looking at the stamp, we prompted the child with the questions, "How do you know?" or "Where does it say so?" before his or her responses were recorded. Only those who cited the right amount and referred to the stamp received credit for a correct answer. Although many children knew the cost of a letter, the low rate of fully correct responses on this question for both cohorts (7% of Cohort 1; 39% of Cohort 2) reflects their limited understanding of stamps or how to read them. Illustrating this problem, 10 children from the Cohort 2 subsample volunteered the correct number on the stamp but gave the wrong denomination (riyals or dirhams instead of centimes).

Similarly, on the electricity billing amount, 10 children in the Cohort 2 subsample read the number correctly but provided the wrong denomination. Conversely, four children not only read the amount correctly in dirhams and centimes but went on to convert this amount to riyals. These children were displaying a skill of special importance in the mediation of monetary literacy tasks within the family: the ability to translate a printed amount into the currency most familiar to the nonliterate adult who would have to pay the bill.

Knowledge of specialized vocabulary. The importance of familiarity with special vocabulary items in order to complete household literacy tasks is illustrated by the medicine-box question that asks about the types of ailments treated (Q.13). Five such ailments were listed on the box, in both Standard Arabic and French. Citing any one of these ailments in Moroccan Arabic was scored as a correct answer; nonetheless, 76% of Cohort 1 and 19% of Cohort 2 could not do so. In the detailed analysis of the subsample, a lack of familiarity with the written terms was reflected both in faulty pronunciation of the Standard Arabic words (in which vowels are not represented in print) and in an inability to demonstrate comprehension (by providing the Moroccan Arabic equivalent), even if they managed proper decoding and pronunciation.[6]

The newspaper headline (Q.7) and article (Q.8) also required knowledge of Standard Arabic terms that lacked close translation equivalents in Moroccan Arabic. To achieve a correct answer on these questions, the student had to read the headline or article in Standard Arabic, then demonstrate comprehension by summarizing the information in Moroccan Arabic. Both cohorts performed relatively well on these questions. Forty-five percent of Cohort 1 and 76% of Cohort 2 gave the correct response to Q.7; 59% of Cohort 1 and 89% of Cohort 2 responded correctly to Q.8. For Cohort 1, as shown in Table 9.3, grade level attained was related to increased performance on both questions; however, for Cohort 2 this association was statistically significant only for Q.7.

Contextual knowledge. Household literacy often requires an understanding of the larger context within which literacy tasks are embedded – the relation of print to the world outside the text. The newspaper headline (Q.7) and article (Q.8) illustrate the role of such contextual knowledge. The headline reads: "Lebanon lives (through) a chain of destruction and death." A correct answer required some mention of the war in Lebanon. Because the word "war" did not appear in the headline, children had to draw on their own knowledge of current world events to understand its reference. Similarly, the short article about an airplane fire at Manchester Airport required some knowledge of geography to avoid confusion about place-names that might otherwise be unfamiliar (e.g., London, northwest England).

The newspaper advertisement provided a combination of real-world reference and the formulaic, telegraphic conventions of advertising language (Q.6). Children were asked to read the advertisement in which a store's business hours were indicated as "9:00 A.M. TO 8:00 P.M." and then to state whether it was possible to shop at that store at 9:00 P.M. Although few children had difficulty decoding the words of the advertisement, 74%

of Cohort 1 and more than 50% of Cohort 2 gave incorrect answers to the test question. Of the subsample of children whose responses were recorded in detail, most of those who answered correctly ("no") referred directly to the advertisement. Others who answered correctly actually gave textually wrong (but socially correct) explanations, such as "My parents won't let me out of the house at night." Most children who responded incorrectly to the question also called on explanations external to the text, such as "I can shop there at night if I need to buy something." In other words, despite having decoded the text of the advertisement correctly (as demonstrated by reading it outloud), many children failed to apply the printed information to circumstances outside the text, responding instead from prior knowledge or concrete social experience.[7]

Similarly, when asked about the proper dosage of medicine (Q.14), a large number of the observed children initially responded "one or two tablets in the morning and at night," without actually consulting the medicine box. For this reason all children were also instructed to "see what it says" before their final response was recorded. Of those who looked for, found, and began to read the printed dosage, the majority still failed to read beyond "one or two pills" to complete the dosage information with "three times a day." Again, grade level attained was positively associated with the frequency of correct responses on this question.

Predictors of household and school literacy skills

We now turn to the analysis of background variables and their importance in the prediction of household and school literacy outcomes. Correlation matrices of key variables revealed strong positive correlations between children's HLA scores and their school reading scores (AR/5; Cohort 1, r = .572; Cohort 2, r = .435; see Table 9.4). Correlations were also substantial between HLA scores and a number of background variables, including factual knowledge, cognitive skills, urban environment, gender (Cohort 2 only), grade level attained, and literacy activity in the home. Parental education, SES, and age were only modestly correlated with HLA scores. Because there were also substantial correlations among a number of key independent variables, including cognitive skills, factual knowledge, grade level attained, and literacy activity in the home, a multivariate statistical approach in the prediction of literacy outcomes was necessary.

The results of linear regression modeling procedures are summarized in Table 9.5. For Cohort 1, gender, age, parental education, and SES contributed little explained variance to the models of either household or school-based literacy and were therefore removed from further analyses in each model. The remaining five variables produced significant regression models for both household and school literacy (36.2% and 52.8% of total variance explained; both $p < .001$). The standard beta weights of the five predictors indicated substantial contributions of cognitive level, urban residence, level of literacy activities in the home, and grade level to both types of literacy measures. There were somewhat greater contributions of factual knowledge and urban environment to household literacy and of cognitive level and grade level to school literacy.

In Cohort 2, linear regression models on older children indicated a more diverse array of predictors across the two types of literacy ability. Again, parental education and SES explained no appreciable amount of variance for either household or school literacy and thus were removed from both models. The resulting eight-variable models explained roughly similar amounts of variance in household and school literacy (31.7% and 35.0%, respectively), although the sources of variance explained for each type of literacy differed considerably, as indicated by the beta weights for individual predictors (Table 9.5b). Cognitive level, factual knowledge, and grade level were significant predictors of both household and school literacy, but urban environment, (male) gender, and literacy activities were substantial predictors of household literacy only, and age and dropout status were important (negative) predictors of school literacy only. The negative influence of age may be understood in terms of the increased number of children who had repeated a grade in this cohort, such that the age variable reflected not only chronological age but also grade failure resulting from poorer overall school performance.

Given the importance usually attributed to school experience in fostering literacy skills, especially in low-literate settings, we also calculated the specific contributions of grade level and school dropout status to performance on household and school literacy tasks. Although grade level achieved was a significant predictor of both types of literacy, the contribution of adding this variable last to the model of school literacy for Cohort 1 was 10.5%, more than twice as high as its contribution to household literacy (4%). For Cohort 2, the unique contribution was about equivalent for household and school literacy (about 1%); school dropout

Table 9.4. Correlation matrix of key variables

(a) Cohort 1 (N = 218)

	1	2	3	4	5	6	7	8	9	10
1 HLA[a]										
2 AR/5	.572[b]									
3 Cog/5	.464	.571								
4 Gen/3	.414	.423	.487							
5 Urban	.285	.188	.216	.243						
6 Gender	.074	.051	.093	.030	-.076					
7 Grade	.412	.598	.418	.273	-.143	.025				
8 LitAct	.395	.480	.333	.317	.095	.094	.477			
9 ParEd	.121	.115	.055	.054	.255	-.014	.101	.167		
10 SES	.142	.105	.129	.163	.116	-.113	.132	.181	.283	
11 Age	-.203	-.186	-.063	-.047	-.271	.005	-.052	-.137	-.205	-.128

(b) Cohort 2 ($N = 453$)[c]

	1	2	3	4	5	6	7	8	9	10	11
1 HLA											
2 AR/5	.435[d]										
3 Cog/5	.335	.364									
4 Gen/5	.436	.437	.270								
5 Urban	.278	.140	.168	.078							
6 Gender	.226	.129	.230	.206	.009						
7 Dropout	-.226	-.404	-.191	-.231	-.081	-.071					
8 Grade	.351	.395	.273	.441	.130	.096	-.454				
9 LitAct	.299	.239	.159	.269	.085	.084	-.239	.210			
10 ParEd	.041	.069	.055	.052	.108	-.036	-.077	.105	.121		
11 SES	.120	.129	.035	.070	.316	-.022	-.117	.160	.064	.345	
12 Age	-.138	-.236	-.046	-.050	-.117	-.046	.416	-.046	-.169	-.198	-.186

[a] Abbreviations as follows: HLA = Household Literacy Assessment; AR/5 = Arabic reading score; Cog/5 = cognitive level; Gen = general knowledge; Urban = urban residence; Gender = male gender; Grade = grade level reached; LitAct = number of self-reported literacy activities in the home; ParEd = level of parents' education; SES = socioeconomic status; Age = child's age at time of HLA; Dropout = school dropout after grade 5.

[b] For $N = 200$, $p < .05$ if $r > .138$; $p < .01$ if $r > .181$.

[c] Due to missing data, all correlations for Cohort 2 that involve AR/5 are based on a pairwise N of 440.

[d] For $N = 400$, $p < .05$ if $r > .098$; $p < .01$ if $r > .128$.

Table 9.5. Predictors of household and school literacy skills

(a) Cohort 1 (N = 218)

Predictors	Household Literacy	School Literacy
Cog/3[a]	.185★★	.271★★★
Gen/3	.152★	.095
LitAct	.139★	.150★★
Urban	.232★★★	.151★
Grade	.260★★★	.408★★★
Adjusted R^2	.362	.528
$F(5,212)$	25.68	49.63

(b) Cohort 2 (N = 440)[b]

Predictor	Household Literacy	School Literacy
Cog/5	.146★★★	.207★★★
Gen/5	.244★★★	.268★★★
LitAct	.144★★★	.055
Urban	.189★★★	.023
Gender	.111★★	.000
Age	−.059	−.121★★
Grade	.134★★	.120★
Dropout	−.017	−.191★★★
Adjusted R^2	.317	.350
$F(8,431)$	26.52	30.59

Note: $★p < .05$; $★★p < .01$; $★★★p < .001$.
[a]Abbreviations: see Table 9.4.
[b]Reduced N is due to missing values.

status contributed about 2% to the variance in school literacy, but almost nothing (0.2%) to household literacy. As one might suppose, school experience factors of grade level (Cohort 1) and school dropout status (Cohort 2) appeared to be more important for the development of school reading skills than for household literacy skills. In sum, the models of household literacy and school literacy shared some important predictors (notably cognitive level and grade level), but they did not share all predictors, and the relative importance of shared predictors differed across the two models for each age and grade level.

What of the commonalities between literacy skills in and out of school?

Our investigation provides both general and specific information regarding the nature of household or functional literacy and how it is related to other factors in the young reader's environment and experience. As shown by the analysis of individual items of the HLA, performance on household reading tasks involves the integration of other types of knowledge – such as knowledge of print conventions, specialized vocabulary, and contextual knowledge – with the text-based reading skills normally stressed in most schools in Morocco and elsewhere. These results suggest that children who remain in school and reach higher grade levels acquire a variety of literacy skills that are also relevant to literacy tasks outside of school. At grade 4, about half of the children could read a newspaper headline and article with understanding, tasks that resembled typical reading exercises encountered in Moroccan schools. A large majority of children, however, were unable to perform tasks requiring knowledge of spatial, monetary, and advertising print conventions (Q.3, Q.6, Q.10, and Q.11), even after reaching grade 5. The performance of children in grade 6 was better on such tasks, however, suggesting that with time and in- and out-of-school experience many children acquire these skills as well. However, because almost half of all Moroccan children never reach grade 6, we can suppose that the large majority of Moroccan youth and adults lack many of such functional literacy skills.

The detailed descriptions of the performance of the Cohort 2 subsample also showed that reading as a means of acquiring information about the world was not a familiar goal for many children. Our informal observations suggest similarly that in Moroccan bus stations, large post offices, and banks, a person is much more likely to seek information by asking another person presumed to be more knowledgeable than by consulting an informational sign or placard. Learning to seek information through literacy – a key dimension of functional literacy – is not an inevitable outcome of school; rather, it may require explicit instruction.

Given the substantial correlations found between school and household literacy skills, it is clear that the two skill domains share important features. Indeed, the results of regression modeling showed that both household literacy and school literacy are supported by the child's cognitive level, factual knowledge of the world around him or her, level of literacy activity outside of school, and grade level reached in school. These results suggest that some school and household literacy skills are acquired to a substantial degree by similar cognitive and learning processes.

However, regression analyses also showed that a number of other factors contributed differentially to the two types of literacy (especially in Cohort 2). School attainment and dropout status, for example, were more potent predictors of school literacy than of household literacy, whereas an urban environment, male gender, and a high level of home literacy activity were more highly predictive of household literacy than of school literacy. It is possible that the urban environment provided more opportunities, and exerted more pressures, for a variety of reading skills outside of school. Newspapers and magazines were more readily available in an urban environment, along with billboards and street signs; and bureaucracies, and the paperwork demanded of their clients, were more plentiful in the urban setting.

The finding that male gender was associated with higher household literacy performance in the older children, despite equivalent performance by both genders on school literacy tasks, may be explained by girls' relative lack of opportunities for the practice of many everyday literacy skills. As they approach adolescence, Moroccan girls are more likely than boys to be constrained by traditional cultural restrictions in their exploration of the urban, literacy-rich street life. Moreover, in both urban and rural settings, traditional gender role expectations tend to result in boys being called upon more often than girls to perform "public" literacy tasks, such as reading bills and medicine prescriptions for other family members. On the other hand, the greater propensity for "private" book reading by adolescent females may allow them to maintain school literacy skills on a par with those of boys and even to improve such skills after leaving school (as we shall see in chapter 10).

That neither parental education nor SES was found to be substantially correlated with either household or school literacy skills lends support to the notion that opposing factors are at work in the Moroccan setting. Although educated parents are typically thought to be important for children's literacy, Moroccan families headed by nonschooled parents are more likely to depend on the literacy skills of their children, creating a practical motivation for the children to exercise such skills and a context in which to do so. The newly literate younger generation in Morocco is now taking on many of the responsibilities of traditional mediators of literacy, as described earlier, and they are also performing new tasks related to the expansion of bureaucratic structures (e.g., post offices, banks, utilities, obligatory national identity cards and family documentation). The acquisition of functional literacy skills among these new mediators of literacy is thus increasingly important in the pattern of statistical relationships.[8] We may expect further intergenerational changes to continue to take place over the coming years.

As for cross-sectional and correlational findings, we can only speculate about causal relationships between specific experiences and skill development. Longitudinal research following children from primary school to adolescence would provide clearer evidence of the apparent progression of household literacy skill acquisition – from schoollike prose skills to other skills that may be commonly employed yet seldom explicitly taught, such as verifying a bill or reading an advertisement with understanding. Experimental or intervention research could test the likelihood and direction of causality among the associations identified here and examine the "teachability" of household literacy skills to low-literates in settings such as rural Morocco. The work presented here may provide useful groundwork for more ambitious studies in this domain.

Implications for literacy in the real world

Our findings suggest that many of the literacy skills called for in everyday life may not be acquired even after 4 or 5 years of formal schooling, the boundary conventionally (and conveniently) used by the United Nations as the pragmatic dividing line between illiteracy and literacy. In Morocco, school experience and proficiency on school literacy tasks were clearly related to proficiency on household literacy tasks. However, such experience and proficiency explained only a portion of the variance in household literacy ability. In other words, although the reading comprehension skills stressed in school may well be necessary for other literacy tasks, they were not sufficient for successful performance of many common literacy tasks in the real out-of-school world.

As noted earlier, most of the Moroccan students in our study belong to the first generation in their families ever to attend public schools. Given the great disparity of literacy skills within these families, it is typical for such children to act as literacy mediators between their families and the society, taking on the new functional literacy tasks related to the continuing expansion of social, political, and economic demands. The acquisition of functional literacy skills among these new mediators of literacy is an increasingly important phenomenon in Morocco and the rest of the developing world.

Moroccan schools go a long way toward imparting the literacy skills needed outside the classroom. Nevertheless, the findings presented here suggest that explicit formal instruction utilizing everyday literacy tasks may be required to ensure the acquisition of these skills by persons who are most in need, especially given their expected roles as literacy mediators for entire families. In settings such as Morocco, women, the rural poor, and others with few opportunities to practice reading skills outside the school classroom appear to be at special risk for functional illiteracy, even if they attend school and even though they may be at little or no disadvantage with regard to school literacy skills. Such groups may require special attention if functional everyday literacy is to be achieved, not only to aid in the development of their own skills but also to provide tangible examples of the real-world functions of literacy in their own children's environment.

Finally, it needs to be underscored that the term *functional literacy* itself is in need of greater specification, as the functionality of a given skill depends on the particular contexts and purposes of its use. Literacy that is truly functional – that is, meaningful, relevant, and useful for accomplishing the tasks of daily life – is obviously difficult to define. Yet it is also clear that the study of school-based skills paints only a limited portrait of how individuals cope with everyday literacy demands. As we shall see in chapter 10, such demands themselves play a role in the maintenance of literacy across time.

Notes

1 The correlation is between what Kirsch and Jungeblut (1986) termed "prose" and "document" literacy, the former being more like school tasks (reading comprehension and interpretation of texts) and the latter understanding materials such as bus schedules and menus.

2 The MLP began long before the NAEP study of American youth (Kirsch & Jungeblut, 1986). But it is pure coincidence that each study developed its own measures of everyday skills: what we called "household literacy" and what they termed "document literacy." Our measures were much more restricted in

scope than the NAEP and were designed to reflect the cultural context of Morocco.

3 Over the 5 years of the study, missing data and the attrition of subjects resulted in sample losses totaling 38 percent of Cohort 1 and 8 percent of Cohort 2. Chi-squares by region, gender, and attrition status indicated that for Cohort 1, attrition of urban males was somewhat greater than that of other groups ($\chi^2 = 7.26$, $p < .10$); Cohort 2 attrition was essentially equivalent across region and gender ($\chi^2 = 1.45$; n.s.). Results of t tests on pre-attrition reading and cognitive scores between lost and retained subjects indicated significantly higher reading scores in the retained sample for both cohorts (Cohort 1, $t = 2.43$, $p < .05$; Cohort 2, $t = 2.488$, $p < .05$) and cognitive scores for Cohort 2 ($t = 2.97$, $p < .01$). Thus, attrition appears to have resulted in retained samples with somewhat higher school reading and cognitive (Cohort 2 only) skills than the original samples.

4 Although Arabic reading assessments were made over several years of the study, only the scores (AR/5) obtained in the spring immediately following the Household Literacy Assessment are discussed in the present chapter. Cognitive assessments utilized in the present study include children's short-term memory, concept identification, visual perception, and factual knowledge. Scores on the first three measures were combined into a single mean cognitive score; the factual knowledge score (based on 20 questions in 4 domains of content knowledge relevant to the Moroccan context) was retained as a separate score in all analyses. Although multiple cognitive assessments were made over the years of the study, only the most recent scores prior to the Household Literacy Assessment (spring of year 3 of the study) were employed in the present analyses.

Data from the structured interviews with parents (Cohort 1 only) and children (both cohorts) were also utilized in the analyses, as shown particularly in the regression statistics. Also utilized were children's self-reports of literacy materials and activities available and practiced in the home. These reports included the number of books in the home, whether the child borrowed or exchanged books with friends, and whether the child engaged in reading and writing activities other than homework.

5 In order to retain as many cases in linear regressions as possible, given randomly missing data points (affecting less than 5% of Cohort 1 and 2% of Cohort 2), we employed the standard practice of replacing missing values on each variable by the mean value of that variable among subjects of the same region and gender. Variables treated in this way included parental education (ParEd), SES, age, and factual knowledge (Gen); the procedure was only applied to independent variables for which the data set was incomplete.

6 As noted in chapter 2, Standard Arabic in everyday texts (e.g., newspapers) is typically unvoweled, rendering even simple decoding much more difficult and

mapping onto oral competency in Moroccan dialect that much more complicated.

7 Such answers evoke the work of Luria (1976) and Scribner (1975) on the responses of unschooled adults to problems posed in the form of logical syllogisms, but which were irrelevant to the commonsense practices of everyday life in their societies. In these cases, subjects tended to respond according to their everyday experiences rather than within the bounds of the problem presented to them.

8 An additional explanation for lack of effects of SES and ParEd is that by year 5 of schooling (for both Cohorts 1 and 2), the effects of background are rather dissipated, especially because of the large number of dropouts, many of whom have marginally lower levels of these two indicators.

10. School dropout and literacy retention: Out of school, out of mind?

Amina has to drop out of school

Four years after she finished her first year of school in al-Ksour, Amina Tamandat found herself in an unenviable situation. Her two older brothers were in *collège* (middle school), and her mother had recently had her fourth child, a baby girl. Amina, unlike some of her classmates, did not have a large number of aunts and female cousins living nearby. Her brothers couldn't help, as they were studying hard and doing part-time work with her father.

Who, then, would help her mother tend the baby, make meals for other extended family members, and generally help around the house? It is an old and familiar story in al-Ksour – and, indeed, across the Third World. Amina had to quit her studies, even though her grades were well above average. She would soon become one of the majority of youth in al-Ksour who drop out of school.

A literacy retention study would seem to be an anomaly. If one learns to read and write, can't we assume that these skills will be retained? As noted in chapter 1, it is not unusual for writers and scholars to say that the world is divided into the haves and have-nots with respect to literacy. Although we have argued that such dichotomies distort reality (as there are many types and levels of literacy), we have not yet addressed the question of skill retention; indeed, almost no one else has either. There has been occasional scholarly speculation as to the maintenance or loss of skill following

209

different types of instruction, even though most of us will remember (often with nostalgia and disappointment) just how much of our first foreign language we have forgotten.

As it happens, it is not all that uncommon for those with a fair amount of formal education to lament how much they no longer remember of what they feel they once "learned" in school. But this complaint usually focuses on facts rather than higher-order skills, such as thinking, problem solving, or literacy. In the West, where public schooling is plentiful, most of these wistful retrospections bring to mind distant memories of youth. In many developing countries, however, where post–primary schooling remains a relatively scarce commodity, skill retention and school dropout have become the center of a major controversy in education.[1] School dropout statistics are important because they are perhaps the best single indicator of the degree of school system efficiency. Dropout statistics are also a prime indicator of human resources development in cross-national comparisons that are issued regularly by international agencies. In this chapter we consider, first, the nature and extent of school dropout as it relates to what is learned in school, and second, the effects of dropping out on the retention of literacy skills.

Grade repetition and dropping out

In many countries the practice of grade repetition is a common means by which school systems attempt to "remedy" students' poor academic performance. It is a practice that can be costly in time and money, both to the repeater and his or her family and to the educational system itself. Evaluation of the relative costs and benefits of grade repetition for children's academic achievement and socioemotional development, therefore, constitutes a research area with important implications for educational policy. While not the main focus of the present analysis, grade repetition is an important aspect of schooling in Morocco, and it has often been linked to school dropout consequences in that country and elsewhere in the developing world.[2]

Grade repetition in Moroccan primary schools is determined by a national policy that combines normative rank ordering on academic performance with consideration of the capacity of higher grade level classrooms to absorb children promoted to the next grade. Through the first 4 years of primary school, grade promotion or repetition is determined on the basis of an annual meeting of classroom teachers. During this year-end meeting, children are ranked by classroom grade point average and then passed or failed according to a system whereby the lowest-ranked 10% to 20% percent of children in each grade level are usually required to repeat the entire (just-completed) year's academic program.[3] Promotion rates are set yearly on the basis of projected space availability in the higher grade levels of each school district, as well as on certain political exigencies.[4]

In the final year of primary school, grade promotion is determined by results on a single standardized examination, again according to space restrictions that may require as much as 50% repetition, as has been often the case over the past 20 years. Though some schools may opt to keep repeaters together in a single class, there is no formal distinction in classroom treatment or curriculum offered to repeaters and nonrepeaters. Only two grade repetitions are allowed by Moroccan law during the primary school years; children exceeding this number are candidates for school expulsion or dropout (though, in practice, some families seem to find ways around such strictures). Thus, the high rates of repetition are a principal cause of dropping out of school, more so than the voluntary (i.e., nonprescriptive) nature of dropouts in the United States, where students "choose" to drop out based on both failure and disinterest.

In sum, our study of school dropouts in the mid-1980s was conducted within a context where grade repetition and dropping out were widespread and unaccompanied by any specific remedial training (such as special education in the United States). Dropout rates were typically determined on the basis of the educational system's material infrastructure (i.e., number of slots available in a given grade for a given year), as well as on the relative academic performance of individual students. As a group, repeaters and dropouts were neither severely stigmatized nor, in many cases, clearly distinguishable by prior academic performance from other, promoted children. Our first effort, therefore, was to determine the extent to which actual academic achievement predicted staying in versus dropping out of school.

Research design for the dropout study

Because large numbers of Moroccan children drop out by the end of primary school (fifth grade), school leavers with about 5 years of primary education were the "typical" schooled individuals in the 1980s. Our data also showed that many of these school leavers were of average or even superior academic ability, though most fell within the lower half of the

Table 10.1. Description of the dropout sample

	Rural		Urban	
	Original	Dropouts	Original	Dropouts
Subsample size	178	31	286	41
Gender				
Boys	92	17	150	14
Girls	86	14	136	27
Mean years of age:	12.9	12.9	12.7	12.7
Cohort 2; total N = 464; total dropouts = 72				

distribution of academic achievement in a given grade. Thus, it would be inaccurate to say that this sample of school leavers was somehow exceptionally disadvantaged or of lower aptitude or intelligence than those children who stayed in school.[5]

The present analysis utilized a 3-year longitudinal comparison of literacy and academic skill retention conducted among fifth-grade school leavers from Cohort 2, whose performance was measured just months before school dropout and again roughly 2 years later (see Table 10.1). This sample of 72 school leavers was derived from a much larger sample of 464 children who were in fifth grade in 1983. As mentioned in chapter 4, an unusually high promotion rate of that year led to only about half the usual percentage of student dropouts; furthermore, quite a few children moved to other locations and thus were lost to the study. Fortuitously, the sample was distributed about evenly by gender and environment (rural vs. urban settings).[6] As with other domains of the project, we were particularly interested in those factors (pre- and postschooling) that might influence individual behavior. Thus, in addition to information on such background variables as parental education, socioeconomic status, and literacy activities in the home, we also included the individual's principal type of postschooling occupation (manual labor, training program, or home/unemployed) following school dropout. These data were supplemented by ethnographic interviews in the home.

Who drops out?

What factors push Moroccan children to leave school after completing primary education? The fact that we were able to obtain a robust matched

Table 10.2. Characteristics of promoted and dropout subsamples by region

	Promoted (in school)						Dropout (out of school)					
	Urban		Rural		Total		Urban		Rural		Total	
N	191		125		316		41		31		72	
%	60.4		39.6		100.0		56.9		43.1		100.0	
	Mean	S.D.	Mean	S.D.	Mean	S.D.	Mean	S.D.	Mean	S.D.	Mean	S.D.
AR/5	85.3	9.9	83.6	8.9	84.6	9.5	69.8	17.4	75.7	10.4	72.4	15.0
FR/5	61.4	16.5	61.0	15.4	61.2	16.1	39.9	14.8	49.2	13.5	44.0	14.9
Per/5	77.2	15.3	75.5	15.7	76.5	15.4	74.2	17.8	67.7	13.9	71.4	16.5
Math/5	81.9	15.2	80.0	13.9	81.1	14.7	69.9	22.3	75.8	11.7	72.5	18.6
Gender	.42	.50	.47	.50	.44	.50	.66	.48	.45	.51	.57	.50
Par Ed	1.57	.76	1.43	.63	1.52	.71	1.40	.59	1.33	.48	1.37	.54
SES	1.94	.65	1.50	.72	1.77	.71	1.82	.56	1.33	.61	1.61	.62
Refrigerator	.57	.50	.40	.49	.50	.50	.48	.51	.23	.43	.37	.49
Water	.90	.30	.73	.45	.83	.38	.85	.36	.50	.51	.70	.46
TV	.92	.27	.69	.47	.83	.38	.85	.36	.50	.51	.70	.46
Material Env	.80	.27	.60	.39	.72	.34	.73	.29	.41	.38	.59	.36
Arabic News	.84	.37	.74	.44	.80	.40	.60	.50	.47	.51	.54	.50
Comics	.78	.41	.76	.43	.77	.42	.56	.50	.47	.51	.52	.50
Books	.44	.50	.42	.50	.43	.50	.15	.36	.33	.48	.23	.42
Lit Env	.65	.24	.57	.25	.62	.25	.46	.23	.44	.28	.45	.25

Cohort 2; N = 388.

Note: Abbreviations are provided in previous chapters and in appendix 2. Sample size is reduced due to missing values.

sample based on year 5 Arabic scores (see note 5) indicates that literacy test performance was not the sole criterion for distinguishing children who remained in school from those who dropped out. For this analysis, then, we also needed to consider background factors that might be additional determinants of school dropout.

For the entire sample of fifth graders who were tested (i.e., before any had dropped out), we found that major differences existed in skill achievement in Arabic and French (see Table 10.2). Yet a variety of other variables also distinguished adolescents who stayed in school from those who dropped out. For example, three measures of home literacy environment produced significant mean differences. In addition to the number of books and magazines in the home (t = 3.52, p < .001), we found that familiarity with (knowledge of) Arabic newspaper titles (t = 4.70, p < .001) and French comic-book titles (t = 4.34, p < .001) were robust measures of how "connected" an individual was to the national (and international) literacy ecology. To understand such specific differences in a broader context, we used a multivariate logit modeling technique appropriate for a categorical dependent variable.

Four main achievement and five background variables were entered into an unordered logit model to measure the likelihood of dropping out.[7] Model A, in Table 10.3, shows that the nine variables accounted for 26.3% of the variance in predicting school leaving, with only three variables reaching statistical significance: French achievement, Arabic achievement, and literacy environment (a composite including number of books and familiarity with publications). When only these three variables were incorporated into logit model B, little of the variance explained was lost. Thus, literacy environment, but not other family or home factors, had the greatest effect on school leaving when controlling for achievement test scores and other background variables. Even though girls were somewhat more likely to become dropouts, these differences were much smaller than would have been expected based on the rhetoric about gender discrimination in Morocco. Regardless of school performance and parents' socioeconomic status, our analyses indicated that a stimulating literacy environment in the home was related to staying in school. Such results support our earlier findings that everyday literacy skills are also influenced by such environmental factors (see chapter 9). Involvement with specific aspects of the literacy environment, represented by indices for knowing the titles of comic books and Arabic newspapers, and the possession of at least 20 books and magazines in the home, was as good at predicting school

Table 10.3. Predictors of school leaving

Model A		Model B	
Predictor		Predictor	
FR/5	3.264[a]	FR/5	3.720[a]
Lit Env	3.010[a]	AR/5	3.488[a]
AR/5	2.918[a]	Lit Env	3.562[a]
Gender	1.384		
Math/5	1.351		
Env	1.075		
SES	.773		
Per/5	.529		
Par Ed	.238		
R^2	.263		.247
Cohort 2; $N = 366$			

Note: All variable statistics are t statistics.
[a]$p < .01$.

promotion as was the combination of all other social variables in the study.

Literacy environment also appears to be particularly important for children who were poor achievers in Arabic literacy. When we compared the lowest third of the dropout sample ($N = 23$) with low-achieving in-schoolers ($N = 20$) who had equivalent scores, the means for literacy environment were significantly different (.409 and .615, respectively; $t = 2.86$, $p < .01$). As might be expected for in-schoolers, literacy environment correlated positively with material environment, parents' education, and SES. However, for dropouts these correlations were negative. Parents with modest resource advantages apparently utilized them to create an enhanced literacy environment, enabling their children to stay in school; but such resource advantages apparently had little effect on the creation of a productive literacy environment for dropouts. For disadvantaged low-literate children, families that managed to keep their children in school created an educational environment that differs importantly from that of families whose children drop out of school, even when controlled for SES level. In other words, there may be substantial individual differences in how families construct learning environments for their children, factors that make a real difference in the future success of their children. These findings are intriguing and merit further investigation with larger samples of children in other countries.

How do dropouts compare to in-schoolers? The marginal value of staying in school

It might seem obvious to assert that by staying in school a child will learn more school-related skills than if he or she were to leave school. Yet, though this assertion is probably true across many different societies, we know relatively little about the relative or marginal value (to use the terminology of economics) for skill acquisition of staying in school compared with dropping out in developing countries.[9] By utilizing the matched subsamples of children, we had a convenient way to address the issue because the two subsamples had equivalent levels of school performance before one of the subsamples dropped out of school. Two years later each child was retested.

Overall, it was found that the in-school group, after two more years, performed significantly better than dropouts on the Arabic achievement tests.[10] But this finding does not tell the whole story. As with most longitudinal studies across the school years, it is necessary to increase the difficulty level of tests in order to accommodate the growing skills of the children in school. In this analysis half the sample did not go on in school; therefore, it was more psychometrically "fair" to retest the dropouts 2 years later on the very same items they were tested on in grade 5. Even though it was impractical to repeat the entire battery of grade 5 tests for the children now in grades 6 and 7 (though we did for the dropouts, as described later), we were able to create a smaller subset of linked items (taken directly from the grade 5 tests used 2 years earlier) that were used to assess both dropouts and in-schoolers.[11] To ascertain the marginal value of staying in school, we sought to analyze whether there were differences in literacy skills as a function of children's original performance level. For this purpose, we divided the grade 5 children into roughly equal sized groups matched for low, medium, and high Arabic reading (AR/5) scores.

As shown in Figure 10.1a, the data suggest that the differences 2 years downstream from fifth grade were somewhat less than one might have expected. For example, in Arabic literacy, there were no dramatic differences overall between children in school and those who had dropped out, but rather consistent gains among the in-school children in Arabic and French literacy.[12] Perhaps most interesting was that the children who were the high performers in Arabic literacy among the dropouts were hardly distinguishable from their in-school counterparts.[13] This analysis

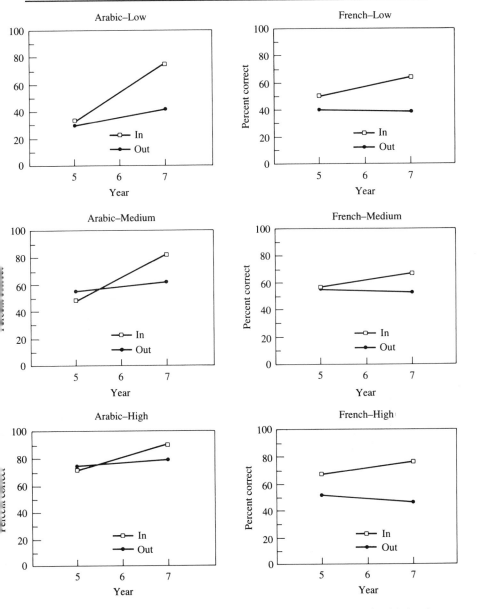

Figure 10.1a. Arabic and French literacy achievement compared across in-school (In) and dropout (Out) children 2 years after first testing, using a subset of linked test items (see text) from grade 5. Children are from subsamples matched (in high, medium and low groups) for equivalence on Arabic reading achievement in grade 5.

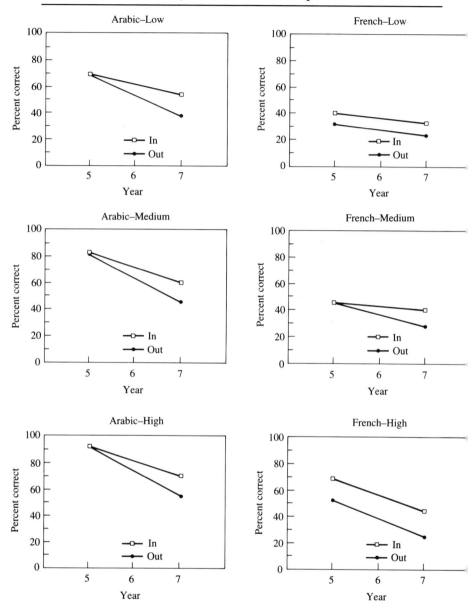

Figure 10.1b. Arabic and French literacy achievement compared across in-school (In) and dropout (Out) children 2 years after first testing, using in year 7 the entire battery of test items from grade 7. Children are from subsamples matched for equivalency on Arabic reading achievement in grade 5.

also provides some preliminary evidence showing that Moroccan children certainly did not "relapse into illiteracy" after 2 years out of school, a point to which we shall return.

With regard to year 7 literacy scores on the entire battery of test items, what is most relevant for our analysis is the achievement gap between in-schoolers and dropouts. Results showed that the gap remained roughly stable across levels: 16.1%, 14.9%, and 16.2% for low, medium, and high levels, respectively (see Figure 10.1b). These difference scores were similar for French achievement as well. Though lower performance (in terms of percent correct) in Arabic and French achievement was anticipated due to the increased difficulty of the year 7 test items, the fact that the lower performing dropouts from grade 5 did not plummet relative to in-schoolers again indicates that they were not in danger of "forgetting" their literacy skills in either language.

In sum, this comparison of matched subsamples of children who stayed in and those who dropped out of school provides some useful information on the marginal effects of schooling on first and second literacy skills in the years following grade 5. As expected, children who stayed in school tended to become more skilled in Arabic and French literacy. What was most surprising is how modest these gains were relative to children who had dropped out 2 years earlier. Such findings should give pause to policy-makers who assume that years in schooling necessarily result in concomitant and significant literacy gains. We return to this topic in chapter 12.

For the study of literacy retention, the present analyses are limited because they compare two groups – in-schoolers versus dropouts – who vary on many other home and individual features. A better approach would focus on a selected group of school dropouts, tracking them over time on both literacy performance and their everyday activities. It is to this analysis that we now turn.

A study of literacy retention

The vast majority of studies of human learning have focused on the acquisition of various skills and abilities. Relatively few have looked at the retention and loss of complex skilled behavior.[14] Indeed, in developmental psychology, the very idea that cognitive skills (as contrasted with specific items of factual knowledge) can be lost is anathema to such contemporary developmental theorists as Piaget and Vygotsky. This observation is supported by the almost complete absence of references to "retention" and "loss" of cognitive skill in Western textbooks on educational psychology. The few discussions available refer to modest "regressions" in psychophysical behavior, owing to the reorganization of specific cognitive functions (Bever, 1982).

In the international education literature, by contrast, retention of complex cognitive skills has been the focus of considerable discussion. For some years now, policymakers in Third World countries have been concerned that the limited years of primary schooling available for children – recall the high dropout rates in Morocco and elsewhere – might be insufficient for them to retain literacy skill. As noted earlier, it is sometimes claimed that at least 4 to 6 years of primary school for children is the intellectual human resources "floor" on which national economic growth is built. The argument is that a *threshold* number of years of education is required for more or less "permanent" literacy to be acquired by the individual (Fagerlind & Saha, 1983; Hamadache & Martin, 1987). In addition, some have suggested that attainment of literacy among 40% of a society's population is a necessary but not sufficient condition for economic growth and that 70% to 80% is required for rapid economic expansion (Anderson & Bowman, 1965). Both of these societal-level claims are based primarily on cross-national comparisons of literacy rates with economic growth (usually GNP), using national statistical sampling. However one calculates the relationships aggregated at the cross-national level, it has been observed that countries with high economic growth rates are those with a highly educated and literate population. And it is for this reason, and others, that international bodies such as agencies of the United Nations and the World Bank have called for greatly increased access to primary schooling in Third World countries.[15]

Within this line of reasoning, the concept of literacy retention (sometimes termed "cognitive retention"; see Simmons, 1976) is central, because what children learn and retain from their primary school years – and likewise for adults in nonformal education programs such as literacy campaigns – is thought to be what can be utilized in productive economic activities later on. When students fail to retain what is taught in an educational program, educational wastage (a term often utilized by international agencies; see UNESCO, 1984b) occurs because those individuals (children or adults) have not reached the presumed threshold of minimum learning that would ensure that what has been acquired would not be lost.

Thus, the retention of literacy is a key goal of educational planners around the world, particularly in Third World societies where only modest amounts of education can be (and are) provided to a large and growing portion of the population. In such contexts, it is critical to know how much is likely to be retained from a given input of instructional time and financial resources. Because basic literacy skills have been the prime educational target for most Third World countries, the possibility of literacy relapse – falling back into a state of illiteracy – has often been mentioned as a major problem in international policy documents (e.g., International Development Research Centre, 1979; Hamadache & Martin, 1987; Lind & Johnston, 1986).

Given the centrality of an assumption of literacy retention in policies governing basic education programs, it is surprising to find that only a small amount of empirical research has dealt directly with skill retention in developing countries (e.g., Cochrane & Jamison, 1982; Gadgil, 1955; Hartley & Swanson, 1986; National Educational Testing Center, 1982; Roy & Kapoor, 1975; Simmons, 1976). Unfortunately, most of these studies had flaws in methodology or project design, and none used a multiyear longitudinal design with subjects as their own controls – a feature that is central to the credibility of the study of skill retention.[16] In the Third World, an appropriate research design for literacy retention is complicated by the fact that primary school leavers may already be assumed to be among the lowest achievers in a school, making it difficult to compare their performance with the performance of those who remain in school.[17] A longitudinal design is required so that an individual's school achievement may be compared with his or her own performance in the years after leaving school.[18]

A second question concerns the "trajectory" of literacy and related skills among primary school dropouts. As noted earlier, fifth-grade achievement was chosen as the target level of school learning because it constitutes the stated minimum amount of schooling desired for the entire population in Morocco and in many other developing countries. Overall, we wanted to know whether students who drop out at the end of fifth grade lose, gain, or simply retain basic skills 2 years after school departure.

Research design

In this part of our work a longitudinal comparison of literacy and academic skill retention was conducted among fifth grade school leavers, whose performance was measured just months before school drop out and again roughly 2 years later. The sample of 72 school leavers (as shown in Table 10.1) was the same as that described earlier in this chapter. Children were assessed on four major types of academic performance: Arabic literacy skills, French literacy skills, mathematics skills, and nonverbal cognitive ability, as measured by the perceptual analogies task (Per; see appendix 2 for detailed descriptions). Additional information from the background survey questionnaires was also utilized. For the retention study, we categorized all individuals in terms of their principal type of post–primary school activity, work (mainly manual labor outside of the home), vocational training, or household work activities (including unemployed).

As discussed, we had hoped to have a substantially larger sample for this study but were hindered by the vagaries of failure rates and by the considerable mobility of these youngsters once they left school. Keeping track of the retention sample over the 2 years of the study, given that all had left school, was no easy task. This requirement is one of the principal reasons why longitudinal skill retention studies are so difficult to achieve.

Do dropouts retain literacy skills?

In order to determine whether the school leavers gained or lost in the four abilities we measured, a retention score was obtained as the difference in percent correct between first and second administrations of the same tests.[19] Curves for each ability are shown in quintiles (20% of the sample in each category) in Figure 10.2. Note that Arabic and French literacy scores tend to be mainly above zero (indicating gain), math scores are mainly below zero (indicating loss), and cognitive skills remain more or less steady around zero. Table 10.4 provides an analysis of overall retention for each skill and shows comparisons of the several sociodemographic contrasts used in the analysis. The most important results are that Arabic literacy was not only retained but actually improved following dropout, with modest significant gains in French literacy as well; math ability showed a significant decline, and the mean of cognitive ability remained unchanged.

Because the finding of significant literacy gains (as opposed to static

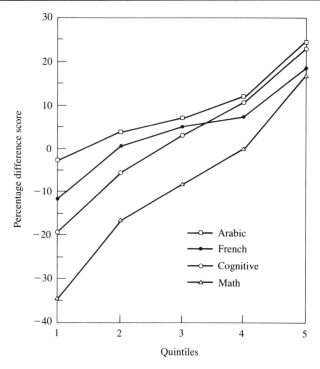

Figure 10.2. Retention curves (based on difference scores) for Arabic literacy, French literacy, cognitive skill (Per), and math. Curves are based on quintiles for each distribution of difference scores; points above zero indicate gain, points below indicate loss, and a score of zero indicates stable retention with neither gain nor loss.

retention or loss) is in stark contradiction to much of the accepted wisdom in the literature, it is important to explore the factors that may influence retention. The urban subsample gained more Arabic literacy than the rural subsample ($F = 6.094$, $p < .016$), and, though not statistically significant (due to the small sample size), female youth gained roughly twice as much as the males. Not surprisingly, school leavers who attended vocational training programs gained the most, most likely due to the additional literacy instruction provided in such nonformal education programs. Less obvious was the finding that female school leavers who stayed at home and were unemployed gained more than twice as much as males who worked as manual laborers.

Based on Western research on foreign language acquisition (Lambert & Freed, 1982), we expected that second (French) literacy would show a

Table 10.4. Retention of skills by subsample groupings of dropouts

Skill type	Sample (N)	Mean % difference	t Score
Arabic literacy	Total (72)	8.34[a]	7.28★★★
	Rural (31)	4.66	3.27★★
	Urban (41)	11.12	7.05★★★
	Male (31)	5.32	3.97★★★
	Female (41)	10.62	6.39★★★
	Vocational (32)	10.36	7.65★★★
	Work (16)	3.47	2.27★
	Home (23)	8.94	3.27★★
French literacy	Total (72)	3.45	2.87★★
	Rural (31)	0.38	0.19
	Urban (41)	5.77	4.14★★★
	Male (31)	0.99	0.54
	Female (41)	5.31	3.40★★
	Vocational (32)	5.71	3.47★★
	Work (16)	−2.07	0.72
	Home (23)	3.91	1.96
Math	Total (72)	−8.10	3.67★★★
	Rural (31)	−9.41	3.91★★★
	Urban (41)	−7.11	2.07★
	Male (31)	−11.29	4.15★★★
	Female (41)	−5.69	1.75
	Vocational (32)	−6.51	2.08★
	Work (16)	−13.02	3.36★★
	Home (23)	−6.52	1.40
Cognitive[b]	Total (72)	2.52	1.44
	Rural (31)	7.97	3.53★★★
	Urban (41)	−1.59	0.67
	Male (31)	2.44	0.90
	Female (41)	2.59	1.11
	Vocational (32)	−0.13	0.05
	Work (16)	3.44	0.98
	Home (23)	5.32	1.63

Note: $^*p < .05$; $^{**}p < .01$; $^{***}p < .001$
[a]Retention is measured by percentage gain or loss.
[b]Measured by perceptual analogies task (Per).

much different retention curve. Because French is not taught until grade 3, and then only for 1 or 2 hours each day, we expected (and found) that French literacy skills in our population samples were considerably inferior to those in Arabic. Yet urban and female dropouts showed gains overall in French literacy ability, with the urban female subsample showing the most impressive increase (7.03%; $t = 4.59$, $p < .001$). In contrast, the math assessment produced an overall performance loss, as well as loss in virtually all subsamples, with male blue-collar workers exhibiting the greatest decrease.[20] Finally, with respect to cognitive skill, there was no overall change, and the only subsample difference was the gain of rural children.

A correlation matrix showing the relationship between the major dependent and independent variables is presented in Table 10.5; regression analyses indicated that among sociodemographic variables, environment and SES were significant predictors of Arabic literacy retention, explaining about 15% of the variance (see Table 10.6).

Interpreting the retention results

Our findings shed new light on the question of literacy retention. In contrast to current belief, significant gains were made in Arabic literacy *after* school dropout, and this was the case for both urban and rural dropouts, males and females, regardless of type of postschooling activity. However, within this trend showing increased Arabic literacy, adolescent females tended to be the biggest gainers. This finding may seem counterintuitive, as it is often assumed that young Moroccan women have fewer opportunities for outdoor activities than men, and may be restricted in this Islamic society to activities in or near the household. However, our ethnographic observations showed that young women are more inclined to book reading than their male counterparts, as a way of having access to the world beyond their homes and via literacy, as one of the few routes to gainful employment. In other words, young Moroccan women have both motivation for and access to Arabic literacy, whereas same-age young men may be obliged to spend their time employed in manual labor with few literacy demands or opportunities.

Perhaps more surprising was the fact that females also gained in French literacy, again in contrast to men. In our ethnographic interviews, women mentioned how the French language helped them to achieve social status, as French presented opportunities to connect with modern life and Western social values. In practice, wage-earning jobs are more available to

Table 10.5. Correlation matrix of variables for dropout subsample

	1	2	3	4	5	6	7	8	9	10	11
1. Ar Ret[a]											
2. Fr Ret	.28										
3. Cog Ret	-.16	-.19									
4. Math Ret	.02	.11	.22								
5. Gender	.27	.21	.01	.15							
6. Environment	.33	.26	-.32	.06	.21						
7. Lit Env	-.07	.04	.09	.20	.16	.03					
8. Par Ed	-.01	.07	.04	-.18	.06	.06	-.15				
9. SES	.37	.10	-.09	-.12	.13	.39	-.30	.35			
10. Voc	.19	.21	-.16	.07	.11	.03	.07	-.09	.02		
11. Work	-.27	-.29	.04	-.15	-.61	-.09	-.21	.08	-.06	-.49	
12. Home	.04	.04	.13	.05	.43	.05	.12	.02	.04	-.63	-.37

Note: N's = 69–72. $r > .23$, $p < .05$; $r > .30$, $p < .01$.

[a] Abbreviations: Ar Ret = Arabic retention; Fr Ret = French retention; Cog Ret = cognitive retention; Math Ret = math retention; Gender (female = +); Environment (urban = +); Lit Env = literacy environment (7-pt. scale); Par Ed = parental education; SES = socioeconomic status; Voc = vocational training (yes = +); Work (employed, manual labor = +); Home (household work, unemployed = +). See text for further details.

Table 10.6. Hierarchical regression model of Arabic literacy retention among dropout subsample

Dependent variable: Arabic retention	Adj. R^2	R^2 chg.	F
Environment	.08	.08	6.80**
Environment + Gender	.10	.02	2.28
Environment + Gender + Par Ed	.09	−.01	0.16
Environment + Gender + Par Ed + SES[a]	.15	.06	6.05*
Environment + Gender + Par Ed + SES + Mat Env	.14	−.01	0.04
Environment + Gender + Par Ed + SES + Mat Env + Lit Env	.13	−.01	0.08
Environment + Gender + Par Ed + SES + Mat Env + Lit Env + Voc	.13	.00	0.93
Dropout Subsample, $N = 67$			

Note: *$p < .05$; **$p < .01$.
[a]When SES is entered first into the hierarchical regression analysis, $F = 9.83$ and adjusted $R^2 = .12$.

moderately educated women in the modern economic sector where literacy (and biliteracy Arabic/French) skills are used as key criteria for employability. Thus, for both social and economic reasons, young women may be more motivated to utilize and practice reading and writing skills than their male contemporaries. It should be noted, however, that French literacy ability among males was retained (i.e., remained stable) 2 years after dropping out, mainly in the urban setting. This environmental effect could not be due to initial differences between the urban and rural samples; indeed, a high initial fifth-grade score would tend to favor a loss in French literacy among urban school leavers. Rather, it would seem that the urban environment, with more French language, media, and print available, afforded more opportunity for practice. In addition, it may be that the relatively modest level of French skill acquired (such as basic decoding and word comprehension) was more resistant to loss.[21]

In contrast to first and second literacy skills, the school leavers showed a significant loss in our measure of math skills. Because the test involved a series of written problems using simple arithmetic notations (+, −, etc.), it may be that such symbols are forgotten, even though mental arithmetic competence is retained. Some evidence for a difference in mental versus written competence in children's math ability has been documented in the case of nonschooled Brazilian street children (Carraher, Carraher, & Schliemann, 1985). It should also be noted that there was no difference between urban and rural environments with respect to math loss, though males lost more than females, and those employed in manual labor lost the most. Overall, the loss in math skill is somewhat counterintuitive, because one would expect that everyday experiences – buying at the market, utilizing the post office, paying bills, and so forth – would favor the use of numbers by many of these youth, perhaps even more so among school leavers than those who stay in school. Further research efforts will need to distinguish between everyday and formulaic schooled-based math skills in order to explain better the present findings.

Finally, there was no overall change in cognitive skill (as measured by our test of perceptual analogy skills) following school drop out. This finding is fortunate, for it supports a major supposition of cognitive psychology, namely, that general intellectual skill is not particularly dependent on specific training or on schooling and therefore should not be especially sensitive to school leaving. In this context the significant gain made by the rural sample would appear to be an anomaly. However, previous research on cognitive development in Morocco also showed a consistent advantage in perceptual skills among rural children (see chapter 5; also Wagner, 1978b).

Cognition and practice

Although this part of the project was undertaken primarily to address the central policy concern of literacy retention, it is also possible to apply our findings to the matter of *practice* theories of cognition. Young adolescents in Morocco with only 5 years of formal schooling apparently received sufficient everyday practice, without continued school instruction in reading and writing, to maintain first and second literacy skills. Two conclusions follow from these results. First, sufficient everyday practice is available even in the low-literate environment of Morocco in order to retain such skills. Metaphorically speaking, if the mind is a muscle, then retention is just as likely with low-impact aerobics as it is with sprinting around a track.[22] Second, the fact that poorly learned and little-practiced second literacy skill in French was retained (and improved upon) indicates that the initial level of expertise attained before ending formal instruction is not necessarily linked to skill retention.

What does this study tell us about developmental and individual differences in cognition? Along with the findings among the Quranic practitioners (described in appendix 1), it supports the proposition that there are differences in cognitive ability as a function of experience and practice. Yet the results also suggest that practice may affect performance differently in conditions of retention from that typically studied in the acquisition of skill. Relatively low levels of practice can apparently be used to maintain low levels of original expertise in literacy. Also, intriguing gender differences were found, particularly in terms of gains in both Arabic and French literacy. These conclusions, based on a limited range of skills and in a milieu quite different from that of Western school culture, are in need of replication and extension across other age and skill levels. More generally, the whole domain of retention studies needs much more exploration – and not only in the Third World, as there are high rates of school dropouts in the United States and in other industrialized countries as well.

Literacy relapse: Myth or reality?

This study is one of the first explorations of the retention of academic skill by primary school dropouts in a developing country. If literacy and mathematics performance can be seen as a set of complex cognitive skills, then the abrupt termination of training may be seen as a test of what loss would occur as a function of little or no practice. This is precisely the form of argument used by international agencies when they talk of literacy relapse as a consequence of too little literacy training to ensure what has been called permanent literacy.

From an international policy perspective, the study provides some of the first evidence that literacy relapse may be a myth, at least if children can acquire a fifth-grade education. It may well be the case that most earlier studies of retention, which used cross-sectional methodologies, tended to miscalculate or exaggerate the degree of literacy relapse, because those who appeared to relapse into illiteracy may not have been literate in the first place. In the present case, Arabic literacy was not only resistant to loss but actually improved significantly for the sample as a whole, and modest gains were also made in French literacy. Particularly important was the finding of gender differences, with adolescent females gaining considerably more than males. This latter finding also calls into question certain prevailing attitudes about female literacy in the Third World, namely, that males make more use of literacy than females. Both ethnographic observations and the empirical results indicate that Moroccan females with a modest fifth-grade education are more engaged in literacy practices (in both Arabic and French) than their male counterparts.

Ramifications for an economics of education

Related to the notion of skill retention is human capital theory – the proposition that increases in such human skills as literacy, numeracy, and cognition have a direct impact on economic productivity (e.g., Behrman & Blau, 1985; Blaug, 1985; Psacharopoulous, 1973; Shultz, 1981). In one typical study it was claimed that "literate and numerate workers are more productive, and that education is valuable to workers because it can give them skills that increase their productivity" rather than simply as a credential (Boissiere, Knight & Sabot, 1985: 1029). The present findings raise an interesting issue made possible by the use of data that are typically unavailable to economists who rely on national samples of labor statistics for regression equations. Specifically, the employed dropouts in the Moroccan sample tended to have lower literacy and numeracy skills than the unemployed (generally female) subsample, even though both groups had the same level of education. Although it is fairly obvious that increased schooling leads to increased academic and cognitive skill levels, and usually to increased wage-earning capacity when analyzed at the national level, at a microanalytic level it seems to be quite possible for those with higher skills to be kept out of the work force on the basis of gender, ethnic, or regional bias. Such was the case for the Moroccan females in our study. Though this finding is not an unreasonable or even unlikely result in Morocco, it should give pause to those who would propose that the universalization and generalization of schooling will naturally (and necessarily) lead to a universalization and generalization of productivity.

When productive jobs are in relative demand, modest advantages in human and intellectual resources may not be the determining factors in obtaining productive work. Thus, making policy at the larger national level may obscure local effects and slippage in the generally strong correlation between education and employment. Because a major goal in international development is to understand parents' motivations for their children's education, it is essential to understand not only global relationships but also the effects on individuals. The present analyses indicate that such individual motivations and their consequences may be quite different from the projections formulated in Washington, Paris, or Rabat. If parents see only the reality of marginal economic utility in increased education for their children, the demand for education may remain lower than that needed for economic growth. This may be one way to explain the apparent leveling off in school enrollments observed in a number of developing countries (King, 1992).

Finally, the present findings suggest that Third World countries like Morocco have probably undertaken a reasonable policy of educational universalization if one goal is instilling "permanent" (even if low-level) literacy skills in children and minimizing wastage, or loss of what is learned. What is still unknown is whether there is a threshold below a fifth-grade education where failure to reach a certain minimum level of literacy will lead to a loss of skill after schooling. Certainly there is logic to this proposition, but one must also consider the fact that although French literacy ability was quite rudimentary after only 3 years of primary school instruction as a foreign language, it did not decline at all 2 years after schooling. Therefore, the hypothesis that the level of competence originally acquired in basic literacy is related to its resistance to attrition or relapse is still open to further inquiry. Another important area of retention research in need of further attention is that of the effects of short-term adult literacy training, for which little is currently known (Wagner, 1990).

As in earlier chapters, the present findings are a function of the particular sample selected, the cultural and linguistic context, and a host of other factors. Thus, it is important to emphasize yet again that literacy is neither a unitary nor unidimensional phenomenon that is either present or absent. Rather, literacy must be understood as a cultural practice that is subject to a wide variety of social and cultural forces that may increase or decrease the level of skill evidenced in any individual at a particular point in time.

Notes

1 The issue of school dropout has become a major interest of American educators as well, as trends of dropping out, particularly from high schools in urban disadvantaged communities, have increased dramatically during the 1980s (e.g., Fine, 1991).

2 For a review of linkages between repetition and dropping out, see UNESCO (1984a, 1984b) and Levy (1971). For an empirical analysis of the academic consequences of grade repetition, see Spratt and Wagner (1992), from which parts of this section were drawn.

3 Since the time that this study was conducted, a program of educational policy changes has been instituted in Morocco to improve the flow of students through the primary years and to reduce what is called "wastage" in educational expenditures. These changes include the gradual lowering of repetition rates at all grade levels and the complete removal of the standardized examination at the end of fifth grade, starting in 1990. There has also been serious discussion of allowing children to repeat only those aspects of their performance in need of remediation, although to our knowledge this has not yet been put into effect.

4 It is not unusual for major political crises, such as a rise in bread prices, to trigger social protests that ultimately have consequences for the rate of promotion in elementary through university classrooms.

5 In the present study, we found it useful to construct a "matched" sample of school dropouts for certain analyses; one finding was that the two subsamples (dropouts vs. those promoted normally) compared quite well with each other on academic skills. A comparison was made of 64 children from the dropouts sample with the same number of children who remained for 2 more years in school with both groups matched on Arabic literacy ability. These matched samples differed only to a minor extent in terms of literacy, math, and cognitive skills. As expected, 2 years later, the in-school group was superior to the matched dropout sample on these same measures, owing to additional instruction in literacy and related skills. Similar results were found (see Spratt & Wagner, 1992) in which children who progress normally to higher grades had consistently higher literacy scores than those children who stayed in school as

many years but had repeated one or more grades at least once, thereby receiving a lower level of curriculum. On the other hand, repeaters performed at least as well as non-repeaters who were in the same *grade* of school – that is, where repeaters had extra years of instruction to learn the same material as the non-repeaters.

6 Six out of the 72 children were assessed only 1 year out of primary school. Because the scores of these 6 did not differ from those of the other 66 children who were tested 2 years beyond school dropout, these 6 children were considered to be part of the larger sample.

7 Logit analysis can be thought of as an approximation of multiple regression analysis when the dependent variable is categorical. Unlike multiple regression, logit produces unbiased estimates of the partial effects on categorical dependent variables. Its main advantage over the more familiar technique for qualitative dependent variables, discriminant analysis, is its ability to generate partial *t* scores. It can also approximate the R^2 in multiple regression based on a similar calculation of explained variance. Table 10.3 presents the partial *t* statistics and the approximate R^2 [1 – (log likelihood at convergence/initial log likelihood)] for the combined set of nine variables and for two selected subsets of predictor variables. My thanks are due to Gary Klein and Jennifer Spratt for their assistance on the statistical analyses in this chapter.

8 Moroccan government data show that girls and rural dwellers are less likely to complete upper levels of education than are boys. Though logical from a socioeconomic and cultural perspective, it is unclear what the national statistics represent. In our study we had considerable difficulty in separating those who simply transferred to other schools from those who truly dropped out for academic reasons, though we tried to do so through personal interviews with students, parents, and teachers. Most government statistics are unable to make such distinctions.

9 We know considerably more about the employment profiles of more highly schooled individuals, most of whom tend to have better paying and professional jobs. For more discussion and details on cross-national comparisons, see World Bank (1980, 1988).

10 By grade 7, the difference between these groups was highly significant (AR/7; $t = 10.1$, $p < .001$).

11 The Arabic and French tests used in this analysis were composed of five Sentence Maze and five Paragraph Comprehension test questions administered in years 5 and 7 in each language. Thus, the number of test items employed here was considerably smaller than for other parts of the retention studies, but a number of findings were, nonetheless, statistically robust.

12 The differences shown were not statistically significant, owing to the variability among the small set of test items.

13 Ceiling effects, as scores approached 90%, may also have obscured real differences among these relatively high-performing children. On the other hand, the rate of achievement gain among dropouts was relatively constant across the different achievement subsamples. Note also that the large gains by the low group could be due to the statistical effect of regression toward the mean.

14 In comparative psychology, specialists have studied learning and forgetting in laboratory animals in mazes, and experimental psychologists, from the days of Ebbinghaus, have employed college sophomores to memorize nonsense syllables in an attempt to discover basic forgetting rates in adults.

15 Others, such as Fuller and Heyneman (1989), claim that it is not only the numbers of children who attend a given level of schooling that matters but the quality of the schooling received as well. They provide strong evidence from a wide variety of countries that suggests major qualitative differences for given levels of schooling achieved.

16 One of the most statistically sophisticated studies of school dropout was conducted by Hartley and Swanson (1986) on Egyptian children. Unfortunately, the operationalization of certain variables in their study, such as intelligence, was based on tests in which we can have only limited confidence. Though verbal intelligence was the most salient predictor of school leaving in their study, it still left about 90% of the variance unexplained. Several other variables depicting school influences, family influences, and attitudes had weak to moderate predictive strength. Their study also failed to follow the trajectory of dropouts beyond a single year out of school, and required excessive statistical controls to overcome serious problems in sampling methodologies.

17 Naturally, this is not always the case. Earlier in this chapter we noted that in many cases school dropouts were as competent in Arabic literacy, at the time they left school, as those who remained in school.

18 Retention of academic skills during the summer months between school years has received some attention, and summer intervention programs in the United States have been suggested as a means of remediation for children at risk for dropping out of school (Heyns, 1987).

19 Due to the possibility of regression toward the mean and to possible ceiling effects in some subjects' scores, a more conservative, adjusted retention score was also calculated that took these potential biases into account. For this purpose, an adjusted score was calculated as follows: (year 7 − year 5)/(N − year 5) for improvers and (year 7 − year 5)/year 5 for decliners. An increment of .01 was added to N to prevent 0 denominators, and balanced with an increment of .01 added to year 7 for improvers and nonchangers. This adjusted score gives less weight to gains made by low year 5 subjects and greater weight to small losses made by them. It also gives greater weight to small gains

made by high year 5 subjects and less weight to small losses made by them. Thus, the measurement is designed in favor of locating a low-level or top-level threshold level. The results using this more conservative measure, however, did not differ significantly from the results that used mean difference scores.

20 It should also be noted that the math test was substantially shorter than the literacy tests, thereby reducing test reliability and statistical variance.

21 Of course, the argument that low levels of French skill are resistant to loss can be pitted against the data for Arabic skill retention, where performance was much higher but where the retention curves were roughly the same as for French. In other words, the present data do not support the notion that either initial high or low skill levels are retained better over time. Though there is a fair amount of research on this topic in foreign language learning and retention (Freed, 1991; Lambert & Freed, 1982), there is almost no relevant information on literacy skill retention in a second language.

22 The concept of mental practice is becoming again a focus of social science research. From such disparate works as sociologist Pierre Bourdieu's *Outline of a Theory of practice* (1977), to anthropologist Jean Lave's *Cognition in Practice* (1988), to psychologist Howard Gardner's *Frames of mind* (1983), we see not only a renewed effort to describe what people do in their everyday lives but also the possible consequences of doing these things repeatedly. Practice, of course, is not an entirely new topic. Ever since the first recorded studies of human psychology (the Greeks' "method of loci" for remembering long folk stories is a well known example) observers have at least implicitly accepted the metaphor of the mind as a muscle – the more you exercise it, the stronger it becomes. From Ebbinghaus's pioneering work on human memory to more recent research on the Suzuki method for learning the violin, it is clear that social scientists have long believed that mental practice is at the heart (or, rather, the head) of skilled behavior.

11. Literacy and poverty

Living in the fonduk

The Benarba family is one of thousands of families who move from the countryside to urban Morocco each year. As in the usual pattern, Mehdi Benarba, the oldest son, preceded the rest of the family, asking them to join him more than 2 years after he got a job working as a waiter in a Marrakech restaurant. In this growing metropolis, once an oasis stopover on the Saharan caravan routes, and where the center of the *medina* has been continuously inhabited for centuries, new migrants from the mountainous (and mainly Berber-speaking) surrounding regions tend to drift into semiabandoned, dilapidated *fonduk*s (literally horse stables), designed long ago for the animals and merchants of the caravans that made their way to do business in the great bazaars of Marrakech.

The Benarba family moved into one of these *fonduk*s, and there seems little chance of their leaving in the near future. Their two younger boys, age 6 and 9, have not gone to school, but are working as apprentices making small tambourines for the tourist trade. No one in the Benarba family has gone to a government school, though most of the men had some Quranic schooling in their youth. The Benarbas know others who have gone to school, but say that most of their *fonduk* neighbors complain that "nothing comes from schooling but laziness, bad attitudes, and lack of useful skills."

The Benarba family is not typical of the statistical economic norm in Morocco, but it represents a stable, 10–20% part of the population that remains in educational poverty. Formal education and literacy are among the ways in which governments strive to develop the human capital of their nations and to improve the productivity of their citizens. In addition, education and literacy have been associated with lowered birth rates, increased life expectancy and reduced infant mortality, and access to general health services. In Morocco, educational investment has constituted the largest portion of government expenditures in the social sector in the years following independence, and few would deny that considerable gains in education have been made. Nonetheless, there are major demographic disparities in educational participation and in literacy, such that large segments of the population, particularly among the poor, have received little or no education.

This chapter examines the available demographic data on the national distribution of education and literacy in Morocco and its relation to the educational needs of the poorest sectors of Moroccan society. In the discussion educational indicators serve as the basis for an analysis of critical policy issues, with a focus on segments of the population currently living in poverty.

The term *educational poverty* is employed here to indicate a level of human capital investment so low that individuals of working age lack the basic literacy and numeracy skills required to enter productive sectors in the labor market. Within the poor and especially the poorest (or what we term the ultra-poor) sectors of society, educational poverty can present a tenacious intergenerational cycle. First, some unschooled parents view schooling as a low-priority activity of questionable value and may not enroll their children in school even when it is available. Second, although many unschooled and illiterate parents desire more and better schooling for their children, nonetheless, they may lack the communication networks required to exert social and political pressure to obtain such schooling. We have already noted that children of educationally impoverished parents, with less home support for their studies, are also at higher risk for grade repetition and early school dropout. Furthermore, families living in educational poverty are least likely to gain access to health and other social services and tend to remain among the least productive elements in the Moroccan economy. Even though increasing numbers of children from poor and ultra-poor households now attend school as a consequence of the dramatic expansion of elementary and secondary schooling that has taken place over the last two decades in Morocco, educational resources for large segments of the population remain limited and underutilized.

Recent studies and our own observations suggest that the ultra-poor, both in urban and rural areas, are at particular risk of continued educational poverty. According to Moroccan government estimates (Direction de la Statistique, 1984), about 90% of heads of the poorest households (defined here as those households expending less than 7,200 dirhams [DH; U.S. $1,000] per annum) reported no formal schooling whatsoever. This exceptionally low level of education not only affects economic productivity but may be assumed to touch younger generations as well, through educationally impoverished environments in the home.

The role of education in the alleviation of poverty and ultra-poverty

The relationship between education and economic development has been the focus of a tremendous amount of attention. Various claims and counterclaims have been offered about the strength and direction of this relationship, but most would agree that education is a central human resource and one that can have particularly positive outcomes among the poor, in terms of fostering literacy, economic growth, reduction of fertility and child mortality rates, and improvements in basic health and nutrition (World Bank, 1980). Furthermore, in a calculation of the economic rates of return (units of output per unit of input) to education, an analysis of 30 developing countries showed that primary schooling produced almost twice the rate of return as secondary and higher education (World Bank, 1980: 17). Such analyses have led many multilateral and bilateral agencies to opt for increased investment in primary education in countries like Morocco. In the same World Bank study, it was also found that, in countries with both high (above 50%) and low (below 50%) adult literacy rates, the rates of return to education remained about constant; this finding indicates that the national level of education (as shown by the adult literacy rate) does not necessarily dilute the impact of marginal improvements in primary education. The latter point is important, as it has been argued in Morocco and elsewhere that additional investments in primary education may have little impact because the level of basic education has grown and there are numerous "educated unemployed." The counterargument in this cross-national analysis is that there may be commensurate shifts in production patterns toward more skill-intensive goods, thus necessitating increased education-related skills.

Though there seems to be consensus on the general importance of education for the alleviation of poverty, there is much less agreement as to specifics. What kinds of education should be available for whom in a country like Morocco is a question that many have sought to answer. However, it is useful at this stage to focus on a second, related issue, that of distinguishing the poor from the ultra-poor with regard to the specific effects that educational factors may have on each group. In other words, to what extent does increased schooling (and concomitant increases in skills such as literacy and numeracy) impact differentially on the poor and the ultra-poor? Evidence suggests that the educational rate of return is relatively constant across countries, but it is less clear that it remains constant across contexts and socioeconomic classes within countries. In Morocco, it is known that the poorest households are also those with the least education. Individual level data are not available, however, on the rate of return from additional inputs of education among the most educationally impoverished.

Taking the household as the unit of analysis, the argument could be made for attaining within each household a minimum level of literacy skill and knowledge necessary for engagement with, say, the literate bureaucracy (such as government agencies) in Morocco. Hypothetically, at least one person in or near each household should be able to read in order to accomplish such elementary tasks as health care (reading/understanding medicine labels), postal services, the use of infant formula, and literacy-based services for the illiterate user. Naturally, a second or third literate household member could further facilitate the process of literacy negotiation through greater availability and would enhance the literacy ecology of the child. However, the benefits gained with each additional literate individual in the household are likely to be of a smaller magnitude (in rate of return) than those obtained from the first literate individual. Because the educationally impoverished are by definition those households with no literate members, it follows that these households should benefit most from even a marginal increase in education and literacy. Over two decades, it is this logic that has driven international agencies to provide significant investments for expanded access to primary education in Morocco.

Current demographics of adult literacy in Morocco

As we described in chapter 2, Morocco has a long history of literacy through the strength of its Islamic educational institutions, though the number of adults capable of using literacy for everyday economic func-

Table 11.1. Principal education indicators at the national level in Morocco, 1970–1988

Indicator	1970	1975	1980	1985	1988
Adult illiteracy rate (% of pop.)	75		65		60
Males (% of male pop.)	63		51		40
Females (% of female pop.)	87		78		80
MOE budget (mil. DH)	669	1,898	4,357	7,697	9,454
Portion of govt. budget (%)	16.0	12.0	18.3	18.4	19.2
Adult educational attainment[a]					
No education (% of pop.)			78		72.2
Islamic education (%)			5		8.1
Primary education (%)			9		8.4
Secondary education (%)			5		8.4
Tertiary education (%)			1		2.4
Unspecified (%)			2		0.5
Public primary education					
Enrollment (% of age group)[b]	46		67		72
Female enrollment (% of students)	31.7	35.5	36.7	38.1	38.4
Dropout rate (% of students)				10.5	9.5
Final examination pass rate (%)			34	49	61
Expenditures (% of MOE budget)		37.1	34.0	33.9	34.4
Per-student recurrent exp. (DH)		395	592	974	1,218
Public secondary education					
Enrollment (% of age group)[b]	11		27		31
Female enrollment (% of students)			37.5	39.6	40.3
Dropout rate (% of students)					11.6
Final examination pass rate (%)					36.1
Expenditures (% of MOE budget)		49.0	48.8	48.6	45.1
Per-student recurrent exp. (DH)		1,392	2,160	2,598	2,622
Tertiary education					
Enrollment (1,000s)		35.0	86.7	143.0	169.2
Enrollment (% of age group)				7.3	
Female enrollment (% of students)		19.5	25.0	33.5	34.2
Expenditures (% of MOE budget)		13.9	17.3	17.5	20.4
Per-student recurrent exp. (DH)		4,682	7,428	7,727	8,457
Vocational and technical education					
Enrollment (1,000s)				66.3	74.2
Female enrollment (% of students)				28.2	35.8

[a]1980 figures actually represent 1982 census figures.
[b]1970 and 1980 figures calculated from 1971 and 1982 censuses; total primary (age 7–12) and secondary (age 13–20) school-age populations estimated from census figures.
Sources: World Bank, 1988, SEP, 1988; SES, 1988; ASM, 1988; census, 1971, 1988.

tions was historically limited to a small proportion of the male population. Current official estimates of adult illiteracy rates in Morocco (estimated as those with less than a fifth-grade education) vary somewhat: from 60% (40% male and 80% female according to the World Bank, 1988; see Table 11.1) to a rate of 65% (51% male and 78% female in the 1982 Moroccan census.). Appreciable reductions in illiteracy are evident when such rates are compared with census data from 1960 (87% total, 78% male, and 96% female over age 10) and 1971 (75% total, 63% male, and 87% female over age 15). Census data also show large differences between urban and rural adult illiteracy rates; in 1971, these rates were 61% and 88% for urban and rural populations, respectively, whereas in 1982, they were 44% and 82%. Though these data must be considered somewhat unreliable because no empirical measurement of literacy was made during the census process, our own fieldwork suggests that it is reasonable to accept the existence of large and persistent differences between male and female and between urban and rural rates of literacy skills. Differences of more than 30% between these aggregate rates remain, despite an overall reduction in the national rate of adult illiteracy through increased school access and participation.

Despite these gains over the past decades, we estimate that the national literacy rate will likely reach asymptote by the year 2000, at about 50% of the adult population. This estimation is based on educational participation statistics for the Moroccan national population of children who reached 7 years of age between 1981 and 1988. Of these children, roughly 25% (principally from rural areas) never enrolled in school; another 20% will have left school before reaching the fifth grade; and 25% will have failed the primary school completion examination (*shahada*), which controls access to secondary school.[1] In other words, 60% to 70% of all children who were of primary school age in the 1980s will not receive more than a fifth-grade education. Given these trends and current budgetary constraints, and despite efforts to increase first grade enrollments and to reduce the fifth-grade failure rate to 20%, it remains unlikely that more than half of the adolescent population in the year 2000 will have received any postprimary education. All indicators suggest, moreover, that this large group of non-schooled and partially schooled adolescents is composed primarily of the poor and the ultra-poor.

In an effort to reduce adult illiteracy, the Ministere de l'Artisanat et des Affaires Sociales (MAAS) has instituted a literacy campaign that has, according to the MAAS (1988), enrolled approximately 120,000 persons since 1981 (about 40,000 persons in 1987 alone). The program consists of

3 contact hours per week over a period of 50 weeks, and the curriculum includes basic literacy and numeracy skills. Unfortunately, as is typical in most campaigns of this kind, virtually no information is available about the effectiveness of this type of program in actually providing needed skills; indeed, it is not clear from the statistics what percentage of enrollees ever completed the literacy program. According to the MAAS, about half the enrollees in the campaign are women, suggesting that such programs do attract women and therefore have the potential to reduce the gender gap in adult literacy.

Educational policy reform trends

Educational policy in Morocco since independence can be characterized as a combination of ambitious planning and changing focus, resulting in both progress and disappointment.[2] As Morocco's economic fortunes have oscillated, so too have educational policy concerns, from the expansion of primary education, to the development of higher education, and back to the current focus on basic education, adult literacy and vocational training, and efficiency in the educational system.

Recent educational reform trends, although not specifically targeted toward the poor, have important potential implications for the educational participation, attainment, and job training of those in poverty. These trends have included efforts to attain universal primary education, to improve the efficiency of the system through increased promotion rates, to extend the length of basic education from 5 to 9 years, and to coordinate the output of educational and training programs with the manpower needs of the nation.

High rates of grade repetition and school dropout, as noted in chapter 10, have led to great inefficiencies, such as the almost 9 years (on average) of educational investment needed to produce a single fifth grade elementary school graduate in the existing educational system. Recent efforts to reduce repetition rates through promotion policy modifications and educational quality improvements are reflected in an increase in the number of students who remain in the system and reach secondary and postsecondary levels of education. Competing concerns, however, such as resistance to lowering grade promotion standards (PDES, 1968: 597; Souali, 1986) and attention to the development of higher education in the 1970s, have tended to slow progress in these areas.

Efforts to generalize primary education fully have been broadened to include extending the length of basic, obligatory schooling. As early as

1973, a long-term goal of 8 to 9 years' obligatory schooling was articulated by the government (Ministry of Education, 1986). The current proposal for 9 years describes a system that would be divided into a 6-year basic cycle and a 3-year specialization in either an academic/technical or a vocational track (for 80% and 20% of first-cycle graduates, respectively). Academic and technical students would be offered a second, optional 3-year cycle leading to the *baccalaureat* (Ministry of Education, 1986). As of 1989, however, obligatory schooling remains at the fifth-grade primary level, although *shahada* passing rates have risen steadily, from a long-stable 35% before 1984 to more than 61% in 1987 (SEP, 1988: 52).

Distribution of educational resources and educational outcomes

Evaluating historical trends and the current distribution of educational resources and educational participation across population sectors requires an examination of both resources provided and outcomes achieved. This section examines such trends and distributions in several ways: at the national level, in international perspective, and by urban and rural environment, economic region, and gender. Educational participation in Morocco tends to vary in relation to the last three factors, owing to differential access to educational resources and to cultural and economic considerations that may influence educational demand and the perceived opportunity costs of education. Thus, an examination of the distribution of education and literacy requires attention to the distribution of resources provided, to the demand for such resources, and to obstacles that impede their utilization.

A variety of indicators are useful in identifying disparities in the distribution of educational resources. Resources reflect the supply, or "input," of educational support provided by the government. The principal indicator of such resources used in the present discussion is the Moroccan education budget, examined with regard to its portion of total government expenditures and its distribution across educational levels and population sectors. The rate of teacher certification is also a useful indicator of educational quality, because it represents a substantial input of government education expenditures.

National educational participation rates and outcomes reflect both supply (i.e., relative ease of access) and individual demand (i.e., the perceived benefits and opportunity costs of education, such as forgoing a job).

Indicators of educational outcomes include estimated adult literacy rates, educational attainment rates, ratio of educational enrollments to the population, dropout rates, and school level completion rates. Each source of data for these analyses has its strengths and limitations. Literacy rates in Morocco, as in most other countries, are based on self-report census information regarding school attendance. It is typically inferred from such data that those who have attended or completed primary school are literate, and that those who have not are necessarily illiterate, resulting in unknown distortions (see further discussion in chapter 12). Educational enrollment figures, similarly, provide an indication of educational participation, but they may overestimate the real level of educational participation because they do not indicate rates of actual school attendance or subsequent dropout. Our observations suggest that school attendance rates differ across population subgroups, sometimes resulting in very different amounts of time actually spent in school despite similar participation rates. Rural areas, such as al-Ksour, also exhibit seasonal attendance fluctuations due to children's participation in agricultural activities.

It must be stressed that the available information, on which the following discussion is based, is insufficient for a comprehensive examination of poor families' access to and participation in public education. Missing are such critical data as school enrollment rates by students' expenditure class (i.e., SES) and within economic subregions or provinces; government budgetary inputs per capita by economic region or province; and person-level (rather than aggregate) analyses of the relationships of education, literacy, and job training to health and employment indicators. Such data would enable researchers and planners to pinpoint better areas in need of special intervention and policy changes. With these limitations in mind, we can still try to identify specific avenues for policy change in education and adult literacy with implications for poverty alleviation.

Government spending and educational participation

The evolution of national budgetary allocations for education is a useful indicator of the supply and expansion of educational programs. In the early 1970s, spending on education was about 16% of total government expenditures, a figure that has risen during the 1980s to more than 19% in 1988 by World Bank estimates (see Table 11.1). Given economic constraints and the already high ratio of education expenditures (relative to most other developing countries), further increases in the education budget seem unlikely. Thus, the more important issue, in our view, is the distribution of spending within the education sector and the extent to which this spending is targeted to programs most likely to benefit the poorest sectors of the population.

Expenditure figures indicate that spending on primary schooling dropped from 37.1% of the education budget in 1975 to 34.4% in 1988. Spending on secondary education also showed a decline from nearly 50% of the budget in 1975 to 45.1% in 1988, whereas expenditure on postsecondary education increased from 13.9% to more than 20% during the same period. This trend exists despite the proclaimed intention of the government to develop primary education and to stabilize university-level expenditures in recent educational reform proposals. Policy recommendations to encourage the development of private education and to transfer a portion of the cost of higher education to the beneficiaries of such education (through tuition fees and more selective scholarship distribution on the basis of need, merit, and performance) have been made; however, there is as yet no discernible shift in education expenditures in favor of primary education. A policy designed to target education for the poor would require a more determined effort to reduce university spending and to increase support for improved primary school access and other educational programs of more direct potential benefit to children from poor households.

As we have seen, clear progress has been made in the extension of literacy and education to greater portions of the population. For example, total primary school enrollments have increased from about 1 million children in the early 1960s to a relatively stable level of 2.1 million in the mid-1980s, representing approximately 72% of the primary school-age population in 1988.

However, according to a 1987 Moroccan government survey, the educational poverty among the poorest economic classes remains severe. For example, heads of household in the low and lowest expenditure classes were disproportionately less likely to have received some formal schooling (17.3% and 10.5%, respectively) than other income groups (37.5%). The disparity was most acute in urban areas, although the overall educational rate in urban areas was more favorable in absolute terms. Not only are the poor in urban areas likely to be poorer in relative buying power than those in rural areas, they are more distinguishable from the nonpoor on the basis of education attained. Thus, there remain substantial disparities in educational enrollment between rural and urban regions, between males and females (especially in rural areas), and across geographic regions and social class. Such national level statistics mirror quite well what we found at the local level in al-Ksour and Marrakech.

Moroccan educational indicators in international perspective

To understand the context of government decision making, it is important to situate Morocco among comparable countries with respect to key educational indicators (see Table 11.2). Among lower middle income countries with comparable GNP or poverty rates, Morocco's expenditures in education (16.6% by Unicef; 19.2% by World Bank estimates) are relatively high, far above the rates for Pakistan, Sri Lanka, Indonesia, Bolivia, and Guyana (from 3.0% to 11.6% of government expenditures) and approximating the rates for the Philippines, Zimbabwe, and North Yemen (from 20.1% to 22.5%). In the face of this significant level, Morocco's performance with regard to primary enrollment rates is substantially lower than that of many comparable countries, especially female enrollments, although the official primary school completion rate of those who do enroll (70%) is relatively high. Morocco's adult literacy rates are also among the lowest within this group, with the exception of those of North Yemen, and secondary school enrollment figures show a similar ranking. Thus, despite relatively high expenditures on education by the Moroccan government, certain measures of educational effectiveness are generally lower than those obtained in other countries with a similar revenue base. Of those countries, it is noteworthy that North Yemen (recently unified with South Yemen), the one country that is consistently worse off in this respect than Morocco, is also most similar to it in cultural terms, as an Arab Islamic state in which the education and literacy training of women have typically been low. With respect to Morocco's cultural and geographic neighbors in the Maghreb – Algeria, Tunisia, Libya, and Egypt – a similar low rate of female literacy and educational participation is evident, lending support to the argument that cultural factors, such as those described in chapters 2 and 3, are at work. Even so, Morocco's rates of adult literacy and school participation remain somewhat lower than those of its Maghreb neighbors.

Despite a low GNP per capita, it is evident that Morocco's difficulties in providing equity in access to educational facilities and to literacy for all segments of the population cannot be attributed entirely to insufficient budget allocations to education. Factors such as culture, policy structure, organization, and planning influence the cross-national diversity of rela-

Table 11.2. Comparison of Morocco's most recent principal education indicators with selected lower middle income (LMI) and neighboring Maghreb countries

Country	1	2	3	4	5	6	7	8	9	10	11	12	13	14
Morocco	590	28	45	84	62	46	16.6	45	22	96/75	62/50	70	39	27
Pakistan	350	32	29	110	58	31	3.2	40	19	55/—	32/—	34	25	10
Sri Lanka	400	—	—	34	71	21	8.4	91	83	104/99	102/99	91	63	70
Philippines	560	50	64	46	64	41	20.1	86	85	107/95	106/94	64	66	69
Peru	1,090	49	—	89	63	69	—	91	78	125/—	120/—	51	68	61
Zimbabwe	620	—	—	73	59	26	20.9	81	67	132/—	126/—	79	55	37
Senegal	420	—	—	129	47	37	—	37	19	66/52	45/36	86	18	9
Indonesia	490	26	44	85	57	27	8.5	83	65	121/99	116/97	80	45	34
Yemen (North)	550	—	—	117	52	22	22.5	27	3	125/—	31/—	15	26	3
Nigeria	640	—	—	106	51	33	—	54	31	103/—	81/—	31	42	14
Bolivia	600	—	85	111	54	49	11.6	84	65	93/83	82/75	32	40	34
Guyana	500	—	—	31	70	33	3.0	97	95	101/—	99/—	84	58	62
Egypt	760	21	25	87	62	48	10.8	59	30	96/—	77/—	64	77	54
Tunisia	1,140	20	15	60	66	54	14.3	68	41	127/99	108/90	78	45	33
Algeria	2,590	20	—	75	63	44	—	63	37	105/96	85/80	83	62	45
Libya	—	—	—	84	62	67	—	81	50	—/—	—/—	82	—	—

Column headings: 1 – GNP per capita ($) (1986). 2 – Urban absolute poverty rate (%) (1977–1986). 3 – Rural absolute poverty rate (%) (1977–1986). 4 – Infant (age 0–1) mortality rate (per 1,000) (1987). 5 – Life expectancy at birth (years) (1987). 6 – Urbanization ratio (%) (1987). 7 – Portion of government expenditures to education (%) (1986). 8 – Adult (age 15+) male literacy rate (%) (1985). 9 – Adult (age 15+) female literacy rate (%) (1985). 10 – Male primary school enrollments (gross/net; % of age group) (1984–1986). 11 – Female primary school enrollments (gross/net; % of age group) (1984–1986). 12 – Portion of grade 1 enrollees to complete. primary cycle (%) (1980–1986). 13 – Male secondary school enrollments (gross; % of age group) (1984–1986). 14 – Female secondary school enrollments (gross; % of age group) (1984–1986).

Note base-year deviations: Bolivia, column 3, 1975 and column 12, 1976; Nigeria, columns 13 and 14, 1982; Guyana, columns 10, 11, 13, and 14, 1980.

Source: UNICEF, 1989.

tionships among inputs such as government expenditures on education and output indicators such as literacy, school enrollment, and school completion rates.

Contrasts in urban and rural demographics

According to recent estimates, the per capita income distribution of the poor and the ultra-poor is roughly equivalent across urban and rural environments (27.5% poor and 15.3% ultra-poor in urban areas and 32.3% poor and 16.1% ultra-poor in rural areas; see Table 11.3). This rough equivalency may be misleading because it does not take into account the cost of living or the cost of education, which may vary by environment, nor does it make clear whether educational changes would have similar consequences in each environment. As expected, there exist substantial disparities in educational enrollments between urban and rural areas (see Table 11.4). Per capita government expenditures on education are significantly higher in urban areas than in rural areas; for example, it is estimated that the share of the education budget received per urban inhabitant is nearly 3.4 times larger than that received per rural inhabitant (Salmi, 1985: 79). In addition, whereas only 43.3% of Morocco's total population in 1988 was living in urban areas, 54.5% of all children in primary school were from urban areas, despite the likelihood of a greater portion of school-age children in rural areas. Schools are still in short supply in rural areas, and those that do exist are less well equipped than are those in urban areas.

Urban-rural disparities in the quality of education are also evident. Academic performance on standardized examinations such as the *shahada* (grade 5) and the *baccalaureat* (grade 12) is generally higher in urban schools than in rural schools. This difference suggests that the academic skills acquired by graduates (and dropouts) of rural schools tend to be weaker than those of urban students at the same grade level, which showed up as well in our own measures of literacy achievement. One consequence is that relatively fewer rural students pass the strict examinations and advance to higher levels of education. Furthermore, the percentage of primary school instructors who are formally certified at the requisite level is higher in urban than in rural schools (98% vs. 89% in 1988; see also Salmi, 1985: 101; el-Farouki, 1977). Conversely, the student-teacher ratio in rural schools is generally lower than in urban schools; but while international studies have shown that the level of teacher training is related to student

Table 11.3. Rates of poverty and ultra-poverty by urban/rural environment and economic region in Morocco

(a) Urban environment

	(Pop.)	Poor		Ultra-poor	
	% of total urban population	% of total urban population	% of region's urban population	% of total urban population	% of region's urban population
Total	(100.0)	27.5	——	15.3	——
Center	(35.1)	8.99	25.6	4.60	13.1
North-west	(25.5)	6.55	25.7	3.60	14.1
Center-north	(8.6)	2.94	34.2	1.80	20.9
Center-south	(7.2)	2.59	36.0	1.63	22.6
East	(6.9)	1.57	22.7	0.75	10.8
South	(6.8)	1.60	23.5	1.00	14.7
Tensift region	(9.9)	3.28	33.1	1.89	19.1

(b) Rural environment

	(Pop.)	Poor		Ultra-poor	
	% of total urban population	% of total urban population	% of region's urban population	% of total urban population	% of region's urban population
Total	(100.0)	32.3	——	16.1	——
Center	(20.1)	5.13	25.5	2.05	10.2
North-west	(17.8)	6.28	35.3	3.04	17.1
Center-north	(13.8)	3.34	24.2	1.24	9.0
Center-south	(7.7)	2.49	32.3	1.52	19.8
East	(7.0)	2.48	35.4	1.41	20.2
South	(15.6)	6.82	43.7	3.78	24.2
Tensift region	(17.9)	5.71	31.9	3.10	17.3

Source: Direction de la Statistique, 1984.

achievement, there is little discernible effect of the student-teacher ratio on student achievement (Fuller, 1988). Thus, rural areas with low population density typically receive relatively more teachers, but these teachers are less likely to be of the appropriate certification level, and it is this latter factor that appears to be more important for educational quality and achievement outcomes.

Table 11.4. Educational indicators by urban/rural environment in Morocco, 1980 and 1988

	1980		1988	
Indicator	Urban	Rural	Urban	Rural
Portion of total population (%)			43.2	56.8
Adult illiteracy rate (%)[a]	44	82		
Males (% of male pop.)[a]	30	68		
Females (% of female pop.)[a]	57	95		
Public primary education				
Students per teacher	40	33	30	22
Female teachers (% of teachers)	40	17	50	18
Certified teachers (% of teachers)			98	89
Enrollment (% of age group)	124	49	96	52
Proportion of enrollments (%)			54.5	45.5
Female enrollment (% of students)	45	24	46	29
Public secondary education				
Students per teacher	– 22 –		– 20 –	
Female teachers (% of teachers)			– 30 –	
Certified teachers (% of teachers)	– 80 –		– 91 –	
Vocational and technical education[b]				
Enrollment (1,000s)			66.3	7.9
Proportion of enrollments (%)			89.3	10.7
Female enrollment (% of students)			37.2	24.7

[a]Figures from 1982 census (Direction de la Statistique, 1984).
[b]Public training facilities only.
Sources: ASM, 1987, 1988; Direction de la Statistique, 1984; MTPFPFC, 1989; SEP, 1988; SES, 1988.

With regard to educational process and outcome indicators, statistics from 1980 indicate 82% adult illiteracy in rural areas, almost twice the urban illiteracy rate (see Table 11.4). In 1987–1988, only 34% of rural girls and 69% of rural boys of age 7 were newly enrolled in grade 1, compared to 85% and 89%, respectively, in urban areas. As to the rate of total enrollments in primary school, whereas urban areas appear to have nearly achieved the stated goal of universal primary school enrollment, rural primary enrollments remain at little more than 50%.[3] Lower attendance rates in rural areas appear to be the result of both lower rates of original school enrollment and higher rates of dropout than in urban areas.

Language is another factor implicated in urban-rural disparities in educational outcomes. As described in chapter 3, the Berber-speaking population resides primarily in rural areas and therefore has less access to education. Furthermore, when they first arrive at school and are confronted with the all-Arabic school curriculum, Berber-speaking children are at a relative disadvantage to Arabic-speaking children, even though many catch up academically (see chapter 8). French language learning may also present problems of educational equity across urban and rural environments. As noted in chapter 2, the French language, formerly obligatory in all aspects of the school curriculum, is now studied as a second language beginning in third grade. Urban children have much more exposure to the French language outside the classroom than rural children do, owing to the importance of French in the modern urban economy and to the differential impact of the French colonial period in urban Morocco. Because the French language is a principal subject area in the *shahada,* the "gatekeeping" exam at the fifth grade level, differences in exposure to French outside the classroom may lead to significant outcome differences, disproportionately limiting rural children's access to upper levels of education in Morocco. This latter topic – differential language contact and school promotion – is one in great need of further study.

In Morocco, as elsewhere, the educational and literacy needs may involve features distinct to urban and rural environments. An educational paradox is that equity may not be achieved through simple instructional equality. Urban dwellers, for example, tend to require higher levels of education and literacy and more industry-oriented training in order to become and remain competitive in the job market. In rural areas, agricultural training is more relevant to local needs. Furthermore, special attention must be paid to issues of transportation and accessibility to schools, the problem of low-density population and potential alternative forms of schooling (such as multigrade teaching), and developing incentives to counteract cultural and economic obstacles to participation.

Gender

As shown in Table 11.1, 80% of the adult female population was reported to be illiterate in 1988, in contrast to 40% of males. Since independence, girls in urban areas have gained rough parity in enrollment in primary schooling, constituting 46% of all urban primary enrollments in 1988. In rural areas, however, boys still outnumber girls at a rate of more than 2 to 1 (boys at 71%, girls at 29%). One factor implicated in the lower rate of girls' participation in rural primary schools is the low proportion of female teachers in such schools; the data show that whereas 50% of urban primary school teachers are female, only 18% of rural teachers are female. Improvement of this ratio could have the important consequence of reducing the reluctance of traditional rural parents to send their daughters to schools and classrooms presided over by single male teachers.

The figures on low female literacy and educational participation in rural areas take on special significance when they are related to such factors as infant mortality and female labor force participation.[4] Aggregate analyses of 1982 Moroccan provincial level data ($N = 40$) showed significant correlations between female illiteracy and infant mortality in urban and rural environments ($r = .46$ and $.45$, respectively), as well as between female schooling (any level) and infant mortality ($r = -.31$ and $-.48$, respectively). In urban areas, literate and educated women were also more likely to participate in the active wage-earning work force ($r = .49$ for literacy and $.56$ for schooling; in contrast, only $.11$ and $.17$ in rural areas). These census data suggest that female literacy and education are implicated in healthy development and in wage-earning employment, but that these relationships vary importantly by environment, supporting our own local observations and survey interviews (see chapter 6).

Obstacles to educational participation of the poor

Despite the fact that education in Morocco is officially free, hidden costs may render school attendance a substantial financial burden. The perceived opportunity costs of education for families depend on a range of cultural, geographic, and ethnic factors. Although generally high demand for (i.e., interest in) the education of their children has been observed at all levels of Moroccan society, as we saw in both Marrakech and al-Ksour, poor families must be especially careful in weighing the perceived benefits of education against its real and perceived costs.

The perceived financial benefits of education may include the long-term possibility of increased salary returns to the family, or at least the possibility that a salaried job might become available if sufficient education is attained. In-kind (non-monetary) benefits may include the acquisition of practical skills such as literacy or numeracy that are useful in the family's everyday transactions; the provision of free lunch, especially for rural children; the provision of child care (by virtue of being in school), especially relevant in the urban setting where both parents might be employed outside the household; and improved access to health care and increased knowledge of preventive health care measures, hygiene, and sanitation. The cultural benefits of education may include a family's gain in social status through educated children, especially sons; gains in access to the outside world of information through expanded language and literacy skills; and gains in religious knowledge and status through Quranic learning and Arabic literacy.

Educational participation also carries with it various costs that may be monetary, in-kind, and cultural. Families, especially poor families, must weigh these costs against the benefits to determine which family members will attend school, and for how long. Real cash costs of "free" public schooling exist in the form of incidental school fees, textbooks, pencils, and other materials, and clothing. Additional cash costs may include transportation to school (especially in remote rural areas), food and lodging in the case of boarding students from rural areas attending urban schools (living stipends exist but are minimal), and the loss of cash income from child wage labor. This last consideration is likely to be most acute in rural areas, where, in 1987, 22.6% of boys and 31.0% of girls under the age of 15 were employed, in contrast with 2.1% employment of urban boys and girls of the same age (ASM, 1987). Among the poorest families, these cash outlays and forgone earnings represent a significant portion of annual income, and thus a real deterrent to school attendance. In-kind costs may include loss of child labor in the home and difficulties in getting to school (mainly in rural areas). Perceived cultural costs to the family can include the risk of "reputation loss," especially in the case of girls from traditionally minded families; the loss of Islamic values and their replacement by secular or Western values; and the straining of family relations, for example, in the case of rural children housed with urban relatives to facilitate school attendance. Literacy itself, in the eyes of some traditional nonliterate parents, is sometimes still viewed as an undesirable skill for daughters because it may provide a "dangerous" communication channel, beyond parental surveillance.

The poor and the ultra-poor: A distinction that makes a difference?

A key assumption is that the poor and the ultra-poor are not equally likely to gain access to additional educational resources even if they were made available, nor do the two groups profit equally from the receipt of such resources. When the marginal returns from additional educational inputs are considered, the ultra-poor may profit more from even small increments in education than the ordinary poor. Though not necessarily the case with additional units of income, additional units of education for the poorest sectors of society may succeed in breaking the cycle of ultra-poverty. This may be so because an educational foothold would enable ultra-poor households to gain greater access to health care information and human service resources in the community through (even minimally) literate family members, steps that could then lead to greater literacy and job access for subsequent generations. The "overeducation" of Moroccan youth relative to employment opportunities is a much-discussed topic. But such a surplus of educational credentials is much less common in rural areas, where a primary school certificate still carries a considerable degree of social and professional importance. Though government statistics show higher rates of unemployment among school leavers than among those without any level of education, especially in urban areas (CERED, 1988), these data probably indicate a poor coordination between education and labor market sectors rather than a generally negative relationship between education and employability.

In a manner similar to Lipton's (1988) argument with respect to the support of health care for the ultra-poor, the provision of basic educational services (primary education and initial literacy training) may have more, and more immediate, utility for the ultra-poor than for the ordinary poor in the population. The ultra-poor, especially women and rural dwellers, remain in need of improved access to basic primary education, as is indicated in the tables presented in this chapter. Conversely, the "ordinary" poor might be better served with the development of vocational training and secondary education to enhance their opportunities for stable employment or other income-generating activities. Such efforts would be especially relevant in urban areas and industrialized regions, where universal primary education has essentially been attained.

Problems in Moroccan educational planning

Although education specialists familiar with Morocco might concur with the recommendations discussed above, there exist major problems in policy making that have limited or inhibited the government's capacity to serve the needs of the poor and the ultra-poor. Many of these problems in the current educational system cannot yet be addressed because of an inadequate information flow, as well as a lack of coherence in educational priorities.

A plan for the reduction of educational poverty requires making difficult choices within a relatively constant budgetary framework. Over a period of decades educational planning in Morocco may be described as multivectored and indecisive at the same time. Considerable progress has been made in increasing overall educational participation since independence, but access to education among the very poor has shown little improvement over the past two decades, and gender and regional gaps in adult illiteracy rates have remained virtually unchanged as well. If this situation is to be altered, a renewed commitment to prioritizing programs that will reach the educationally impoverished is critical.

Better communication and coordination between education and the labor market are needed in order to allocate support for programs that are likely to increase productivity. Recognition of this problem is not new; indeed, the coordination of educational outputs with manpower needs has been a persistent theme of planning efforts in Morocco and elsewhere. Analyses of educational wastage typically utilize as outcome variables grade repetition and school dropout rates, but data on postgraduation employment are seldom collected at all in Morocco. The lack of infrastructure to allow intersectoral exchange of information has probably contributed to inadequate planning on the one hand and to inefficient duplications of effort on the other.

Contextual factors also contribute to the success or failure of the implementation of policy initiatives in important ways (Fuller & Heyneman, 1989). Whereas cross-national comparisons are essential for determining the merits of overall planning, country-specific and within-country variations in characteristics such as language background, level of teacher certification, and the availability of textbooks can constrain or enhance a particular intervention. Within the present discussion, it should be evident that enhancing school access for the ultra-poor will require attention not only to the obvious differences between urban and rural life (such as distance to schools and expenses for school materials) but also to cultural and economic differences by gender and across geographic regions (such as variations in school attendance as a function of different agricultural cycles).

Naturally, the problems enumerated could be addressed more directly and effectively if a more complete and reliable data base were available. An infrastructure for the collection of basic educational statistics is in place, but the information gathered is often irrelevant to the most pressing matters of policy. In some cases, the data simply have not been gathered (such as rates of school enrollment per school-age population by expenditure class); in other cases, the data may be available but are very difficult to retrieve or are long out of date (as reflected in the dates of the tables in this chapter). Furthermore, the current data-gathering infrastructure is "inflexible" in the sense that while efforts are made to continue gathering the same statistics, there is little or no capacity to carry out ad hoc case studies in order to pinpoint viable policy options and to provide relatively timely answers. This situation is exacerbated by the lack of interministerial coordination of data bases that do exist but that remain difficult or impossible to integrate.

Beyond the glass ceiling

Considerable progress has been made in the expansion of educational participation in Morocco. Yet, if present educational policies are maintained and budgetary limitations remain unchanged, it is estimated that the national rate of literacy (defined here as at least a fifth-grade level of measurable skills) will remain at a "glass ceiling" of about 50% of the adult population well beyond the year 2000. This situation of an asymptotic status quo of a low national rate of literacy should raise serious concern, especially because it is the poorest sectors of Morocco that are most affected.[5]

Therefore, reducing obstacles to educational participation and literacy, especially among the poor, therefore should be an important dimension of future policy planning. As noted earlier, obstacles can involve issues of access as well as the opportunity costs of education and literacy training. Achieving a supply of educational resources sufficient to reduce educational poverty on a national scale may lie not so much in an absolute quantity of classrooms or teachers but rather in the distribution and redirection of educational resources to the poorest sectors of society. Demand for education can and should be improved by providing better indications of the utility of education and literacy and more direct paths to the workplace. Finally, reductions in the opportunity costs of education involving monetary and in-kind incentives, such as free lunches and school materials, female teachers, and geographically convenient schools, may go far in reducing the low rates of participation in rural areas, among girls, and within ultra-poor families.

Concomitantly, existing supports for education may be capitalized upon as footholds for development and the redirection of policy. Such supports may include the public perception that literacy is a valuable and accessible personal and family resource, that educational credentials are important in determining employment options, and that educational access and quality are essentially egalitarian. Popular support for higher school promotion rates might be more forthcoming if parents felt that educational quality was being enhanced. Improvements in educational effectiveness also require more consideration. Especially for the poorest families, Morocco's traditionally high rates of grade repetition and school dropout have represented a considerable and frustrating expenditure of time and money for parents and communities. To break the cycle of family illiteracy and educational poverty will, as we have shown, require attention more targeted to the particular needs of the ultra-poor. Whether government policymakers will be able to make the necessary improvements to alter a situation in which ultra-poverty and educational poverty are reproduced across generations remains a major question.

In summary, though few would dispute the real gains in educational development since Moroccan independence, tremendous disparities in educational participation are likely to remain throughout the 1990s and beyond. Even with a well-educated elite, Morocco is burdened with great numbers of illiterate and low-literate adults and non- or partially schooled youth. The future of economic development in Morocco will depend critically on government policies that affect the capacity of the poor and the ultra-poor to break the cycle of educational poverty.

Notes

1 These figures are estimated from statistics on net enrollment ratios in grade 1 for urban and rural 7 year olds combined (range 50% to 74.5%, average ratio 65.5%; World Bank, 1989, annex 4); school dropout rates in grades 1–4 (roughly 7% per year from each grade level between 1982 and 1988; SEP, 1988); and the primary to lower secondary promotion rate of fifth graders (estimated to average 60% of fifth graders each year between 1985 and 1991; see World Bank, 1989).

2 Long-term educational reform planning in Morocco falls under the jurisdiction of the Conseil Superieur de l'Enseignement. Members of the council include governmental authorities, members of parliament, the deans and directors of higher educational institutions, provincial representatives, and representatives of the teacher corps, university students, the Association de

l'Enseignement Superieur, and the private sector (Baina, 1981: 34–36). The council meets once a year and in extraordinary sessions to review proposals for educational reform. Proposals may originate from the Ministry of Education's (MEN) Division of General Inspection (Inspection Generale) or from the MEN Bureau of Planning (Direction de la Planification) (see also Radi, 1983: 126–129).

3 These figures themselves are likely to be inflated (especially 1980 figures), due to migration of rural children to urban areas for the purpose of schooling, the presence of overage repeaters in total enrollments, and a total school-age population denominator uncorrected for the extended age range of children in school.

4 These analyses were undertaken by Jennifer Spratt as part of an internal report to the World Bank (Wagner and Spratt, 1989).

5 It should be mentioned that this situation may be much more common cross-nationally than is generally realized. Many specialists concur that literacy levels in the United States, in spite of a major renewed effort toward adult literacy service provision, are unlikely to change in the near term.

12. Linking research and policy

When you don't know which way to go, any road will take you there.
(Lewis Carroll, *Alice in Wonderland*)

Our work began with a primary emphasis on understanding the acquisition and retention of literacy in cultural context. Scholarly interests followed in the intellectual tradition of trying to be sensitive to differences and specificities within a culture – the *emic* perspective – while at the same time attempting to achieve a more general and generalizable understanding of literacy across settings and cultures – the *etic* perspective. As work progressed we observed that numerous educational, social and economic policy questions began to take shape, all depending in one way or another on solid data about literacy. Thus, it became clear early on that we had an unusual opportunity to chart new ground in the interface between literacy research and literacy policy. We can now review some of the policy questions that are often raised about literacy and development and that may be addressed by the data collected in Morocco.

Literacy definitions and data collection

There are many possible definitions of literacy, as well as ways to categorize the skills that are present or absent in children and adults. In Morocco, we sought to utilize broad domains of literacy (such as reading and writing), but to base all classifications and quantitative analyses on the direct measurement of a variety of observed, surveyed, or tested skills. For example, we avoided labeling unschooled or religiously schooled individuals as illiterate, even though they may possess few of the literacy skills required for "economic productivity." Indeed, we used the term *literacy* as a descriptor that encompassed many types of skills, behaviors, and attitudes. The result of this open-ended approach was that we had more opportunity for the inclusion of culturally specific skills than would have been the case had we adopted some a priori definition. We also could take a fresh look at ways to quantify the various dimensions of skill that could generalize our findings more broadly.

This led to our first conclusion: to reject the idea that individuals can be described as literacy haves and have nots. We found that it was far from sufficient simply to ask individuals whether or not they are or are not literate, as is still being done in many national studies and within international agencies. Whereas the concept of a literacy dichotomy may be the least expensive method of literacy categorization, it is also likely to be the least accurate and subject to all kinds of variations that are virtually impossible to predict or to measure. Nevertheless, we cannot conclude that in-depth and theoretically derived methodologies for research, such as those utilized in the Morocco Literacy Project (which was expensive in terms of the data collected and time spent on research), are always needed. Rather, for contexts such as Morocco, the Third World generally, or low-literate ethnic communities in industrialized countries, it may be most useful to employ qualitative approaches and categorical breakdowns that provide just enough information for use by policymakers. With the data from Morocco, we believe that more easily and simply constructed and less expensive tools for literacy measurement can be produced in the future.

In line with this thinking, a "midlevel" method of assessment may be more appropriate for future policy work, as exemplified in the model developed under the auspices of the UN National Household Survey Capability Program (United Nations, 1989; Wagner, 1990).[1] In this model four main skill classifications are utilized: *nonliterate,* for a person who cannot read a text with understanding, write a short text in a significant national language, recognize words on signs and documents in everyday contexts, or perform such specific tasks as signing his or her name or recognizing the meaning of public signs; *low-literate,* for a person who cannot read a text with understanding or write a short text in a significant national language, but who can recognize words on signs and documents in everyday contexts and can perform such specific tasks as signing his or her name or recognizing the meaning of public signs; *moderate-literate,* for a person who can, with some difficulty (i.e., making numerous errors), read a text with understanding and write a short text in a significant national language; and *high-literate,* for a person who can, with little difficulty (i.e., making few errors), read a text with understanding and write a short text in a significant national language. (See Wagner, 1990, for more details on this schema for literacy surveys in developing countries.) By employing a selection of the tests for early reading and writing, word-picture matching and paragraph comprehension, it is possible to produce an inventory of skills that will give policymakers a much better idea of the literacy situation in a given country.

Furthermore, whether the context is Morocco or the United States, a household literacy survey, which gathers information on a representative sample of individual households in a society, may be the most effective method for gathering information required for policy decision making of the sort described in chapter 11. Although such surveys are not without cost (and are probably more expensive than equivalent testing among in-school student populations), they enable one to determine how literacy varies by age, grade, geographic region, and language group. This approach to evaluation is one of the major lessons of our work in Morocco. Though we needed, for scholarly purposes, to gather a considerable range of detailed information on literacy, it appears that a more focused survey-oriented, minimalist data collection approach could go a long way toward providing low-cost and effective information for policy-making purposes. At the same time, such surveys will need to be delivered with a sensitivity to the particular social and cultural contexts that are the focus of policy decision making.

Literacy practices and beliefs

Another fundamental policy concern is how and when literacy skills are employed. In the opening vignette of the book, we observed that Oum Fatima was illiterate in the traditional sense of the word but, nonetheless, was able to employ literate behaviors to solve problems associated with print. Recall that she knew which piece of mail went to whom based on the script utilized by the sender. We also found that school-going youth, even though literate enough to pass school-based literacy tests in Arabic, were often unable to solve the problem of interpreting instructions on a medicine box for the common cold. It is becoming increasingly apparent that the academic skills learned in school may not transfer directly or easily to everyday literacy needs. Indeed, for youths who are not expected to pursue further education, additional training on everyday literacy uses may be worth serious consideration.

In addition, we found that children, youth, and parents – with widely varying backgrounds of experience with written language – have diverse patterns of beliefs about what it takes to be literate. For example, children generally believe that those who need to work hard to become literate are, in fact, those who do become most skilled in literacy. The policy implications of beliefs and attitudes about literacy are many and serious. Motivation, or the lack of it, is one primary factor in the failure to learn in and out of school. To enhance motivation is to alter belief systems and attitudes toward learning and the contexts in which people are likely to learn. In spite of this well-known fact about learning in general and literacy learning in particular, relatively few programs for literacy have made the necessary and substantial efforts associated with the affective side of literacy. Much attention has focused on grandiose and politicized notions of "empowerment," but only minuscule attention has been directed toward understanding the belief systems associated with the ethnic, linguistic, and social contexts in which *individuals* live and practice literacy.

Literacy acquisition

Since World War II, educational development efforts focused first on building infrastructure for schools and schooling in developing countries. By the 1960s, emphasis was put on trying to increase primary school enrollments to more than 50% of the school-age population in the world's poorest countries. It was a widely held assumption that this augmented school attendance would lead to the end of the "scourge" of illiteracy. As we have seen, this assumption was flawed in at least two respects. First, skill achievement in school depends on many factors, and school attendance is far from sufficient to ensure the learning of basic literacy skills. Second, the types and levels of literacy skills once thought to be crucial have changed over time.

From a policy perspective, and evidenced in the 1990 Jomtien conference on Education for All (United Nations, 1990), there is now a very real concern over what is learned in the classroom, as contrasted to simply tracking school attendance records. The Morocco Literacy Project adds support to this same concern. Even within a relatively homogeneous sample of children from the Moroccan *classes populaires,* there were very wide differences in literacy acquisition and school achievement. Large numbers of children succeeded in learning the fundamentals of reading, writing, and arithmetic, but equally large numbers did not, even if they remained in school (and almost 50% of our sample, as with national level statistics, dropped out of school before completion of the fifth-grade certificate). Furthermore, even children who had achieved relatively well in school tended to perform poorly on many of the household literacy tasks in our study. Finally, parental education, socioeconomic status, literacy materials in the home, and household amenities (such as electricity and water) all had predictive power on subsequent literacy achievement (chapter 6). Nonetheless, much of the statistical variance in literacy acquisition could not be accounted for by these background factors, which are so often put forward as "explanatory" in Western research.

Are these results, then, peculiar to the Moroccan context? In our view, such a conclusion is unlikely. Similar findings are beginning to appear in many industrialized countries as well. With dropout rates approaching 50% in many of America's urban secondary school systems, and with achievement test scores dropping, ever more attention is being focused on what is, and is not, learned in formal schooling and beyond. In Morocco, we found that many of the factors at work in predicting learning were similar to those described in Western schools, such as the importance of parental values, as well as the values, attitudes, and motivations of the children themselves. Indeed, it is our sense that motivation and values may be a crucial missing link in much educational policy work, particularly in the Third World. Yet the question of practical intervention is an issue that remains to be explored.

We must also stay cognizant of the cultural specificities at work in Morocco. It was found that Quranic preschools played a particularly crucial role in children's learning of literacy skills, skills that follow children into the primary school classroom and on into later school success. In addition, such traditional schools were helpful to Berber-speaking children learning to read in Arabic. The finding that Berber-speaking children caught up to their Arabic-speaking classmates is one of the most significant empirical findings of the project, as it stands in contradiction to widely held views on multilingual language and literacy acquisition. Furthermore, our data suggest that proficiency in the Moroccan dialect of Arabic was helpful to all children learning to read in Standard Arabic, contrary to some earlier speculation on this issue. Another crucial element was the importance of the Arabic language and orthography in the culture outside public schooling, a factor in second language and second literacy learning that distinguishes the Moroccan case from many others in the developing world. Our evidence on literacy acquisition in Arabic suggests as well that much greater attention needs to be devoted to the scripts and cultural beliefs about specific languages. As noted earlier, there is a tremendous gap in our understanding of cultural variations in literacy across the globe.

Literacy retention

Literacy retention, which received its first serious exploration in this project, appears a fertile area for linking research and policy. Because educational policymakers need to plan as a function of expectations about individual competencies in postschooling activities, the measurement of skill gains and losses within and beyond the schooling process is central to decision making. As we have seen, the area of literacy retention held a number of surprises, such as females' skill gain in Arabic and French literacy, the relatively poor skill retention among working males, and the contrast between skill gains in literacy and in numeracy. Overall, it appears that the practice of literacy skills after schooling (sometimes referred to as "postliteracy") is in particular need of further exploration.

As policymakers consider the differential impacts of primary and secondary schooling, along with vocational and nonformal campaigns, the issue of retention will continue to move to the forefront of policy debate. How effective are short-term campaigns on a per-hour basis relative to in-classroom instruction? What are the costs and benefits of different learning contexts when seen in the light of what skills are retained following instruction? Based on the Moroccan results, we have more confidence in saying that five grades of primary schooling is sufficient for the retention of a reasonable level of basic literacy skills. There was, in fact, little loss of either Arabic or French literacy over the 2 years following fifth-grade dropout. Nonetheless, the long-term consequences of dropout or of the possible impact of fewer than 5 years of primary schooling are issues that remain to be investigated. Our study consisted of a relatively modest sample size from particular schools in a particular country. There is every reason to believe that considerable variation in retention curves would obtain from country to country, as well as across skill domains.

Pedagogical ideologies and educational achievement

Millions of children in dozens of countries attend religious schools for either part or all of their formal education. In Morocco, despite a central focus on the study of Quranic texts, the traditional Quranic preschools have adapted to changes in contemporary social life. With the advent of increased primary school enrollments, a large majority of Moroccan children now attend Quranic preschools as preparation for formal schooling; the traditional schools for older children are disappearing. The scathing commentaries about stern conditions and rigid memorization are far less accurate today than they once were. In addition, the changes in populations served (now predominantly very young children), backgrounds of the teachers (now younger and better educated), and pedagogy (now with some emphasis on the academic skills of reading, writing and math) have placed Quranic schooling in more direct contact (and competition) with the modern preschool school system.

Findings concerning the enhancement of preschool literacy skills among the most disadvantaged sectors of the population raised several policy issues. First, and most obvious, is that the claims of negative academic consequences of Quranic preschooling need to be reconsidered and probably rejected. Even without positive effects, the availability of a preschool situation that provides a safe and stimulating place for children to be, with the increasing numbers of parents who both work, is becoming a practical necessity. Second, given the paucity of financial support provided to such traditional schools, we can only imagine how good they could become if more investment were made in terms of materials and personnel. Finally, because such schools are socially embedded in precisely the areas where populations are most disadvantaged, their infrastructure could be of tremendous value to other types of multisectoral community development work, such as health or infant care.

It is important to emphasize that the "consequences issue" is crucial to any policy initiatives with respect to Quranic schooling. As long as it could be maintained that Quranic schools had a negative cognitive impact, it was possible – based on such "scientific arguments" even without data – to ask for their demise. It now appears that findings such as those from the present study can help to turn around attitudes based only on an individual's or agency's pedagogical ideology. Our data, including those in appendix 1, suggest that Quranic schools can be a particularly good investment of community resources as well as children's time and effort.

Literacy, poverty, and economic development

It is often taken as a given that literacy is "good" in the sense that it helps to bring economic well-being to individuals and societies. We have reviewed some of the research on this relationship, and have suggested in chapter 11 that the Moroccan case demonstrates rather starkly the role that literacy plays in the intergenerational cycle of educational and economic poverty. When seen in historical terms, and in relation to other developing countries, it is reasonable to conclude that Morocco will be unable to become much more literate on a societal level, or more economically self-sufficient, unless dramatic changes take place. This is not news to those who, over many years, have been calling for major changes in the educational and economic policies in Morocco.

Yet our inquiry has less to do with the options for political reform than for an improved understanding of the role that literacy might play in economic productivity. Overall, it is difficult to dispute the assertion that those Moroccan adolescents who were able to achieve greater literacy skills in school were more able to stay in the highly selective educational system and, hence, had greater access to the limited job opportunities in the modern economic sector. However, we also found (chapter 10) that adolescents who were moderately literate had a roughly equal chance of finding a modern sector job whether or not they had stayed in school. This finding reflects the saturation of the job market with schooled youth; having a little more literacy or a little more schooling helps relatively little when there are no jobs to be had.

This is not to say that literacy is unimportant – to the contrary. It appears that the credentialing system of school certificates and diplomas is fast becoming less effective for securing a job. Literacy and other basic skills seem to be what employers in all parts of the world are still looking for, and our evidence did not disconfirm this hypothesis (even though we could not directly test it with our data). What we did learn is that there is tremendous fluidity in the schooling–employment relationship in Morocco. There is considerable room for literacy skills to play a role independent of schooling. And, as already mentioned, employment is only part of the rationale for literacy, as other societal consequences include health, nutrition, civic participation, and the like.

Future initiatives in research and policy

The problems associated with illiteracy, low-literacy, and poverty exist on such a vast scale in developing countries, and lead to such emotional reactions, that national policymakers and multilateral agencies are often tempted to commit virtually all available resources to programs that can have direct impact on the needy. Though such reactions are understandable, it is unlikely that this way of thinking will be as useful as its advocates might suggest. Social programs in the twentieth century have been fraught with failure or at least low rates of success. Reaction to such failures can lead, in turn, to an elimination of financial support because a given social program "didn't work well" and a tendency to move on to a completely new approach to the social problem.

The effort to reduce illiteracy, among children or adults, is no exception. We are beginning to understand better the causes and consequences of literacy and illiteracy in countries like Morocco, but much remains to be understood. Even within Morocco, we have had to take into account an incredibly complex set of sociocultural factors and contexts, in a study that took years to achieve. To acquire a comprehensive understanding of the issues we addressed will be a major challenge for many countries – and, of course, we attempted to study only a subset of critical issues in literacy research and policy. Among other questions in urgent need of exploration: How effective are adult literacy campaigns as contrasted with programs for school-aged children in producing socially desirable consequences (e.g., improved health, lowered fertility, etc.)? Should education programs focus principally on reading/writing, or should equal (or greater) emphasis be placed on mathematics or other skills? Is literacy retained (and, if so, how much) following a limited number of years of primary schooling or short-term campaigns? Is it important to teach literacy in the individual's mother tongue, and, if so, at what point in the educational process? What are the most efficient and cost-effective ways to measure literacy attainment in and out of school settings?

These and similar questions (only some of which we addressed in the project) – so central to the core of education in all countries – remain without definitive answers, in spite of the occasionally strong rhetoric in support of one position or another. Basic and applied research, along with effective program evaluation, can provide critical information that will lead not only to greater efficiency in particular educational programs but also to greater public support of such programs in times of economic constraints. Moreover, such research will inevitably lead to a better and broader understanding of the complex reality in which literacy, culture and development are interconnected.

Notes

1 The first household survey to utilize this model was undertaken in Zimbabwe in 1986–87 under the UNHSCP program, but due to follow-through problems, a comprehensive data analysis was never completed. For one perspective on that study, see Wagner (1987a). A second study was undertaken in Morocco in the early 1990s under the auspices of the World Bank, using many of the assessment materials developed from our work. While the data analysis is not yet complete, one important preliminary finding suggests that biases in the self-reporting of literacy abilities vary significantly by the age, gender, and background of the individual surveyed.

13. Literacy, culture, and development: Concluding thoughts about a changing society

Revisiting Oum Fatima

Oum Fatima is now in her mid-60s. Still a lady of considerable local re-spect, she can no longer put in the long hours of housework and marketplace. Bargaining for prices remains an important traditional skill, and one in which Oum Fatima takes great pride. But times are changing. The literacy knowledge that Oum Fatima learned in the street is now considered of only marginal practical value in an evolving and moderniz-ing economy. Letters, government documents, and jobs requiring writing are intruding on what was once a flourishing commerce in traditional lit-eracy. Oum Fatima, herself, is beginning to realize that being viewed as illiterate (even if she is skilled and highly thought of in her *derb*) can affect her life and the economic existence of her family.

The Morocco Literacy Project took most of the 1980s to complete. During that decade, Moroccan society went through major changes, as did many of the actors and societal norms described in this book. As we have argued throughout, literacy and society are bound together and evolve together. What once seemed to be taken for granted (such as a world of literates and illiterates) is no longer so, given rapidly changing societies. So we come to an important practical question: To what extent can this kind of research be made relevant to today's social scientists, educators, policymakers, and interested laypersons? The principal difficulty in analyzing and relating our research findings is that, even though each of these audiences may find something of use, each also comes to the work with a different frame of reference. For example, not every policymaker cares very much about the relationship between ethnographic and psychometric research designs, or about the orthographic properties of the Arabic script. And not every reading specialist is going to be fascinated by the problems that Berber-speaking children encounter in learning to read in the Quranic schools of Morocco. And will laypersons be much interested in the degree to which socioeconomic factors predict reading achievement among fifth graders? The success of a project (and a book) like this one will reside, then, in its ability to appeal to individuals with rather different outlooks on what counts in literacy and education, without falling (too far) between the proverbial chairs.

The combined ethnographic and experimental approach we utilized to study literacy in Morocco was one of the project's most distinctive features. The varied levels and methods of data collection and data analysis were designed to address specific theoretical concerns that could shed light on the complex reality of literacy in cultural context. As have others with an ethnographic lens, we found it necessary to remind ourselves constantly of the bounded nature of our inquiry. The sample population was drawn from particular sectors of Moroccan society where the widespread appearance of first-generation literacy is still taking place. It entailed a number of significant sociological features, such as increasing Arabization within long-standing bilingual communities and the appearance of a growing number of Quranic and modern preschools. Furthermore, even though adult literacy skills were not common at the socioeconomic level of our sample population, knowledge about literacy and access to it through formal and informal intermediaries were. Moroccan society, once characterized by a pattern of "restricted" social distribution of both literate skills and literate practice, is now moving steadily in the direction of generalized, diffused, and popularized literacy. International statistics still show that more than half the adult Moroccan population is "illiterate," and our own analyses (chapter 11) suggest that this statistic will likely remain roughly the same for years to come. However, use of our broader definition, which includes skills, knowledge, and beliefs about literacy, would bring a major drop in the official illiteracy rate, a change that would more accurately characterize the Moroccan situation.

This is not to say that there is no literacy problem in Morocco, any more than one can say that there is no literacy problem in the United States, where a national survey found that illiteracy was present in less that 5% of

American youth but where "low" literacy affected almost 25% of the survey population (Kirsch & Jungeblut, 1986). What can be said is that literacy, like health, will always be a problem, precisely because, in a changing world, needs and desires will change as well. There is no minimum level that will remain fixed in stone for policymakers. Each survey, each estimate, each policy decision will need to be based on agreed-upon definitions, and these may need to be reconsidered at least as often as national censuses are undertaken.

As we have argued, to study literacy in Morocco is to discover that the concept of literacy itself may be defined by knowledge and belief as well as by the presence or absence of particular skills. How the former are related to the latter is a topic only beginning to be addressed, as we found in the work on beliefs and attributions. In addition, we should be careful not to treat literacy as a monolithic entity, as we have multiple languages and scripts, as well as multiple levels of skills, knowledge, and beliefs within each language and/or script domain. Thus, within a complex society, be it Morocco or the United States, literacy is not an "object" that can be mandated by government authorities; but, rather, its acquisition and maintenance are surely dependent on the cultural beliefs, practices, and history within which it resides. This perspective, a central outcome of our findings from Morocco, clearly puts constraints on many of the generalizations about literacy that have appeared over the past century.

Yet constraints need not only constrain. They can also lead to new areas of scientific inquiry and to innovation in educational policy. Knowing that a second language can be a useful vehicle for literacy learning in certain contexts opens up, rather than closes down, policy options for formal and nonformal educational programs. Realizing that the retention of skill may be more prevalent among young women than men, even though the former are unemployed, raises important issues about job opportunities that may vary by gender. Understanding the multiple roles that beliefs and attitudes play in literacy acquisition among preschoolers as well as their low-literate parents can provide new opportunities for utilizing mass media to help influence parenting and family support mechanisms.

These and related findings from projects like this one can serve as the stimuli for fresh visions about literacy work. Although international literacy statistics remain as bleak as ever, there is renewed energy in the air. By linking solid research with political vision, the possibilities for becoming a more literate world have never been better.

Appendix 1. Cognitive consequences of Quranic preschooling

For many people, rote learning evokes recollections of Latin lessons, unending biological terminology, perhaps even the nine-digit U.S. postal zip codes. It may bring to mind the drudgery of elementary and high school lessons, even though rote learning was supposed to have been eliminated from so-called modern schools in most countries many decades ago. The word *rote,* a variant on the words *route* and *routine,* is defined by *Webster's Dictionary* as "learning mechanistically, by memory alone, or without thought." As is evident from the scientific literature, memory often has been seen to have a dual and even paradoxical role in education: first, as a low-level skill that replaces thought, and second, as a basic skill necessary for all types of school learning.[1]

The history of rote learning and memory is surprisingly rich and diverse. Prior to the advent of writing systems, keeping track of accumulated bits of information contributed to an increasing burden on human memory. The oral tradition, which relied on the individual's memory, helped promote the use of mnemonics or specialized strategies that improved on earlier methods of rote memorization. Yet one apparent cause for the rise of formal educational settings (where students are explicitly taught a given body of knowledge) followed directly from the fact that haphazard remembering was an inefficient manner of storing and conveying large amounts of information (e.g., Goody, 1977; Yates, 1966).

Given that written religious texts, such as the Quran, were at the historical origins of this kind of memorization, it might be expected that

271

memorized oral traditions would be replaced by written materials over the centuries. Once it became possible to record information for posterity, traditional memory specialists (poets, bards, and religious reciters such as Islamic *fqihs*) would no longer need formidable memories and complex mnemonics to encode, maintain, and retrieve large amounts of information from memory. This, as we have seen in Morocco, was not to happen. Although, in contemporary Western societies, one is often impressed with the capacity to store and process information outside of our heads (through individual literacy and now especially through computers), oral traditions have not disappeared with the advent of widespread literacy; instead, memorization and literacy have coexisted more or less happily to the present (Havelock, 1976; Lord, 1960).

Just as many contemporary educators have bemoaned the overuse of memory at the expense of higher-order thinking skills in contemporary American classrooms, so too have some modern observers decried the continuation of Quranic schooling for promoting and reinforcing rote recitation. There are two principal questions embedded in this discussion of traditional schooling and memorization. One is whether or not Quranic schooling really has an effect on the memory skills of children who attend them. And the other is whether there are negative effects of Quranic schooling on subsequent learning in school. Both of these are empirical questions, yet neither has received adequate attention. One goal of our project was to add some meat to these old bones of contention.

The first claim – on memory effects of traditional schooling – stems from a relatively long tradition of work in culture and psychology that presumes a critical cognitive dichotomy between Western and "preliterate" societies and where considerable research attention has already been devoted to the study of whether formal schooling has an impact on cognitive growth. For more than a century and up to the present, research has taken place in a number of countries in the Third World, where schooling is not available for large numbers of children and adults. There is, at present, a consensus that formal schooling along the Western model, which has been the focus of virtually all of the studies to date, affects a variety of cognitive skills ranging from logic and reasoning to memory and perceptual skills (Cole & Scribner, 1974; Nerlove & Snipper, 1981; Rogoff, 1981).

Until the Morocco Literacy Project, we knew of only one other empirical study of Islamic schooling and its cognitive consequences, the research on literacy in Liberia undertaken by Scribner and Cole (1981).[2]

In one widely cited example from their research, Liberian adults who had attended Quranic schools in their youth were found to have better incremental memory skills (words remembered in increasing long strings) as a consequence of years of Quranic study, particularly when compared with Vai (tribal) literates who never attended Quranic schools. Nonetheless, the Quranic-schooled adults did not possess better general memory or other cognitive skills than adults who became literate either in the indigenous Vai script or in English (in the modern public schools). Scribner and Cole claimed that the enhanced incremental memory skills were evidence that literacy per se did not affect memory (since all three groups were literate), but rather the differences were due to the nature of the practice involved in learning to read and write. However, because the Liberian adults had completed their Quranic schooling and literacy learning many years before the research was conducted, it was impossible to know precisely which antecedent factors really led to the differences found.[3] Our work in Morocco attempted to close this research gap, as we had access to children who were in the process of Quranic instruction and memorization.

Research design and experimental measures

The children who participated in this specific study were part of Cohort 1 and were selected from the first year of primary school such that the following principal contrasts could be made: no preschool versus Quranic preschool versus modern preschool; Arabic versus Berber maternal languages; urban versus rural environment; and boys versus girls (as shown in Table 4.2). The main contrast in this analysis was between children who had 1 to 2 years of Quranic preschooling before entering primary school and those who had little or no Quranic preschooling.

Because we hoped to replicate the Scribner-Cole study, we needed a broad sampling of children's memory skills, particularly those involving rote memory. Other cognitive skills, including perceptual development and logic, were measured as well in order to determine whether the effects would be general or specific to the type of intellectual practice children received. Quranic schooling, according to the Scribner-Cole work, should affect rote-type memory skills more than other types of memory and cognitive skills. Finally, we included in this analysis children's results on tests of logical reasoning, as well as the effects on Arabic reading achievement in years 1–5 of primary school.[4]

For this brief research summary, only the Arabic-speaking children are compared across environment and type of preschooling experience; a detailed analysis of the work, including Berber-speaking children, is provided in Wagner and Spratt (1987). The measures of memory ability we developed are described in the following discussion.

1. Serial memory. Because a major interest was to consider the specific effects of Quranic rote pedagogy, we developed four contrasting types of serial memory tasks, each one more closely related, so we hypothesized, to the memory practices of children studying the Quran. The description of Liberian Quranic schooling provided by Scribner and Cole (1981) was only partly applicable to Morocco. Though Moroccan children learn series of phrases in longer and longer strings, they do not typically repeat sentences lengthened one word at a time at each repetition, as described for Liberia. Nonetheless, because the Liberian memory data showed a positive relationship between prior Quranic schooling and superior incremental serial memory performance among adults, we sought to replicate this finding with Moroccan children.

The span and incremental memory tasks were also useful in that they seemed to epitomize the notion of rote memory and because there was a long history of their use in intelligence testing. In year 1, children were presented with all four serial memory tasks, as shown in Figure A1.1. In year 3, children were assessed on only one of these tasks (Span Digit).

a. Span digit memory (Span Digit). Children were presented with an IQ-type digit span task: A random series of digits is presented for oral repetition, increasing in length on successive trials. In this and the other serial memory tasks, the child was allowed a second attempt on each string of numbers if he or she failed to repeat the sequence correctly on that trial. Testing was stopped if the second attempt at repetition of a given string was incorrect. The score was calculated as the longest sequence of digits repeated correctly.

b. Incremental digit memory (Incr Digit). This task was similar to Span Digit, except that each string built incrementally on the prior string. Scribner and Cole (1981) had hypothesized that Quranic learning would favor the acquisition of longer and longer strings of information, thus favoring learning by increments.

c. Span name memory (Span Name). While studying the Quran, children do not spend time memorizing digits. However, they often have occasion to memorize Muslim names, as well as sometimes lengthy strings of God's attributes (such as *Allah ar-Rahman ar-Rahim* "God, the Benefi-

a. Span digit memory

trial 1	7	9			
trail 2	6	1	5		
trial 3	9	3	4	2	
trial 4	8	2	5	1	9

b. Incremental digit memory

trial 1	7	9			
trial 2	7	9	2		
trial 3	7	9	2	4	
trial 4	7	9	2	4	3

c. Span name memory

trial 1	Ahmed ben	Abdullah			
trial 2	Salim ben	Hamid ben	Jamil		
trial 3	Abdul ben	Jamil ben	Hussein ben	Boubker	
trial 4	Jamil ben	Ahmed ben	Abdullah ben	Salim ben	Hussein

d. Incremental name memory

trial 1	Ahmed ben	Abdullah			
trial 2	Ahmed ben	Abdullah ben	Jamil		
trial 3	Ahmed ben	Abdullah ben	Jamil ben	Hussein	
trail 4	Ahmed ben	Abdullah ben	Jamil ben	Hussein ben	Salim

Figure A1.1. Design of serial memory tests.

cent, the Merciful"). In addition, there is a long history of the memorization of sequences of names, or chains of sources (*isnad*), in the study of
Islamic tradition (Hadith). While not typical in the Quranic preschools in
Morocco, the study of *isnad* is quite common in higher-level Islamic
education, and it is a well-known cultural form in Morocco. This cultural
tradition fit well into our plan to approximate Quranic-based memory
skills in the experimental measures. The Span Name task was constructed
of a random series of Muslim names, increasing in length on successive
trials. The particle *ben* between items connotes a kinship relationship
(literally son of) and served, for testing purposes, to separate one name
from the next.

   d. Incremental name memory (Incr Name). If the Scribner-Cole hypothesis is correct, the Incr Name task, more than the other serial memory

tasks, ought to show the clearest advantage for Quranic schooled children. This task is identical to the Incr Digit task, except that Muslim names, rather than digits, are presented in incrementally longer strings.

    e. Mean serial memory (Mean Serial). This score was calculated from the mean of the four memory tests, in year 1 only.

2. Other memory tasks. These memory tasks, typical in the literature on children's memory, were hypothesized to be relatively less susceptible to the specific effects of Quranic study.

    a. Discourse repetition memory (Discourse). This task measured children's ability to repeat increasingly long and complex segments of connected and understandable text in their native language. Children were required to repeat them verbatim, with both length and number of correctly repeated sentences scored. If Quranic schooling helps in serial rote memory, one might wonder if similar differences would occur in memory for connected discourse. The Discourse task consisted of increasingly longer meaningful sentences on each trial (e.g., trial 1: Mokhtar took his nephew to the market; trial 2: Nadia asked her friend to teach her embroidery). Number of correctly repeated sentences (trials) was the child's score on this task.

    b. Pictorial memory (Pictorial). This task consisted of a series of pictures of well-known animals, randomly arranged in lines of five on single sheets of cardboard. Each cardboard sheet was presented for a few seconds and then covered; over 10 trials the child was shown a target item and had to point to where that animal was located among the five covered pictures on the cardboard. While equivalent tasks have been used as a measure of verbal labeling and rehearsal among older primary and secondary school children (Hagen, Meacham, & Mesibov, 1970; Wagner, 1974, 1978a), the pictorial task was used as a measure of short-term pictorial, as opposed to verbal, memory in young children.

Results

Mean z-scores were calculated on each of the contrast groups on all tasks.[5] There was variation across tasks within subsamples, but the Quranic (and modern preschool) groups generally outperformed the non-Quranic groups (see Table A1.1). Not surprisingly, the average score of the serial tasks (Mean Serial) confirmed the superiority of Quranic schooled children relative to non-preschooled children, and data from Span Digit/3

Table A1.1. Environment and Quranic preschool: ANOVAs on experimental measures

Measures	N	Environment[a]		Quranic preschool[b]		Env. × QS
		F	Direction of Effect	F	Direction of Effect	F
1. Serial memory						
Span Digit/1	(168)	.141		6.861***	QS > N	.044
Incr Digit/1	(168)	.016		3.880**	QS > N	.002
Span Name/1	(168)	.014		1.416		.185
Incr Name/1	(168)	.062		7.346***	QS > N	3.709**
Mean Serial/1	(168)	.056		9.858***	QS > N	.629
Span Digit/3	(134)	2.872*	U > R	7.808***	QS > N	4.115
2. Other memory						
Discourse/1	(168)	.295		.250		1.222
Pictorial/1	(169)	6.348***	R > U	2.443		.480

Note: *significant at .10 level; **significant at .05 level; ***significant at .01 level. Direction of contrasts are indicated by U (Urban), R (Rural), QS (Quranic preschool), and N (no Quranic preschool).

[a]The environment contrast compares Arabic-speaking urban children (UQA + UNA) with Arabic-speaking rural children (RQA + RNA). UMA was also removed from the urban sample to allow for a balanced 2 × 2 ANOVA.

[b]The Quranic preschool contrast compares the Arabic-speaking Quranic preschool (QS) group (UQA + RQA) with the Arabic-speaking non-Quranic preschool (N) group (UNA + RNA).

showed that this advantage was maintained into year 3 of the study.[6] Neither Discourse nor Pictorial memory showed significant effects of Quranic preschooling, though for Pictorial memory rural children were superior to urban children.[7]

Are there cognitive consequences?

The main results may be summarized most clearly by considering the two main questions raised earlier. First, are there cognitive consequences to Quranic pedagogy and learning? Our results lend support to the Scribner-Cole hypothesis that Islamic schooling has a significant effect on serial memory and does not generalize to other kinds of memory or cognitive skills (such as discourse and pictorial memory). However, our attempt to link the specific nature of the memory task to particular practices of Quranic schooling met with less success. According to the Scribner-Cole hypothesis, we would expect that Quranic preschooled children would do relatively better on the two incremental memory tasks, and especially on the incremental name task, which most approximated the *isnad* tradition of religious study. But the incremental tasks were not systematically easier than span tasks for children who attended Quranic preschooling. Furthermore, the effects of Quranic preschooling were roughly equivalent whether using digits or names as items to be remembered. Finally, the average serial memory scores (Mean Serial) of urban groups who attended either Quranic or modern preschool (UQA and UMA) were quite similar, even though explicit Quranic recitation occurs more often in Quranic schools. Potential explanations for the latter results may be understood in light of two ethnographic findings we noted earlier: (1) Quranic learning of texts in Morocco does not typically involve incremental strings of single words but rather of phrases; and (2) even the modern preschools in Morocco provide a certain amount of recitation practice. Nonetheless, the overall trend favoring Quranic preschooled children on serial memory is striking, especially given that no other cognitive task showed a major effect of Quranic schooling.[8]

Second, does Quranic schooling stultify the mind, as has been claimed by some observers, and does it lead to poor school performance in children? The evidence we collected clearly rejects this joint hypothesis. Although the Quranic preschooled groups do no better on reasoning tasks than their counterparts without such schooling, neither do they do any worse. In the domain of school performance, whereas there were no differences overall, the Berber-speaking rural subsamples who attended Quranic school actually showed increased reading achievement.[9] In sum, there is little empirical basis for the speculation that Quranic preschool is "bad for the mind."[10]

A final comment on the study of Quranic pedagogy

Consistent but distinct patterns of cognitive performance were found for children with different kinds of pedagogical experience. Although no subgroup was found to be superior on all types of tasks, Quranic pre-schooled children outperformed non–preschooled children on tests of serial memory, providing a replication and ontogenetic extension of the work of Scribner and Cole (1981).

Such studies of cognition and schooling are important pieces in the complex puzzle that is educational development. Many opinions (and biases) continue to exist in the realm of learning, and especially so in traditional settings such as Morocco's Quranic preschools. It is no surprise that many well-educated Moroccans view such traditional schools as anachronisms of the past. Whether the future will treat such schools as potential resources for development (as proposed elsewhere; see Wagner, 1989a) or as relics to dismiss will be an interesting and important saga to follow over future decades.

Notes

1 For a review of the literature on culture and memory development, see Wagner (1980).

2 The research of Scribner and Cole (1981) was devoted primarily to whether (or how much) individual literacy skills affect individual cognitive development. Based on earlier, predominantly historical research (e.g., Goody & Watt, 1968; Havelock, 1976), Scribner and Cole sought to disentangle the effects of literacy from other social factors (such as schooling and social class) on adult cognition in Liberia. They tested mainly for adult cognitive skills and attempted to correlate these with self-reported schooling histories.

3 This gap between the time of the experience and the time of testing leaves open many alternative explanations for the findings reported. We found that the information gathered on Quranic schooling of Moroccan fathers was not particularly reliable, because attendance was often only sporadic over the childhood years, and information was often obtained from mothers not the fathers. The fact that the Scribner-Cole study found a significant (even if modest) effect of Quranic schooling on certain memory abilities leads to at

least one of three possible conclusions: (1) The Liberian context of Quranic schooling is very different from that of Morocco; (2) the findings are really more robust than that claimed by Scribner-Cole, inasmuch as they overcame "noisy" data; or (3) the findings are spurious. We will probably never be able to resolve this issue, though it is fair to say that studies that attempt to measure the consequences of childhood socialization would be considerably enhanced if they provided ontogenetic evidence of their developmental claims. See Wagner (1982a) for a broader review of this issue.

4 As described in chapter 3, the curriculum of Quranic preschooling may vary across teachers to a certain extent, but usually includes a large amount of memorization and group recitation of verses of the Quran, along with some teaching of the Arabic alphabet and basic numeracy skills. Modern preschools, by contrast, emphasize preparation for primary school with such activities as beginning reading and arithmetic.

5 The raw score means, equivalent to what is commonly termed the "memory span" of the four serial tasks over all subsamples were Span Digit = 3.89, Incr Digit = 4.73, Span Name = 3.37, and Incr Name = 3.38. These scores approximate U.S. norms for same-age children (Stigler, Lee, & Stevenson, 1986). Digit Span was superior to Name Span ($F = 225.60$, $p < .01$); and incremental presentation of items helped performance on the digit task ($F = 484.44$, $p < .01$) but not on the name task. The raw score superiority of digit over name memory is not surprising, for Baddeley, Thomson, and Buchanan (1975) have shown that the vocalized duration of items in a digit span test is inversely related to the number of digits recalled.

6 The overall patterns of scores for Mean Serial and Span Digit/3 are similar, especially considering the 2-year gap between testing; furthermore, the scores on these two measures were significantly correlated ($r = .36$, $p < .01$).

7 While Discourse memory scores were significantly correlated with Serial memory tasks ($r > .30$, $p < .01$), Pictorial memory scores were not ($r < .08$, $p > .10$). These findings are consistent with the hypothesis that verbal memory abilities are related more to each other than to visual memory skills. General information task scores were unaffected by preschool or environment. By contrast, the results of the Children's Embedded Figures Test (CEFT) indicated that rural groups outperformed urban groups, again with no effect of Quranic preschooling. The Concept Identification task also produced a significant advantage for the Rural groups. As with Concept Identification, rural children were superior on the CEFT, as found by Wagner (1978b), even though the causes (socialization, differentiation, perceptual disembedding practice, or other) remain elusive. In that study, Wagner hypothesized that rural children were socialized in a more "independent" fashion than urban children, and also had more opportunities to use perceptual disembedding skills in such household chores as shepherding. Because the CID and CEFT

tasks involved perceptual acuity, this constitutes additional support for a perceptual superiority explanation.

8 See note 7.

9 For more detail on Berber-speaking children in Quranic schools, see chapter 8; see also Wagner and Spratt, 1987.

10 Of course, one can criticize such schools on other grounds, such as the poverty of their circumstance (lack of tables, chairs, sanitary facilities, and so forth) or the lack of formal training of the *fqihs*, but these domains are quite another thing from the kinds of cognitive claims that have been made. Furthermore, such criticisms could be easily rectified with better funding support.

Appendix 2. Details of test construction

In order to create tests appropriately adapted for Morocco, we had to deal with a number of complex methodological problems. Testing instruments had to make sense to the Moroccan children and their parents, as well as be of relevance to the scientific community (the emic-etic dilemma discussed in chapter 1). Second, the project studied literacy in Standard Arabic and Arabic orthography, for which the scientific literature on testing is extremely limited. Further, we worked with sample populations in Morocco who speak a varied mix of languages (Moroccan Arabic, Standard Arabic, Berber, and French), and had to prepare instruments in at least two and, in some cases, all four languages in order to gather needed data. Needless to say, problems of translation and back-translation, and pilot testing, took a great deal more time and effort than in the typical research project in the United States.

Such inherent difficulties also led to increased vigilance concerning the validity of the test instruments, and to a number of innovative approaches. For example, because of the nature of Arabic orthography and Arabic writing (such as differing forms of a given letter depending on its place in a word), we were able to develop several new ways of studying children's early prereading knowledge (see chapter 5). In addition, because we observed the style of rote memorization in the Quranic school, we were able to create cognitive tasks that could mimic, to a greater or lesser extent, the possible consequences of this practice (see appendix 1).

In sum, the variability and complexity that are part of such a cross-cultural, multilingual, and multidisciplinary research project was an integral part of the challenge and excitement of the Morocco Literacy Project.

Scoring methods used in analyses

Because of the variety of tests used in the project, and because the tests varied in content and length across the years of research, contrasts were sometimes made using standardized z-scores calculated for each task in a given year. In addition, overall or global scores for reading and cognitive abilities were constructed from the average of the standard scores on these tasks. Thus, a single overall z-score mean for reading was utilized for each subject in a given year in some of the large complex analyses requiring a simple literacy outcome variable. The creation of such overall scores was supported by the high average correlations found among the individual test pairs used to make up the overall scores (Arabic, year 1: $N = 166$, mean $r = .542$; year 3: $N = 130$, mean $r = .634$; year 5: $N = 117$, mean $r = .668$; French, year 3: $N = 62$, mean $r = .367$; year 5, $N = 116$, mean $r = .514$).

Description of individual tests for Cohort 1

A summary listing of all instruments presented to Cohort 1 is provided in Table A2.1. Further details on some of the measures are provided in the specific chapters in which the test data are presented.

A. Arabic reading measures

In years 1 and 2 of the study (1983–1984), all reading tests were presented to children individually. The test battery generally took 25 to 35 minutes per child to complete. Each child received a small gift for his or her participation. Most tests were developed in two forms, so that longitudinal test-retest administration across the first 2 years of the study would be possible.

For testing sessions in years 3 and 5 (1985–1987), a second battery of Arabic reading tests was constructed to sample the curricula of third-, fourth-, and fifth-grade level Arabic courses provided in the Moroccan school system. The battery included tests of word decoding, word-picture matching, sentence maze, paragraph comprehension, oral reading, and dictation. Due to problems of psychometric reliability, the oral reading

Table A2.1. Cohort 1 instruments: summary listing

Instrument	Abbreviation	Year(s) administered
A. Arabic Literacy Tests		
Morocco Picture Vocabulary Test 1	(MPV/1)	Spring 1983
Early Reading Test 1/2	(ERT/1,2)	Spring 1983; 1984
Word Decoding 1/2	(WD/1)	Spring 1983
Word-Picture Matching 1/2	(WPM/1)	Spring 1983
Quranic Verse Completion 2	(QV/2)	Spring 1984
Word Decoding Arabic 3	(WDC/3)	Spring 1985
Arabic Oral Reading 3	(ORA/3)	Spring 1985
Word-Picture Matching Arabic 3/5	(WPM/3,5)	Spring 1985; 1987
Sentence Maze Arabic 3/5	(SM/3,5)	Spring 1985; 1987
Paragraph Comprehension 3/5	(PC/3,5)	Spring 1985; 1987
Arabic Dictation 3/5	(DCA/3,5)	Spring 1985; 1987
Household Literacy Assessment	(HLA/5)	Fall 1986
Arabic Reading Achievement	(AR/1,3,5)	1983, 1985, 1987[a]
B. French Literacy Tests		
Letter Recognition French 3	(LRF/3)	Spring 1985
Word Decoding French 3	(WDF/3)	Spring 1985
Word-Picture Matching French 3/5	(WPMF/3,5)	Spring 1985; 1987
Sentence Maze French 3/5	(SMF/3,5)	Spring 1985; 1987
Paragraph Comprehension 3/5	(PCF/3,5)	Spring 1985; 1987
French Reading Achievement	(FR3/5)	1985, 1987[b]
C. Cognitive Tests		
Math 1	(MA/1)	Spring 1983
Children's Embedded Figures Test 1	(CEFT/1)	Spring 1983
Concept Identification 1	(CID/1)	Spring 1983
General Information 1	(GEN/1)	Spring 1983
Span-Digit Memory 1/3	(SpanD/1,3)	Spring 1983; 1985
Span-Name Memory 1	(SpanN/1)	Spring 1983
Incremental-Digit Memory 1	(IncrD/1)	Spring 1983
Incremental-Name Memory 1	(IncrN/1)	Spring 1983
Discourse Repetition Memory 1	(DISC/1)	Spring 1983
Pictorial Visual Memory 1	(PICT/1)	Spring 1983
Math 3	(MA/3)	Spring 1985
Concept Identification 3	(CID/3)	Spring 1985
General Information 3	(GEN/3)	Spring 1985
Perception 3/5	(PER3,5)	Spring 1985; 1987
Math 5	(MA/5)	Spring 1987
Span-Digit Memory 5	(SpanD/5)	Spring 1987
Logic 5	(LOG/5)	Spring 1987

Table A2.1. *(cont.)*

Instrument	Abbreviation	Year(s) administered
D. Metacognitive and Attitudinal Indices		
Metacognitive Stories	(CGR, HGR/1)	Spring 1983
Reading Awareness Index	(RAI/5)	Fall 1986
Causal Attributional Indices	(IE, EA)	Fall 1986
E. Interviews		
Student Selection Questionnaire		Spring 1983
Parental Questionnaire		Fall 1983–Spring 1985
Student Interview		Fall 1986
Teacher Questionnaire		Fall 1983–Fall 1984

Note: As noted in the text not all test variables (or abbreviations) were included in the statistical analyses and the text. Also, some of the abbreviations listed here are more specific and/or not identical to those used in the text. Suffixes appended to abbreviations indicate the year(s) in which the particular form of a test was administered.
[a]The Arabic reading (AR) achievement score is derived from selected Arabic reading tests, as described in chapter 5.
[b]The French reading (FR) achievement score is derived from standardized results from French reading tests, as described in chapter 8.

and dictation measures were not part of the statistical analyses presented in this volume.

1. Morocco Picture Vocabulary (MPV) test. The MPV test, an adaptation of the Peabody Picture Vocabulary Test for the Moroccan setting and the age range of our subjects, was administered in year 1 only. It is basically a measure of knowledge of Moroccan Arabic vocabulary. The stimulus pictures were taken from the picture glossary of a Moroccan government Arabic primer for first graders. Moroccan Arabic names for the pictures were collected in pilot sessions in the field, ranked for familiarity and level of difficulty, and finally, certain of these terms were selected for inclusion as the target words in one of the two forms of the test. Though it has been found that spoken vocabulary ability correlates with reading comprehension, for our purposes this task was used primarily to corroborate or support evidence of the child's maternal language. As expected, self-reported Moroccan Arabic speakers performed far better on this task than self-reported Berber speakers. These data were essential in checking the placement of individual subjects in maternal language-based sample groups within our rural sample.

2. Early Reading tests (ERT). The Early Reading tests (composed of the Letter Concept task, Word Concept task, Letter Boundary task, and the Letter Knowledge task) were designed to evaluate the child's prereading knowledge about the Arabic writing system at the single-letter and complete-word levels. The test is divided into eight sections, each of which is intended to measure a discrete set of reading subskills, some general and some specific to Arabic orthography, that some have claimed to be important in the learner's interaction with print (Chall, 1983; Clay, 1979; Feitelson, 1966, 1967). Because of the lack of other such prereading-level measurements for the Arabic language, the tasks described here, prepared with the assistance of Moroccan colleagues specializing in reading, language, and education (A. Ezzaki, F. Badry, M. Nejmi, B. Ben-Omar, and M. Mellouk), are not only innovative but unique. These prereading tasks promise to be useful in indicating new avenues of exploration in an attempt to understand reading acquisition in the Arabic language and script (see also Wagner & Spratt, in press). Detailed descriptions of the tasks of the ERT are provided in chapter 5.

3. Word Decoding (WD). For testing in 1983–1984, the WD task was the first of the whole-word reading tasks in which decoding skills were involved. The child was asked to decode orally each of 16 words presented in writing on individual cards. The words for the two forms of the task were chosen from two separate lexicons compiled from (1) vocabulary appearing in the shortest 15 chapters of the Quran (those most likely to have been studied in the Quranic preschool) and (2) vocabulary appearing in a Moroccan reading primer used in the first year of primary school and in some cases in the modern preschool. These lexicons were accordingly labeled "Quranic" and "secular," primarily for analytical purposes, but sample group differences were not found by vocabulary type. It should be recalled that despite the claim that Standard Arabic covers both classical and modern Standard varieties of Arabic, the two are essentially overlapping word pools of a larger whole.

The last 10 items of the WD1/2 task, which did not provide such vocalization diacritics, required the child to rely more heavily on whole word recognition; unless she or he is a good guesser, the child would probably not be able to provide the correct voweling patterns between the letters except through prior (and remembered) exposure to the word. (See Feitelson, 1966, 1967, 1980, for discussions of the special features of

Hebrew and Arabic scripts and their implications for reading achievement.)

The 1985–1987 WD task drew words from a sampling of chapters from third- to fifth-grade reading textbooks used in the Moroccan schools. While the content of the test differed from that of the WD tests administered in 1983 and 1984, procedures of presentation remained the same.

4. Word-Picture Matching (WPM). This task assessed comprehension at the single word level. In the 1983–1984 version of this task, the child was required to choose from among three written words the one that named or described the picture presented with them. Target and foil words used in the 12 items of each form of the task were chosen from the "Quranic" and "secular" lexicons.

For the 1985–1987 version, target words were chosen from Moroccan third-, fourth-, and fifth-grade primers, as in the WD task, with the additional criterion that they be depictable, familiar, and culturally intelligible concepts. Pictures were replicated from Moroccan French and Arabic textbooks and the Peabody Picture Vocabulary Test, and some were drawn by hand. Each picture was presented with the correct lexical choice and three foil words. Foils were chosen to be semantically, syntactically, or orthographically similar to the correct lexical choice; the orthographic distinction was found to be particularly important (see chapter 5). The 30 items presented on each form of the test equally represented words drawn from third-, fourth-, and fifth-grade level primers. In years 3 and 5, the WPM was presented in a paper-and-pencil, multiple-choice format to groups of about 20 children at a time.

5. Sentence Maze (SM). The Sentence Maze test required the child to supply, from a list of three words, the one word that best completed each of 16 sentences. This test included items and foils that tested primarily vocabulary rather than grammatical structures.

In 1985–1987, the sentences for this task were drawn from an equal distribution of sentences from chapters throughout third-, fourth-, and fifth-grade primers. For each form, the task consisted of 10 fill-in-the-blank sentences to be completed by nouns and an equal number to be completed by verbs. Each item presented one correct and three foil words to be chosen to complete the sentence. The foils were chosen to represent syntactic, semantic, or phonetic confusions, as noted in chapter 5. Because of resource limitations, a detailed analysis of foil error types was never completed, leaving open the question of whether such a typology could help pinpoint learning problems among beginning readers of Arabic.

6. Paragraph Comprehension (PC). The Paragraph Comprehension test presented the child with a series of short paragraphs followed by three to five comprehension questions to be answered by multiple choice. Further details are provided in chapter 5.

7. Oral Reading Arabic (ORA). A test of oral reading was administered in 1985 only. The task, presented to each child individually, was derived from a fourth-grade primer text. The tester followed the child's individual oral reading of the text, marking omissions, misreadings, and insertions on a separate score sheet. A series of orally administered yes–no questions followed the child's oral performance as a measure of overall comprehension. The results of this test was found to be very dependent on the individual who administered it, thereby producing too much variability to be acceptable for analytic purposes. Thus, data from this test were not included.

8. Dictation (DCA). Dictation, or writing down from the teacher's oral discourse, is a very common practice in Morocco, inherited from the French colonial school system. Dictation tasks, based on the same procedure, were presented in 1985 and 1987. The passage used for 1985 testing, about 40 words in length, was derived from a fourth-grade primer text. The 36-word text for the 1987 Arabic dictation was chosen from the children's magazine *Majid* (No. 400, 22 October 1986, p. 20). In both years the task was administered to subjects in a group format. The passage was read slowly twice, and children were instructed to reproduce it word for word in writing in their textbooks. As with the ORA, the administration and scoring of the DCA was found to be too subjective and variable to be included in the statistical analyses.

9. Quranic Verse (QV) Completion. This task, administered in 1984 only, required the child to read outloud and complete (from memory) unfinished Quranic verses, presented on individual cards. The eight verses chosen for each form of this task were selected from among the 15 shortest chapters of the Quran, chapters which children were most likely to have encountered in their Quranic or modern preschool careers. The task, therefore, required both the display of decoding and memory skills, as well as prior exposure to the verses sampled. We had anticipated, of course, that

Quranic preschooled children would excel at this task. However, owing to the limited number of test items and the large variability with the QV, this task was eliminated from subsequent analyses.

10. Household Literacy Assessment (HLA). In year 5, an assessment of everyday or household literacy skills was administered, as described in chapter 9. The HLA item selection was based on our observations concerning the types of tasks that young schooled family members were likely to be called upon to perform in the household.

B. French reading measures

Instruction in French language and literacy is introduced into the Moroccan public school curriculum at the third grade. Thus, in year 3 of the study, a battery of French reading tests was added to the assessment measures administered to those sample subjects who had reached third grade in that year. French language versions of Word Decoding (WDCF), Word-Picture Matching (WPMF), Sentence Maze (SMF), and Paragraph Comprehension (PCF) were developed, drawing vocabulary and themes from the third-, fourth-, fifth-, and sixth-grade textbooks used in Moroccan classrooms. The format and administration of these tasks paralleled those of the equivalent Arabic reading tasks. The Letter Recognition (LRF) task presented strings of five Latin alphabet lowercase letters on separate white cards. The child was required to read off the names of each letter in each string as the tester noted the number of correctly named letters. Instructions for all French tasks were provided in Moroccan Arabic so as to ensure comprehension.

C. Cognitive measures

A variety of cognitive tasks were administered in years 1, 3, and 5 of the study. In addition, mathematics skills were assessed in year 2. The 1983 battery of cognitive measures consisted of 10 separate tasks administered individually. The battery consisted of four measures of general cognitive abilities (Concept Identification, General Information questions, Children's Embedded Figures test, and Math tasks) and six memory tasks (four incremental and span tasks, a Discourse Repetition task to measure auditory and semantic short-term memory, and a Pictorial Memory task). The Perception task was administered in years 3 and 5, while the Logic task was given in year 5 only.

Notebooks of 5 × 8 and 8 × 11 cards held the materials for the tasks requiring a visual stimulus. In year 1, all tasks were presented to the children in their language of greatest competence (Moroccan Arabic or Berber) as determined through the sample selection procedure; in subsequent years, Moroccan Arabic was used. Assistants used stopwatches to keep track of the time limits for certain tasks; in general, assistants were instructed to wait a reasonable amount of time until the child made some response before continuing to the next item. In a small number of isolated cases, perhaps five in each site, a child was too frightened or otherwise unable to respond to certain tasks, particularly those requiring a verbal response. Only one subject refused to participate in all tasks and had to be dropped from the study.

All tasks administered in year 1 were pretested, and the testers trained, during a 1-week session in November 1982, at the Bab Marrakech School in Rabat. A subject pool of 27 six-year-old students was tested at that time. Each testing period was followed by discussions with the testers on both procedural and content issues, and the final tasks reflected revisions made based on results and suggestions that emerged from this training session.

1. Concept Identification (CID). This task is a version of a common nonverbal subtest of many IQ tests adapted for Moroccan children. It was chosen as a nonverbal measure of reasoning ability. The child has to point to the unique item among five small pictures that doesn't fit the pattern (e.g., four drawings of a right hand and one drawing of a left hand are presented).

The Concept Identification task was increased to 20 items in the year 3 administration (CID3); the first 12 items consisted of pictures of objects, and the remaining 8 items employed geometrical forms. New items used to extend the original test were drawn from the Test of General Ability, Levels 3 and 4 (Guidance Testing Associates, 1962), and the Kuhlmann-Anderson Test, Booklet K (7th ed., 1963). Items were presented roughly in order of ascending difficulty, according to results of itemization analysis of the previous CID task.

2. General information (GEN). This type of task is also commonly found in IQ tests and was adapted to the Moroccan context. The task consisted of 20 orally presented questions sampling four subject categories: history and geography, culture and religion, science, and everyday knowledge. Questions from each subject category were evenly distributed through the test. Subjects' responses were scored correct, partially correct, or incorrect by the testers, according to preestablished criteria. Such information tasks are usually highly correlated with reading and IQ.

The year 3 version of the test, identical in format to the year 1 task, retained eight questions from the previous test, eliminating those that were too easy for third to fifth graders. Twelve new questions were added to maintain a total number of 20 questions. The questions were ordered by level of difficulty, as determined by the results of item analysis of the GEN/1 test.

3. Memory tasks. A series of short-term serial and other memory tasks was constructed especially for the study of memorization in traditional Quranic schools. Details on these memory tasks are contained in appendix 1. In year 5 of the study, the span digit task, previously presented orally and individually, was revised to permit group testing. Children were presented with forms, including lines of boxes of increasing length, and were instructed to hold their hand and pencil high in the air as the tester read off once the list of numbers for each trial. At the signal, children were required to write the numbers they had heard in the order presented, one digit to a box in the line for that trial.

4. Children's Embedded Figures Test (CEFT). The CEFT is a well-known measure of cognitive style in perceptual development and is often considered to be correlated with general intellectual ability (cf. Witkin et al., 1971). The task, administered in year 1 only, was used in a slightly shortened form in the present study. It consisted of locating the outline, embedded in a series of complex pictorial arrays, of particular geometric shapes (labeled "tent" and "mosque" for the Moroccan sample) within a prescribed time limit.

5. Mathematics (MA). The math tests for years 1 and 2 consisted of a variety of simple arithmetic questions, presented in both written (e.g., $2 + 5 = ??$) and oral story problem formats. Questions assessed simple counting, addition, and subtraction skills. The year 3 arithmetic task (MA/3) consisted of 6 individually presented oral story problems and a written section of 12 items. The written section was administered in a group format; of the 12 equations, 4 were presented horizontally (1 equation each of simple addition, subtraction, multiplication, division) and 8 in columns (2 of each operation, with increasing difficulty). The year 5 test (MA/5) was essentially identical to the 12-item written section of the year 3 test except that different numbers were used.

6. Perception task (PER). This task of perceptual discrimination, administered in years 3 and 5 of the study, was drawn from the Primary Mental Abilities Test, Grades 2–4 (Science Research Associates, 1962). The test, containing 49 items in our slightly edited version, was a paper-and-pencil group-administered test. Each item presented the child with a row of four geometric forms; the child was required to find and circle the two forms that were exactly alike. Children were allowed 5 minutes to complete the task, so there was an element of speed involved as well.

7. Logic task (LOG). This task, administered in year 5 only, was a slightly abridged version (22 items) of the paper-and-pencil Serial Matrices task (Scale 4) from the Culture Fair Test series (Cattell & Cattell, 1961). In each trial, children were required to select the one box out of five choices that best completed the pattern of a 2 × 2 or 3 × 3 matrix in which one cell was missing. Apart from the abridgment, the only other change was that children were instructed to circle their response choice rather than to copy its referent letter in a response column at the far left margin of the page (as required in the original test), in order to minimize the number of steps required to complete the task. Pilot testing served to train the testers in its administration and explanation to subjects; results from pilot testing also revealed a satisfactory range of better than chance level correct responses, indicating that the goal of the task was generally understood by the large majority of subjects.

D. Metacognitive and attributional indices

1. Metacognitive stories (CGR, HGR). Seven metacognitive stories were designed to explore the child's view of differing popular Moroccan conceptions and values with regard to reading. This task was administered in year 1 only. For more detail, see chapter 7.

2. Reading Awareness Index (RAI). In year 5, a second assessment of metacognitive beliefs and reading awareness, geared to older children, was administered to Cohort 1. The questions in this measure were derived from the work of Paris and his colleagues (Paris & Oka, 1986) and adapted for the Moroccan context. For more detail, see chapter 7.

3. Causal Attribution scales (IE, EA). A measure of children's causal attributions, presented in an oral forced-choice format, was designed to examine the child's tendency to cite ability, effort, or external rationales for hypothetical positive and negative experiences. This measure was administered in year 5, during the course of the student interview. Derived from Crandall, Katkovsky, and Crandall's (1965) Intellectual Achievement Responsibility scale, the original IAR scale was modified to incorporate situations pertinent to the Moroccan experience and to differentiate between ability and effort attributions (confounded in the Crandall, et al. scale). The resulting 24-item measure allowed for the analysis of two main contrasts: effort versus ability (AE, 7 items) and internal versus external (IE, 17 items) attributions. See chapter 7 for more detail.

E. Interviews

1. Student selection interview. In order to select a sample that would represent the contrast groups required by the project design (male-female; urban-rural; preschool experiences; maternal language), a student selection interview was developed to ascertain first graders' status with regard to these contrasts. The instrument was administered to all first graders in four urban primary schools in Marrakech and five schools in rural al-Ksour. Information from students themselves regarding preschool background was checked with the school administration, preschool authorities, and parents when possible, as were the child's age and prior first-grade repetition history. Maternal language information was based on self-report and verified within the interview itself with short conversational tests of Moroccan Arabic and Berber. To avoid threats to the validity of the experimental contrasts in the study, children with multiple preschooling experiences, first grade repetition prior to year 1 of the study, and/or bilingual (Arabic/Berber) proficiency were eliminated from participation in the study.

2. Parent interview. Beginning in the fall of year 1, 2-hour (or more) interviews were conducted with the primary caretaker (usually the mother) of most children (90%) in the study. In the course of this structured interview, administered by Moroccan-American researcher pairs in the parent's preferred language (Moroccan Arabic or Berber), family history was obtained, including education of parents, grandparents, and siblings of the target child and language(s) used in the home. Parents' and siblings' literacy levels (on a 3-point scale) were reported by the family member interviewed. No direct measurement of literacy was undertaken because mothers were, in the large majority, unschooled and claimed they could neither read nor write. Detailed sibling information was gathered for the two oldest siblings of the sample child.

During the same interview, mothers were asked 30 questions concerning attitudes about the development and education of their children. These questions were aimed at discovering how individual parents conceived of the complementary roles of parents, teachers, and schools in the instruction of children. A subset of these questions paralleled the metacognitive questions asked of the children themselves, such as the importance of studying alone versus with other children (see chapter 7). An English translation of the parent interview is provided in appendix 3.

3. Student interview. In year 5, structured interviews similar to those administered to parents were conducted with the Cohort 1 children themselves, by then 12 years of age. Apart from the household literacy assessment, reading awareness, and causal attributions instruments, the student interview included questions regarding the child's family background, attitudes about reading, writing, and schooling generally, home literacy and material environment, travel experience, and mass media exposure and preferences. An English translation of the student interview is provided in appendix 4.

4. Teacher interview. All first-grade teachers whose pupils were subjects in the study were individually interviewed in year 1. Basic personal data (age, marital status, linguistic background, education of family members) were gathered, as well as information on the individual's teacher training, certification status, and experience, the school establishment, class size, teaching responsibilities and methods, and reflections on teaching. Results from the teacher interview provided supporting information for our ethnographic observations. Table 6.3 presents some of the key questions (and results) of the teacher interview.

Design and construction of instruments for Cohort 2

A summary listing of all instruments presented to Cohort 2 is provided in Table A2.2.

A. Arabic reading measures

In years 3 and 4 of the study, Cohort 2 received the same Arabic reading measures as those administered to Cohort 1 in year 3. Individual children

Table A2.2. Cohort 2 instruments: summary listing

Instrument	Abbreviation	Year(s) administered
A. Arabic Literacy Tests		
Word Decoding Arabic 5/6	(WD/5)	Spring 1985
Word-Picture Matching Arabic 5/6	(WPM/5)	Spring 1985
Sentence Maze Arabic 5/6	(SM/5)	Spring 1985
Paragraph Comprehension 5/6	(PC/5)	Spring 1985
Arabic Dictation 5/6	(DCA/5)	Spring 1985
Arabic Oral Reading 5	(ORA/5)	Spring 1985
Sentence Maze Arabic 7	(SM/7)	Spring 1987
Paragraph Comprehension 7	(PC/7)	Spring 1987
Arabic Writing Task 7	(WRA/7)	Spring 1987
Household Literacy Assessment	(HLA/5)	Fall 1985
Arabic Reading Achievement	(AR5/7)	1985, 1987[a]
Dropout supplement to 1987 tests		
Word-Picture Matching Arabic 5/D	(WPMAD/7)	Spring 1987
Sentence Maze Arabic 5/D	(SMAD/7)	Spring 1987
Paragraph Compehension Arabic 5/D	(PCAD/7)	Spring 1987
Arabic Dictation 5/D	(DCAD/7)	Spring 1987
B. French Literacy Tests		
Letter Recognition French 5	(LRF/5)	Spring 1985
Word Decoding French 5/6	(WDF/5)	Spring 1985, 1986
Word-Picture Matching French 5/6	(WPMF/5)	Spring 1985, 1986
Sentence Maze French 5/6	(SMF/5)	Spring 1985, 1986
Paragraph Comprehension 5/6	(PCF/5)	Spring 1985, 1986
Sentence Maze French 7	(SMF/7)	Spring 1987
Paragraph Comprehension 7	(PCF/7)	Spring 1987
French Writing Task 7	(WRF/7)	Spring 1987
French Reading Achievement	(FR5/7)	1985, 1987[b]
Dropout supplement to 1987 tests		
Word-Picture Matching French 5/D	(WPMFD/7)	Spring 1987
Sentence Maze French 5/D	(SMFD/7)	Spring 1987
Paragraph Comprehension French 5/D	(PCFD/7)	Spring 1987
C. Cognitive Tests		
Math 5	(MA5,7)	Spring 1985, 1987
Span-Digit Memory 5	(SpanD/5)	Spring 1985
Concept Identification 5	(CID/5)	Spring 1985
General Information 5	(GEN/5)	Spring 1985
Perception 5/7	(PER/5,7)	Spring 1985, 1987
Math 7	(MA/7)	Spring 1987
Span-Digit Memory 7	(SpanD/7)	Spring 1987
Logic 7	(LOG/7)	Spring 1987

Table A2.2. *(cont.)*

Instrument	Abbreviation	Year(s) administered
D. Metacognitive and Attitudinal Indices		
Reading Awareness Index	(RAI/6)	Fall 1985
Causal Attributional Indices	(IE, EA)	Fall 1985
E. Interviews		
Student Selection Questionnaire		Spring 1985
Student Interview		Fall 1985
Dropout Fact Sheet		Fall 1983–Fall 1984

Note: As noted in the text not all test variables were included in the statistical analyses and the text. Also, some of the abbreviations listed here are more specific and/or not identical to those used in the text. Suffixes appended to abbreviations indicate the year(s) in which the particular form of a test was administered.

[a]The Arabic reading (AR) achievement score is derived from selected Arabic reading tests, as described in chapter 5.

[b]The French reading (FR) achievement score is derived from standardized results from French reading tests, as described in chapter 8.

received opposite forms of the tasks across the 2 years. For year 5 test administration, however, new higher-level tests were required for Cohort 2 in-school children (who were now in sixth and seventh grades) because the Arabic reading tests used in years 3 and 4 represented curriculum spanning the primary school years but not beyond. The one-word level of the Word-Picture Matching test was found to be, on the average, too simple for these children and was therefore dropped from the year 5 testing of in-school children. Furthermore, Sentence Maze and Paragraph Comprehension tasks were also revised to make them more difficult. Incorporated into these new reading tests were a number of "linking" items from previous years' tests (see chapter 10); however about two thirds of each test is entirely new material. In addition, the Dictation task of previous years was replaced by a new writing task (see item 3 below).

Most of the tests for Cohort 2 were derived from previous use with Cohort 1. Where tests have been altered to increase difficulty, or for other reasons, these changes are described.

1. Sentence Maze Arabic (SMA). The SM/7 task comprised 30 items divided into three subsections: 10 linking items from previous tests (5 items from each form); 10 newly created vocabulary items, in which the correct answer is distinguishable from the foils on semantic grounds only; and 10 new grammar items, in which the answer must be chosen on the basis of syntactic correctness.

2. Paragraph Comprehension (PC). As with the Sentence Maze task, a linking subsection and a new subsection were combined to create the final 6-text, 26-question (5 questions for each of 2 linking texts; 4 questions for each of the 4 new texts) year 5 Paragraph Comprehension test. One linking text with questions was selected from each form of the year 3 test, on the basis of its overall statistical reliability level and moderate difficulty level according to year 3 item means.

3. Writing (WRA). For the in-school subjects of Cohort 2, a more free-form writing task in Arabic was chosen to replace the Dictation task of earlier years. For this task, children were given a series of four drawings arranged vertically on a page, with space to write a story to the right of the pictures. The drawings (taken from "guided composition" exercises used in first- and second-year English language courses in Morocco high schools) presented a progression of action that clearly told a story. Children were instructed to write one or two sentences for each picture, so that the entire text would tell the story of the pictures. In pretests, equal numbers of subjects were given one of two sets of pictures that were used to eliminate the set that appeared to be less well understood. Pretesting also raised questions of evaluation of the writing samples, such as in the case of students who used colloquial rather than literary Arabic lexical items and syntactic forms. For the final task it was decided that two evaluators would each assign a score of 0 to 4 for each paper; discrepant scores would be remedied by the input of a third evaluator. Even with all this work on pilot testing, the results were so variable, and interrater reliability so low that the WRA was excluded from further analyses.

B. French reading measures

The administration of French reading tests to Cohort 2 in years 3, 4, and 5 was analogous to that of Arabic tasks for the same years and also utilized with Cohort 1. The tests administered in years 3 and 4 were identical to the French test received by Cohort 1 in year 3, in opposite forms across years; in year 5, tests involved the same in-school/dropout distinctions as described for Arabic tasks. Following is a description of the new French tests developed for year 5 testing. The development, administration, and evaluation of the French writing task (WRF) were identical to those of the Arabic in-school writing task, except that children were instructed to produce stories written in French. The picture set employed in this task also differed from that of the Arabic task. As with the WRA, the WRF was found to be psychometrically unreliable and was not used in subsequent analyses.

C. Cognitive measures

The cognitive tasks administered to Cohort 2 in years 3, 4, and 5 were identical to those received by Cohort 1 in the same years, with the exception of the math tasks administered in year 5. In year 5, Cohort 2 school dropouts received the same 10-item math task that they had received in year 3, whereas in-school subjects received a new math task, which was revised to increase the length of the basic functions sections and to reduce or eliminate sections involving complex higher algebraic functions not central to the purposes of the test. The resulting 42-item draft was pilot-tested, and the most difficult items eliminated, so that a final 20-item test was produced. The final format of this test paralleled that of the earlier math test administered in year 3.

D. Metacognitive and attributional scales

In year 5 of the study, Cohort 2 subjects received the same reading awareness and causal attributional measures as those described for Cohort 1.

E. Interviews

1. Student selection interview. A student selection interview, utilized primarily for sample placement, was administered to all fifth graders in four Marrakech primary schools and all three primary schools in the rural research site. This short interview gathered basic data on pupils' age and prior school experience, including grade repetition history; those pupils who had already repeated the fifth grade were eliminated from participation in the study.

2. Student interview. This interview, administered to Cohort 2 in the fall of year 3 of the study, was essentially identical to the Cohort 1 student interview.

3. Dropout fact sheet. In year 5 of the study, those children who had dropped out of school were interviewed to ascertain their primary postschooling activities (e.g., employment, vocational training, etc.) and self-reported reading and writing behavior.

4. Parent interview. The parent interview was the same as that presented to the parents of the children in Cohort 1 and was undertaken during the first year of the study involving Cohort 2.

Appendix 3. Parent interview

Note: English translation; interview was given in Moroccan Arabic or Berber, as required.

Abbreviations:

C:	Child	R = Respondent (if not MC or FC)
MC:	Mother of child	Sibs[a]: Siblings of child (up to 9)
FC:	Father of child	

----

1. What is family relationship of Respondent to the child?

  1 = MC
  2 = FC
  3 = Uncle
  4 = Aunt
  5 = GFC (grandfather)
  6 = GMC (grandmother)
  7 = Brother
  8 = Sister
  9 = Other

----

2. What is C's birth order?

  Range = 1–9

----

3. How often watch television?

  . = NA
  1 = Never
  2 = Once a year
  3 = Once a month
  4 = Once a week

5 = 2 to 3 times/wk
6 = Every day

----

4. How often does FC go to Mosque?

1 = Never
2 = Once a year
3 = 2 to 4 times/yr
4 = Once a month
5 = Once a week
6 = 2 to 4 times/wk
7 = Once a day
8 = Twice or more/day
9 = Ramadan only

----

5. Who is the principal worker?

1 = FC
2 = MC
3 = GFC
4 = GMC
5 = Brother of C
6 = Sister of C
7 = Cousin of C
8 = Uncle of C
9 = Other

----

6. Job of principal worker in the family?

0 = Unemployed
1 = Retired
2 = Small Farmer
3 = Servant/Chaouch
4 = Artisan/Laborer
5 = Small Business
6 = Military/Police
7 = Govt. Worker
8 = Big Business/Farm
9 = Other

----

7. House has running water?

1 = No
2 = Yes

----

8. House has electricity?

    1 = No
    2 = Yes

---

9. Maternal language of MC/FC

    1 = NA/don't know
    2 = Berber
    3 = Arabic
    4 = French
    5 = Other

---

10. How well does C/MC/FC speak Arabic?

    . = NA/don't know
    1 = Not at all
    2 = Very little
    3 = Moderately well
    4 = Well
    5 = Fluently

---

11. Size of the town the student presently lives in

    1 = Isolated home
    2 = Rural cluster
    3 = Small city
    4 = Large city

---

12. Number of years lived in present town?

    1 = One year
    2 = Two years
    3 = Three years or more

---

13. Size of the town previously lived in

    1 = Isolated home
    2 = Rural cluster
    3 = Small city
    4 = Large city

---

14. Are both parents alive?

    1 = Yes
    2 = Father only
    3 = Mother only
    4 = Neither one are alive

---

15. Birthplace of C/MC/FC

---

16. Age of MC/FC as of 1984, in years

----

17. Marital status of MC/FC?

   1 = Single
   2 = Married
   3 = Widowed
   4 = Divorced
   5 = Other

----

18. Are birth certificates available?

   1 = Uncertain
   2 = No
   3 = Yes

----

19. Household size

   02 = Two people
   03 = Three people
   04 = Four people
   etc.

----

20. How well does C/MC/FC/Sibs/R speak Berber?

   . = Uncertain
   1 = Not at all
   2 = A little
   3 = Average
   4 = Well
   5 = Fluently

----

21. How well does C/MC/FC/Sibs/R speak French?

   . = Uncertain
   1 = Not at all
   2 = A little
   3 = Average
   4 = Well
   5 = Fluently

----

22. How well does C/MC/FC/Sibs/R speak another language?

   . = Uncertain
   1 = Not at all
   2 = A little
   3 = Average
   4 = Well
   5 = Fluently

----

23. How often does C/MC/FC/R visit the countryside?

    1 = Never
    2 = Once a year
    3 = Once a month
    4 = Once a week
    5 = Two to three times/week
    6 = Every day

----

24. How often does C/MC/FC/R visit a large city?

    1 = Never
    2 = Once a year
    3 = Once a month
    4 = Once a week
    5 = Two to three times/week
    6 = Every day

----

25. Why does C/MC/FC/Sibs/R go into the large city?

    1 = Uncertain
    2 = Shopping
    3 = Visit relatives
    4 = Work
    5 = For religious reasons
    6 = For studies
    7 = Vacation
    8 = Return to homeland
    9 = Other

----

26. Has C/MC/FC/Sibs/R traveled abroad?

    1 = No
    2 = Yes

----

27. Why has C/MC/FC/Sibs/R traveled abroad?

    1 = Uncertain
    2 = Shopping
    3 = Visit relatives
    4 = Work
    5 = For religious reasons
    6 = For studies
    7 = Vacation
    8 = Return to homeland
    9 = Other

----

28. How long has the principal worker been employed?

        . = Uncertain
        1 = Less than one year
        2 = One to five years
        3 = Six to ten years
        4 = Ten to twenty years
        5 = More than twenty years

---

29. Did the principal worker have special training for his/her present job?

        1 = No
        2 = Yes

---

30. What is/was the principal general employment of:

        Maternal grandfather of C
        Maternal grandmother of C
        Paternal grandfather of C
        Paternal grandmother of C

        0 = Unemployed
        1 = Retired
        2 = Small Farmer
        3 = Servant/Chaouch
        4 = Artisan/Laborer
        5 = Small Business, service
        6 = Military/Police
        7 = Teacher, other mid-level gov't worker
        8 = Big Business/big farm owner
        9 = Other

---

31. Number of family members working?

---

32. What is specific employment of: Primary worker in the family
                          Maternal grandfather
                          Maternal grandmother
                          Paternal grandfather
                          Paternal grandmother

00-unemployed

10 = Farming	*60 = government salaried*
11 = large farm owner	61 = military
12 = animal husbandry	62 = police
13 = agriculture	63 = PTT, Commune rurale, baladiya, J&S, travaux publiques
	eaux et forets
20 = labor	64 = muqaddem
21 = factory worker	65 = caid/cadi
22 = restaurant worker	66 = teacher/school admin.
23 = charcoal worker	67 = nurse/pharmacist

24 = farm laborer
25 = gas station attendant
26 = works abroad (laborer)
27 = silver cleaner

30 = skilled worker
31 = shoemaker/leathermaker
33 = metalworker (blacksmith,
   welder, brass maker)
34 = tailor/embroiderer
35 = mechanic
36 = construction
   (carpenter/mason)
37 = plumber
38 = weaver/wool worker
39 = electrician

40 = commerce
41 = clothes/fabric
42 = henna, ghasoul, spices
43 = vegetables
44 = butcher
45 = cafe-owner
46 = wood, charcoal
47 = tiles
48 = animals
49 = bread

50 = services
51 = rental agent (simsar)
52 = chauffeur (taxi/truck)
53 = porter/water carrier
54 = maid
55 = cafe waiter
56 = barber/coiffeur
57 = gardien/chaouch
58 = entertainer (dancer/prostitute)
59 = housewife

68 = doctor/veterinarian
69 = city bus system

70 = traditional professions
71 = fqih
72 = taleb/katib
73 = 'alim
74 = imam
75 = traditional doctor

80 = student
81 = modern preschool/nadi
82 = P1 to P3
83 = P4 to P5
84 = S1 to S3
85 = S4 to S5
86 = S6 to S7
87 = U1 to U3
88 = U4 to
89 = Quranic preschool

90 = other
91 = inherited property
92 = beggar
93 = retired/unspecified
94 = retired/gov't
95 = retired/private company
96 = bathhouse owner
97 = hotel worker
98 = cinema
99 = deceased

----

33. Number of C's siblings in school?

----

34. Number of months C spent in preschool?

----

35. Population of birthplace of C/FC/R in 1000's (based on 1982 Census figures; thus does not take into account the size of the place at time of birth)

Range: 1–1000

----

36. How well does MC/FC/Sibs/R read literary Arabic?

   . = NA/Don't know
1 = Not at all
2 = Very little
3 = Moderately
4 = Well
5 = Fluently

----

37. How well does MC/FC/Sibs/R write literary Arabic?

   . = NA/Don't know
1 = Not at all
2 = Very little
3 = Moderately
4 = Well
5 = Fluently

----

38. How well does MC/FC/Sibs/R read French?

   . = NA/Don't know
1 = Not at all
2 = Very little
3 = Moderately
4 = Well
5 = Fluently

----

39. How well does MC/FC/Sibs/R write French?

   . = NA/Don't know
1 = Not at all
2 = Very little
3 = Moderately
4 = Well
5 = Fluently

----

40. Types of Arabic written matter at home (number of types)

Range = 0–8

----

41. Types of French written matter at home (number of types)

Range = 0–8

----

42. Whom do you ask for help in reading and writing?

   1 = NA
   2 = Inside family
   3 = Outside family
   4 = Both
   5 = No need for help

----

43. Inside family, whom do you ask?

   1 = NA
   2 = Son/daughter
   3 = Brother/sister
   4 = Spouse
   5 = Other

----

44. Outside family, whom do you ask?

   1 = NA
   2 = Fkih
   3 = Public writer
   4 = Adil (notary)
   5 = Civil servant
   6 = Modern school teacher
   7 = Literate neighbor
   8 = Literate friend
   9 = Other

----

45. Can you read and write numbers?

   . = NA/don't know
   1 = Neither R nor W
   2 = Read only
   3 = Write only

----

46. Number of years MC/FC/Sibs/R attended QS?

   Range = 0–9

----

47. Level of schooling reached by MC/FC/Sibs/R in MPS?

   0 = None
   1 = MPS
   2 = P1 to P3 (primary)
   3 = P4 to P5 (primary)
   4 = S1 to S3 (primary)
   5 = S4 to S5 (secondary)
   6 = S6 to S7 (secondary)
   7 = U1 to U3 (university)
   8 = U4 and up (university)

----

48. How many grandparents are literate in Arabic?

        0 = None
        1 = One grandparent
        2 = Two grandparents
        3 = Three grandparents
        4 = Four grandparents

----

49. How many grandparents are literate in French?

        0 = None
        1 = One grandparent
        2 = Two grandparents
        3 = Three grandparents
        4 = Four grandparents

----

50. Are there texts once memorized but now forgotten?

        = Missing
        1 = Yes
        2 = No

----

51. Do you calculate numbers in your head or on paper?

        1 = Uncertain
        2 = Neither one or other
        3 = Head only
        4 = Paper only
        5 = Both

----

52. Where did you learn math?

        1 = Uncertain
        2 = Studied independently
        3 = Parent
        4 = Friend
        5 = Teacher at school
        6 = Friend at work
        7 = Not sure
        8 = Other

----

53. What is the best age for a boy to marry?

        . = No best age/missing
        1 = Puberty (14 yrs. or less)
        2 = 15 to 17 yrs.
        3 = First job
        4 = In high school
        5 = 18 to 21 yrs.
        6 = Over 21 yrs.

----

54. What is the best age for a girl to marry?

. = No best age/missing
1 = Soon as possible
2 = 14 yrs. or less
3 = 15 to 17 yrs.
4 = 18 to 21 yrs.
5 = After studies
6 = 22 to 25 yrs.
7 = 26 to 35 yrs.

55a. Why send C to QS?
55b. Why send C to MPS?

1 = NA/didn't go
2 = Prep for MPS
3 = Learn R and W
4 = Advance SES
5 = Soc/Fam reasons
6 = Religion/Quran
7 = Legally required
8 = Day case
9 = Other

---

56. Why learn to read?

1 = NA
2 = Religion
3 = Employment
4 = Daily use
5 = Baraka/blessing
6 = General knowledge
7 = Prestige
8 = Other

---

57. Desired academic level for C?

1 = Elem Q studies
2 = P5 certificate
3 = P4 certificate
4 = Baccalaureate/S7
5 = Advanced Q study
6 = University
7 = Other

---

58. Do boys and girls need same level of education?

1 = Yes, same
2 = Boys more
3 = Girls more

---

59. Who does better in school: boys or girls?

        1 = No difference
        2 = Boys
        3 = Girls
        4 = Depends on child
        5 = Other

----

60. What is the best number of children to have?

        Range = 1–9

----

61. Should women work outside of the home?

        1 = No opinion
        2 = Work outside
        3 = Stay at home
        4 = Either is OK
        5 = Other

----

62. Did C receive help in reading before school? From whom?

        1 = NA
        2 = Parent
        3 = Brother/sister
        4 = GP
        5 = Other relative
        6 = Friend
        7 = Other

----

63. Is school success due more to ability or effort?

        1 = Ability (gifted)
        2 = Effort
        3 = Other

----

64. Is school success due more to teacher or parent?

        1 = Good teacher
        2 = Good parents
        3 = Other

----

65. Is it best for a child to study alone or with others?

        1 = No opinion
        2 = Alone
        3 = With others
        4 = Other

----

66. Is it best to study by memorizing or by trying to understand?
   1 = No opinion
   2 = Memorize
   3 = Understand
   4 = Other

---

67. Is it better to learn from self-experience or by following the guidance of others?
   1 = No opinion
   2 = Self-experience
   3 = Guidance by others
   4 = Other

---

68. Why did MC/FC/Sibs/R go to Quranic school?
   1 = Didn't attend
   2 = Prep for school
   3 = To learn to read/write
   4 = To advance financially
   5 = Social reasons/family
   6 = Religious reasons
   7 = Legal duty
   8 = Day case
   9 = Other

---

69. Why did MC/FC/Sibs/R go to modern school?
   1 = Didn't attend
   2 = Prep for school
   3 = To learn to read/write
   4 = To advance financially
   5 = Social reasons/family
   6 = Religious reasons
   7 = Legal duty
   8 = Day case
   9 = Other

---

70. How do you follow C's school progress?
   1 = I don't
   2 = Speak with teacher
   3 = Speak with principal
   4 = See notices from school
   5 = Speak with child
   6 = View child's homework
   7 = Other

---

71. What is your response when the child receives a good report card? (note 1st and 2nd responses)

    1 = Nothing
    2 = Verbal appreciation
    3 = Grant privileges
    4 = Gifts
    5 = Other

----

72. What is your response when child received a poor report card? (note 1st and 2nd responses)

    1 = Nothing
    2 = Verbal punishment
    3 = Remove privileges
    4 = Physical punishment
    5 = Other

----

73. What is the average number of days per week that the child studies?

    1 = One day
    2 = Two days
    3 = Three days

----

74. What is the average number of hours per day that the child studies?

    1 = Not applicable
    2 = Half-hour
    3 = One hour
    4 = One and a half-hour
    5 = Two hours
    6 = Three or more
    7 = Uncertain

----

75. Who usually helps child with homework?

    1 = Uncertain
    2 = Alone
    3 = Friend
    4 = Mother
    5 = Father
    6 = Sibling
    7 = Other relative
    8 = Other

----

76. What is the number of school days the student has been absent within the last year?

    . = Uncertain
    1 = Never
    2 = Less than one week
    3 = Less than two weeks

4 = Less than one month

5 = More than one month

---

77. What was the most frequent reason for absence?

1 = Uncertain

2 = Sickness

3 = Family reasons

4 = Other

---

78. How much time does C/R spend listening to the radio?

1 = Uncertain

2 = Never

3 = Once a year

4 = Once a month

5 = Once a week

6 = Two or three times a week

7 = Every day

---

79. What language does C/R usually listen to on the radio?

1 = Uncertain

2 = Berber

3 = Moroccan Arabic

4 = Classical Arabic

5 = Literary Arabic

6 = French

7 = Not important

8 = Other

---

80. What language does C/R usually listen to on the TV?

1 = Uncertain

2 = Berber

3 = Moroccan Arabic

4 = Classical Arabic

5 = Literary Arabic

6 = French

7 = Not important

8 = Other

---

81. How often does C/R go to the movies?

. = Uncertain

1 = Never

2 = Once a year

3 = Once a month

4 = Once a week
5 = Two or three times a week
6 = Every day

---

82. Movies in what language does C/R usually watch?
1 = Uncertain
2 = Berber
3 = Moroccan Arabic
4 = Classical Arabic
5 = Literary Arabic
6 = French
7 = Not important
8 = Other

---

83. What is your favorite type of radio program?
1 = Uncertain
2 = News
3 = Music
4 = General exposes
5 = Religious lectures
6 = Other

---

84. What family members have made the pilgrimage to Mecca? (Up to 3 responses)
1 = Uncertain
2 = Father
3 = Mother
4 = Grandmother
5 = Grandfather
6 = Sibling
7 = Uncle
8 = Aunt
9 = Other

---

85. Does anyone recite the Quran in the home?
1 = No
2 = Yes

---

86. Who recites the Quran in the home?
1 = Uncertain
2 = Father
3 = Mother
4 = The whole family
5 = Fqih or tolba
6 = Other

---

87. Who in the family prays regularly? (Up to 3 responses)

    1 = Uncertain
    2 = Father
    3 = Mother
    4 = Grandmother
    5 = Grandfather
    6 = Sibling
    7 = Uncle
    8 = Aunt
    9 = Other

----

88. Were your parents more or less strict than you are in observing religious practices?

    . = Uncertain
    1 = Less strict
    2 = The same
    3 = More strict

----

89. Are your children more or less strict than you are in observing religious practices?

      = Uncertain
    1 = Less strict
    2 = The same
    3 = More strict

----

90. What is the best age for a child to learn to read and write?

    1 = Uncertain
    2 = As early as possible
    3 = Three to four years
    4 = Five years of age
    5 = Six years
    6 = Seven years
    7 = Eight or more years
    8 = Depends on child
    9 = Other

----

91. What type of preschool would you prefer to send your child to?

    1 = Quranic school
    2 = Modern public
    3 = Modern private
    4 = Other

----

92. What are the fqih's most important responsibilities? (Up to 3)

    1 = Uncertain
    2 = Discipline the child
    3 = Teach reading
    4 = Teach religion

5 = Teach morals
6 = Be a model for the student
7 = Keep the child during the day
8 = Prepare the child for scholastic entrance
9 = Other

---

93. What are the modern preschool teacher's most important responsibilities? (Up to 3)

1 = Uncertain
2 = Discipline the child
3 = Teach reading
4 = Teach religion
5 = Teach morals
6 = Be a model for the student
7 = Keep the child during the day
8 = Prepare the child for scholastic entrance
9 = Other

---

94. Whose duty is it to teach the child morals?

1 = Neither one
2 = Parents
3 = Mother
4 = Father
5 = Teacher
6 = All three

---

95. Whose duty is it to punish the child?

1 = Neither one
2 = Parents
3 = Mother
4 = Father
5 = Teacher
6 = All three

---

96. Whose duty is it to teach the child to read?

1 = Neither one
2 = Parents
3 = Mother
4 = Father
5 = Teacher
6 = All three

---

97. Whose duty is it to teach the child religion?

1 = Neither one
2 = Parents
3 = Mother

4 = Father
5 = Teacher
6 = All three

---

98. Whose duty is it to teach the child how to behave properly in public?
1 = Neither one
2 = Parents
3 = Mother
4 = Father
5 = Teacher
6 = All three

---

99. Is it better to read aloud or silently?
1 = Uncertain
2 = Out loud
3 = Silently

---

100. Who helps you the most in raising your children?
1 = No one
2 = Grandmother
3 = Older children
4 = Aunt
5 = Father
6 = Other parent
7 = Friend or neighbor
8 = House servant
9 = Other

---

101. What is the worst behavior trait of your child?
1 = Uncertain
2 = Lack of respect
3 = Disobedience
4 = Laziness
5 = Lying
6 = Stealing
7 = Other

---

102. How do you usually punish your child?
1 = Uncertain
2 = Verbal reprimand
3 = Physical correction
4 = More tasks

5 = Take away privileges
6 = Other

---

103. What is the frequency of punishments?

. = Uncertain
1 = Never
2 = Once a year
3 = Six times a year
4 = Once a month
5 = Twice a month
6 = Once a week
7 = Twice a week
8 = Once a day

---

104. Will a child learn better through punishment or praise?

1 = Uncertain
2 = Punishment
3 = Praise

---

105. Who chose your spouse?

1 = Both parents
2 = Mother
3 = Father
4 = Other parents
5 = Intermediary
6 = Personal choice
7 = Other

---

106. Who is your preference for your child's spouse?

1 = Maternal cousin
2 = Paternal cousin
3 = Neighbor
4 = School mate
5 = Work mate
6 = Member of tribal group
7 = Other

---

107. Is it better to have more boys or more girls in a family?

1 = Uncertain
2 = More boys than girls
3 = More girls than boys
4 = It doesn't matter

---

108. What career do you prefer for your sons?

    1 = Farmer
    2 = Merchant
    3 = Artisan
    4 = Soldier
    5 = Teacher
    6 = Government worker
    7 = Clergyman
    8 = Professional
    9 = Other

---

109. What career do you prefer for your daughter?

    0 = Housewife
    1 = Farmer
    2 = Merchant
    3 = Artisan
    4 = Soldier
    5 = Teacher
    6 = Government worker
    7 = Clergyman
    8 = Professional
    9 = Other

---

110. Why did MC/FC/Sibs/R not go/stop going to Quranic school?

    1 = NA
    2 = Poor grades
    3 = School too far
    4 = Money problems
    5 = Social reasons/marriage
    6 = Poor health
    7 = Reached required level
    8 = Not found useful
    9 = Other

---

111. Why did MC/FC/Sibs/R not go/stop going to modern school?

    1 = NA
    2 = Poor Grades
    3 = School too far
    4 = Money problems
    5 = Social reasons/marriage
    6 = Poor health
    7 = Reached required level
    8 = Not found useful
    9 = Other

---

[a]Only the two oldest siblings of target child (C) were asked certain questions. Each of these siblings had a data profile parallel to that of C.

Appendix 4. Student interview

Note: English translation; interview as given in Moroccan Arabic or Berber as required.

Abbreviations:

C:	Child in the sample	QS:	Quranic school
MC:	Mother of child	MPS:	Modern public school
FC:	Father of child		
Sibs[a]:	Siblings of child (up to 9)		

----

1. How long have you lived in Marrakech/al-Ksour?

$1 = 1$ yr. or less

$2 = 2–5$ yrs.

$3 = 6–10$ yrs.

$4 =$ Always

----

2. Where did you live before?

$1 =$ Rural area

$2 =$ Small town

$3 =$ Big town

$4 =$ City

----

3. Gender of Sibs

$1 =$ M

$2 =$ F

----

4. Age of C, FC, MC, Sibs

Age in years

----

5. Did C, FC, Sibs attend Quranic school?

    1 = No

    2 = Yes

----

6. What level has FC, MC, Sibs (1–9) reached in schooling?

    0 = No MPS

    1 = MPS

    2 = P1-P3

    3 = P4-P5

    4 = S1-S4

    5 = S5-S7

    6 = Univ.

----

7. First language of FC/MC

    1 = Berber

    2 = Arabic

    3 = Both

----

8. Present activity of FC/MC/Sibs1–9 (by category type)

00-unemployed

10-Farming	*40-Trade*	*70-Traditional profession*
11-shepherd	41-vegs/spices	71-fqih
12-orchard work	42-store owner	72-imam
	43-butcher	73-shikhat
	44-clothes/material	
	45-carpets	
	46-buyer	
	47-medicine	
20-Unskilled labor	*50-Services*	*80-Student*
21-café/hotel worker	51-lottery worker	87-university
22-chaouch	52-maid	88-professional school
23-miller	53-bus station	89-vocational school
24-factory worker	54-driver	
25-gas station attendant	55-agent (simsar)	
26-painter	56-baker	
27-porter	57-barber	
28-woodcutter	58-photographer	
29-shop assistant	59-housework	
30-Skilled labor	*60-Modern profession*	*90-Other*
31-mechanic/solderer	61-functionary	91-disabled
32-tailor/weaver/knitter	62-teacher	92-cinema
33-airport worker	63-police/gendarme	93-hotelier
34-carpenter/mason	64-military	94-cycliste

35-builder	65-office work
36-electrician	66-nurse
37-shoemaker	67-Eaux et Forets/OCP
38-plumber	68-mudir
	69-ca'id

---

9. Does FC, MC, Sibs 1–9 live with you?

> 1 = No
> 2 = Yes

---

10. How many other people live with you?

> Range: 0–9

---

11. What language is spoken at home?

> 1 = Berber
> 2 = Arabic
> 3 = Both

---

12. Is there running water in your house?

> 1 = No
> 2 = Yes

---

13. Is there electricity in your house?

> 1 = No
> 2 = Yes

---

14. Does your family own a car?

> 1 = No
> 2 = Yes

---

15. Does your family own a mobylette?

> 1 = No
> 2 = Yes

---

16. Do you have a radio in your house?

> 1 = No
> 2 = Yes

---

17. Do you have a refrigerator in your house?

> 1 = No
> 2 = Yes

---

18. Do you listen to it just about every day? Once a week? Or less?

        1 = Never
        2 = Less than once a week
        3 = About once a week
        4 = Every day

---

19. Do you have a television?

        1 = No
        2 = Yes

---

20. Did you just buy the television this year or has it been longer?

        0 = Not applicable
        1 = Bought this year
        2 = Over a year old

---

21. Do you watch TV just about every day, once a week, or less?

        1 = Never
        2 = Less than once a week
        3 = About once a week
        4 = Every day

---

22. Do you ever watch TV at another's? Is that just about every day, once a week, or less?

        1 = Never
        2 = Less than once a week
        3 = About once a week
        4 = Every day

---

23. Language of favorite TV program

        1 = MA (Mor. Arabic)
        2 = SA (Standard Arabic)
        3 = Egyptian Arabic
        4 = French
        5 = MA/SA mix
        6 = Any language
        9 = Other

---

24. Do you have a favorite TV program? What is it?

        1 = News/Info.
        2 = Drama/Comedy
        3 = Cartoon
        4 = Sports
        5 = Religious
        9 = Other

---

25. Did you watch TV last night? How many hours, approximately?

$$0-9 \text{ hrs.}$$

---

26. Have you ever gone to a big city?

1 = No

2 = Yes

---

27. What one(s)?

1 = Big town (e.g. Beni-Mellal)

2 = City (e.g. Agadir or larger)

---

28. How often do you go in a year?

1 = Once a year or less

2 = Twice a year, etc.

9 = 9 times a year or more

---

29. How long do you usually stay?

1 = Less than a week

2 = A week or two

3 = A month or two

4 = Several months

5 = A year or more

---

30. Has anyone in your household gone abroad?

1 = Father

2 = Mother

3 = Sibling

4 = Grandparent

5 = Self

6 = Cousins, aunts, uncles

8 = None

9 = other

---

31. Where did they go?

1 = Europe

2 = Other Arab country

9 = Other

---

32. Why did they go?

1 = Visit

2 = Study

3 = Work

4 = Hajj (pilgrimage)

5 = Accompanying immigrant worker
9 = Other

---

33. Does anyone in your house ever buy or bring home a newspaper or magazine?
1 = No
2 = Yes

---

34. How often?

1 = Never
2 = Less than once a month
3 = About once a month
4 = About every week
5 = Every day

---

35. What language?

1 = Arabic
2 = French
3 = Both
4 = Other

---

36. Do you ever read in your spare time?

1 = No
2 = Yes

---

37. If so, what do you read?

0 = nothing
1 = Newspaper/magazine
2 = Quran
3 = Cineroman
4 = Bande déssinée
5 = Novel/storybook
6 = Letter
9 = Other

---

38. Other than homework, did you read anything last night?

1 = No
2 = Yes

---

39. What did you read last night?

0 = nothing
1 = Newspaper/magazine
2 = Quran
3 = Cineroman
4 = Bande déssinée

5 = Novel/storybook
6 = Letter
9 = Other

---

40. What language was it in?

0 = none
1 = Arabic
2 = French
3 = Both
9 = Other

---

41. Have you ever written a letter?

1 = No
2 = Yes

---

42. To whom have you written most often?

0 = no one
1 = Relative
2 = Friend
3 = Boss
4 = Teacher
5 = Government office
9 = Other

---

43. Did you write anything last night?

1 = No
2 = Yes

---

44. What was it?

0 = nothing
1 = Letter
2 = Homework
3 = Diary
4 = Scrapbook
5 = Official forms/papers
9 = Other

---

45. In what language?

0 = none
1 = Arabic
2 = French
3 = Both

---

46. How many books and magazines would you say you have in your house?

$$0 = 0$$
$$1 = 20 \text{ or less}$$
$$2 = 21 \text{ or more}$$

----

47. Do you ever rent books or magazines, or exchange them with friends?

$$1 = \text{No}$$
$$2 = \text{Yes}$$

----

48. Do/did other people sometimes help you with homework?

$$1 = \text{No}$$
$$2 = \text{Yes}$$

----

49 Who helps you, usually?

$$0 = \text{no one}$$
$$1 = \text{Parent}$$
$$2 = \text{Sibling}$$
$$3 = \text{Friend}$$
$$4 = \text{Teacher}$$
$$9 = \text{Other}$$

----

50. Do you usually study alone or with others?

$$1 = \text{Alone}$$
$$2 = \text{With others}$$

----

51. How long does/did it take you to get to school?

$$1 = \text{Less than 15 min.}$$
$$2 = 15–30 \text{ min.}$$
$$3 = 30 \text{ min. to an hour}$$
$$4 = \text{Over an hour}$$

----

52. How do/did you usually get there?

$$1 = \text{Walk}$$
$$2 = \text{Bike}$$
$$3 = \text{Bus}$$
$$4 = \text{Car}$$
$$5 = \text{Mobylette}$$
$$9 = \text{Other}$$

----

53. How many Arabic newspapers can you name? Total number of Arabic newspaper titles mentioned.

Range: 0–9

----

54. How many French newspapers can you name? Total number of French newspaper titles mentioned.

Range: 0–9

55a. Do you ever read cineromans or bandes déssinées?

1 = No
2 = Yes

55b. In what language?

0 = none
1 = Arabic
2 = French
3 = Both

---

56. Do you read them just about weekly or more? Once a month?

0 = never
1 = Less than once a month
2 = About once a month
3 = Weekly or more

---

57. How many comic books can you name? Total number of comic book titles named.

Range: 0–9

---

58. Do you like school a lot or a little?

1 = A little
2 = A lot

---

59. What do/did you like most about school?

1 = Friends
2 = A specific subject
3 = Job preparation
4 = Provides general knowledge
5 = Freedom from chores
6 = Discipline
7 = Teacher
9 = Other

---

60. What do/did you dislike most about school?

1 = Difficult
2 = Boring
3 = Teacher too strict
4 = Too far away
5 = Not useful
6 = Social problems
9 = Other

---

61. Would you prefer to be studying in school or not?

      1 = No
      2 = Yes

---

62. Who usually gets better results in school, girls or boys?

      1 = Girls
      2 = Boys
      3 = Both

---

63. How far do you hope to go in school?

      1 = P5
      2 = Brevet (S4)
      3 = Bac (S7)
      4 = University
      5 = God's will, as far as possible
      9 = Other

---

64. What is the main reason that some girls don't finish school?

      1 = Low academic performance
      2 = Get a job
      3 = Marriage
      4 = Parent's decision
      5 = Dislike of schooling
      9 = Other

---

65. What is the main reason that some boys don't finish school?

      1 = Low academic performance
      2 = Get a job
      3 = Marriage
      4 = Parent's decision
      5 = Dislike of schooling
      6 = Lack of discipline
      9 = Other

---

66. Why do you think you passed last year?

      1 = Hard work
      2 = Innate ability
      3 = Easy test
      4 = Good luck
      5 = Good preparation by teachers
      9 = Other

---

67. Why do you think you failed last year?

    1 = Did not study
    2 = Lack of ability
    3 = Difficult test
    4 = Bad luck
    5 = Poor preparation by teachers
    6 = God's will
    9 = Other

----

68. Why do people learn how to read? What will they do with it?

    1 = Read street signs
    2 = Read for knowledge
    3 = Read letters
    4 = Read bills and forms
    5 = Job requirement
    6 = Learn to talk correctly ("ulsub")
    9 = Other

----

69. What language do you enjoy reading more, Arabic or French?

    1 = Arabic
    2 = French
    3 = Both

----

69. Why?

    1 = More proficient in that language
    2 = Better subject matter available
    3 = Esthetic pleasure
    9 = Other

----

70. In your opinion, which language is more important to be able to read in Morocco?

    1 = Arabic
    2 = French
    3 = Both

----

71. What kinds of things do people write?

    1 = Letters
    2 = Records
    3 = Form-filling
    4 = Work-related uses
    5 = Diary/journal
    6 = Signature
    9 = Other

----

72. In your opinion, is it better for a person to remain living with his family in the same town throughout his life, or to move to another place to work or marry?

1 = Stay
2 = Move away
3 = God's will

----

73. Is it better for a Moroccan boy to choose his bride, or should the parents choose her for him?

1 = Self
2 = Parents
3 = Other

----

74. Who should get more education: boys or girls, or is it the same for both?

1 = Boys more
2 = Girls more
3 = Both the same

----

75. What's the most important quality you want to have when you grow up?

1 = Famous
2 = Rich
3 = Popular
4 = Respected
5 = Religious
6 = Content
7 = Powerful
8 = Honest/sincere
9 = Other

----

76. What do you most hope for in your life?

1 = Good job
2 = Family/marriage
3 = Education
4 = Money/possessions
5 = Fame
9 = Other

----

77. What do you expect you will be doing when you grow up?

1 = Spouse/parent
2 = Farming
3 = Labor (factory/artisanal)
4 = Small services
5 = Commerce
6 = Mid-level civil or military

7 = Teacher
8 = Profession (doctor, etc.)
9 = Other

---

78. Where do you want to be living when you grow up?

1 = same town/city
2 = (other) small town in Morocco
3 = (other) big city in Morocco
    (Rabat, Casablanca, Fes, etc.)
4 = Very rural area
5 = Abroad
9 = Other

---

79. Do you ever read anything for people who can't? What?

0 = Nothing
1 = Newspaper/magazine
2 = Quran
3 = Bande dessinee
4 = Novel/story book
5 = Letter
6 = Medicine
7 = Forms and papers
9 = Other

---

80. Do you ever write anything for people who can't? What?

0 = Nothing
1 = Write letters
2 = Keep records
3 = Form-filling
4 = Work uses
5 = Keep diary/scrapbook
6 = Math
9 = Other

Note: The questionnaire is shown in slightly abridged form because of space limitations.
*a*Only the two oldest siblings of the target child (C) were asked certain questions. Each of these siblings had a data profile parallel to that of C.

References

Aaron, P. G., & Joshi, M. (Eds.). (1989). *Reading and writing disorders in different orthographic systems.* Netherlands: Kluwer Academic.

Adams, M. J. (1990). *Beginning to read: Thinking and learning about print.* Cambridge, MA: MIT Press.

Anderson, C. A., & Bowman, M. J. (1965). *Education and economic development.* London: Frank Cass.

Anzalone, S. J. (1981). Why Abu can't read: A critique of modern literacy doctrine. Doctoral dissertation, University of Massachusetts.

Anzalone, S. J. & McLaughlin, S. (1983). *Making literacy work: The specific literacy approach.* Amherst: Center for International Education, University of Massachusetts.

Aries, P. (1962). *Centuries of childhood.* London: Jonathan Cape.

Armer, M. (1977). Education and social change: An examination of the modernity thesis. *Studies in Comparative International Development, 12,* 86–99.

Arnove, R. F. and Graff, H. J. (Eds.). (1988). *National literacy campaigns.* New York: Plenum.

ASM. (1987). *Annuaire Statistique du Maroc.* Rabat.

ASM. (1988). *Annuaire Statistique du Maroc.* Rabat.

As-Said, L. (1975). *The recited Koran: A history of the first recorded version.* Princeton, NJ: Darwin.

Ayache, G. (1981). *Les origine de la guerre du Rif.* Paris: Publications de la Sorbonne.

Azzam, R. (1989). Orthography and reading in the Arabic language. In P. G. Aaron & M. Joshi (Eds.), *Reading and writing disorders in different orthographic systems.* Netherlands: Kluwer Academic.

Baddeley, A. D., Thomson, N., & Buchanan, M. (1975). Word length and the structure of short-term memory. *Journal of Verbal Learning and Verbal Behavior, 14,* 575–589.

Badry, F. (1983). Acquisition of lexical derivational rules in Moroccan Arabic: Implications for the development of Standard Arabic as a second language through literacy. Ph.D. dissertation, University of California, Berkeley.

Baina, A. (1981). *Le systeme de l'enseignement au Maroc.* Tome 2: *L'enseignement humain et materiel.* Rabat: Editions Maghrebines.

Baker, L., & Brown, A. L. (1984). Metacognitive skills of reading. In D. Pearson, R. Barr, M. Kamil, & P. Mosenthal (Eds.), *Handbook of reading research* (pp. 353–394). New York: Longman.

Bandura, A. (1977). *Social learning theory.* New York: Wiley.

Batmaz, V. (1986). Television and achievement in Morocco. Paper presented at the International Congress of Cross-Cultural Psychology, Istanbul, July.

Becker, G. S. (1975). *Human capital* (2nd ed.). New York: Columbia University Press.

Behrman, J. R., & Blau, D. M. (1985). Human capital and earnings distributions in a developing country: The case of prerevolutionary Nicaragua. *Economic Development and Cultural Change, 34,* 1–31.

Bennett, J. A. H., & Berry, J. (1987). The future of Cree syllabic literacy in northern Canada. In D. A. Wagner (Ed.), *The future of literacy in a changing world.* New York: Pergamon.

Berry, J. W. (1980). Social and cultural change. In H. Triandis (Ed.), *Handbook of cross-cultural psychology.* New York: Allyn & Bacon.

Berry, J. W., & Dasen, P. (1974). Introduction. In J. W. Berry & P. Dasen (Eds.), *Culture and cognition: Readings in cross-cultural psychology.* London: Methuen.

Berstecher, D. (1985). *Education and rural development: Issues for planning and research.* Paris: UNESCO/IIEP.

Bever, T. G. (1982). *Regressions in mental development: Basic phenomena and theories.* Hillsdale, NJ: Erlbaum.

Bhola, H. S. (1984). *Campaigning for literacy: Eight national experiences of the twentieth century, with a memorandum to decision-makers.* Paris: UNESCO.

Bijeljac-Babic, R. (1983). Les langues maternelles et nationales dans les politiques d'alphabetisation. *Enquetes et etudes,* ED-83/WS-84. Paris: UNESCO.

Blaug, M. (1985). Where are we now in the economics of education? *Economics of Education Review, 4,* 17–28.

Boas, F. (1940). *Race, language and culture.* New York: Free Press.

Boissiere, M., Knight, J. B., & Sabot, R. H. (1985). Earnings, schooling, ability, and cognitive skills. *American Economic Review, 75,* 1016–1030.

Boukmaj, Ahmad. (n.d.). *'Iqra': Al-Juz' al-Khamis li-l-Qism al-Mutawassit ath-Thani* ("Read!: Volume V, for the second-intermediate (fifth grade) class"). Tangier: Dar al-Fikr al-Maghribi.

Boukous, A. (1977). *Langage et culture populaires au Maroc: essai de sociolinguistique.* Casablanca: Dar el Kitab.

Bourdieu, P. (1977). *Outline of a theory of practice.* Cambridge: Cambridge University Press.

Bradley, L., & Bryant, P. E. (1983). Categorising sounds and learning to read: A causal connection. *Nature, 301,* 419–421.

Brown, A. L., Armbruster, B. B., & Baker, L. (1984). The role of metacognition in reading and studying. In J. Orasanu (Ed.), *A decade of reading research: Implications for practice.* Hillsdale, NJ: Erlbaum.

Brown, G., & Hiskett, M. (Eds.). (1975). *Conflict and harmony in education in tropical Africa.* London: Allyn & Unwin.

Campbell, D. T., & Stanley, J. C. (1963). *Experimental and quasi-experimental designs for research.* Chicago: Rand McNally.

Carnoy, M. (1974). *Education as cultural imperialism.* New York: David McKay.

Carraher, T. N., Carraher, D. W., & Schliemann, A. D. (1985). Mathematics in the streets and in the schools. *British Journal of Developmental Psychology, 3,* 21–29.

Cattell, R. B., & Cattell, A. K. S. (1961). *Test of "g": Culture Fair Scale 2, Form B.* Champaign, IL: Institute for Personality and Ability Testing.

CERED. (1988). *Relation entre l'education et l'activite.* Rabat: Centre d'Etudes et de Recherches Demographiques, December.

Chall, J. S. (1983). *Stages of reading development.* New York: McGraw-Hill.

Charlton, S. E. M. (1984). *Women in third world development.* Boulder, CO: Westview.

Clanchy, M. T. (1979). *From memory to written record.* Cambridge, MA: Harvard University Press.

Clarke, M. (1980). The short-circuit hypothesis of ESL reading – or when language competence interferes with reading performance. *Modern Language Journal, 64,* 203–209.

Clay, M. M. (1979). *Reading: The patterning of complex behavior.* Exeter, NH: Heinemann.

Cochrane, S. H., & Jamison, D. T. (1982). Educational attainment and achievement in rural Thailand. In A. Summers (Ed.), *New directions for testing and measurement: Productivity assessment in education.* no. 15. San Francisco: Jossey-Bass.

Cole, M. (1975). An ethnographic psychology of cognition. In R. W. Brislin, S. Bochner, & W. J. Lonner (Eds.), *Cross-cultural perspectives on learning.* Beverly Hills, CA: Sage.

Cole, M., Gay, J., Glick, J., & Sharp, D. (1971). *The cultural context of learning and thinking.* New York: Basic Books.

Cole, M., & Means, B. (1981). *Comparative studies on how people think.* Cambridge, MA: Harvard University Press.

Cole, M., & Scribner, S. (1974). *Culture and thought.* New York: Wiley.

Coleman, J. S., et al. (1966). *Equality of educational opportunity.* Washington, DC: U.S. Government Printing Office.

Coombs, P. H. (1985). *The world crisis in education: The view from the eighties.* New York: Oxford University Press.

Coombs, P. H., & Ahmed, M. (1974). *Attacking rural poverty.* Baltimore: Johns Hopkins University Press.

Crandall, V. C., Katkovsky, W., & Crandall, V. J. (1965). Children's beliefs in their own control of reinforcements in intellectual-academic achievement situations. *Child Development, 36,* 91–109.

Cummins, J. (1979). Linguistic interdependence and the educational development of bilingual children. *Review of Educational Research, 49,* 222–251.

Cziko, G. A. (1978). Differences in first- and second-language reading: The use of syntactic, semantic and discourse constraints. *Canadian Modern Language Review, 34,* 473–489.

Dalby, D. (1985). *The educational use of African languages in sub-Saharan Africa: The state of the art.* Document ED/85/WS/62. Paris: UNESCO.

Darnton, R. (1990). *The kiss of Lamourette: Reflections on cultural history.* New York: Norton.

Davis, S. S. (1984). *Patience and power: Women's lives in a Moroccan village.* Cambridge, MA: Schenckman.

Davis, S. S., & Davis, D. A. (1989). *Adolescence in a Moroccan town.* New Brunswick, NJ: Rutgers University Press.

Deshen, S., & Zenner, W. P. (1982). *Jewish Societies in the Middle East: Community, culture and authority.* New York: University Press of America.

Diaz, R. M. (1985). Bilingual cognitive development: Addressing three gaps in current research. *Child Development, 56,* 1376–1388.

Dichter, T. W. (1976). The problem of how to act on an undefined stage: An exploration of culture, change, and individual consciousness in the Moroccan town of Sefrou – With a focus on three modern schools. Ph.D. dissertation, University of Chicago.

Direction de la Statistique. (1984). *Caracteristiques socio-economiques de la population d'apres le recensement general de la population et de l'habitat de 1982.* Rabat: Ministere du Plan, Direction de la Statistique.

Downing, J. (1973). *Comparative reading.* New York: Macmillan.

Downing, J. (1984). A source of cognitive confusion for beginning readers: Learning in a second language. *The Reading Teacher.* January, 366–370.

Dunn, L. M. (1959). *Peabody Picture Vocabulary Task (Plates).* Circle Pines, MN: American Guidance Service.

Dunn, L. M. (1965). *Peabody Picture Vocabulary Task (Manual).* Circle Pines, MN: American Guidance Service.

Dutcher, N. (1982). The use of first and second languages in primary education:

Selected case studies. World Bank Staff Working Paper No. 504. Washington, DC: World Bank.

Dweck, C. S., & Bempechat, J. (1983). Children's theories of intelligence: Consequences for learning. In S. G. Paris, G. A. Olson, & H. W. Stevenson(Eds.), *Learning and motivation in the classroom* (pp. 239–256). Hillsdale, NJ: Erlbaum.

Dweck, C. S., & Bush, E. S. (1976). Sex differences in learned helplessness: Differential debilitation with peer and adult evaluators. *Developmental Psychology, 12,* 147–156.

Dwyer, D. H. (1978). *Images and self-images.* New York: Columbia University Press.

Eickelman, D. F. (1978). The art of memory: Islamic education and its social reproduction. *Comparative Studies in Society and History, 20,* 485–516.

Eickelman, D. F. (1983). Religion and trade in Western Morocco. *Research in Economic Anthropology, 5,* 335–348.

Eickelman, D. F. (1985). *Knowledge and power in Morocco.* Princeton, NJ: Princeton University Press.

Eisenstein, E. L. (1979). *The printing press as an agent of change.* Cambridge: Cambridge University Press.

El-Farouki, H. (1977). *Deperditions et inegalites dans l'enseignement primaire publique au Maroc.* Memoire de fin d'etudes en vue de l'obtention du diplome d'Ingenieur Statisticien Economiste. Rabat: INSEA.

Engle, P. L. (1975). Language medium in early school years for minority language groups. *Review of Educational Research, 45,* 283–325.

Engle, P. L. (1976). The language debate: Education in first or second language? In P. Sanday (Ed.), *Anthropology and the public interest* (pp. 247–272). New York: Academic Press.

Ezzaki, A. (1988). An historical survey of literacy education in Morocco: A sociocultural perspective. Paper presented at the World Congress on Reading, Australia, July.

Ezzaki, A., Spratt, J. E., & Wagner, D. A. (1987). Language differences, preschool experience, and literacy acquisition among children in rural Morocco. In D. A. Wagner (Ed.), *The future of literacy in a changing world.* London: Pergamon.

Ezzaki, A., & Wagner, D. A. (1992). Language and literacy in the Maghreb. *Annual Review of Applied Linguistics* (special issue on literacy), 7.

Fagerlind, I., & Saha, L. J. (1983). *Education and national development: A comparative perspective.* New York: Pergamon.

Feitelson, D. (1966). The alphabetical principle in Hebrew and German contrasted with the alphabetic principle in English. In P. Tyler (Ed.), *Linguistics and reading.* Newark, DE: International Reading Association.

Feitelson, D. (1967). The relationship between systems of writing and the teaching of reading. In M. Jenkinson (Ed.), *Reading instruction international forum.* Newark, DE: International Reading Association.

Feitelson, D. (1980). Relating instructional strategies to language idiosyncrasies in Hebrew. In J. F. Kavanaugh & R. L. Venezky (Eds.), *Orthography, reading and dyslexia*. Baltimore: University Park Press.

Ferguson, C. (1959). Diglossia. *Word, 15,* 325–340.

Ferreiro, E., & Teberosky, A. (1982). *Literacy before schooling*. Exeter, N. H.: Heinemann.

Fine, M. (1991). *Framing dropouts*. Albany: SUNY Press.

Fitouri, C. (1983). *Biculturalisme, bilinguisme et education*. Paris: Delachaux & Niestle, Editeurs Neuchatel.

Flavell, J. H. & Ross, L. (1981). *Social cognitive development: Frontiers and possible futures*. New York: Cambridge University Press.

Forrest-Pressley, D. L., & Waller, T. G. (1984). *Metacognition, cognition, and reading*. New York: Springer-Verlag.

Freed, B. F. (Ed.). (1991). *Foreign language acquisition research and the classroom*. Lexington, MA: Heath.

Freire, P. (1972). *Pedagogy of the oppressed*. London: Penguin.

Freire, P., & Macedo, D. (1987). *Literacy: Reading the word and the world*. South Hadley, MA: Bergin and Garvey.

Fuller, B. (1988). *Raising school quality in developing countries: What investments boost learning?* World Bank Discussion Papers, 2. Washington, DC: World Bank.

Fuller, B., & Heyneman, S. (1989). Third World school quality: Current collapse, future potential. *Educational Researcher, 18,* 12–19.

Gadgil, D. R. (1955). Report of investigation into the problem of lapse into illiteracy in the Satara District. In D. R. Gadgil & V. M. Dandekar (Eds.), *Primary education in the Satara Districts: Reports of two investigations*. Publication No. 31. India: Gokhale Institute of Politics and Economics.

Galand, L. (1979). *Langue et litterature berberes*. Paris: Editions CNRS.

Gardner, H. (1983). *Frames of mind*. New York: Basic Books.

Gardner, R. C., & Lambert, W. E. (1972). *Attitudes and motivation in second-language learning*. Rowley, MA: Newbury House.

Garner, R. (1987). *Metacognition and reading comprehension*. Norwood, NJ: Ablex.

Gates, A. I., & MacGinitie, W. H. (1965). *Gates-MacGinitie Reading Tests: Primary A, Primary B, Primary C*. New York: Teachers College Press.

Gillette, A. (1987). The Experimental World Literacy Campaign: A unique international effort revisited. In R. F. Arnove, & H. J. Graff, (Eds.), *National literacy campaigns: Historical and comparative aspects*. New York: Plenum.

Ginsburg, H. P., Posner, J. K., & Russell, R. L. (1981). The development of mental addition as a function of schooling and culture. *Journal of Cross-Cultural Psychology, 12,* 163–178.

Goodnow, J. J. (1984). Parents' ideas about parenting and development: A review of issues and recent work. In M. E. Lamb, A. L. Brown, & B. Rogoff (Eds.),

Advances in developmental psychology (Vol. 3, pp. 193–242). Hillsdale, NJ: Erlbaum.

Goody, J. (1968). *Literacy in traditional societies.* Cambridge: Cambridge University Press.

Goody, J. (1977). *The domestication of the savage mind.* Cambridge: Cambridge University Press.

Goody, J., & Watt, I. (1968). The consequences of literacy. In J. Goody (Ed.), *Literacy in traditional societies.* Cambridge: Cambridge University Press.

Gould, S. J. (1985) Mysteries of the panda. *New York Review of Books, 32,* 13, 12–14.

Graff, H. J. (1981). *Literacy and social development in the West: A reader.* Cambridge: Cambridge University Press.

Graff, H. J. (1987). *The legacies of literacy.* Bloomington: Indiana University Press.

Grandguillaume, G. (1983). *Arabisation et politique linguistique au Maghreb.* Paris: Maisonneuve.

Gray, W. S. (1956). *The teaching of reading and writing.* Paris: UNESCO.

Guidance Testing Associates. (1962). *Test of General Ability, Levels 3 and 4.* Austin, TX.

Hagen, J. W., Meacham, J. A., & Mesibov, G. (1970). Verbal labeling, rehearsal, and short-term memory. *Cognitive Psychology, 1,* 47–58.

Hakuta, K., & Diaz, R. M. (1985). The relationship between the degree of bilingualism and cognitive ability: A critical discussion and some new longitudinal data. In K. E. Nelson (Ed.), *Children's language.* (Vol. 5). Hillsdale, NJ: Erlbaum.

Hamadache, A. & Martin, D. (1987). *Theory and practice of literacy work: Policies, strategies and examples.* Paris: UNESCO/Code.

Hammoud, M. S. (1982). Arabicization in Morocco: A case study in language planning and language policy attitudes. Ph.D. dissertation, University of Texas, Austin.

Hardy, G., & Brunot, L. (1925). *L'enfant marocain.* Rabat-Paris: Edition du Bulletin de l'enseignement du Maroc, no. 63.

Harman, D. (1970). Illiteracy: An overview. *Harvard Educational Review, 40,* 226–243.

Harter, S. (1982). The perceived competence scale for young children. *Child Development, 53,* 87–97.

Hartley, M. J. (1984). Achievement and wastage: An analysis of the retention of basic skills in primary education. Final report of the international study of the retention of literacy and numeracy: An Egyptian case study (preliminary version). Washington, DC: World Bank, June.

Hartley, M. J., & Swanson, E. V. (1986). Retention of basic skills among dropouts from Egyptian primary schools. Education and Training Series Report No. EDT40. Washington, DC: World Bank.

Havelock, E. A. (1976). *Origins of Western literacy.* Toronto: Ontario Institute for Studies in Education.

Heath, S. B. (1980). The functions and uses of literacy. *Journal of Communication,* Winter, 123–133.

Heath, S. B. (1982). What no bedtime story means: Narrative skills at home and at school. *Language in Society, 11,* 49–76.

Heath, S. B. (1983). *Ways with words.* New York: Cambridge University Press.

Henderson, L. (1984). *Orthographies and reading: Perspectives from cognitive psychology, neuropsychology, and linguistics.* Hillsdale, NJ: Erlbaum.

Heyneman, S. (1976). Influences on academic achievement: A comparison of results from Uganda and more industrialized societies. *Sociology of Education, 49,* 200–211.

Heyns, B. (1987). Schooling and cognitive development: Is there a season for learning? *Child Development, 58,* 1151–1160.

Hornberger, N. H. (1989). Continua of biliteracy. *Review of Educational Research, 59,* 271–296.

Huston, A. C. (1983). Sex-typing. In P. Mussen (Ed.), *Handbook of child psychology* (Vol. 4, IV, 4th ed.). New York: Wiley.

Illich, I. (1970). *Deschooling society.* New York: Harper & Row.

Inkeles, A., & Smith, D. H. (1974). *Becoming modern.* Cambridge, MA: Harvard University Press.

International Development Research Centre. (1979). *The world of literacy: Policy, research and action.* Ottawa.

Jacobs, J. E., & Paris, S. G. (1987). Children's metacognition about reading: Issues in definition, measurement, and instruction. *Educational Psychologist, 22,* 255–278.

James, C. (1980). *Contrastive analysis.* London: Longman.

Jamison, D., & Lau, L. (1982). *Farmer education and farm efficiency.* Baltimore: Johns Hopkins University Press.

Jencks, C., et al. (1972). *Inequality: A reassessment of the effect of family and schooling in America.* New York: Basic Books.

Johns, J. L. (1980). First graders' concepts about print. *Reading Research Quarterly, 15,* 539–549.

Kaestle, C. F. (1991). *Literacy in the United States.* New Haven, CT: Yale University Press.

Kavanaugh, J. F., & Venezky, R. L. (Eds.). (1980). *Orthography, reading and dyslexia.* Baltimore: University Park Press.

King, K. (1992). *Aid and education in the developing world.* London: Longman.

Kirsch, I. and Guthrie, J. T. (1977). The concept and measurement of functional literacy. *Reading Research Quarterly, 4,* 485–507.

Kirsch, I., & Jungeblut, A. (1986). *Literacy: Profiles of America's young adults.* Final report of the National Assessment of Educational Progress. Princeton, NJ: ETS.

Kleinbaum, D., Kupper, L., & Muller, K. (1988). *Applied regression analysis and other multivariate methods* (2nd ed.). Boston: PWS-Kent.

Klineberg, O. (1935). *Race differences.* New York: Harper & Row.

Koda, K. (1987). Cognitive strategy transfer in second language reading. In J. Devine, P. L. Carrell, & D. E. Eskey (Eds.), *Research in reading English as a second language.* Washington, DC: Teachers of English to Speakers of Other Languages.

Labov, W. (1982). Objectivity and commitment in linguistic science: The case of Black English trial in Ann Arbor. *Language in Society, 11,* 165–201.

Lado, R. (1959). *Linguistics across cultures.* Ann Arbor: University of Michigan Press.

Lambert, R. D., & Freed, B. F. (Eds.). (1982). *The loss of language skills.* Rowley, MA: Newbury House.

Lambert, W. E. (1967). Social psychology of bilingualism. *Journal of Social Issues, 23,* 91–109.

Lambert, W. E., & Tucker, G. R. (1972). *Bilingual education of children: The St. Lambert Experiment.* Rowley, MA: Newbury House.

Laosa, L. M., & Sigel, I. E. (Eds.). *Families as learning environments for children.* New York: Plenum.

Laraoui, A. (1977). *The history of the Maghrib.* Princeton, NJ: Princeton University Press.

Lave, J. (1988). *Cognition in practice: Mind, mathematics and culture in everyday life.* New York: Cambridge University Press.

Lerner, D. (1963). *The passing of traditional society: Modernizing the Middle East.* New York: Free Press.

Levine, K. (1982). Functional literacy: Fond illusions and false economies. *Harvard Educational Review, 52,* 249–266.

Levine, K. (1986). *The social context of literacy.* London: Routledge & Kegan Paul.

Levy, M. B. (1971). Determinants of primary school dropouts in developing countries, *Comparative Education Review, 15,* 44–58.

Levy-Bruhl, L. (1910/1966). *How natives think.* New York: Washington Square Press.

Lind, A. (1988). *Adult literacy: Lessons and promises. The Mozambican literacy campaigns, 1978–1982.* Stockholm: Institute of International Education.

Lind, A., & Johnston, A. (1990). *Adult literacy in the Third World: A review of objectives and strategies.* Stockholm: Swedish International Development Agency.

Lipton, M. (1988). *The poor and the poorest: Some interim findings.* World Bank Discussion Papers, 25. Washington, DC: World Bank.

Lord, A. B. (1960). *The singer of tales.* Cambridge, MA: Harvard University Press.

Luria, A. R. (1976). *Cognitive development: Its cultural and social foundations.* Cambridge, MA: Harvard University Press.

Maamouri, M. (1983). Illiteracy in Tunisia: An evaluation. In R. M. Payne (Ed.), *Language in Tunisia.* Tunis: Bourguiba Institute of Modern Languages.

MAAS (1988). *Le programme d'alphabetisation des adultes.* Rabat: Ministere de l'Artisanat et des Affaires Sociales.

McClelland, D. (1961). *The achieving society.* New York: Free Press.

McLaughlin, B. (1985). *Second language acquisition in childhood.* Vol. 2: School-age children. Hillsdale, NJ: Erlbaum.

MacDonald, D. B. (1911). *Aspects of Islam.* New York: Macmillan.

Macnamara, J. (1966). *Bilingualism in primary education.* Edinburgh: Edinburgh University Press.

Macnamara, J. (Issue Ed.). (1967). Problems of bilingualism. *Journal of Social Issues, 23,* 2.

Mason, J. M., & Allen, J. B. (1986). A review of emergent literacy with implications for research and practice in reading. In E. Z. Rothkopf (Ed.), *Review of research in education.* Washington, DC: American Educational Research Association.

Meakin, B. (1902). *The Moors.* New York: Macmillan.

Mehryar, A. H. (1981). The role of psychology in national development: Wishful thinking and reality. *International Journal of Psychology, 19,* 159–168.

Mernissi, F. (1975). *Beyond the veil: Male-female dynamics in a modern Muslim society.* Cambridge, MA: Schenckman.

Messick, B. M. (1983). Legal documents and the concept of 'restricted' literacy in a traditional society. *International Journal of the Sociology of Language, 42,* 41–52.

Messick, B. M. (1993). *The calligraphic state.* Berkeley: University of California Press.

Micholowski, P. (1993). Early literacy revisited. In D. Keller-Cohen (Ed.), *Literacy: Interdisciplinary conversations.* New York: Hampton.

Mikulecky, L. (1982). Job literacy: The relationship between school preparation and workplace actuality. *Reading Research Quarterly, 17,* 400–419.

Miller, S. A. (1986). Parents' beliefs about their children's cognitive abilities. *Developmental Psychology, 22,* 276–284.

Mincy, R. B., Sawhill, I. V. & Wolf, D. A. (1990). The underclass: Definition and measurement. *Science, 248,* 450–453.

Ministry of Education, Kingdom of Morocco. (1982. 1986). *Statistiques de l'Enseignement Primaire.* Rabat.

Ministry of Education, Kingdom of Morocco. (1983a). *Qira'ati: As-Sanat ath-Thalithat al-'Ibtida'iya* (My reading: Third year primary). Rabat: Maktabat al-Ma'arif.

Ministry of Education, Kingdom of Morocco. (1983b). *Qira'ati: As-Sanat ar-Rabi'at al-'Ibtida'iya* (My reading: Fourth year primary). Rabat: Maktabat al-Ma'arif.

Ministry of Education, Kingdom of Morocco. (1986). *Le mouvement educatif au Maroc 1984–1985; 1985–1986*. Rabat.

Moatassime, A. (1974). Le "bilinguisme sauvage": Blocage linguistique; sous-developpement et cooperation hypotheque; l'exemple maghrebin; cas du Maroc. *Tiers Monde, 15,* 619–670.

Modiano, N. (1968). National or mother tongue language in beginning reading: A comparative study. *Research in the Teaching of English, 2,* 32–43.

Montagne, Robert. (1931/1973). *The Berbers: Their social and political organization*. London: Frank Cass.

MTPFPFC. (1988). La formation professionnelle en chiffres. Rabat: Ministere des Travaux Publics de la Formation Professionnelle et de la Formation des Cadres.

Murugaiyan, A. (1985). *Enseignement des langue natinales et maternelles dan cinq pays d'Asie: Problems et perspectives*. Document ED/85/WS/63. Paris: UNESCO.

Myers, M., & Paris, S. G. (1978). Children's metacognitive knowledge about reading. *Journal of Educational Psychology, 70,* 680–690.

Myers, R. G. (1992). *The twelve who survive: Strengthening programmes of early childhood development in the Third World*. London: Routledge & Kegan Paul.

Myers, R. G., & Hertenberg, R. (1987). *The eleven who survive: Toward a re-examination of early childhood development program options and costs*. World Bank Education and Training Report No. EDT 69. Washington, DC: World Bank.

National Educational Testing Center et al. (1982). *Literacy retention among dropouts from the Philippine elementary schools*. Manila: Philippine Ministry of Education, Culture and Sports.

Navon, D., & Shimron, J. (1984). Reading Hebrew: How necessary is the graphemic representation of vowels? In L. Henderson, (Ed.), *Orthographies and reading: Perspectives from cognitive psychology, neuropsychology, and linguistics*. Hillsdale, NJ: Erlbaum.

Nerlove, S., & Snipper, A. S. (1981). Cognitive consequences of cultural opportunity. In R. H. Monroe, R. L. Munroe, & B. B. Whiting (Eds.), *Handbook of cross-cultural human development*. New York: Garland.

Nicholls, J. G. (1983). Conceptions of ability and achievement motivation: A theory and its implications for education. In S. G. Paris, G. A. Olson, & H. W. Stevenson (Eds.), *Learning and motivation in the classroom* (pp. 211–238). Hillsdale, NJ: Erlbaum.

Ogbu, J. (1978). *Minority education and caste: The American system in cross-cultural perspective*. New York: Academic Press.

Okedara, J. T., & Okedara, C. A. (1992). Mother-tongue literacy in Nigeria. In D. A. Wagner & L. Puchner (Eds.), *World literacy in the year 2000. Annals of the American Academy of Political and Social Science.* Newbury Park, CA: Sage.

Oxenham, J. (1980). *Literacy: Writing, reading and social organization.* London: Routledge & Kegan Paul.

Paris, S. G., & Jacobs, J. E. (1984). The benefits of informed instruction for children's reading awareness and comprehension skills. *Child Development, 55,* 2083–2093.

Paris, S. G., & Lindauer, B. K. (1982). The development of cognitive skills in early childhood. In B. Wolman (Ed.), *Handbook of developmental psychology.* Englewood Cliffs, NJ: Prentice Hall.

Paris, S. G., Lipson, M. & Wixson, K. K. (1983). Becoming a strategic reader. *Contemporary Educational Psychology, 8,* 293–316.

Paris, S. G., & Oka, E. R. (1986). Children's reading strategies, metacognition, and motivation. *Developmental Review, 6,* 25–56.

PDES. (1968). *Plan de developpement economique et sociale, 1968–1972.* Rabat: Ministere du Plan.

Pearson, P. D. (Ed.). (1984). *Handbook of reading research.* New York: Longman.

Pike, K. L. (1966). *Language in relation to a unified theory of the structure of human behavior.* The Hague: Mouton.

Porteus, S. D. (1937). *Intelligence and environment.* New York: Macmillan, 1937.

Psacharopoulos, G. (1973). *Returns to education: An international comparison.* Amsterdam: Elsevier.

Quasem, M. A. (1982). *The recitation and interpretation of the Qur'an: Al-Ghazalis's theory.* London: Kegan Paul International.

Rabinow, P. (1977). *Reflections on fieldwork in Morocco.* Berkeley: University of California Press.

Radi, M. (1983). La planification de l'enseignement au Maroc: Analyse du processus de cette planification. In Enseignement et systeme scolaire. *Bulletin Economique et Social du Maroc, 149–150,* 121–138.

Reder, S. M. (1987). Comparative aspects of functional literacy development: Three ethnic American communities. In D. A. Wagner (Ed.), *The future of literacy in a changing world.* New York: Pergamon.

Reder, S. & Green, K. (1983). Contrasting patterns of literacy in an Alaska fishing village. *International Journal of the Sociology of Language, 42,* 9–40.

Resnick, D. P., & Resnick, L. B. (1990). Varieties of literacy. In A. E. Barnes & P. N. Stearnes (Eds.), *Social history and issues in human consciousness: Some interdisciplinary connections.* New York: New York University Press.

Rivers, W. H. R. (1905). Observations on the sense of the Todas. *British Journal of Psychology, 1,* 321–396.

Rogoff, B. (1981). Schooling and the development of cognitive skills. In H. C. Triandis & A. Heron (Eds.), *Handbook of cross-cultural psychology* (Vol. 4). Boston: Allyn & Bacon.

Rogoff, B., & Lave, J. (Eds.). (1984). *Everyday cognition: Its development in social context.* Cambridge, MA: Harvard University Press.

Rogosa, D., Brandt, D., & Zimowski, M. (1985). A growth curve approach to the measurement of change. *Psychological Bulletin, 92,* 726–748.

Roy, P., & Kapoor, J. M. (1975). *The retention of literacy.* Delhi: Macmillan of India.

Salmi, J. (1985). *Crise de l'enseignement et reproduction sociale au Maroc.* Casablanca: Editions Maghrebines.

Salmi, J. (1987). Language and schooling in Morocco. *International Journal of Educational Development, 7,* 21–31.

Santerre, R. (1973). *Pedagogie musulmane d'Afrique noire.* Montreal: Presses de l'Universite de Montreal.

Saville, M. R., & Troike, R. C. (1971). *A handbook of bilingual education.* Washington, DC: Teachers of English to Speakers of Other Languages.

Saxe, G. B. (1985). Effects of schooling on arithmetical understandings: Studies with Okaspmin children in Papua New Guinea. *Journal of Educational Psychology, 77,* 503–513.

Schieffelin, B., & Cochran-Smith, M. (1984). Learning to read culturally. In H. Goelman, A. Oberg, & F. Smith (Eds.), *Awakening to literacy* (pp. 3–23). Exeter, NH: Heinemann.

Scholastic Testing Service. (1963). *Kuhlmann-Anderson Test, Booklet K* (7th ed.). Bensenville, IL.

Science Research Associates. (1962). *Primary Mental Abilities Test, Grades 2–4.* Chicago.

Scribner, S. (1975). Recall of classical syllogisms: A cross-cultural investigation of error on logical problems. In R. Falmagne (Ed.), *Reasoning: Representation and process.* Hillsdale, NJ: Erlbaum.

Scribner, S. (1984). Studying working intelligence. In B. Rogoff & J. Lave (Eds.), *Everyday cognition.* Cambridge, MA: Harvard University Press.

Scribner, S. (1987). Introduction to 'Theoretical perspectives on world literacy.' In D. A. Wagner (Ed.), *The future of literacy in a changing world.* London/New York: Pergamon.

Scribner, S., & Cole, M. (1981). *The psychology of literacy.* Cambridge, MA: Harvard University Press.

Seckinger, B. (1988). Implementing Morocco's Arabization policy: Two problems of classification. In F. Coulmas (Ed.), *With forked tongues: What are national languages good for?* Ann Arbor, MI: Karoma Press.

Segall, M., Campbell, D. T., & Herskovits, M. J. (1966). *The influence of culture on visual perspection.* Indianapolis, IN: Bobbs-Merrill.

SEP. (1988). *Statistiques de l'enseignement primaire, 1987–1988.* Rabat: Ministere de l'Education Nationale, Secretariat Generale, Direction de la Planification, Division des Statistiques.

SES. (1988). *Statistiques de l'enseignement secondaire, 1987–1988.* Rabat: Ministere de l'Education Nationale, Secretariat Generale, Direction de la Planification, Division des Statistiques.

Sheffield, J. (1977). The retention of literacy and basic skills: A review of the literature. Unpublished manuscript. Teachers College, Columbia University.

Shokeid, M. (1980). Principales orientations des recherches consacrées en Israel aux juifs d'origines marocaines. In *Juifs du Maroc: Identité et dialogue.* Paris: La Pensée Sauvage.

Shultz, T. W. (1981). *Investing in people: The economics of population quality.* Berkeley: University of California Press.

Sigel, I. (Ed.). (1985). *Parental belief systems.* Hillsdale, NJ: Erlbaum.

Sigel, I. E., McGillicuddy-DeLisi, A. V., & Goodnow, J. J. (Eds.). (1992). *Parental belief systems: The psychological consequences for children* (2nd ed.). Hillsdale, NJ: Erlbaum.

Simmons, J. (1976). Retention of cognitive skills acquired in primary school. *Comparative Education Review, 20,* 79–93.

Simmons, J. (1980). *The education dilemma.* New York: Pergamon.

Skoyles, J. (1988). Vowels of civilization. *New Scientist, 24,* 69–73.

Skutnabb-Kangas, T., & Toukomaa, P. (1976). *Teaching migrant children's mother tongue and learning the language of the host country in the context of the socio-cultural situation of the migrant family.* Helsinki: Finnish National Commission for UNESCO.

Smilansky, M. (1979). Priorities in education: Preschool; evidence and conclusions. *World Bank Working Paper* No. 323, April.

Snow, C. E., Barnes, W. S., Chandler, J., Goodman, I. F., & Hemphill, L. (1991). *Unfulfilled expectations: Home and school influences on literacy.* Cambridge, MA: Harvard University Press.

Souali, M. (1986). *Enseignement: De l'ecole nationale a l'ecole de base.* Lamalif (Morocco), 173 (January), 16–19.

Souali, M., & Merrouni, M. (1981). Question de l'enseignement au Maroc. *Bulletin Social et Economique du Maroc,* 143–146.

Spratt, J. E. (1988). Passing and failing in Moroccan primary schools: Institutional and individual dimensions of grade repetition in a selective school system. Doctoral dissertation, University of Pennsylvania.

Spratt, J. E., Seckinger, B., & Wagner, D. A. (1991). Functional literacy in Moroccan school children. *Reading Research Quarterly, 26,* 2, 178–195.

Spratt, J. E., & Wagner, D. A. (1986). The making of a *fqih:* The transformation of traditional Islamic teachers in modern times. In M. White & S. Pollack

(Eds.), *The cultural transition: Human experience and social transformation in the Third World and Japan* (pp. 89–112). New York: Routledge & Kegan Paul.

Spratt, J. E., & Wagner, D. A. (1992). *Grade repetition and reading achievement in Morocco.* Staff Working Paper. Center for International Development. Raleigh, NC: Research Triangle Institute.

Sraieb, N. (1974). *Colonisation, decolonisation et enseignement: l'exemple tunisien.* Tunis: Institut National des Sciences de l'Education.

Stein, N. L., & Glenn, C. G. (1979). An analysis of story comprehension in elementary school children. In R. O. Freedle (Ed.), *New directions in discourse processing,* Vol. 2. Norwood, NJ: Ablex.

Stevenson, H. W., Lee, S.-Y., & Stigler, J. W. (1986). Mathematics achievement of Chinese, Japanese, and American children. *Science, 231,* 693–699.

Stevenson, H. W., & Stigler, J. W. (1992). *The learning gap. Why our schools are failing and what we can learn from Japanese and Chinese education.* New York: Summit.

Stevenson, H. W., Stigler, J. W., Lucker, G. W., Lee, S., Hsu, C. C., & Kitamura, S. (1982). Reading disabilities: The case of Chinese, Japanese, and English. *Child Development, 33,* 1164–1181.

Sticht, T. G. (Ed.). (1975). *Reading for working: A functional literacy anthology.* Alexandria, VA: Human Resources Research Organization.

Stigler, J. W., Lee, S.-Y., & Stevenson, H. W. (1986). Digit memory in Chinese and English: Evidence for a temporally limited store. *Cognition, 23,* 1–20.

Stigler, J. W., Shweder, R. A., & Herdt, G. (1990). *Cultural psychology: Essays on comparative human development.* New York: Cambridge University Press.

Street, B. V. (1984). *Literacy in theory and practice.* London: Cambridge University Press.

Stromquist, N. P. (1990). Women and illiteracy: The interplay of gendered subordination and poverty. *Comparative Education Review, 34,* 95–111.

Szwed, J. F. (1981). The ethnography of literacy. In M. F. Whiteman (Ed.), *Writing: The nature, development, and teaching of written communication* (Vol. 1). Baltimore: Erlbaum.

Teale, W. H., & Sulzby, E. (1987). Literacy acquisition in early childhood: The roles of access and mediation in storybook reading. In D. Wagner (Ed.), *The future of literacy in a changing world.* New York: Pergamon.

Tyan, E. (1959). *Le notariat.* Harissa, Lebanon: St. Paul.

UNESCO. (1953). The use of vernacular languages in education. *Monograph on fundamental education,* No. 8. Paris.

UNESCO. (1957). *World illiteracy at mid-century.* Paris.

UNESCO. (1973). *Practical guide to functional literacy: A method of training for development.* Paris.

UNESCO. (1976). *The experimental world literacy program: A critical assessment.* Paris.

UNESCO. (1983). *Statistics of educational attainment and literacy.* Paris.

UNESCO. (1984a). *The drop-out problem in primary education: Some case studies.* Bangkok.

UNESCO. (1984b). *Evolution of wastage in primary education in the world between 1970 and 1980.* Document ED/BIE/CONFINTED/39/Ref. 2. Paris.

UNESCO. (1992). *World education report.* Paris.

UNICEF. (1989). *The state of the world's children, 1989.* Oxford: Oxford University Press.

United Nations. (1989). *Measuring literacy through household surveys.* New York: United Nations Statistical Office.

United Nations. (1990). *World Declaration on Education for All.* New York (Jomtien, Thailand): UNICEF.

Venezky, R. L. (1970). Nonstandard language and reading. *Elementary English, 47,* 334–345.

Venezky, R., Wagner, D. A., & Ciliberti, B. (Eds.) (1990). *Toward defining literacy.* Newark, DE: International Reading Association.

Verhoeven, L. T. (1990). Acquisition of reading in a second language. *Reading Research Quarterly, 25,* 90–114.

Vygotsky, L. (1978). *Mind in society.* Cambridge, MA.: Harvard University Press.

Wagner, D. A. (1974). The development of short-term and incidental memory: A cross-cultural study. *Child Development, 45,* 389–396.

Wagner, D. A. (1978a). Memories of Morocco: The influence of age, schooling and environment on memory. *Cognitive Psychology, 10,* 1–28.

Wagner, D. A. (1978b). The effects of formal schooling on cognitive style. *Journal of Social Psychology, 106,* 145–151.

Wagner, D. A. (1980). Culture and memory development. In H. Triandis & A. Heron (Eds.), *Handbook of cross-cultural psychology* (Vol. 4). New York: Allyn & Bacon.

Wagner, D. A. (1982a). Ontogeny in the study of culture and cognition. In D. A. Wagner & H. W. Stevenson (Eds.), *Cultural perspectives on child development.* San Francisco: Freeman.

Wagner, D. A. (1982b). Quranic pedagogy in modern Morocco. In L. L. Adler (Ed.), *Cross-cultural research at issue.* New York: Academic Press.

Wagner, D. A. (1983a). Indigenous education and literacy in the Third World. In D. A. Wagner (Ed.), *Child development and international development: Research-policy interfaces.* San Francisco: Jossey-Bass.

Wagner, D. A. (Ed.). (1983b). *Child development and international development: Research-policy interfaces.* San Francisco: Jossey-Bass.

Wagner, D. A. (1983c). (Issue Ed.). Literacy and ethnicity. *International Journal of the Sociology of Language, 42.*

Wagner, D. A. (1983d). Rediscovering "rote": Some cognitive and pedagogical preliminaries. In S. Irvine & J. W. Berry (Eds.), *Human assessment and cultural factors.* New York: Plenum.

Wagner, D. A. (1985). Islamic education: Traditional pedagogy and contemporary change. In T. Husen & T. N. Postlethwaite (Eds.), *International Encyclopedia of Education: Research and Studies.* New York: Pergamon.

Wagner, D. A. (1986a). When literacy isn't reading (and vice-versa). In M. E. Wrolstad & D. F. Fisher (Eds.), *Towards a new understanding of literacy.* New York: Praeger.

Wagner, D. A. (1986b). Child development research and the Third World: A future of mutual interest? *American Psychologist, 41,* 298–301.

Wagner, D. A. (1987a). Literacy assessment in Morocco and Zimbabwe: Political priorities and research responsibilities. Paper presented at the Annual Meeting of the Comparative and International Education Society, Washington, DC.

Wagner, D. A. (Ed.). (1987b). *The future of literacy in a changing world.* New York: Pergamon.

Wagner, D. A. (1988). "Appropriate education" and literacy in the Third World. In P. Dasen, J. W. Berry, & N. Sartorious (Eds.), *Psychology, health and culture.* Beverly Hills, CA: Sage.

Wagner, D. A. (1989a). In support of primary schooling in developing countries: A new look at traditional indigenous schools. *World Bank Background Paper Series,* Doc. No. PHREE/89/23. Washington, DC: World Bank.

Wagner, D. A. (1989b). Literacy campaigns: Past, present and future. *Comparative Education Review, 33,* 256–260.

Wagner, D. A. (1990). Literacy assessment in the Third World: An overview and proposed schema for survey use. *Comparative Education Review, 33,* 112–138.

Wagner, D. A. (1992). *Literacy: Developing the future.* UNESCO Yearbook of Education, Vol. 43. Paris.

Wagner, D. A. (1993). Life-span and life-space literacy. In D. Keller-Cohen (Ed.), *Literacy: Interdisciplinary conversations.* Cresskill, NJ: Hampton Press.

Wagner, D. A., & Lotfi, A. (1980). Traditional Islamic education in Morocco: Socio-historical and psychological perspectives. *Comparative Education Review, 24,* 238–251.

Wagner, D. A., & Lotfi, A. (1983). Learning to read by "rote." *International Journal of the Sociology of Language, 42,* 111–121.

Wagner, D. A., Messick, B. M., & Spratt, J. E. (1986). Studying literacy in Morocco. In B. B. Schieffelin & P. Gilmore (Eds.), *The acquisition of literacy: Ethnographic perspectives.* Norwood, NJ: Ablex.

Wagner, D. A., & Paris, S. G. (1981). Problems and prospects in comparative studies of memory. *Human Development, 24,* 6, 412–424.

Wagner, D. A., & Spratt, J. E. (1987). Cognitive consequences of contrasting pedagogies: The effects of Quranic preschooling in Morocco. *Child Development, 58* (5): 1207-1219.

Wagner, D. A., & Spratt, J. E. (1988). Intergenerational literacy: Effects of parental literacy and attitudes on children's reading achievement in Morocco. *Human Development, 31,* 359–369.

Wagner, D. A., and Spratt, J. E. (1989). Education, literacy and the poor. *Morocco: Economic growth and social welfare.* (Draft internal report). World Bank Report No. 7903-MOR. Washington, DC: World Bank.

Wagner, D. A., and Spratt, J. E. (1993). Arabic orthography and reading acquisition. In J. Altarriba (Ed.), *Cognition and Culture.* Amsterdam: Elsevier.

Wagner, D. A., Spratt, J. E., & Ezzaki, A. (1989). Does learning to read in a second language put the child at a disadvantage? Some counter-evidence from Morocco. *Applied Psycholinguistics, 10,* 31–48.

Wagner, D. A., Spratt, J. E., Gal, I., & Paris, S. G. (1989). Reading and believing: Beliefs, attributions, and reading achievement among Moroccan school children. *Journal of Educational Psychology, 81,* 283–293.

Wagner, D. A., Spratt, J. E., Klein, G. D., & Ezzaki, A. (1989). The myth of literacy relapse: Literacy retention among Moroccan primary school leavers. *International Journal of Educational Development, 9,* 307–315.

Wagner, D. A., & Stevenson, H. W. (1982). *Cultural perspectives on child development.* San Francisco: Freeman.

Wakin, J. (1972). *The function of documents in Islamic law.* Albany: SUNY Press.

Weber, R. M. (1970). *Linguistics and reading.* Washington, DC: ERIC Clearinghouse in Linguistics.

Wechsler, D. (1974a). *The Wechsler Intelligence Scale for Children-Revised.* New York: Psychological Corporation.

Wechsler, D. (1974b). *Manual for the Wechsler Intelligence Scale for Children-Revised.* New York: Psychological Corporation.

Weiler, H. N. (1978). Education and development: From the age of innocence to the age of scepticism. *Comparative Education, 14,* 179–198.

Weiner, B. (1983). Some thoughts about feelings. In S. G. Paris, G. M. Olson, & H. W. Stevenson (Eds.), *Learning and motivation in the classroom.* Hillsdale, NJ: Erlbaum.

White, M. (1987). *The Japanese educational challenge: A commitment to children.* New York: Free Press.

Witkin, H. A., Oltman, P. K., Raskin, E., & Karp, S. A. (1971). *A manual for the Embedded Figures Test.* Palo Alto, CA: Consulting Psychologists Press.

Witkin, H. A., Price-Williams, D., Bertini, M., Christiansen, B., Oltman, P. K., Ramirez, M., & Van Meel, J. (1974). Social conformity and psychological differentiation. *International Journal of Psychology, 9,* 11–29.

Woodhead, M. (1988). When psychology informs public policy: The case of early childhood intervention. *American Psychologist, 43,* 443–454.

World Bank. (1980). *Poverty and human development.* Washington, DC: Bank.

World Bank. (1988). *World development report 1988.* New York: Oxford University Press.

World Bank. (1991). *World development report 1991.* New York: Oxford University Press.

Yates, F. A. (1966). *The art of memory.* Chicago: University of Chicago Press.

Zafrani, H. (1969). *Pedagogie juive en terre d'Islam.* Paris: Librairie D' Amerique et D'Orient.

Zerdoumi, N. (1970) *Enfants d'hier: L'education de l'enfant en milieu traditional algerian.* Paris: Maspero.

Zigler, E., & Valentine, J. (1979). *Project Head Start: A legacy of the war on poverty.* New York: Free Press.

Name index

Aaron, P. G., 83
Abdullah, Si, 140
Adams, M. J., 100
Allen, J. B., 35
Anderson, C. A., 220
Anzalone, S. J., 6, 39n6
Armbruster, B. B., 141
As-Said, L., 47
Ayache, G., 38n2
Azzam, R., 102n1, 106n22

Baddeley, A. D., 280n5
Badry, F., 102n1, 173, 286
Baina, A., 258n2
Baker, L., 141, 142
Bandura, A., 143
Barnes, W. S., 9
Behrman, J. R., 230
Bempechat, J., 142–3, 154
Bennett, J. A. H., 8
Ben-Omar, B., 286
Berry, J. W., 3, 8
Berstecher, D., 138n4
Bever, T. G., 220
Bijeljac-Babic, R., 171
Blau, D. M., 230
Blaug, M., 230
Boissiere, M., 230
Boukous, A., 16
Bourdieu, P., 24, 235n22

Bowman, M. J., 220
Bradley, L., 100
Brandt, D., 78n4
Brown, A. L., 141, 142
Brunot, L., 48
Bryant, P. E., 100
Buchanan, M., 280n5
Bush, E. S., 158

Campbell, D. T., 65
Carraher, D. W., 228
Carraher, T. N., 228
Cattell, A. K., 292
Cattell, R. B., 292
Chall, J. S., 87, 100, 286
Chandler, J., 9
Charlton, S. E. M., 121
Ciliberti, B., 9
Clanchy, M. T., 4
Clarke, M., 172
Clay, M. M., 83, 141, 142, 286
Cochrane, S. H., 221
Cochran-Smith, M., 111
Cole, M., 3, 7, 8, 65, 134, 272, 273, 274, 275, 278, 279, 279nn2, 3
Coleman, J. S., 107–8
Crandall, V. C., 150, 293
Crandall, V. J., 150, 293
Cummins, J., 181
Cziko, G. A., 172

353

Subject index

abstract thinking, 65

Abu Dhabi, 106n22

academic achievement: and dropping out, 212; grade repetition and, 210; sense of self-competence and, 142–3; *see also* school achievement

adult literacy, 242; demographics of, 239–42

adult literacy rates, 244n, 246

adult literacy training, 231; *see also* literacy campaigns

Africa, 171, 183; regional map of northwest, 16f

age, 12; and household literacy, 198–9

age grouping (schools), 51

Algeria, 17, 20, 21, 185n9, 246

alphabet: Arabic, 28, 81, 82f; Berber script, 17; knowledge of, 97; mastery of, 98, 191; teaching, in Quranic schools, 44

alphabetic orthography/scripts, 80–1, 95

ambient literacy, 35

amulets, 29, 30

Andalusian Muslims, 38n2

anthropological methods, 10, 64–5, 66

Arab League, 106n23

Arabic language, 16, 17, 38, 125; dialects, 19–20; government policy and, 23; and Islam, 19–20, 101; language of literacy in public sector, 32; learning to read in, 79–106; in Morocco, 21–3; in schools, 20, 21; *see also* Moroccan Arabic; Standard Arabic

Arabic letters: knowledge of, 100

Arabic literacy, 254, 264; retention of, 222, 223, 225, 227t, 229, 230; in traditional Morocco, 23–6

Arabic literacy achievement: and school dropout, 214, 216–19, 217f, 218f

Arabic literacy acquisition, 180; L1/L2 in, 172

Arabic literacy skills, 72

Arabic orthography, 282; concept and boundary tasks in, 84f; and reading, 80–3, 101–2

Arabic reading achievement, 174–75, 177f; Arabic decoding skill in, 180

Arabic reading (AR) achievement score, 91–2

Arabic reading acquisition, 66, 67; preliminary conclusions regarding, 99–101; understanding, 101–2

Arabic script, 39n4, 66, 79, 81–2, 83, 102, 180; emic characteristics of, 83; learning to read in, 101–2; orthographic features of, 98; simplified, 106n23

Arabic-speaking children, 118, 263; academic achievement, 171; and Arabic literacy acquisition, 172, 173, 174, 175–6, 180, 181–2; educational outcomes, 251; and French reading achievement, 178–80; reading achievement, 150, 155

Arabic-speaking world, 19, 20

Arabization, 22n, 39n5, 52, 269

Arabs, 16

357